Blockchain Foundations
for the
Internet of Value

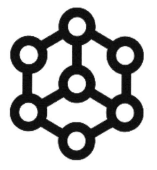

Blockchain Foundations
for the
Internet of Value

Mary C. Lacity

An imprint of The University of Arkansas Press
Arkansas, USA

An Epic Books publication
(Imprint of The University of Arkansas Press)

Cover design:
Nick Sample
www.nicksample.co.uk

Editor & layout designer:
Steve Brookes
SB Publishing
Stratford-upon-Avon, UK
www.sbpublishing.org

Cover artwork image:
Synchonicity of Colour: Blue by Margo Sawyer, 2008
www.margosawyer.com
Installation at Discovery Green, Houston, Texas, USA
www.discoverygreen.com

Author:
Mary C. Lacity

Published in 2020 by:
Epic Books (an imprint of University of Arkansas Press)

ISBN: 978-1-682261-57-6

Printed and bound in the USA by University of Arkansas Press

Contents

Contents

Figures

Tables

Foreword by Don Tapscott

Blockchain: An idea that has become a necessity

This is one of those rare turning points in history and Mary Lacity's enormously helpful and instructive book *Blockchain Foundations for the Internet of Value* is a timely one. The COVID-19 pandemic will profoundly change our behavior and society. Many institutions will come under scrutiny and, we hope, change for the better.

At the Blockchain Research Institute, we're doing our part to facilitate positive change. Technologies like artificial intelligence, the Internet of Things, augmented/virtual reality, and above all, blockchain, are more relevant than ever—not just to business and the economy but to the future of public health and the safety of global populations. Traditional systems have failed us and it's time for a new paradigm. To build on Victor Hugo, *"Nothing is more powerful than an idea that has become a necessity."* To avoid and manage pandemics the world needs the Internet of Value. It's time for a new paradigm.

In Blockchain Revolution, Alex Tapscott and I argued this Internet of Value represents a second era of the Internet. The first era was defined by information—the Internet of Information, a peer-to-peer mechanism for communicating information and collaborating online. While it has enabled companies to interact directly with consumers, take orders online, and deliver digital goods, services, and experiences, it has not fundamentally changed how we do business. Companies and markets are still vertically or horizontally integrated hierarchies, relatively opaque and insular, and relatively slow to change. We can say the same of public institutions.

With the Internet of Information, we have to rely on powerful intermediaries to exchange things of value. Governments, banks, digital platforms such as Amazon, eBay, and AirBnB, and universities do the work of establishing our identity, vouching for our trustworthiness, and helping us to acquire and transfer assets and settle the transactions.

Overall, they do a pretty good job—but there are limitations. They use centralized servers, which can be hacked. They take a piece of the value for performing this service—say 10 percent to send some money internationally. They capture our data, not just preventing us from using it for our own benefit but often undermining our privacy. These intermediaries are sometimes unreliable and often slow. They exclude two billion people who don't have enough money to justify a bank account, let alone an education. Most problematic, they are capturing the benefits of the digital age asymmetrically.

We posed the question: *"What if there was an Internet of value—a global, distributed, highly secure platform, ledger, or database where we could store and exchange things of value and trust each other without powerful intermediaries?"* That is the blockchain. Collective self-interest, hard-coded into this new native digital medium for value, would ensure the safety, security, and reliability of our exchanges online. Trust is programmed into the technology, which is why we call blockchain the Trust Protocol.

Combine AI and Machine Learning with blockchain and this represents the second era of the digital age. Every institution will change profoundly. How about the corporation, a pillar of modern capitalism? With the rise of a global peer-to-peer platform for identity, trust, reputation and transactions, we will be able to re-engineer deep structures of the firm, for innovation and shared value creation. We're talking about building 21st century companies that look more like networks rather than the vertically integrated hierarchies of the industrial age. The whole financial service industry is already being reinvented by blockchain and others will soon follow. How well does today's university prepare students for such a future?

How about the Internet of Things? In the not-too-distant future, billions of smart things in the physical world will be sensing; responding; communicating; sharing important data; generating, buying and selling their own electricity; and doing everything from protecting our environment to managing our health. It turns out, this Internet of Everything needs a Ledger of Everything.

One of the biggest opportunities is to free us from the grip of a troubling prosperity paradox. The economy is growing but fewer people are benefiting. Rather than trying to solve the problem of growing social inequality through redistribution alone, we can change how wealth—and opportunity—is predistributed in the first place, as people everywhere, from farmers to musicians, can use this technology to share more fully in the wealth they create.

Blockchain and Pandemics

Given the urgent need for global solutions to the Covid-19 pandemic, the Blockchain Research Institute convened a virtual roundtable of 30 experts from five continents. We discussed the challenges of COVID-19 and the possibilities of using blockchain in areas of need. In our special report, *Blockchain Solutions in Pandemics*, we developed a framework for facing pandemics together in these five areas.

1. Self-sovereign identity, health records, and shared data

Data is the most important asset in fighting pandemics. If any useful data exists now, it sits in institutional silos. We need better access to the data of entire populations and a speedy consent-based data sharing system. To accelerate discovery, the blockchain start-up, Shivom, is working on a global project to collect and share virus host data in response to a call for action from the European Union's Innovative Medicines Initiative. In Honduras, Civitas—an app developed by the start-up Emerge—is linking Hondurans' government-issued ID numbers with blockchain records used to track medical appointments. Doctors simply scan the app to review a patient's symptoms verified and recorded by telemedicine services. And Dr. Raphael Yahalom of MIT and Oxford-Hainan Research Institute is working on Trustup, a trust-reasoning framework that can systematically highlight the ways in which health data recorded on a blockchain ledger is more trustworthy than data stored in conventional databases. The trade-off between privacy and public safety need not be so stark. Through self-sovereign identities where individuals own their health records and can freely volunteer it to researchers, we can achieve both.

2. Just-in-time supply chain solutions

Supply chains are critical infrastructure for our globally connected economy, and COVID-19 has put them under tremendous strain, exposing potential weaknesses in their design. We must rebuild supply chains to be transparent, where users can access information quickly and trust that it's accurate. The start-up, RemediChain, is doing just that for the pharmaceutical supply industry. One of its co-founders, Dr. Philip Baker, was interested in tracking down and recycling unused but still efficacious medications, such as those used for cancer. He saw blockchain as means of recovering their chain of custody:

> *"By posting the medication and its expiration date, people all over the country can create a decentralized national inventory of surplus medication. When there is a sudden run on a previously ubiquitous medication like hydroxychloroquine, healthcare professionals can call on this surplus as a life-saving resource. The same principle applies for ventilators and PPE."*

Blockchain serves as a 'state machine' that gives us visibility into the state of our suppliers as well as the assets themselves. When COVID-19 hit, the start-up VeriTX—a virtual marketplace for digital assets like patented design files—pivoted to medical supplies, so that medical facilities could print the parts needed at one of the 180 3D printing facilities in VeriTX's network.[i] VeriTX can reverse-engineer a part and then build it much faster and at a lower cost than getting it from the original manufacturer or replacing the equipment.

---

[i] See Chapter 5 for an in-depth case study on VeriTX

3. Sustaining the economy: How blockchain can help

If supply chains are the machinery of global commerce, then money is its lubricant. Yet, money as a carrier of the disease has been a stressor during this pandemic. We highlight the what, why, and how of digital cash as an alternative. Costs are also an issue. The Ethereum-based Solve.Care platform is dramatically lowering healthcare administrative costs so that more of a patient's medical budget goes directly to care. The health crisis has also become a financial crisis, closing off access to supply chain credit. We look at blockchain-based financing solutions such as Chained Finance and fundraising efforts like that of the Binance Charity Foundation. Finally, decentralized models of governance such as those created by blockchain start-ups Abridged and Aragon can transform how NGOs, governments, and communities respond to the crisis.

4. A rapid response registry for medical professionals

Front-line medical professionals are the heroes and our last line of defense. Yet hospitals can't onboard people fast enough. This is not for lack of talent; it's the inability to find those with proper credentials. Blockchain platforms such as Dock.io, ProCredEx, and Zinc.work help to streamline coordination among different geographies, departments, and certification bodies so that supply and demand for healthcare workers—as well as the process for verifying their skills—becomes more efficient and transparent.

5. Incentive models to reward responsible behavior

People respond to incentives. Blockchain serves as a mechanism to up the incentives of stakeholder groups around issues and activities, changing patterns of behavior in the process. For example, the Heart and Stroke Foundation of Canada collaborated with Interac to micro-motivate healthy lifestyles, and Toronto's University Health Network teamed up with IBM to put the control over health records into patients' hands.

An action plan for the new paradigm

Many of these changes are beyond the timeframe of this round of COVID-19. But many can be implemented quickly. Governments must wake up to the blockchain opportunity. Every national government should create an emergency task force on medical data to start planning and implementing blockchain initiatives. They can stimulate the development of technology firms working on the solutions described here. They should partner with medical professional associations and other players to implement blockchain credential systems.

The private sector affected by COVID-19 must still lead the way. They must start today by incorporating blockchain into their infrastructures. Companies need to continue their work on pilots framed around medical records, credentialing systems, incentive structures, and other sovereign identity solutions. When designing pilots, companies could consider embedding incentive systems for socially responsible behavior.

Emergencies turbocharge the pace of historical progress. Businesses like Zoom, once used mostly by technology companies, have become ubiquitous tools of daily life. Meanwhile, 20th century titans are asking for bailouts. By necessity, human behavior— from where we work and when to how we socialize—changes overnight. Add to this mix the exponential properties of blockchain, and we're setting ourselves up for a cataclysm of some kind.

We anticipate a real crisis of leadership as the new digital-first and digital-only models conflict with the old industrial tried-and-true. Maybe this awful crisis will call forth a new generation of leaders who can help us finally get the digital age on track for promise fulfilled? Who among us will step up?

This book

It is in this context that we're delighted to see Mary Lacity's lucid book. If there was ever a topic that needed de-obfuscation, blockchain is one. The book clearly explains key blockchain concepts and the global blockchain landscape. It's not a book about crypto or digital currencies, but rather one that will be of considerable help to strategists, and implementors within enterprises and government, laying out a solid framework for applications and outlining a plethora of great use cases in the financial services industry, supply chains, and credentials for talent. It's also a practical book with real down-to-earth approaches and even tactics on how to make it happen in your organization.

Read on, enjoy, prosper, lead the change.

Don Taspscott

Don Tapscott is the author of 16 books about the Digital Age. His most recent, **Blockchain Revolution***, he wrote with his son, Alex, with whom he co-founded the Blockchain Research Institute. He is an Adjunct Professor at INSEAD, the Chancellor Emeritus of Trent University and a member of the Order of Canada.*

Author's Acknowledgements

Many people informed and shaped this research program. I am especially thankful to all of the executives interviewed for this research. I hope this guide fittingly trumpets your visions and achievements.

In June of 2018, I became the Director of the Blockchain Center of Excellence (BCoE) at the Sam M. Walton College of Business at the University of Arkansas. It was an opportunity of a lifetime to work with fellow blockchain enthusiasts including Professor Matt Waller, the Dean of the Walton College; Professor Rajiv Sabherwal, Chair of the Information Systems (ISYS) Department; Professor Paul Cronan, Director of Management Information Systems (MIS) graduate programs; and Dr. Zach Steelman, Assistant Professor of IS (and resident blockchain guru). They laid the groundwork for the BCoE.

I relied on insights and inspiration from our exceedingly capable BCoE team: Kathryn Carlisle, BCoE Senior Managing Director; Professor Dan Conway, BCoE Associate Director; Professor Remko Van Hoek, BCoE Advisor; and Andrea Morgan, ISYS Department Assistant. A special thanks to Jacob Yates, our rock-star graduate MIS student, for updating statistics and uses cases. Jacob, you have all the makings of a University Professor, and I look forward to future collaborations as you pursue a Ph.D. with us.

Before coming to the University of Arkansas, I had the full support of the University of Missouri-St. Louis for over a quarter century. Dr. Dinesh Mirchandani, Chair of the Information Systems Department, and Charles Hoffman, Dean of the College of Business, supported every request to enable our blockchain research. Other colleagues engaged in thoughtful conversations about the research, most notably, Dr. Nasser Arshadi, Professor of Finance; Dr. Tom Eyssell, the Associate Dean and Director of Graduate Studies at the time; Dr. Shaji Khan, Associate Professor of Information Systems; and Dr. Steve Moehrle, Chair of the Accounting Department. Dr. Joseph Rottman, Associate Dean, has been my longtime collaborator, confidant, and friend.

Many thanks to Epic Books, SB Publishing, and the University of Arkansas press. My gratitude to Matt Waller for launching the Epic book series and for his vision, kindness, and leadership. SB Publishing, whose editing and production services bring our best work to market faster than any traditional publishing route, has been a great partner for years. Thank you to Mike Bieker, Director of the University of Arkansas Press, for understanding and accommodating the unique needs of business publications.

I express my heartfelt gratitude to my circle of family and friends. This work consumed much of my time, resulting in neglect on my part to people who enrich my life in every way. Thank you to my long-time colleague, coauthor and friend, Professor Leslie Willcocks at the London School of Economics. Christine Emma Cotney Benson, thank you for entertaining me during my many research trips to New York City. My thanks to my parents, Dr. Paul and Joan Lacity, my sisters Karen, Diane (always close) and Julie, and my dear friends, Michael McDeviitt, Beth Nazemi, and Val Graeser for your unwavering support and humor. To my son, Michael Christopher, whom I hold in my heart every hour of every day. Finally, to the man who makes all this worthwhile, Jerry Pancio, my past, present, and future.

The Book's Cover Art

Margo Sawyer is Professor of Sculpture and Assistant Chair of Studio in the Department of Art & Art History at the University of Texas at Austin. A graduate of Chelsea School of Art in London and Yale University, Sawyer is an internationally artist. Honored by: John Simon Guggenheim Fellowship, Louis Comfort Tiffany Foundation, NEA, Japan Foundation, American Academy in Rome, Fulbright Grant to India and Japan.

Sawyer's artistic work *Synchronicity of Color: Blue*, 2008 at Discovery Green in Houston, Texas, has become the beloved icon for the city of Houston, and an image of the artwork is used on the cover of this book.

Synchronicity of Color: Blue, by Margo Sawyer
Installation at Discovery Green, Houston, Texas
Source: www.margosawyer.com

Publication Credits

Earlier versions of our work have been revised and updated for this guide, including:

Lacity, M. (2020), 'Crypto and Blockchain Fundamentals', *Arkansas Law Review*, 73.

Lacity, M. (2020), *Re-inventing Talent Acquisition: The SmartResume® Solution,* Blockchain Center of Excellence Case Study Series, BCoE-2020-01, University of Arkansas.

Van Hoek, R., and Lacity, M. (April 27, 2020), 'How the Pandemic Is Pushing Blockchain Forward,' *Harvard Business Review*, https://hbr.org/2020/04/how-the-pandemic-is-pushing-blockchain-forward

Lacity, M. (2019), *An Overview of the Internet of Value, Powered by Blockchains*, Blockchain Center of Excellence white paper, BCoE-2019-03, University of Arkansas.

Lacity, M., Zach, S., Paul, C. (2019), *Blockchain Governance Models: Insights for Enterprises.* Blockchain Center of Excellence white paper, BCoE-2019-02, University of Arkansas.

Lacity, M., Zach, S., Paul, C. (2019), *Towards Blockchain 3.0 Interoperability: Business and Technical Considerations*, Blockchain Center of Excellence white paper, BCoE-2019-01,University of Arkansas.

Lacity, M., Steelman, Z. R., Yates, J., Wei, J. (2019), 'US and China Battle for Blockchain Dominance', *CoinTelegraph.*

Lacity, M., Allee, K., Zhu, Y. (2019), 'Blockchain in Business: What do Companies' 10-K Reports Say About DTL?', *CoinTelegraph.*

Lacity, M. (2018), 'Addressing Key Challenges to Making Enterprise Blockchain Applications a Reality', *MIS Quarterly Executive*: (3), Article 3.

Lacity, M. (2018), *A Manager's Guide to Blockchains for Business*, SB Publishing, Stratford-Upon-Avon, UK

About the Research

About the Research

Think back to the early 1990s. Are you old enough to remember the first time you saw the Internet through the friendly interface of a web browser? I do. It was 1994. I was sitting in my office at Templeton College when my colleague showed me Mosaic, one of the first web browsers. I viewed it with curiosity for a few moments, but then went back to my 'day job'. I venture to say I was not alone in initially ignoring—and certainly underestimating—the Internet's long-term economic, social and political effects.

Jump ahead to 2009 when Bitcoin, the first blockchain application, was released. Many visionaries saw its value long before I did. Finally, Lee Coulter, CEO of Ascension Shared Services at the time, explained blockchains to me on the back of a napkin during a dinner in San Francisco in May 2016. I went home and read Don and Alex Tapscott's forward-thinking book, *The Blockchain Revolution: How the Technology Behind Bitcoin is Changing Money, Business, and the World*. The authors described how Bitcoin and other blockchain innovations were moving us from an 'Internet of Information' to an 'Internet of Value' where people transact value—i.e. money and other assets—in new ways. I could see the promise, and blockchains for business became my primary research focus.

I spent the first six months learning about the protocols that specify the rules for blockchains like Bitcoin; Ethereum; Ripple; Stellar; Corda; Fabric; and Quorum. The learning curve was brutal—it's easy to fall down the technical rabbit hole. Terms like elliptic curve cryptography; proof-of-work; mining; digital wallets; native digital assets; smart contracts; hashing; Merkle roots; Byzantine Fault Tolerance; and zero-knowledge proofs, make it difficult to climb out and really understand what the technology enables for businesses. I developed and taught blockchain modules to Masters' students at the University of Missouri-Saint Louis (UMSL) in the fall of 2016. One of the aims of the course was to shortcut the technical learning curve for students and business professionals.

In 2017, I joined MIT's Center for Information Systems Research (CISR), housed in the Sloan School of Management, as a Visiting Scholar to study how enterprises were exploring blockchains. The research team included Dr. Jeanne Ross, Principal Research Scientist, and Kate Moloney, Research Specialist. During interviews, we asked managers about their blockchain adoption journeys, their participation in blockchain ecosystems, and the practices and lessons they have learned so far. We asked the following types of questions:

What strategies are being considered? How is the organization building blockchain capabilities? Which applications are deemed to be the most promising, are already under development, or have been deployed?

Does the organization participate in industry consortia? Open-source projects? Invest in startups or FinTechs? What needs to happen to create the minimum viable ecosystem for applications relevant to the organization?

What challenges do organizations need to overcome to deploy blockchain applications? What are the key project and change management practices? How well have expectations been met so far? What are the preliminary outcomes and lessons learned?

We interviewed executives from global enterprises currently exploring blockchains; from the professional services firms that sell services to them; and from the startups that want to disrupt them. The enterprises we studied primarily represent global financial services, but also included manufacturing and healthcare firms. The professional services firms included representatives from large organizations like Deloitte, KPMG, Capgemini, IBM, and Wipro, as well as boutique consulting firms. The startups included companies seeking to advance general blockchain technical capabilities and specific business-focused blockchain applications. In 2017, these enterprises were participating actively in industry blockchain consortia and developing many proof-of-concepts; none had deployed live production systems. In 2017 and 2018, I also participated in (or more accurately *observed)* the Center for Supply Chain's three studies to define blockchain standards for tracking and tracing pharmaceuticals.[iii] Bob Celeste leads the group of about 100 participants who represent pharmaceutical manufacturers, wholesalers, distributors, and retail and hospital pharmacies. This experience helped me to understand the perceived benefits and concerns that supply chain partners have about shared blockchain applications.

From 2018 forward, our research has been supported by the Blockchain Center of Excellence (BCoE) at the University of Arkansas. We work with the Executive Advisory Board members on blockchain research, which include ArcBest; Ernst & Young (EY); FIS; Golden State Foods; IBM; JB Hunt; McKesson; Microsoft; Tyson Foods; and Walmart. We meet in closed workshops to hear from experts, which then informs our white paper and research briefing series. So far, we have investigated blockchain interoperability; shared governance models; messaging the C-suite; IoT and other enabling technologies; and digital identities. Overall, members are interested in deploying technologies to deliver real business value; blockchains are just one component that enable new solutions.

Other BCoE blockchain research projects include:

Blockchain Indices

We are working with a number of University of Arkansas faculty and students to assess blockchain's impact, including the reporting of blockchain activities in accounting reports and patent applications and awards in China and the US. Research team members

---

[iii] See Center for Supply Chain's website at https://www.c4scs.org/

include Dr. Dan Conway; Dr. Zach Steelman; Dr. Kris Allee; Jacob Yates; Jia Wei; and Yaping Zhu. Results are presented in Chapter 2.

Poultry Excellence in China

This project aims to improve food safety for poultry in China. It is funded by the Walmart Foundation. The project entails collecting data on the salmonella and antibiotic residues using bio-sensor IoT devices; developing risk assessment and cost-benefit analyses; and tracing vital information from poultry breeding to retail outlets using blockchain technologies. The project is led by Yanbin Li, Distinguished Professor, Tyson Endowed Chair in Biosensing Engineering at the University of Arkansas. The University of Arkansas' blockchain portion of the project is led by Kathryn Carlisle, Senior Managing Director of the BCoE and Professor John Kent, Supply Chain Management. The project is quite large, with leaders from Walmart Food Safety Collaboration Center; South China Agricultural University; Zhejiang University; Zhejiang Academy of Agricultural Sciences; Agricultural Technology; and China Agricultural University.

Consumer Economics

This project investigates US consumers' willingness to pay for blockchain traceability for beef. It is being led by Dr. Aaron Shew, Assistant Professor of Agricultural Economics, Arkansas State University; Rudy Nayga, Distinguished Professor and Tyson Chair in Food Policy Economics and Heather Snell, Program Associate for the University of Arkansas. Based on 1,000 participants, we found that respondents valued blockchain and digital ledger tech names similarly and were willing to pay a premium for the information compared to the current meat labeling system.

More blockchain-related projects are underway. See https://blockchain.uark.edu/

Why executives, professionals, and students should learn about blockchains

"Whereas most technologies tend to automate workers on the periphery doing menial tasks, blockchains automate away the center. Instead of putting the taxi driver out of a job, blockchain puts Uber out of a job and lets the taxi drivers work with the customer directly."

Vitalik Buterin, co-founder Ethereum

"Bitcoin doesn't do anything. It just sits there. It's like a seashell or something, and that is not an investment to me."

Warren Buffet, Chairman and CEO of Berkshire Hathaway.

"Maybe I'm just too old, but I'm going to let this mania go on without me."

Jeffrey Gundlach, DoubleLine Capital CEO

There's no question that blockchain is an exciting new development. Executives must decide whether to lead blockchain development; participate in the development with ecosystem partners; or wait until others develop the platforms and applications and join later. As the first quote above from Vitalik Buterin attests, blockchains promise to radically disrupt some business models. Therefore, blockchain's threat of taking third-parties out of the equation opens up a whole new world of automation and efficiency that should (rightly) have most C-suite executives doing their homework. The second quote from Warren Buffet expresses a rather impotent view of Bitcoin, and seems to suggest it's not worth an executive's time (at least not yet). In our research, blockchain's dissenters made similar statements, such as *"there are no legitimate use cases"*, and *"blockchains are over-hyped"*. The third quote seems to suggest blockchains are best left to the younger generation. Which opinions are most compelling? Wading through the arguments and evidence, we grant that, as we enter 2020, blockchains for business are indeed following a traditional technology hype cycle. However, the point is that most technologies eventually do mature; managers eventually learn to adapt them for purposeful use; and ultimately, innovations like blockchains become institutionalized as part of our technical architecture. This is already happening for the early-adopters discussed throughout this guide. Bottom line: we believe executives need to give blockchain technologies even more attention than they are giving to other technological innovations, like analytics or artificial intelligence. Why? Whereas most innovation decisions happen within the boundaries of the firm, blockchains are shared applications that require shared decision making with ecosystem partners. It requires an unprecedented level of cooperation with competitors and other mindshifts that only an executive can champion efficaciously.

As for professionals and students, the 'Internet of Value' will change the tasks and thus the skills needed for IT; finance; accounting; supply chains; marketing; law; and healthcare:

Information Technology

Blockchain IT skills are in high demand from enterprises of all sizes and from across industries and geographies. According to LinkedIn, ***blockchain was the most in-demand technical skill*** for 2020 in the United States; United Kingdom; France; Germany; and Australia. Information technology professionals will need to learn how to develop, test and integrate decentralized applications (dApps). Additionally, blockchain technologies likely will represent only 20 to 30 percent of an end-to-end-system, so IT students and IT professionals must learn how to integrate dApps with traditional applications. Specifically, dApps will be integrated with data collection devices like Internet-of-Things (IoT) and Radio Frequency Identification (RFID); with existing systems of records like Enterprise Resource Planning (ERP) and Customer Relationship Management (CRM) software; and with web-based and mobile user interfaces. Chapters 3 and 8 will be of particular interest to IT professionals and students.

Finance

JP Morgan has already issued its own stablecoin; Santander has already issued and settled a bond on a public blockchain; R3, a blockchain consortia for financial services firms, has already released Corda—its blockchain code base for confidential transactions. Finance students and professionals will need to understand new financing models like Initial Coin Offerings, Security Token Offerings, Initial Exchange Offerings and peer-to-peer lending, which are covered in Chapter 2. Finance students and professionals need to understand how blockchain technologies will improve or disrupt traditional financial services for remittances; cross-border payments; bond issuances and settlements; derivatives; equities; trade finance and so much more. Chapter 4 covers specific blockchain applications for financial services.

Accounting

Blockchains move us from the longstanding double-entry bookkeeping system to triple-entry booking in which every transaction has three entries: the credit, the debit, and the public receipt stored on a shared ledger (see Figure 0.1). With blockchain technologies, every transaction in the ledger is already verified, balances are guaranteed to be correct and current, and everything is transparent. Accountants will need to understand the implications on bookkeeping, reconciliations, audits, and accounts payable and receivable. Mike Walker, Senior Director of Applied Innovation and Digital Transformation for Microsoft said, *"Reconciliations are on the endangered species list"*. However, this does not mean that the demand for accounting skills will decrease.

29

Blockchain technologies could actually create more value-added work for accountants by freeing them up to tackle tasks that require judgement and advice. According to the Institute of Chartered Accountants in England and Wales (ICAEW):

"The spectrum of skills represented in accounting will change [because of blockchains]. Some work such as reconciliations and provenance assurance will be reduced or eliminated, while other areas such as technology, advisory, and other value-adding activities will expand. To properly audit a company with significant blockchain-based transactions, the focus of the auditor will shift. There is little need to confirm the accuracy or existence of blockchain transactions with external sources, but there is still plenty of attention to pay to how those transactions are recorded and recognized in the financial statements, and how judgmental elements such as valuations are decided."

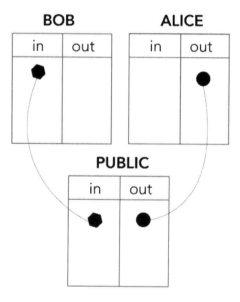

Figure 0.1: Blockchain ledgers use triple-book accounting

Source: Adapted from https://miro.medium.com/max/4724/1*c3OFdrYqUO2ZqO1-E7nMkQ.png

Supply Chain Management (SCM)

For the past three decades, companies have been improving *internal* operations through (1) the adoption of ERP and other IT systems; (2) the application of Six Sigma quality improvement programs; and (3) improved inventory management practices. Many operations are lean, but only *within* the boundaries of the firm. There is still plenty of opportunities to improve the efficiency and effectiveness of operations *across* supply chain partners. Today's global supply chains are a complex web of trading partners and trusted third-parties. Each party maintains its own centralized systems and subsequently partners face significant challenges trying to synchronize the *data* about the flow of physical goods and services, with the actual flow of goods and services. By sharing a blockchain application, supply chain partners can all partake in the benefits of decreased administrative costs; increased supply chain visibility; verification of sustainable practices; fewer lost goods; and fewer counterfeit products, to name but a few. Put simply:

> *"The future of supply chain management will include blockchain."*
>
> **Remko Van Hoek et al. 2019, p. 215**

Chapter 5 covers a number of blockchain applications for supply chains.

Marketing

Social media and digital marketing are now mainstream marketing strategies, but blockchain technologies have the power to disrupt them. Perry Drake, Professor of Digital and Social Media Marketing at the University of Missouri-St. Louis said, *"This new blockchain technology will not only disrupt and change the way we conduct everyday business but also how marketers interact with customers. These new security applications are highly needed now if we want to continue to expand our use of technology into our everyday lives."*

According to *Forbes* contributor, Daniel Newman, *"While Artificial Intelligence and analytics have arguably benefited businesses more than consumers, blockchain may level the playing field by giving the power of data back to consumers themselves."* When the 'Internet of Value' becomes ubiquitous, individuals will be in charge of their data; they will decide its worth and with whom they will share it. Instead of paying Google or Facebook to post advertisements, marketers likely will pay consumers directly to watch an advertisement. Marketers will have to employ new methods to find consumers and to gain their attention and trust. Social media platforms, like the blockchain-based Steemit, already allow the community to decide the payments made to content curators.

Law

Blockchains have significant implications for the practice of law. According to Jaliz Maldonado, author for the *National Law Review, "Blockchain technology is the most transformative technology to emerge since the advent of the Internet."* According to Dale Chrystie, Blockchain Strategist at Federal Express, legal professionals will have to become bi-lingual in 'smart contracts' (see Chapter 3) and 'legal contracts'. Professor Carol Goforth from the University of Arkansas and author of *Regulation of Cryptotransactions*, explained what legal professionals need to know: *"Legal needs go far beyond awareness of the bitcoin phenomenon or even knowing how cryptocurrencies are regulated. Understanding blockchain and how clients are integrating the new technology into their day-to-day operations is essential in order to provide competent legal advice about business planning and strategy, risk management, and compliance for all kinds of businesses."* Legal professionals will need to understand how blockchain technologies affect corporate filings; criminal and civil cases; dispute resolution; document notarizations; intellectual property rights; land registries and property deeds; and law firm operations.

Healthcare

In the US, blockchain technologies could potentially save the healthcare industry $100 to $150 billion in administrative costs. For example, a shared blockchain application could streamline claims adjudication.

Beyond the use cases for institutions *within* the healthcare industry, blockchain technologies promise patient empowerment. From a patients' perspective, our confidential healthcare data—like immunizations; blood tests; diagnoses; allergies; prescription medicines; treatments; surgical procedures; behaviors (like smoking or exercising)—are in the possession of doctors, governments, health care providers, employers, and insurance providers. Increasingly, people are concerned about what TTPs and governments might do with their healthcare data. For example, millions of people have given their DNA to 'find their ancestors', but what if the data was sold to insurance companies? Might they use genetic weaknesses to determine coverage and insurance rates or to decline coverage altogether? Alternatively, if everyone's healthcare data were stored on a blockchain, individuals could decide with whom to share their information. This model may be a way off, but there are many startups working on doing just that. MedRec, a startup from the MIT Media Lab, provides a patient-centered electronic health record sharing platform. According to an article in the *Harvard Business Review*, *"it doesn't store health records or require a change in practice. It stores a signature of the record on a blockchain and notifies the patient, who is ultimately in control of where that record can travel."*

Beyond IT, finance, accounting, supply chains, marketing, law, and healthcare, blockchain applications are underway for governments, media, entertainment, manufacturing, education, and other sectors. Wherever there is a need for a tamper-resistant record of transactions among multiple parties who do not trust each other, we are sure to see blockchain-based solutions.

Overview to this guide

While there are many books on blockchains, this guide focuses on ***blockchain applications for business***. The target audience is business students, professionals, and managers who want to learn about the overall blockchain landscape—the investments, the size of markets, major players and the global reach—as well as the potential business value of blockchain applications. Readers will learn enough about the underlying technologies to speak intelligently to technology experts in the space, as the guide also covers the blockchain protocols, code bases and provides a glossary of terms.

Depending on one's needs, the guide may be read in parts or in its entirety. There is some purposeful redundancy of content so that chapters can standalone to service the needs of different audiences. **Part I** covers blockchain foundations and provides answers to these questions:

- Chapter 1: How did Bitcoin launch the Internet of Value?
- Chapter 2: How big is the blockchain landscape today? Which players are leading?
- Chapter 3: What exactly are blockchain applications? What value do they promise and how do they work?

In **Part II**, we take a deeper dive into real enterprise blockchain solutions for financial services, supply chains, energy and credentialing. We'll get to know the organizations leading these efforts, including: traditional enterprises; spinoffs from traditional enterprises; partnerships; private startups; non-profits; and industry consortia. Within these cases, we meet visionary leaders who are not just waiting for blockchains to mature— they are actively working to ripen the technology, define industry standards, create new models of shared governance, and lobby for new laws and regulations. These leaders remain resolute during the long implementation journeys. Specifically, the chapters answer the following questions:

- Chapter 4: What are examples of actual blockchain applications for financial services?
- Chapter 5: What are examples of actual blockchain applications for supply chains?
- Chapter 6: What are examples of actual blockchain applications for energy?
- Chapter 7: What are examples of actual blockchain applications for credentials?

From the in-depth cases, we gain a deeper appreciation for the technical and business challenges of moving blockchain applications from innovation labs and proof-of-concepts to market-ready platforms. The common thread is that the leaders are solving real business problems that just happen to be well-suited for blockchain enabled solutions.

In **Part III**, we examine the technical, data, legal, ecosystem, strategy and management challenges and emerging solutions to address them (see Figure 0.2).

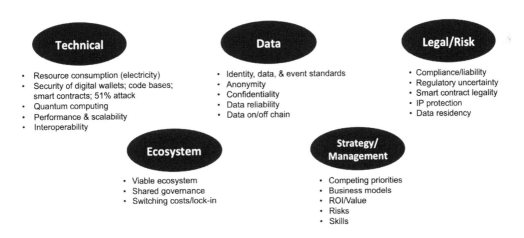

Figure 0.2: Challenges to realizing an 'Internet of Value', particularly for enterprises

Specifically, the chapters answer the following questions:

- Chapter 8: What are the technical challenges and emerging solutions?
- Chapter 9: What mind shifts, strategies and action principles should an enterprise consider?
- Chapter 10: What is the future of blockchains?

While it is too soon to foresee all that will unfold, we've learned that despite the billions of dollars in blockchain investments worldwide, the thousands of proofs-of-concepts across all industries, and the high-profile groups working to define standards and to develop code, *enterprise* blockchains applications really only ramped up production in 2018-2019. Some platforms, like the IBM Food Trust, TradeLens, and EY WineChain have processed millions of transactions with hundreds of platform participants. However, many other blockchain solutions have yet to scale, but ecosystem participants are getting value and their networks of participants are growing. So, while we agree it is early days before the full vision of an 'Internet of Value' is upon us, it's time to learn about blockchains now.

Citations:

[1] Marr, B. (August 15, 2018), '23 Fascinating Bitcoin And Blockchain Quotes Everyone Should Read', *Forbes*, https://www.forbes.com/sites/bernardmarr/2018/08/15/23-fascinating-bitcoin-and-blockchain-quotes-everyone-should-read/#74a245e57e8a

[2] Li, Y. (May 4, 2019),'Warren Buffett says bitcoin is a 'gambling device' with 'a lot of frauds connected with it', *CNBC* https://www.cnbc.com/2019/05/04/warren-buffett-says-bitcoin-is-a-gambling-device-with-a-lot-of-frauds-connected-with-it.html

[3] Marr, B. (August 15 , 2018), '23 Fascinating Bitcoin And Blockchain Quotes Everyone Should Read', *Forbes*, https://www.forbes.com/sites/bernardmarr/2018/08/15/23-fascinating-bitcoin-and-block-chain-quotes-everyone-should-read/#74a245e57e8a

[4] Anderson, B. (January 9th 2020), *The Most In-Demand Hard and Soft Skills of 2020*, https://business.linkedin.com/talent-solutions/blog/trends-and-research/2020/most-in-demand-hard-and-soft-skills Yuji Ijiri (1989), 'Momentum accounting and triple-entry bookkeeping: exploring the dynamic structure of accounting measurements', *Studies in Accounting Research*, American Accounting Association, Sarasota (31).

[5] Lacity, M., Zach, S., Paul, C. (2019). *Blockchain Governance Models: Insights for Enterprises* (2nd ed., vol. 2019). Blockchain Center of Excellence.

[6] ICAEW (2018), *Blockchain and the future of Accountancy*, https://www.icaew.com/-/media/corporate/Files/technical/information-technology/thought-leadership/blockchain-and-the-future-of-accountancy.ashx

[7] Van Hoek, R., Fugate, B., Davletshin, M., and Waller, M. (2019), *Integrating Blockchain into Supply Chain Management*, Kogan Press, London.

[8] Newman, D. (September 18, 2019), 'How Blockchain is Changing Digital Marketing', *Forbes*, https://www.forbes.com/sites/danielnewman/2019/09/18/how-blockchain-is-changing-digital-marketing/#6a68af7f16eb

[9] Maldonado, J. (2018), *10 Ways Blockchain Technology Will Change the Legal Industry,* The National Law Review, https://www.natlawreview.com/article/10-ways-blockchain-technology-will-change-legal-industry

[10] Gofoth, C. (2020). *Regulation of Cryptotransactions*, West Academic, St. Paul Minnesota.

[11] Arsene, C. (February 21, 2019), *Blockchain in Healthcare: An Executive's Guide for 2020*, https://www.digitalauthority.me/resources/blockchain-in-healthcare/

[12] Halamka, J., Lippman, A., and Ekblaw, A. (March 2017), 'The Potential for Blockchain to Transform Electronic Health Records', *Harvard Business Review*, https://hbr.org/2017/03/the-potential-for-blockchain-to-transform-electronic-health-records

[13] CB Insights (October 2017) *Blockchain in Review: Investment Trends and Opportunities*.

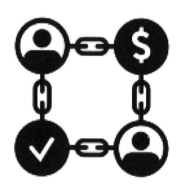

PART I

Blockchain Foundations

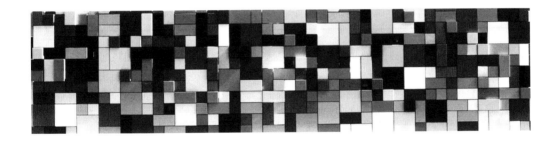

Chapter 1

Moving to the 'Internet of Value'

"I believe that Blockchain will do for trusted transactions what the Internet has done for information."

Ginni Rometty, CEO of IBM[1]

"Blockchain represents the second era of the Internet. The first era for decades was the Internet of information. Now we're getting an Internet of value. Where anything of value which including money, our identities, cultural assets like music, even a vote can be stored, managed, transacted and moved around in a secure private way."

Don Tapscott, Chairman and Founder of the Blockchain Research Institute[2]

1.1. Something big is afoot

Since the 1990s, we have had an 'Internet of Information' that allows us to seamlessly share *information*—such as documents, images, emails, and videos—over the Internet. While most Internet users do not need to understand the details of the technical protocols operating underneath user-friendly interfaces, it is helpful to understand how they work at a high-level. With the 'Internet of Information', *copies* of information are routed over the Internet.[i]   If you email a friend, you keep the original email and your friend receives a copy of the email. We take this all for granted now, but the Internet changed everything, everywhere.

Bitcoin, the first blockchain application released in January of 2009, and other blockchain innovations that followed, are moving us from an 'Internet of Information' to an 'Internet of Value' where people transact value, i.e., money and other assets, directly with each other. The pivot to an 'Internet of Value' requires innovative solutions to some very old problems—like double-spending, identity, credentials, bookkeeping and a medium of exchange (i.e., money!)—as well as to newer problems like cybercrime. Before blockchains, we rely on institutions to solve these problems. After blockchains, we rely on technologies like cryptography, distributed ledgers, digital assets, and smart contracts to solve these problems.

So how would an 'Internet of Value' work for an average person? We can imagine a scenario where Alice is enjoying a visit to her favorite art museum and decides she would like two pints of fresh organic strawberries to be delivered to her smart refrigerator, which is located by her back door. She uses her phone to place the order and elects to pay with a stable coin—a cryptocurrency that is pegged to the US dollar—from her digital wallet. With one click, her order and payment option request is matched with a reliable supplier with available inventory, and with an authorized and available logistics operator. A smart contract is automatically generated to code the terms of the transaction for Alice, the supplier, and the logistics operator. The three parties authorize the agreement, either automatically or by human review, depending on their preferences. By authorizing the smart contract, Alice allows the smart contract to hold her payment to the supplier in escrow until the transaction is complete; she has also granted access rights for the logistics operator to verify the location and access code of her smart outdoor

---

[i] Transmission Control Protocol/Internet Protocol (TCP/IP) is the Internet's primary protocol. It breaks messages into packets and routes them to their destination as defined by a unique address called an 'IP address'. Every device connected to the Internet has a unique IP address including computers; mobile phones; laptops; printers; IoT devices; servers; routers, etc.

refrigerator. An hour later, a drone arrives at Alice's smart outdoor refrigerator. The drone electronically unlocks the smart refrigerator with a one-time access key. Alice's refrigerator scans the package, verifies receipt against the smart contract's requirements, sends a receipt confirmation message to the smart contract, which then automatically releases the payment to the supplier's digital wallet. Alice's phone notifies her of the delivery and she is delighted to see exactly where and when the fruit was harvested, its certifications for organic and sustainable production, the temperature and pitstops during its entire journey through the supply chain, ending with its final delivery to her smart refrigerator. Meanwhile, the drone shuts the refrigerator, sends a message of successful delivery and requests instructions for its next flight plan. When Alice gets home, she enjoys her strawberries so much that she uses her digital wallet to tip the farmer. She also decides to give her supplier and drone operator top ratings for their services. In turn, the supplier awards her three tokens which she can redeem on future purchases.

In this scenario, one can imagine that a number of applications are working behind the scenes, such as an e-commerce platform to match Alice's order to the supplier and logistics operator; a food traceability application to track the strawberries from the farm to Alice's refrigerator; a cold chain application that signals any temperature deviations and durations along its journey from the farm; a logistics application for scheduling and routing drones; a home appliance application for Alice's refrigerator, a payments application using digital currencies, and a universal identity application to verify credentials and access rights for all of the individuals, organizations, and objects in this story. How realistic is this scenario? As of 2020, we have the components for each application in Alice's story, but they are not yet scaled or interoperable. When the full vision for the 'Internet of Value' is realized, these applications will be interoperable, secure, confidential, trustworthy, and most importantly, decentralized—no one institution or government will own or control any of it. They will run on blockchain technologies.

Something big is indeed afoot; blockchains have the potential to change everything, everywhere. While the blockchain learning curve can be challenging, this guide aims to hasten the journey. We begin with Bitcoin because it is the first blockchain application; it created a fascinating new solution to some very old problems. Every student and manager should know Bitcoin's story because all subsequent blockchains are an extension of, or departure from, the original Bitcoin blockchain.

1.2. Bitcoin: A new solution to some very old problems

"Bitcoin is a remarkable cryptographic achievement and the ability to create something that is not duplicable in the digital world has enormous value."

Eric Schmidt, CEO of Google[3]

"I think the fact that within the bitcoin universe an algorithm replaces the functions of [the government] ... is actually pretty cool. I am a big fan of Bitcoin."

Al Gore, 45th Vice President of the United States[4]

"As bitcoin becomes more mainstream, the social consensus around what bitcoin should be may change. If this occurs, we may not see the libertarians turn on bitcoin so much as bitcoin turn on the libertarians. It is for this reason that I believe it is incredibly important that we teach bitcoin users the history behind cryptocurrency in order to instill Cypherpunk values in them."

Jameson Loop, Coindesk[5]

Satoshi Nakamoto, the inventor of Bitcoin, approached some very old problems in a remarkably new way. Nakamoto—a pseudonym used by an unknown person or persons who remains anonymous to this day—imagined a world where people could safely, securely, and anonymously transfer value directly with each other (1) without using government-issued currencies; (2) without relying upon trusted third parties (TTPs) like banks; and (3) without the need to reconcile records across trading partners. His (or her) innovation is Bitcoin, described in a white paper posted to a cryptographic mailing list on October 31, 2008.[6]

The timing of Bitcoin was no accident. After the 2008 Global Financial Crisis people became increasingly distrustful of financial institutions. Movements like Occupy Wall Street ranted against wealth inequality and the influence of large financial institutions on government policy. People rallied against the government's power to control money. Bitcoin has its roots in Libertarian and Cypherpunk values, which aim to create social and political change by circumventing governments and large financial institutions through privacy-enhancing technologies.[7]

Satoshi Nakamoto's nine-page white paper specified the technical requirements for the 'Internet of Value'. What's remarkable is that Nakamoto used existing algorithms, but assembled them in a way to do something entirely new. Quite simply, Nakamoto proposed *"a purely peer-to-peer version of electronic cash [that] would allow online payments to be sent directly from one party to another without going through a financial institution."*[8] Bitcoin achieves this by tackling some very old problems with algorithms and behavioral incentives (See Figure 1.1). Let's begin with the 'double spend' problem, the risk that value might be sent twice (or more).

Double spending and other counter-party risks

To transact *value,* i.e. money, over the Internet, one cannot send a copy. Instead, after the transfer of value is complete, the sender should no longer have the money, the recipient should. Today, a messy network of global financial systems and regulators prevent double spending. They also mitigate other counter-party risks—the risk each trading party bears that the other party will not fulfill its contractual obligations. Banks, credit card companies, money transmitters, notaries, lawyers, and other trusted third parties (TTPs) provide independent 'truth attestations' such as notarizing signatures; verifying identity; verifying ownership; authenticating assets; and attesting that agreements have been properly executed. TTPs provide these and many other vital services to facilitate trade (the advantages), for which they earn significant transaction fees (the major disadvantage). Transaction costs for remittances are typically about eight percent of the value of the transaction.[9] Before an 'Internet of Value', the process to transact value

Problems with establishing trust among trading partners	Current solution with TTPs and Governments	Bitcoin solution
Double spending and other counter-party risks (e.g. counterfeit assets; illegimtimate ownership)	Trusted third parties (TTPs) mitigate counter-party risks	Computer algorithms and an incentivized community mitigate counter-party risks
Bookkeeping errors and reconciliations	Each party keeps and reconciles their own records	A digital ledger (called a blockchain) that is verified, transparent and immutable is shared, so reconciliations are not needed
Mediums of exchange	Parties use fiat money, regulated by sovereign governments	Parties use a cyptocurrency, governed by software
Cyber threats	Each party protects its IT permimeter or relies on a TTP to do it for them	Cryptography and other computer algorithms secure the data and network

Figure 1.1: Trusted-Third Parties & Governments *vs.* Bitcoin: Different solutions to old and new problems

is expensive, and it is often opaque in that tracking transactions once they leave the boundaries of the firm can be difficult.

Bitcoin solved the double spend and other counter-party risks by automating some of the services normally done by TTPs, and by engaging a community to perform other services. For an automation example, Bitcoin (and many blockchain applications that followed) rely on cryptographic private-public key pair to verify account ownership; whoever is in possession of the private key is assumed to be the legitimate owner of the account (explained more deeply in Chapter 3). Validating transactions to prevent double spending was a bit trickier to solve without trusted third parties. Senders cannot be trusted to verify that they have enough cryptocurrency in their accounts to fund their transactions. An independent verifier is needed, but Nakamoto did not want to rely on traditional financial institutions to provide the validation. Here was Nakamoto's brilliant solution: reward other people in the network (called 'miners')[ii] with newly issued

---

[ii] The Bitcoin protocol is based on a gold mining metaphor. Just as gold miners *work* using physical resources to

bitcoins to validate all the recently submitted transactions. The economic incentives of the Bitcoin network motivate validators to play by the rules.[iii]

Bookkeeping errors and reconciliations

We also have the ancient challenge of bookkeeping. We need a record for every transfer of value upon which all parties agree. Before an 'Internet of Value', every party manages its own systems of records (software and data, including ledgers) within the boundaries of the firm or relies on a TTP. Across firm boundaries, parties have to reconcile information about the transaction. Reconciliations are expensive and time-consuming. Once reconciled, there is nothing to prevent trading partners from modifying records after the fact; partners cannot be confident they are dealing with the same historical record of transactions through time. This is why we have millions of people with accounting skills working on processing everyday receipts and payables.

Nakamoto solved the bookkeeping problem by moving from party-level record keeping to shared record keeping. The Bitcoin network maintains a digital ledger, called a *blockchain*, to serve as the universal bookkeeping record; no more need to reconcile records because every party agrees 'this is what transpired'. The ledger is distributed to all the host computers (called nodes) that run the Bitcoin network. There were over 9,000 Bitcoin nodes as of December 2019, each with its own identical copy of the ledger.[10] The nodes in the Bitcoin network constantly chatter with each other to make sure no party tampers with the records after-the-fact. If anyone cheats, the other parties' nodes automatically ignore it.

---

excavate gold from gold mines, bitcoin miners *work* using computer resources to release new bitcoins; Bitcoin, like gold, has a limited supply, making it a rare commodity. Just as it gets harder to mine gold as a gold mine is depleted, bitcoin releases fewer new digital coins over time.

[iii]Nakamoto (2008) wrote this about the economic incentives to motivative miners to behave honestly: *"If a greedy attacker is able to assemble more CPU power than all the honest nodes, he would have to choose between using it to defraud people by stealing back his payments, or using it to generate new coins. He ought to find it more profitable to play by the rules, such rules that favour him with more new coins than everyone else combined, than to undermine the system and the validity of his own wealth."* p. 4.

Acceptable medium of exchange

We also have the ancient problem of an acceptable medium of exchange. Money was invented over 10,000 years ago to facilitate trade. Money serves three functions: as medium of exchange for the payment of debts; as a common measure of value; and as a store of value that aims to retain its worth over time. Primitive moneys included whale's teeth, shells, and stones. Metal coins were invented in about the 6th century BC and paper currency in about 1,000 AD.[11] Today, we have government-issued currencies, of which the United Nations recognizes 180 as legal tender.[12] Most sovereign currencies are now *fiat*, backed solely on the promises of governments rather than by gold reserves as was common in the past.

Granted, fiat currencies have a number of advantages. Fiat currencies have defined laws and regulations, so individuals and enterprises know how to be compliant when using them. Many currencies are reasonable stable stores of value that hold their worth over time (of course there are exceptions like the Venezuelan bolívar fuerte). People understand fiat currencies as a unit of measure. (To illustrate this last point, ask a few neighbors if $1.00 for a loaf of bread is reasonable; then ask them if 1 bitcoin for a loaf of bread is reasonable. What types of answers did you elicit?) However, fiat currencies have a number of disadvantages. Governments can print fiat money at will, causing inflation and can change regulations on a whim. Governments can also freeze, seize, or restrict access to one's assets.[13] Criminals can counterfeit currencies, and according to one website, the most counterfeited currencies are the Chinese yuan, United States dollar, United Kingdom pound, Indian rupee, New Zealand dollar, and Mexican peso.[14]

Rather than using a government-issued currency, Nakamoto created a new *cryptocurrency*—a digital currency secured by cryptography that makes it nearly impossible to counterfeit.[15] Bitcoin is not controlled by any government or institution. Rather, bitcoin's monetary policies are programmed in the software. Specifically, Bitcoin's software capped the total monetary supply at 21 million bitcoins, and has an automatic monetary distribution schedule. The last bitcoin will be released in 2140.[16]

Cyber threats

Lastly, cybersecurity is a newer problem that needs to be overcome to realize the 'Internet of Value'. If we are sending value over the Internet, how do we prevent someone from stealing it? Or stealing our identity? Today, individuals rely on Internet providers, financial institutions, software providers, retailers, and other institutions with whom they transact to protect their identities and assets. Enterprises either secure their own information technology (IT) perimeters or outsource to a TTP. It's a daunting task for whoever is responsible for cybersecurity. Scams included phishing, where a cyber thief poses as somebody you trust; tech support fraud, where someone pretends to be from an IT department and needs access to your account; extortion, where someone seizes control of your digital assets and demands a ransom; and payroll diversion, where someone hijacks your paycheck and deposits it in their account. According to the US Federal Bureau of Investigation (FBI), cybercrime cost businesses $2.7 billion in 2018—double the costs from 2017.[17]

Bitcoin uses a number of sophisticated algorithms to secure the data and the network. Readers will learn about private-public-key pairs, hashing algorithms, and consensus algorithms used to secure transaction data stored on the blockchain ledger in Chapter 3.

Bitcoin's legacy

Bitcoin tackled some old and new problems to create peer-to-peer payments. To recap, Bitcoin achieved this by shifting (1) from government-issued currencies to a cryptocurrency; (2) from trusted third parties to automated and community-driven counter-party risk mitigation and (3) from party-level record keeping to shared record keeping. Bitcoin is important because it is the most visible on-going, live experiment for an open, public, secure, non-governmental, non-TTP reliant application, pointing us towards an 'Internet of Value'. All are welcome to participate. Millions of people use it—over 32 million Bitcoin wallets have been created.[18] Thousands of people help secure it by being miners. Bitcoin proves that the 'Internet of Value' is technically feasible and that a shared digital ledger is highly secure.

However, Bitcoin—like all innovations—has limitations and there is room for improvement. Bitcoin has been a poor store of value because of its high price volatility. For example, Bitcoin was worth $14,112 on January 1st 2018; $3,747 on January 1st 2019; and $7,194 on January 1st 2020. (Although my friend Professor Dan Conway counters that Bitcoin is completely stable, it's the US dollar that fluctuates wildly!) Bitcoin has limited functionality … it is just a payment system to send and receive bitcoins; it cannot do much else. It's rather pokey, only capable of processing about two to six transactions per second (TPS). It's not yet user-friendly, so most people end up relying on a trusted third party anyway, called an exchange, to transfer their bitcoins. The miners who operate computers to secure the Bitcoin network consume *a lot* of electricity. Bitcoin was designed as a standalone application, which is a long way off from a seamless, interoperable 'Internet of Value'.

To overcome these (and other) limitations, thousands of innovations have followed. In this guide, readers will learn about altcoins; privacy coins; stablecoins; crypto-tokens; exchanges; smart contracts; public platforms; private platforms, and more. Besides the need for technical innovations, the 'Internet of Value' also requires the development of:

- ***Standards*** for the identity of individuals, organizations, devices, and assets; standards for data structures and events.

- ***Regulations*** that will serve to protect citizens, consumers, investors, and the environment without stifling innovation.

- ***Shared governance*** models with verifiable controls to prevent the rise of powerful alliances.

Furthermore, technical innovations, standards, regulations, and shared governance models all need to co-evolve to realize the 'Internet of Value'. It requires communities to work together.

1.3. Blockchain communities

As of 2020, the global blockchain population falls, roughly, into three community types:

Public blockchain communities

As noted above, Bitcoin has its roots in Libertarian and Cypherpunk principles, which value anonymity, inclusion, and public and open access. One often hears the term *'permissionless'* to describe public blockchains, meaning that anyone can transact in the network and anyone can run validator nodes. Many other innovators share Bitcoin's values and have sought to improve upon and extend Nakamoto's ideas, including the inventors of altcoins, privacy coins, and public platforms with smart contracting capabilities, like Ethereum and EOS (see Chapter 3). The public blockchain community is filled with exciting startups, non-government organizations and even traditional enterprises. They have social missions to bring financial services to the 1.7 billion people who lack access; to democratize software development; to protect the property rights of people with low economic status; to ensure the integrity of political elections; and to enable self-sovereignty over one's identity and personal data, to name but a few.

Private blockchain communities

Most traditional enterprises do not see use cases for public blockchains like Bitcoin (at least not yet). Traditional enterprises need confidentiality, not anonymity, so that information about their transactions are visible, but only to authorized parties. Working with ecosystem partners, most enterprises are interested in private platforms, called *'permissioned'* platforms, where joining the network is by invitation-only, and where only authorized members validate transactions. They see value coming from sharing blockchain-enabled systems with ecosystem partners, such as lower costs; better transaction visibility; faster settlement times; immutability and auditability of records; less vendor opportunism; and better cybersecurity. Private blockchains are already in production and delivering value to participants, including the IBM Food Trust for food quality and traceability; MediLedger for pharmaceutical supply chain tracing; and TradeLens for tracking shipping containers (see Chapter 3).

Boundary Spanners

Boundary spanners believe the public and private platforms will amalgamate by bringing the best innovations from each community to create the 'Internet of Value'. Specifically, boundary spanners believe public platforms can be used for private transactions. They foresee that today's private blockchains will migrate to or will interoperate with public platforms once the technologies, standards, regulations, and governance models mature. This view is supported by history. Just as traditional enterprises first adopted *intranets* before the standards were in place to secure the 'Internet of Information'; traditional enterprises may continue to adopt private blockchains until public blockchain standards and technology mature enough to ensure confidentiality, security, scalability, and interoperability. Many see the shift from private to public blockchains as inevitable. Paul Brody, Principal & Global Innovation Leader, Blockchain Technology for Ernst & Young (EY) is betting on this. His team has developed a number of open-access innovations that allow private transactions on public blockchains.

1.4. Beyond Bitcoin

"We don't want [centralized databases], because when you are the center of the universe, you can play God and change history in destructive ways, and control who gets to write and not write in ways that are hard to detect. Instead, we want records to be tracked, verifiable and distributed among a crowd—not just for cryptocurrency but also for supply chains, provenance tracking and finance... We want to know what to audit and where information has flowed. This goes for education records, prison records, births, property titles and other ecosystems that act as central registries. There are other situations too, where registries are not yet centralized, and rather than create an eBay or an Uber, you want something more distributed. This is what blockchain [technology] is uniquely positioned to support."

Brian Behlendorf, Executive Director, Hyperledger Project[19]

Brian Behlendorf provides a compelling vision for the types of applications we'll have for the 'Internet of Value'. He's leading one of the most visible communities in the space, the Hyperledger Project, supported by the Linux Foundation. The Hyperledger Project and other global blockchain communities are working to develop the technologies, standards, regulations and governance needed for an 'Internet of Value'. In the next chapter, we'll see their progress as of the start of 2020.

Citations:

[1] Quote from CEO's speech at IBM's Interconnect Conference, March 21, 2017.

[2] Quote from an Interview with Don Tapscott (April 5 2018), *52 Insights*, https://www.52-insights.com/don-tapscott-blockchain-represents-the-second-era-of-the-internet-interview/

[3] Quotes are from the website, *Best Bitcoin Quotes,* posted on https://www.weusecoins.com/best-bitcoin-quotes/

[4] Quotes are from the website, *Best Bitcoin Quotes*, posted on https://www.weusecoins.com/best-bitcoin-quotes/

[5] Loop, J. (July 23, 2016), *Bitcoin: The Trust Anchor in a Sea of Blockchains*, Coindesk, https://www.coindesk.com/bitcoin-the-trust-anchor-in-a-sea-of-blockchains/

[6] Nakamoto, S. (2008). *Bitcoin: A Peer-to-Peer Electronic Cash System*, p. 1. https://bitcoin.org/bitcoin.pdf

[7] Lacity, M. (2018). *A Manager's Guide to Blockchain for Business: From Knowing What to Knowing How*, SB Publishing, Stratford-Upon-Avon, UK.

[8] Nakamoto, S. (2008). *Bitcoin: A Peer-to-Peer Electronic Cash System,* p1.https://bitcoin.org/bitcoin.pdf

[9] The World Bank estimated that sending remittances cost an average of 7.99 percent of the amount sent; *Navigating the world of cross-border payments,* http://www.iqpc.com/media/1003982/57107.pdf. The administrative costs for tracking containers in the global supply chain was roughly 22 percent of the retail costs according to Anderson, J., & Van Wincoop, E. (2004). 'Trade Costs', *Journal of Economic Literature, 42*(3), 691-751. Retrieved from http://www.jstor.org/stable/3217249

[10] The actual number of Bitcoin nodes is difficult to track because some nodes operate behind fire walls. This site tracks 'reachable' nodes: https://bitnodes.earn.com/

[11] https://en.wikipedia.org/wiki/History_of_money

[12] Sawe, B. (2018). 'How Many Currencies Exist in the World?', *WorldAtlas,* https://www.worldatlas.com/articles/how-many-currencies-are-in-the-world.html.

[13] For example, the Greek banks would not allow account holders to withdraw more than 60 euros a day in 2015; Associated Press (June 28, 2015), 'The Latest: Strict limits on bank withdrawals will not apply to foreign credit cards', *US News,* https://www.usnews.com/news/business/articles/2015/06/28/the-latest-greece-wants-ecb-to-keep-giving-emergency-help

[14] (April 6, 2018). The world's most counterfeited currencies, https://www.lovemoney.com/www.love-money.com

[15] **Cryptography** is *"a method of protecting information and communications through the use of codes so that only those for whom the information is intended can read and process it"* https://searchsecurity.techtarget.com/definition/cryptography

[16] https://en.bitcoin.it/wiki/Controlled_supply

[17] US Federal Bureau of Investigation (2018). Internet Crime Report, https://pdf.ic3.gov/2018_IC3Report.pdf

[18] Lielacher, A. (2019). *How Many People Use Bitcoin in 2019,* https://www.bitcoinmarketjournal.com/how-many-people-use-bitcoin/

[19] MacKenna, J. (January 10th 2018), *Hyperledger's Brian Behlendorf and How Blockchains Will Change the Enterprise World,* Nasdaq http://www.nasdaq.com/article/hyperledgers-brian-behlendorf-and-how-blockchains-will-change-the-enterprise-world-cm903367

Chapter 2

The Blockchain Landscape

"I'm a big believer in the ability of blockchain technology to effect fundamental change in the infrastructure of the financial service industry."

Bob Greifeld, CEO of NASDAQ in 2015[1]

"The only way we are going to get value for the whole industry is to think differently about working together. I've been calling blockchain a 'team sport' for a few years now. We have to work with our competitors on things that improve the entire industry, like safety, quality, and reducing barriers to trade across borders."

Dale Chrystie, Blockchain Strategist at FedEx,
Chair of BiTA Standards Council[2]

2.1. Overview of the landscape

In this chapter, we map the size, players, and trends emerging across the global blockchain landscape as of 2020 (see Figure 2.1). Cryptocurrencies continue to dominant the landscape, representing the largest share of the market at about $1/4 trillion. Investors using conventional equity investment models, including venture capital (VC) and Initial Public Offerings (IPOs), have funneled billions of dollars into the blockchain landscape, but so too have investors using three new investment models: Initial Coin Offerings; Security Token Offerings; and Initial Exchange Offerings. In total, between $32 and $45 billion have been invested in new blockchain projects.

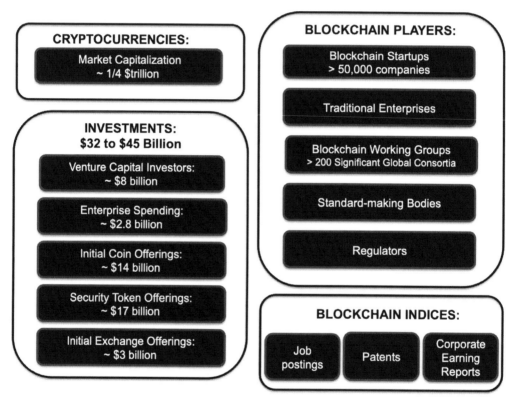

Figure 2.1: The global blockchain landscape as of Q1 2020

In addition to startups and investors, there are other important players shaping the blockchain landscape. We focus on blockchain working groups, traditional standards-making bodies and regulators in this chapter, but academics; philanthropists; meet-up groups; technology journalists; politicians; lawyers; and other stakeholders are making significant contributions as well. We present three indices to help track the landscape— job postings, patents, and blockchain mentions in US corporate earnings reports.

We conclude the chapter with Gartner's assessment of where blockchains are in the technology hype-cycle. The overall takeaway is that, beyond the wild fluctuations in the cryptocurrency market, blockchain players are in this space for the long-term by helping to build the blockchain foundations for the 'Internet of Value'.

2.2. The cryptocurrency market

By February of 2020, there were over 5,000 cryptocurrencies trading on popular exchanges. Where did all these digital coins come from? How much are they worth? In this section, we explore the types of cryptocurrencies and the overall market value. Contrary to popular belief, Bitcoin was not the first cryptocurrency. David Chaum launched DigiCash in 1990—the first live cryptocurrency of significance.[3] While an important breakthrough, DigiCash was centrally controlled in that the company's system performed the validations. Nakamoto resurrected Chaum's idea of blind digital signatures as a way to verify asset ownership, but this time with distributed validation.[4] After Bitcoin, a Cambrian explosion of new cryptocurrencies emerged on the market.

2.2.1. Types of cryptocurrencies

Altcoins

After bitcoin, new coins were often created by downloading the Bitcoin Core, altering the programming code, and launching a 'fork' (see Glossary) to Bitcoin. These are called 'altcoins' because they are alternatives to Bitcoin. Altcoins aimed to either improve on bitcoin, such as increasing data storage or decreasing settlement times, or to serve different purposes, such as funding a new platform.[5] Namecoin and litecoin—both launched in 2011—are two early examples. *Namecoin* was designed by the Bitcoin community as a way to register names on the Bitcoin blockchain. One of its unique features is that Namecoin merged mining functions of Bitcoin and Namecoin to allow simultaneous mining of both coins, instead of making miners choose between the two. *Litecoin* was created by Charlie Lee to improve Bitcoin's settlement times by a factor of four; Litecoin creates a new block every 2.5 minutes instead of every ten minutes, as

Bitcoin does. Its money supply is 84 million litecoins, which is four times greater than Bitcoin's money supply. Most notably, it uses a different hashing algorithm ('Scrypt' rather than SHA-256), which at the time was designed to allow miners to mine litecoin without the need for specialized hardware.[6] Readers will learn about mining and hashing in the next chapter.

Privacy coins

With Bitcoin, any person with access to the Internet may view transactions stored on Bitcoin's digital ledger. The identities of the public address holders are not known, except to the two parties of the transaction. However, one of the parties may follow all of the subsequent transactions associated with the addresses, which is why Bitcoin is considered to be 'pseudo-anonymous'. Several cryptocurrencies were developed to increase anonymity even more than Bitcoin. These so called 'privacy coins' include monero and zcash. *Monero*, launched in 2015, is a cryptocurrency with increased data obfuscation compared to Bitcoin using ring signatures and stealth addresses.[7] *Zcash* is another major privacy coin, launched in 2016. Designed by professors from Johns Hopkins, MIT, Technion, and Tel Aviv University, Zcash uses a cryptographic zero-knowledge proof which allows users to mask their addresses.[8] Chapter 8 will cover these privacy coins in more detail.

Stablecoins

Several cryptocurrencies aim to create a more stable store of value compared to Bitcoin by pegging the coin to a stable asset outside of the network, such as pegging a digital coin to a fiat currency or to commodity like gold or a barrel of oil. *Tether* was the first stablecoin, launched in 2014, by a company called Tether Limited. Buyers exchange one US dollar for one tether coin, with Tether Limited allegedly storing each US dollar in a bank reserve.[i] Cryptotraders use tethers to take advantage of the price arbitrage across

---

[i] Tether Limited promised that at any time, a buyer could get its US dollar back and the coin would be destroyed. In 2017, however, the company could not meet withdrawal demands; it stands accused of currency manipulation and fraud. It has never provided a legal audit, despite many promises to do so. Despite the risks, nearly 75 percent of all bitcoin trades were still facilitated by Tether in 2019.

cryptocurrency exchanges; they can buy cryptocurrencies at a lower price with tethers on one exchange without having to first withdraw fiat currency from another exchange.[9]

Other notable stablecoins pegged to fiat currencies have launched since tether, including USD Coin and Gemini in 2018; JPM Coin in 2019; and the proposed Libra coin, which is supposed to launch in 2020. The *USD Coin*—created by Coinbase and Circle— launched the coin as part of a consortium, promising transparency over its US dollar reserve management.[10] *Gemini* was founded by Cameron and Tyler Winklevoss; the gemini coin is another 1-to-1 peg with the US dollar.[11] JP Morgan uses its *JPM Coin* to facilitate institution-to-institution transfers; it is also pegged to the US dollar. When one JP Morgan client sends money to another JP Morgan client over the blockchain, it uses the digital coin to speed settlement times, which are immediately redeemed for US dollars.[12] *Libra*, the new token proposed by Facebook, will be pegged to a basket of fiat currencies (or perhaps to a local currency) and will be managed by the Libra Association, a non-profit membership organization based in Switzerland.[13] The US Congress has fiercely questioned Facebook founder Mark Zuckerberg and David Marcus, Head of Calibra (Facebook's spinoff that operates the digital wallet for libra coins) about libra, so its future is uncertain.[14]

Besides pegging to fiat currencies, some stablecoins are pegged to commodities. For example, *DGX* pegs one coin to one gram of gold; Venezuela's government pegged the *petro* to one barrel of oil.[15, 16] Some stablecoins are pegged to other cryptocurrencies; *dai,* launched in 2017, is pegged to the US dollar but is backed also by *ether,* Ethereum's cryptocurrency.[17] In the future, some cryptocurrencies may use algorithms to maintain a stable base price by automatically adjusting supply and demand.

2.2.1. Cryptocurrency market value

So what are all these virtual currencies worth? The market capitalization of existing cryptocurrencies—calculated by multiplying the price in US dollars times the number of coins in circulation—is one way to size the market. On February 9, 2020, there were

5,099 cryptocurrencies with a total market capitalization of $287 billion, according to coinmarketcap.com.[ii] *Bitcoin* continues to dominate the market, representing over 63 percent of the entire market with a market capitalization of over $183 billion. The cryptocurrencies with the next five largest market capitalizations on this day were *ethereum* ($25 billion); *ripple* ($12 billion), *bitcoin cash* ($8 billion); *bitcoin SV* ($6 billion), and *litecoin* ($5 billion).[18] However, market prices fluctuate considerably, sometimes rising or falling by hundreds of billions of dollars within a few weeks. For example, 1,320 cryptocurrencies had a combined market capitalization of $324 billion on December 2nd 2017 and just 30 days later, the market cap exceeded $800 billion.[19, 20]

Certainly, Bitcoin's price breaking marks dominated news cycle when it reached $1,000 per bitcoin in November 2013;[21] $2,000 per bitcoin in May 2017;[22] $10,000 in November 2017[23] and then over $19,000 in December 2017.[24] A month later, Bitcoin fell back to about the $10,000 range. Bitcoin was not the only cryptocurrency to see wide spreads in price. In general, the prices of most cryptocurrencies rise and fall in unison. For example, Ethereum's price fluctuated between $7.13 and over $800 in 2017.[25] Litecoin started out at $4.51 in January 2017 and hit over $370 by December 2017.[26]

By February 2018, the crypto market crashed, falling by more than $550 billion. Theories to explain the crash include:

1. Fear of regulatory restriction, particularly in Asia;

2. Manipulation of the market by 'whales';

3. The proper functioning of markets to reset prices from hyper-inflated values.

As far as the first theory, South Korean and Chinese government cracked down on virtual currencies, prompting other governments to consider regulations for virtual currencies. This caused uncertainty among crypto-holders, so they began exiting the market due to rumors of potential bans occurring in main contributing countries.

[ii] Coinmarket.com and openmarketcap.com are two websites that track the total value of the cryptocurrency market. Openmarketcap.com screens exchanges for inflated volumes, so the two sites vary considerably on reported trade volumes.

The second theory asserts that Bitcoin's price was manipulated by one or more 'whales'—individuals with large bitcoin holdings of over $1 billion in value. Whales can sell a large enough portion of their bitcoins at a lower than market price to prompt a panic sell-off, which lowers the price further.[27] When the price falls low enough, the whales swoop in and buy more bitcoins at a reduced price. Prices rise soon after. Two university professors suspect that a single Bitcoin whale manipulated prices in 2017.[28]

Another explanation: with Bitcoin rising in value by over 200 percent between October and December of 2017 along with other cryptocurrencies rising as well, analysts argued that the market became unsustainable due to the influx of new investors to the cryptocurrency market as a whole.[29]

Assuming the crypto market doesn't crash before *this* publication, it's helpful to place the size of the market in context. Figure 2.2 compares the values of the world's money supply; stock market; physical money supply; gold supply; Apple; Amazon; the entire cryptocurrency market; and Bitcoin.

As of January 2020, ***the value of all the cryptocurrencies combined equaled only about .025 percent of the global money supply.***

While the cryptocurrency market cap tracks the *current market value*, the investment market captures the initial dollars invested in blockchain technologies with the hopes of *future* returns.

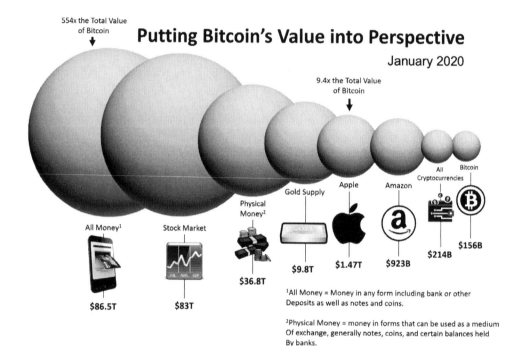

Figure 2.2: Market size comparisons

Source: Jacob Yates, with permission

2.3. Blockchain investment

Investors have been actively funding blockchain projects and startups since about 2014. Here, we examine four investment models: conventional venture capital (VC) equity investment and three new funding models that generate new tokens: Initial Coin Offering; Security Token Offerings; and Initial Exchange Offerings. According to TeqAtlas, $32.3 billion has been invested into blockchain by the first half of 2019, with record amounts occurring in 2018.[30] Figure 2.3 compares traditional investment with token generation investment.

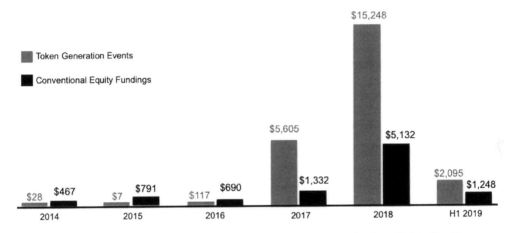

Data as of July 2019; Source: teqatlas.com; Conventional Equity Fundings include Angel/Seed, Early Stage VC, Later Stage VC Other VC Deals, and Private Equity. Early Stage VC deals include Series A, B, and C, while Later Stage – all above Series D venture deals

Figure 2.3: Traditional vs. new funding models in blockchain startups

Source:https://www.crowdfundinsider.com/2019/08/150513-research-since-2014-32-3-billion-has-gone-into-blockchain-investments-with-record-amount-in-2018-during-first-half-of-2019-blockchain-deals-have-dropped/

In 2019, there was a drop off in investment spending the first half of the year mostly due to Initial Coin Offerings being scrutinized by regulatory bodies.

2.3.1. Venture capital investment

In a venture capital (VC) deal, private investors buy ownership shares of a startup. Since 2014, venture capitalists have invested nearly $8 billion in blockchain technology, with $5.5 billion of the investment coming in 2018.[31] Early investments focused on public blockchain technologies like digital wallets and currency exchanges—few of which prevailed. Only 28 percent of startups were able to achieve additional funding after the initial angel investments, according to CB Insights.[32] Later, investments focused on private blockchains for business.

Eight of the top ten largest venture capital investments for blockchain companies occurred in 2018 with the largest being for Bitmain that provides crypto-mining hardware (see Figure 2.4). Advocates of the technology believe having more investors will bring credibility to the market and potentially entice a broader adoption of crypto-assets.[33]

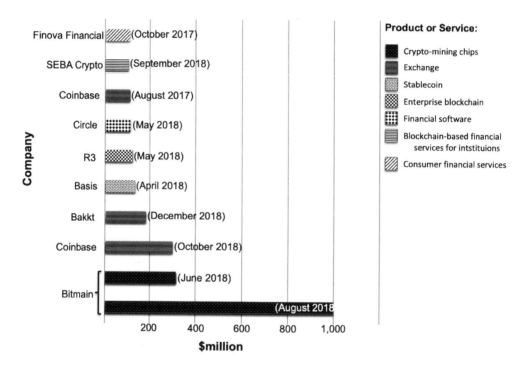

Figure 2.4: Ten largest VC blockchain deals

Source: https://www.technologyreview.com/s/613247/venture-capitalists-are-still-throwing-hundreds-of-millions-at-blockchains/

While the US investment market is by far the largest, equity investors are funding startups all over the world. For example, The Digital Currency Group has made investments in companies in Africa, Asia, Australia, Europe, North America and South America.[34]

2.3.2. New investment models

The blockchain landscape saw new financing mechanisms such as Initial Coin Offerings (ICOs), Security Token Offerings (STOs) and Initial Exchange Offerings (IEOs) (see Table 2.1 for a comparison).

	ICOs	STOs	IEOs
Commonality	Projects raise funds by issuing a new crypto-token		
Fundraising managed by	The project's developers	Capital investor firms	A cryptocurrency exchange
Investors	Anyone	Accredited investors only	Customers of the exchange
Pre-screening	None in countries where ICOs are not regulated	Full pre-screening; compliant and fully regulated	The exchange screens projects before they are willing to risk their reputation
Relative investor risk	Highest	Lowest	Medium

Table 2.1: Comparison of ICOs, STOs, and IEOs

Initial Coin Offerings (ICOs).

With an ICO, people exchange money (typically bitcoins) for new coins released by the project's founders. Investors buy the coins, but not shares in a company, which for a long time bypassed many onerous regulations. *Mastercoin* was the first ICO, which raised $5.5 million in 2014.[35] *Ethereum* was the second ICO, raising $18 million in 2014. The largest ICOs include:

- *EOS*, a blockchain platform to build and launch smart contracts, raised $4.1 billion;

- *Telegram Open Network* raised $1.7 billion to build a peer-to-peer messenger app;

- *Dragon Coin* raised $320 million for a decentralized currency for gambling;

- *Huobi* raised $300 million for its Singapore-based cryptocurrency exchange;

- *Hyundai Digital Asset Currency* (HDAC) raised $258 million for an Internet of Things (IoT) contract platform;

- *Filecoin* raised $257 million to store files on a distributed network analogous to the way Bitcoin stores transactions; and

- *Tezos* raised $232 million to put more governance around blockchains to prevent forks such as occurred at Ethereum (a story told later in this guide).[36]

Overall, ICOs raised over $14 billion dollars from 2014-2019.[37] As a new funding tool, the risks around ICOs are significant. By 2018, the top ten ICO scams swindled over $687 million from investors.[38] At the top of this list was *Pincoin* and *iFan*, two ICOs run by the same company— Modern Tech—in Vietnam; its seven executives defrauded 32,000 investors of over $660 million.[39] They closed shop, kept the websites up, fled the country and disappeared.[40]

How do you spot an ICO scam? For the casual investor, Techcrunch contributor Deep Patel identified these red flags to detect ICO scams: the early release of coins goes primarily to the founders, not investors or miners; the founders are anonymous or have little credible experience; the project's white paper is missing details; the project has no clear timelines; the project claims the programming code will be open sourced but it does not exist on GitHub—the de facto repository for open-sourced blockchain source code. In short, *caveat emptor*.

When regulators around the world started intervening, the ICO market fell precipitously.[42] In 2019, ICOs raised only $371 *million* compared $7.8 *billion* worldwide 2018.[43] In the US, the SEC deemed that many of the ICO projects' tokens were securities, and thus subject to all SEC regulations.[44] The SEC has also halted ICOs, including *Plexcoin*, which raised $15 million by promising a 1300 percent return on investment within a month.[45] By 2019, the SEC had brought a number of charges and penalties to companies that raised money with an ICO, including *Bitqyck; Block.one; ICOBox; UnitedData*; and *XBT*.[46] Some countries, most notably China and South Korea, have banned or imposed strict restrictions on ICOs.[47]

While ICOs fell in popularity, two new funding models rose in popularity: Security Token Offerings (STOs) and Initial Exchange Offerings (IEOs).

Security Token Offerings (STOs)

STOs are legally compliant, licensed ICOs which protect investors against fraud. The value of the token is based on the company's valuation. STOs are only available for accredited investors. In 2018, 119 security tokens were launched by capital investor firms, raising over $17 billion, with the majority of that in the last quarter of the year.[48] A number of STO standards are emerging, which will make it easier for investors to liquidate.[49]

Initial Exchange Offerings (IEOs)

IEOs are a funding round conducted on a cryptocurrency exchange. Investors fund their exchange wallets with coins and use those funds to buy the fundraising company's tokens. Many exchanges now comply with Anti-Money Laundering (AML) and Know Your Customer (KYC) regulations and also vet the fundraisers, making IEO investments less risky than ICOs. *Binance, Huobi, OKEX, KuCoin*, and *BitMax* are examples of exchanges with IEO services.[50] As of February 2020, the countries with the greatest number of IEOs were the US, Estonia and Singapore, with 27 IEOs in each country. There were 18 IEOs in the United Kingdom (UK); 11 in Malta; and nine in Switzerland. By May 2019, IEOs had raised over $3 billion.[51]

Next we examine the global blockchain players.

2.4. Blockchain players

According to the Blockchain Council—a member network of 1500 blockchain experts, the ten countries most active in blockchain technologies are Australia; China; Estonia; Japan; Malta; Singapore; Switzerland; United Arab Emirates (Dubai); United Kingdom; United States.[52] Blockchain startups, traditional enterprises, blockchain working groups, traditional standards-making bodies, and regulators are the major players shaping the blockchain landscape. Blockchain startups and traditional enterprises are helping to build blockchain technologies *within* the boundaries of the firm. Blockchain working groups and traditional standards-making bodies are developing blockchain foundations *across* firm boundaries. Regulators across the globe struggled to keep pace, but several governments have passed pro-crypto laws, while others have cracked down.

2.4.1. Blockchain startups

While it's difficult to identify a precise number of blockchain startups, there are a number of websites that attempt to do just that. Here we examine startups in the US, China, and Europe. As of January 2020, the US website www.angel.co identified 4,237 blockchain startups, with an average valuation of $4.9 million.[53] LongHash, a platform for accelerating the development of blockchain technology, reported over 79,000 registered startups in China alone, although only 26,057 were still in operations as of February 2020.[54] Many had their licenses revoked after the Chinese government took a firmer stance against ICOs. However, in November of 2019, Chinese President Xi Jinping stated that blockchain technologies (rather than cryptocurrencies) were a major strategic thrust for the country, and subsequently there were 800 new blockchain startups in China during the first three weeks of 2020.[55] In Europe, the European Commission reported the number of blockchain startups to be 184 as of 2019, with the United Kingdom, Germany, France, and Estonia having the most number of startups. However, this number seems underreported. According to Crunchbase, there were 750 blockchain startups within the European Union.[56] Across the globe, blockchain start-ups are found across every industry: financial services; insurance; healthcare; real estate; supply chain; Internet of Things (IoT); FinTech; identity; energy; retail; music; food; and legal services.

Crypto exchanges

Crypto exchanges were among the early startups that were vital to the diffusion of cryptocurrencies. Initially, the only way to interact with the Bitcoin network was to become a miner and to manage one's own digital wallet, which requires significant technical skills. Many people saw the need for an exchange where users could easily buy and sell bitcoins with fiat currency. The first Bitcoin exchange was ***Bitcoin Market***, launched in March of 2010 by a Bitcoin Talk member using the pseudonym 'dwdollar'.[57] Jed McCaleb (born in Little Rock Arkansas), soon after launched the most famous Bitcoin exchange called *Mt. Gox* in 2010. McCaleb sold the site to Mark Karpelès in 2011. Early exchanges operated under the radar of regulatory bodies, and many consumers were at risk for shams and heists. Mt. Gox—and other exchanges that followed—were lucrative targets for hackers because exchanges controlled the users' private keys. One of the largest heists occurred in August of 2014 when 850,000 bitcoins worth $450 million was stolen from the wallets managed by Mt. Gox.[58]

Today, there are over 260 cryptocurrency exchanges, including *Coinbase* (founded in 2012 in the US); *Huobi* (founded in China in 2013); and *Binance* (founded in China in 2017 but it has since moved to Malta).[59] Many exchanges now comply with regulations, including Know Your Customer (KYC) and Anti-Money Laundering (AML) requirements. For example, Coinbase had money transmitter licenses from 45 US States and a New York State Virtual Currency License by 2019. Coinbase also has commercial criminal insurance that is greater than the value of digital currency maintained in online storage (98 percent of the private keys are stored offline). Increased compliance means a loss of user anonymity, a consequence counter to the Cypherpunk values of the initial Bitcoin adopters.

Considering all startups, which are the leaders in 2020? Rise.global lists 100 of the most influential blockchain companies based on Kred scores (Kred is a social media community that tracks and scores social media influencers); tweets; retweets; and Linkedin mentions. As of January of 2020, its top blockchain influencers were *Blockchain* (focused on the future of finance); *CoinTelegraph* (blockchain news); *Ripple* (financial services application); *Coindesk* (blockchain news); *Binance* (crypto exchange); *NEM* (asset management on a blockchain); *Stratisplatform* (enterprise platform); *Bitcoin News* (blockchain news); *Bitstamp* (crypto exchange); and *Stellar* (open network for moving money).[60] We'll encounter several of these startups throughout this guide.

2.4.2. Traditional enterprises

Several research firms have estimated the spending on blockchain services by traditional enterprises, and their estimates vary widely. In 2018, HfS (a UK-based consulting firm) estimated the blockchain market for enterprise services to be $1 billion.[61] In 2019, Grand View Research, a US-based market research and consulting company, valued the global blockchain market at $509 million in 2015 and $605 million in 2016 and could be worth as much as $7.59 billion by 2024.[62, 63] According to IDC, enterprises spent $2.8 billion on blockchain technologies in 2019 and likely will spend $12.4 billion by 2020. The biggest spenders are from financial services; the United States (US) will spend most (about $1 billion), followed by western Europe (about $700 million) and China (about $320 million).[64]

A number of surveys report a slow and steady march of support and adoption of blockchain technologies by traditional enterprises. According to Gartner, a global research and advisory firm, 60 percent of Chief Information Officers (CIOs) expect to deploy blockchains in the next three years.[65] Deloitte's 2019 survey of 1,386 senior managers in 12 countries found that 86 percent believe blockchains are broadly scalable and will achieve mainstream adoption.[66] In a 2019 survey done by Forrester Research and EY of 233 decision makers, 66 percent were planning to implement private blockchains and 35 percent were planning to implement public blockchains within the next two years.

Who is leading? Lots of websites rate the top traditional companies using blockchain technologies. For example, Reality Shares, in 2019, created a blockchain score based on blockchain R&D; blockchain product stage; blockchain economic impact; patents; filings; and the role in the blockchain ecosystem. Reality Shares rated the top five companies at the forefront of blockchains as *IBM*; *Alibaba Group*; *Fujitsu*; *Mastercard*; and *ING*. IBM, which states that it has helped to launch more successful blockchain initiatives than any other company, believes that investments from corporations in financial services will continue to see an increase throughout 2020. In 2019, Forbes highlighted the blockchain technology platforms used by 50 traditional global companies (see Figure 2.5).[67] Consistent with Forrester Research and EY's survey, Forbes found that companies were using more private platforms like Hyperledger Fabric, Corda, SawTooth and Quorum compared to public blockchains like Ethereum and Bitcoin.

Although firms from all sectors are exploring blockchain technologies, we'll focus on the two most active industries, namely, financial services and professional and information technology (IT) services.

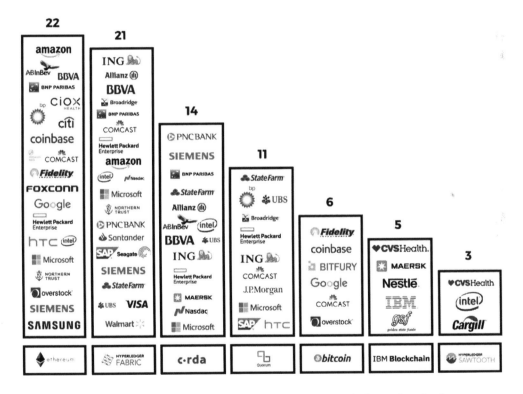

Figure 2.5: Global companies adopting blockchain technologies.

Source: https://medium.com/blockdata/breaking-down-the-forbes-blockchain-50-2f44e9902537

Financial services

According to Gartner and Deloitte, financial services firms continue to lead the way in blockchain advancements. Financial services firms were the first to recognize Bitcoin as a potential threat or opportunity.[68] Since 2014, more than 50 of the world's largest financial services companies have made direct investments in blockchain startups. Financial services firms were the early investors, including such companies as *American Express; Banco Santander; BNP Paribas; Citi; CME Group; DTCC; Goldman Sachs; JP Morgan; MasterCard; Morgan Stanley; NYSE; USAA; Visa;* and *Wells Fargo* to name just a few.[69] Most of these blockchain projects aim to improve (rather than disrupt) traditional financial services. Financial services firms are seeking to lower transaction costs and to speed settlement times for remittances; cross-border payments; bond issuances and settlements; derivatives; equities; and trade finance.

Professional and IT services

Many of the large professional and IT services firms have vibrant blockchain practices. Some firms report having hundreds of employees focused on blockchains. Many of these companies are helping their clients explore blockchain technologies by offering strategy; opportunity analysis; development; and implementation services. Some firms, like *Microsoft* and *Alibaba*, are focused on Blockchains as a Service. *IBM* focuses on both. Table 2.2 highlights examples of the professional and IT services firms with blockchain practices, along with their websites to keep track of this rapidly evolving space.

2.4.3. Blockchain working groups

Working groups, including private and public consortia and non-profits, are defining blockchain standards, developing code bases and exploring use cases for business applications. According to a survey by Deloitte, enterprises join working groups to achieve cost savings; to accelerate learning; to share risks; to build a critical mass of adoption; to maintain relevance; and to influence standards.[70]

Company	Blockchain Practice Website
Alibaba	https://www.alibabacloud.com/products/baas
Accenture	https://www.accenture.com/us-en/services/blockchain-index
Capgemini	https://www.capgemini.com/beyond-the-buzz/blockchain/
Cognizant	https://www.cognizant.com/enterprise-blockchain-solutions
Deloitte	https://www2.deloitte.com/us/en/pages/consulting/topics/blockchain.html
EY	https://www.ey.com/en_us/blockchain
KPMG	https://advisory.kpmg.us/services/digital-transformation/blockchain.html
IBM	https://www.ibm.com/blockchain
Infosys	https://www.infosys.com/blockchain.html#infosys-blockchain
Microsoft	https://azure.microsoft.com/en-us/services/blockchain-service/
PwC	https://www.pwc.com/gx/en/issues/blockchain.html
Wipro	https://www.wipro.com/en-US/blockchain/blockchain-platform-services/

**Table 2.2: Examples of professional and IT services firms
with blockchain practices**

By 2020, there were over 220 major blockchain consortia (see Figure 2.6). The banking and financial services sector constituted nearly 31 percent of the blockchain consortia by the end of 2018 but declined to less than 25 percent of the overall consortia by the end of 2019. This relative decline indicates a wider adoption of blockchain technology outside of banking and financial services. For example, healthcare became the third largest sector of blockchain consortia at eight percent. From 2014 to 2019, there has been continuous growth in the number of consortia formed year over year, with 2019 having nearly 80 blockchain consortia formed.[71]

To get a sense of these working groups, we will briefly cover R3; Hyperledger Project; B3i; Enterprise Ethereum Alliance; Blockchain in Transportation Alliance (BiTA); and the Oil & Gas Blockchain Consortium (OOC).

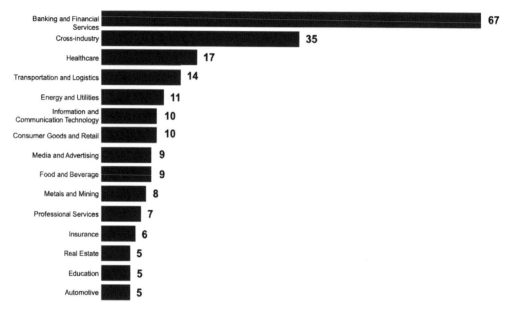

Figure 2.6: Blockchain consortia by industry

Source: Drawn by Jacob Yates drew using data from ESL Intelligence (2020), https://esg-intelligence. com/access-enterprise-blockchain-intelligence/list-of-all-blockchain-consortia/

R3

Founded in 2014 by David Rutter in New York City, R3 is one of the first consortia of significance. R3 was launched with nine large banks: ***Barclays; BBVA Francés; State Street; JP Morgan; Commonwealth Bank of Australia; Goldman Sachs; Royal Bank of Scotland; Credit Suisse***; and ***UBS***—eventually growing to 60 members. In 2017, R3 released Corda, a peer-to-peer code base aimed at enterprises that want strict data and transaction privacy. Corda is designed to increase privacy, reduce data redundancy (not everyone needs to see a transaction), and scalability (see Glossary for more on Corda).[72] Figure 2.5 also identifies companies that are using Corda.

Hyperledger Project (HLP)

The Linux Foundation launched this non-profit organization with 30 corporate founders in December of 2015. Brian Behlendorf, the developer of the Apache Web server, serves as Executive Director. As of January 2020, 275+ corporate members are listed on its website. It aims to advance the application of enterprise-grade blockchains across industries.[73] Its four-part mission is to:

4. create an enterprise grade, open source distributed ledger framework and code base, upon which users can build and run robust, industry-specific applications, platforms and hardware systems to support business transactions;

5. create an open source, technical community to benefit the ecosystem of HLP solution providers and users, focused on blockchain and shared ledger use cases that will work across a variety of industry solutions;

6. promote participation of leading members of the ecosystem, including developers, service and solution providers and end users;

7. (host the infrastructure for HLP, establishing a neutral home for community infrastructure, meetings, events and collaborative discussions and providing structure around the business and technical governance of HLP.[74]

Thus far, HLP oversees six major distributed ledger projects: Fabric (see Glossary for overview); Sawtooth; Iroha; Burrow; Indy; and BESU (see Figure 2.7). Fabric, much of whose code was donated by IBM, is commonly used by enterprises, including **IBM, Walmart**, and **Maersk** (see Figure 2.5 above).[75] HLP is also developing five tools (Avalon, Cactus, Caliper, Cello, and Explorer) and building libraries (Quilt for blockchain interoperability; Ursa for cryptography; Transact for smart contracts; and Aries for digital credentials).[76] Finally, Hyperledger GRID was donated by Cargill to serve as a reference implementation for supply chains and includes data types, data models, and smart contract business logic.[77]

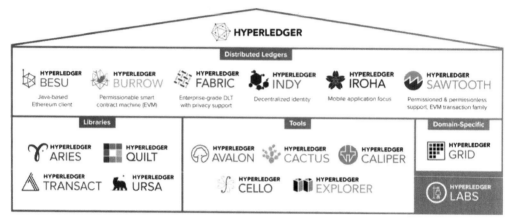

Figure 2.7: Hyperledger's projects as of 2020

Source: https://www.hyperledger.org/

B3i

B3i was founded in October 2016 in Zurich, Switzerland to focus on blockchain standards for the insurance sector. By 2017, it had 15 members: *Achmea; Aegon; Ageas; Allianz; Generali; Hannover Re; Liberty Mutual; Munich Re; RGA; SCOR; Sompo Japan Nipponkoa Insurance; Swiss Re; Tokio Marine Holdings; XL Catlin;* and *Zurich Insurance Group*. In March 2017, B3i began working on a proof-of-concept for catastrophic property insurance. The product, called Property Cat XOL contract, was officially released on the Corda Network in August 2019; it is designed to make the insurance process faster, cheaper, and better.[78]

Enterprise Ethereum Alliance (EEA)

Many companies want an enterprise-grade blockchain based on the Ethereum protocol. To help make that a reality, *Microsoft; Accenture; JP Morgan; BNY Mellon; CME Group; MasterCard; Santander; Wipro* and 26 other enterprises founded the Enterprise Ethereum Alliance in February 2017.[79] Within the first year, 200 organizations joined the alliance. The alliance is seeking solutions to Ethereum's scalability, performance and privacy challenges.[80] To help make progress, given the size of the alliance, working groups focus on particular areas of interest. As of mid-2017, the active working groups focused on the advertising industry; banking; healthcare; insurance; legal industry; supply chain; and token working groups.[81] The EEA's major project is the Token Taxonomy Initiative, with aims to help *"developers to create new types of tokens from a set of reusable, cross-industry components—all without requiring an understanding of industry jargon or coding."* [82] The Token Taxonomy Framework overview and specification drafts were published in November 2019. EEA announced a collaboration with HLP in October of 2018 to accelerate mass adoption of blockchain technologies for enterprises.[83]

The Decentralized Identity Foundation (DIF)

Many experts view 'identity' as the pre-cursor and necessary foundation for an 'Internet of Value'. Ideally, people, groups, organizations, devices, and objects can become uniquely identified and recognized across blockchain applications. To that end, DIF was founded in 2017. By 2020, it had over 60 members and is working on standards that *"enable creation, resolution, and discovery of decentralized identifiers and names across underlying decentralized systems, like blockchains and distributed ledgers."*[84] By 2020, they published overviews for 'the Universal Resolver' and 'Sidetree Protocol'.

The Blockchain in Transportation Alliance (BiTA)

BiTA was launched in 2017 to develop data standards for the entire transportation industry. Its website reports members from 25 countries. The BiTA Standards Council, a separate not-for-profit organization, is chaired by Dale Chrystie, a business fellow and blockchain strategist at **FedEx**. So far, standards for tracking data and location components have been released.[85] The standard is designed to answer the question, *"Where is my shipment?"*

Oil & Gas Blockchain Consortium (OOC)

More recently, the OOC launched in 2019 in Houston Texas with ten founding members: *Chevron; ConocoPhillips; Equinor; ExxonMobile; Hess; Marathon Oil; Nobel Energy; Pioneer; Repsol;* and *Shell.* Members are collaborating on four use cases pertaining to trucking; joint operating agreements; and seismic data management.[86]

While our coverage above is far from exhaustive, it underscores the point that people are taking blockchains for business seriously across sectors and across the globe. Some consortia are working well, with competitors learning to work in the spirit of 'coopetition'—defined as collaboration between traditional competitors in the hopes of obtaining mutually beneficial results.[87] However, members of some consortia are frustrated as traditional companies struggle with the notion of 'coopetition'. For example, we have observed that many companies join consortia because they claim they value 'transparency', but what many companies really want is access to ecosystem partners' data without revealing their own.

2.4.4. Standards-making bodies

"The nice thing about standards is that you have so many to choose from."

Andrew S. Tanenbaum and David Wetherall (1981), p. 702[88]

Traditional standard-making bodies are also major players in the blockchain landscape. They have the experience, legitimacy, and recognition to establish technical standards for an 'Internet of Value.' Some have been around for over one hundred years. As a quick history, the Engineering Standards Committee, established in London in 1901, was the first standards organization.[89] Since then, international, national and regional standards-making bodies proliferate.

In the world of digital business communications, the machine-readable barcode was invented in 1952; the Universal Product Code (UPC) was adopted in the retail sector in

1973; and the United Nations passed Electronic Data Interchange for Administration, Commerce and Transport (EDIFACT) in 1987. Since the 1990s we've had eXtensible Markup Language (XML) standards—to pass business documents in both human and machine-readable form over the Internet. We've had industry specific standards from International Organization for Standards (ISO), GS1, and the IEEE for decades. For example, GS1's Electronic Product Code Information Services (EPICS) has been widely adopted in the pharmaceutical industry to track major events in the supply chain, capturing the 'what, when, where, and why' of a business transaction.[90] Given all these existing standards, why do blockchains require more?[91] According to GS1's (2018) report, *Bridging Blockchains: Interoperability is Essential to the Future of Data Sharing*:

> *"It will not be enough to only leverage existing GS1 standards for identification, data capture and sharing as a best practice [to achieve blockchain interoperability]. Industry and the consortiums that serve industry will also need to collaborate on answers to some entirely new questions around governance and interoperability."* [92]

Organizations with blockchain standards initiatives	Reference sites to blockchain projects
GS1	https://www.gs1.org/
IEEE Blockchain Initiative (BCI)	https://blockchain.ieee.org/ https://blockchain.ieee.org/standards
International Organization for Standards (ISO) TC 307	https://www.iso.org/committee/6266604.html
National Institute of Standards & Technology (NIST)	https://www.nist.gov/publications/blockchain-technology-overview
China Electronics Standardization Institute (CESI)	http://www.cc.cesi.cn/english.aspx
Object Management Group (OMG)	https://www.omg.org/hot-topics/distributed-immutable-data-object.htm

Table 2.3: Blockchain standards initiatives

Many traditional standards organizations are tackling blockchain extensions and adaptations, but few have produced final reports (see Table 2.3). These include:

- *GS1*—a neutral not-for-profit standards organization—is working to enhance its existing standards to apply to blockchain applications.[93]

- *The IEEE*—a globally recognized standards-setting body—started a blockchain group (BCI) in January of 2018. The IEEE BCI has over 25 active standards projects pertaining to blockchain technology including the launch of the world's first *Advancing HealthTech for Humanity*™ with the five most recent standards as of 2019 pertaining to the healthcare sector.[94]

- The *International Organization for Standards (ISO)* launched the Technical Committee (TC) 307 on blockchains and distributed ledgers in 2016. Representatives from 44 countries are participating, including the *American National Standards Institute (ANSI)* and the *British Standards Institution (BSI)*. As of 2020, it has eleven major blockchain projects. The first standard, called ISO/TR 23455, was published in 2019; it provides an overview of interactions between smart contracts and distributed ledger technology systems.[95]

- The *National Institute of Standards and Technology (NIST)* is looking into blockchains and published a primer in 2018.[96]

- *China Electronics Standardization Institute (CESI)* released four domestic blockchain standards in 2019 on: smart contracts implementation; blockchain privacy protection; blockchain in evidence deposition; and blockchain security.[97]

- The *Object Management Group (OMG)* published a discussion paper on distributed immutable data objects.

To get a better understanding of existing standards and how they are being adapted for blockchains, we'll focus on GS1's efforts. As noted above, GS1 is a not-for-profit organization that develops and maintains data standards for business communications. It was founded in 1969 by US retailers searching for ways to speed up checkout. Today, GS1 is a global entity. Its management board includes *Amazon; Alibaba Group;*

Carrefour; eBay; Google; Independent Grocers Association; Johnson & Johnson; Mondelez; Nestlé; Procter & Gamble; Smuckers; Walgreens; and *Walmart.* GS1's global standards are widely adopted in supply chain contexts. The individual standards work in concert to facilitate the tracing of products through a supply chain. For example, Figure 2.8 shows a hierarchy of codes comprising GLN, GSIN, SSCC, and GTIN data standards can be seen in Table 2.4.

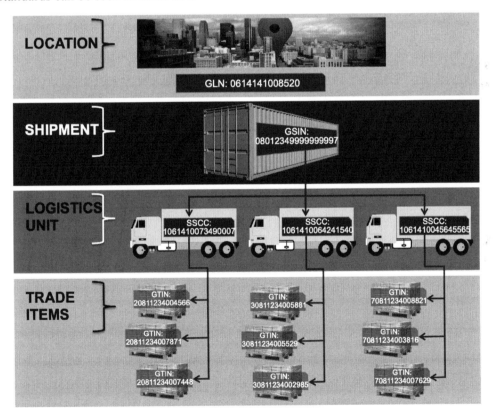

Figure 2.8: Example of how GS1 standards work in concert to track items through a supply chain

Source: https://www.gs1si.org/CashEDI/Doc/GSIN_Intro.pdf

Sample GS1 Standards	Describes	Description
Global Location Number (GLN)	Parties and locations	Includes codes for company prefix and location reference; Example locations are: a room within a building, a dock door, and accounts payable department.
Serial Shipping Container Code (SSCC)	Logistical units	Includes codes for company prefix and serial reference. It's an 18-digit barcode, preceded by a '(00)', placed on the outside of a shipping container/pallet that uniquely identifies the contents.
Global Shipping Identification Number (GSIN)	Shipments	Includes codes for application identifier, company prefix, shipping reference. Example of a GSIN with a 7-digit GS1 Company Prefix (402) 0801234 999999999 7 Application Identifier — GS1 Company Prefix — Shipper Reference — Check Digit
Global Trade Item Number (GTIN)	Products and services	GTIN includes codes for company prefix, item reference. For example, the GTIN number 038900006198 maps to 'Dole Crushed Pineapple in Its Own Juice, 8 oz'

Table 2.4: Examples of GS1 data standards

GS1's EPCIS and EDIFACT standards help trading partners execute business transactions (see Table 2.5).

GS1 is working to enhance these standards to apply to blockchain applications. As an easy step, GS1 is creating a JavaScript Object Notation (JSON) version, which is the emerging standard for blockchain APIs. (The current EPCIS standard is enabled by XML.) More importantly, GS1 is working with industry partners like IBM and Microsoft to enhance the additional business steps needed for blockchain solutions. For the US pharmaceutical sector, GS1 is adding a return verification event to its Electronic

Product Code Information Services (EPCIS), as return verification is emerging as one of the first use cases the ecosystem partners are exploring with a blockchain solution. In addition to the pharmaceutical sector, GS1 is also working closely with IBM Food Trust to understand enhancements required for food traceability. According to Melanie Nuce, Senior Vice President, Corporate Development at GS1 US, blockchain solutions require additional data fields to be included in GS1 standards:

> *"The primary use cases we've been addressing are in the pharmaceutical and food safety sectors. There's a lot of missing data that's going to prevent companies from building these really large ecosystems. Most enterprises are not capturing the data, so it cannot be shared. We've really been trying to emphasize the fundamental messages of: 'You have to know what you're trying to share, with whom you're trying to share it, and how you're going to go about sharing it, regardless of the technology you use.'"[98]*

Standards-making bodies typically need about three years from the time proposals are announced until standards are published.[99] The time is needed to ensure broad stakeholder input and review.

Electronic Product Code Information Services (EPCIS)	Event data	*"Product X with serial numbers 111, 112, and 113 were observed at 10:23am on April 2017 at Location ABC, during a 'shipping' operation."*
Electronic Data Interchange for Administration, Commerce and Transport (EDIFACT)	Documents, messaging	EDIFACT comprises an interchange header; functional group header; message header; user data types; message trailer; functional trailer and interchange trailer.

Table 2.5 Examples of GS1 electronic standards[iii]

[iii] Tables 2.4 and 2.5 were extracted from Lacity, M., Zach, S., Paul, C. (2019). Towards Blockchain 3.0 Interoperability: Business and Technical Considerations. Blockchain Center of Excellence white paper, BCoE-2019-01, University of Arkansas.

2.4.5. Regulators

"Regulators are still trying to manage this machine with rules devised for
the industrial age."

Don and Alex Tapscott, authors of *Blockchain Revolution*[100]

While blockchain innovators will sometimes lament that regulators are 'clueless' or 'stifle innovation', most people agree that reasonable regulations are needed to protect consumers, investors, workers, and the environment. Governments all over the world are examining the blockchain space. Some governments like Malta, Switzerland, and Gibraltar are supportive, some governments like Egypt and Pakistan are not, and still others have yet to deliberate.[101] We first examine US Federal and State regulations.

Government regulation in the US

Given that financial services are one of the most heavily regulated industries, it's apt to focus upon it. A complex web of federal and state regulators oversees financial services in the United States (see Figure 2.9). At the Federal level, the US Treasury Department was one of the first regulators to enact a cryptocurrency policy. In 2013, it classified Bitcoin as a convertible, decentralized, virtual currency, and therefore subject to property taxes. Subsequently, the Internal Revenue Service (IRS) treats cryptocurrencies as property for Federal income tax purposes. People must report gains or losses on their US tax returns.[102]

We have already noted above that the US Securities and Exchange Commission (SEC) has intervened on a number of ICOs. It's useful to understand how the SEC guides its rulings. The SEC applies the 'Howey Test' to determine whether an investment is considered a security and thus subject to SEC regulations. The 'Howey Test' comes from a 1946 Supreme Court case where the SEC sued the Howey Company of Florida. The Howey Company was a citrus farm that leased land to raise investment funds, but it did not register transactions with the SEC. The Supreme Court deemed that the transactions were indeed securities based on a four-part test. A transaction is considered a security investment if: (1) it includes an investment of money (2) in a common enterprise (3) with an expectation of profit (4) based solely on the efforts of a promoter or third party. Based on this test, mostly all new investments in cryptocurrencies are now viewed as securities.[103] However, the SEC deemed that Bitcoin is NOT a security; by the time the SEC examined Bitcoin, the governance was so decentralized that the SEC could not find an identifiable promoter or third party.[104]

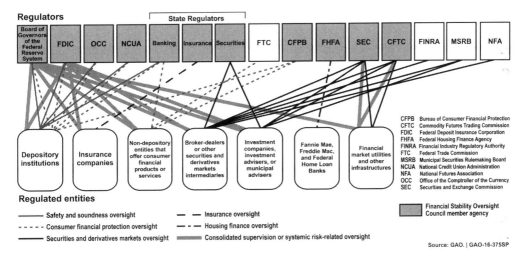

Figure 2.9: US GAO map of US regulatory environment[105]

Soutrce: http://www.gao.gov/modules/ereport/handler.php?1=1&path=/ereport/GAO-16-375SP/data_center/General_government/5._Financial_Regulatory_Structure

Besides US federal regulations, US States agencies can also impose cryptocurrency and blockchain regulations. In 2019, 28 US States introduced legislation related to blockchain with a total of 27 bills and resolutions being adopted or enacted according to the National Conference of State Legislatures.[106] Some US State laws are quite controversial. One notable example was a regulation published in June of 2015 by the Department of Financial Services (DFS) for New York State, which required companies to get a BitLicense for virtual currencies. Many small firms found compliance to be too expensive (or too invasive) and stopped operating in the state. A further controversy happened when the chief architect of the regulation, Benjamin Lawsky, left the DFS to start his own consulting process to help clients maneuver through the onerous process to obtain a BitLicense.[107] The arguments for regulations are reasonable—the BitLicense, for example, required companies to: store transaction receipts; disclose risks; publish a customer complaint policy; maintain a cybersecurity program; hire a compliance officer; and abide by anti-money-laundering rules.[108] For startups, complying with such regulations can cost hundreds of thousands of dollars, prompting them to establish their businesses in other US states with more welcoming regulations. So far, the State of Wyoming is leading in pro-crypto laws. Among them is a law that allows companies to charter Special Purpose Depository Institutions (SPDIs), *"a new type of fully-reserved fiat bank that can also custody crypto assets."*[109] Wyoming's law aims to allow companies to access customers in New York without having to apply for a BitLicense.[110]

Nearly every month, new Federal or State regulations are announced from various regulatory bodies. For example, on the day of this writing, the US Treasury Department's Financial Crimes Enforcement Network (FinCEN) announced that it is preparing to unveil new regulations around cryptocurrencies.[111] To help guide startups through the regulatory tangle, Marco Santori, President and Chief Legal Officer of Blockchain.com, spearheaded the Simple Agreement for Future Tokens (SAFT) project to establish a compliant token sale framework. The goal is *"to develop an industry standard that protects the interests of network creators, investors, and users."*[112]

Government regulation in China

Beyond the US, China was one of the first countries to ban financial institutions from accepting, using, or selling virtual currencies in 2013. A year later, China required financial institutions to close bitcoin trading accounts. By July of 2019, China forced the closure of 173 cryptocurrency exchanges and many bitcoin mining operations.[113] When China's President Xi Jinping announced strong support for blockchain technologies in October of 2018, it was clear that China's government wanted control over the space;

China will likely issue a tokenized Chinese yuan by mid 2020.[114] Many see China's move as an attempt to usurp the US dollar as the world's dominant currency.[115]

Government regulation in the United Kingdom (UK)

In 2017, the UK government treated bitcoin as foreign currency for the purposes of taxation. No value-added taxes (VAT) are due when exchanging bitcoin for other currencies, but profits and losses are subject to capital gains taxes. Cryptocurrency mining and getting paid in cryptocurrencies may be subject to income tax and national insurance contributions.[116] Beyond taxation, Naseem Naqvi, President of the British Blockchain Association, points out that the UK is a pioneer in the blockchain landscape. He notes that the UK government was among the first to create a national roadmap for distributed ledgers, back in 2015.[117]

Government regulation in Estonia

Estonia is one of the more forward-thinking countries when it comes to cryptocurrecies and blockchain technologies.[118] Bitcoin is legal, provided the trader identifies the buyer for any transaction over 1,000 euros.[119] Although Estonia does not recognize cryptocurrencies as a legal tender within the country, Estonia remains open and innovative to the idea by recognizing cryptocurrency as *"value represented in digital form"*. In June 2018, Estonia attempted to introduce a national cryptocurrency known as 'estcoin' through a government plan but the plan was ultimately criticized by the European Union (EU), sending the Estonia government back to the drawing board.[120]

Government regulation in other countries

Algeria; Bangladesh; Bolivia; Ecuador; Egypt; Kyrgyzstan, Morocco; Nepal; and Pakistan explicitly banned bitcoins.[121] Russia banned cryptocurrencies in 2016, but allowed crypto mining in 2018, treating bitcoins as property.[122] Saudi Arabia has warned investors that cryptocurrencies are a high-risk asset. Japan recognizes Bitcoin as a method of payment and allows crypto exchanges provided that they are registered and comply with all regulations. For specific regulations by country, the US Library of Congress maintains a list of cryptocurrency regulations around the world.[123]

2.5. Blockchain indices

The Blockchain Center of Excellence (BCoE) at the University of Arkansas aims to build a dynamic blockchain index to help track the overall global blockchain landscape. This index will include measures such as the number of blockchain job listings; patent applications and awards; mentions in corporate earnings reports; number of transactions on major blockchain networks; and other indices. Here, we provide snapshots of three such measures. What's interesting is that they each provide different insights. From job listings, we learn that blockchains are among the hottest skills in demand in 2020. From patent awards, we learn which countries and companies are most active in inventing blockchain innovations. From US corporate earnings reports for public companies, we learn that blockchains are still immature, posing negligible risks to shareholders.

2.5.1. Job listings

LinkedIn identified 'blockchains' as the most in-demand technical skill for 2020 in the United States; United Kingdom; France; Germany; and Australia.[124] This number-one slot was surprising given that LinkedIn did not even identify blockchain skills among the top 25 skills the prior year.[125] According to Glassdoor, a jobs review site, blockchain demand within the US was highest in the cities of New York; San Francisco; San Jose; Chicago and Seattle. High demand is driving up wages; blockchain developers, on average, command $15,000 to $40,000 more than other software developers with comparable years of experience. The average salary ranges for blockchain developers as of June 2019 was between $150,000 and $175,000.[126]

Which blockchain skills do job recruiters need the most? According to the Blockchain Council, the top five in-depth skills a blockchain developer needs are:

1. Knowledge of data structures
2. Understanding of the workings of a blockchain architecture
3. Understanding of smart contracts
4. Web development skills
5. Cryptography concepts[127]

Upwork, a global freelancing platform, posted the top *50* blockchain skills, of which experience with Ethereum; Bitcoin; JavaScript; cryptography; PHP; Node.js; cryptocurrency; content writing; website development; and Python were in the top ten.[128]

2.5.2. Patents awarded

A number of innovators are seeking patents for blockchain-related inventions. The BCoE at the University of Arkansas examined blockchain-related patents granted from January 2014 to October 2019 by China's patent office (CNIPA),[129] and the US Patent and Trademark Office (USPTO). China is clearly outpacing the US on blockchain inventions: the CNIPA awarded 2,218 blockchain patents compared to 227 by the USPTO (see Figure 2.10).[130]

The difference in numbers—in comparing US *vs* China patents—is slightly misleading, as the CNIPA awarded nearly 40 blockchain-related patents to US-based global companies such as Goldman Sachs; IBM; Intel; JP Morgan; Mastercard; Microsoft; and Visa. In contrast, the USPTO had not awarded blockchain-related patents to any Chinese-based organizations. This pattern holds more widely; according to one study published by the Federal Reserve Bank of Saint Louis, in 2016 only 4.17 percent of 1.2 million Chinese patent applications were filed overseas, whereas 43 percent of 521,802 US patent applications were filed overseas.[131] Perhaps US organizations worry more about protecting their IP overseas than Chinese organizations, or perhaps this trend reflects a distrust in the patentability of the Chinese applications overseas. Only 6.31 percent of the overseas patent applications filed by Chinese firms are granted.

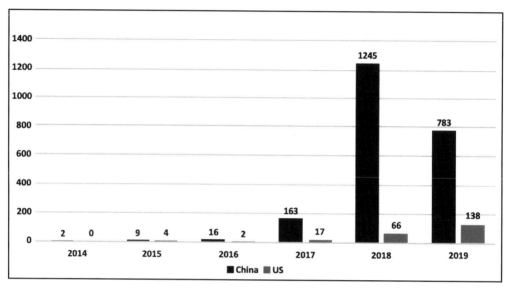

Figure 2.10: Blockchain patents awarded in China and the US

Source: Lacity, M., Steelman, Z. R., Yates, J., Wei, J. (2019). US and China Battle for Blockchain Dominance. https://cointelegraph.com/news/us-and-china-battle-for-blockchain-dominance

Furthermore, the Chinese patent office expedited the patent process more quickly than the US; it took China, on average, just six months from patent filing to patent acceptance, compared to 20 months in the US. Several explanations are possible: China may have more resources devoted to patent processing or China's patent process might not be as rigorous as the US patent process. According to Meredith Lowry, a patent attorney for Wright Lindsey Jennings, *"blockchain patent applications in the US patent process face additional hurdles to show the invention is patentable subject matter and more than the use of an algorithm. The bar for patentable subject isn't as high in other countries like China."* [132]

The European Patent Office (EPO) is another important source for protecting intellectual property pertaining to blockchain technology. The EPO hosted its first major conference on patenting blockchain in December 2018. The EPO noted that the number of blockchain patents were rising rapidly and that they needed to constantly review and adapt to ensure a sound process for both the examiners and the external stakeholders.[133] According to Statista, the largest EPO patent owners were nChain with 31 patents; Siemens with 19 patents; and MasterCard with 18. The German government had seven blockchain-related patents by 2020.[134]

2.5.3. Corporate earnings reports

How seriously are enterprises committed to blockchain technologies? Are blockchain technologies materially significant yet? One place to answer these questions is the US Securities and Exchange Commission (SEC) Form 10-K. The 10-K report contains much more detail than a company's annual report. Some of the information a company is required to disclose in the 10-K includes information on the nature of its business; risk factors; financial data; organizational structure; subsidiaries; and management's discussion and analysis about the financial and operational results. Because it is regulated by the SEC, audited by an independent auditor, and scrutinized by market participants, such as analysts and institutional investors, the 10-K is perceived as a credible report and source of information on the operations and financial performance of the firm. Given its inherent credibility compared to, say, a marketing campaign; social media post; or talk at a technology conference, we examined companies' propensity to discuss blockchains in their 10-Ks to measure the degree of their investment in this technology.

The BCoE at the University of Arkansas extracted 10-K reports from the years 2014 to 2018 that mentioned the terms 'blockchain' or 'distributed ledger' and counted the number of times a corporation used these terms.[135] We found very modest results. Of the 36,836 10-K reports in the database over five years, only 242 reports—representing a little more than ½ of a percent—mentioned blockchains or distributed ledgers. Thus, most of corporate America was silent on blockchains in 10-K reports—they were not yet materially significant enough to alert investors. Some companies that mentioned blockchains or distributed ledgers expressed positive statements about their blockchain services, investments, patents, and products while other corporations identified blockchains/distributed ledgers as a risk that could adversely affect their financial and operational performance. *Among the positive statements about blockchains in 10-K reports:*

- **Accenture** cited blockchains as one of its core consulting capabilities.

- **FedEx** announced it joined the Blockchain in Transportation Alliance.

- **IBM** identified 'blockchain' as one of its core technologies, along with analytics, artificial intelligence, security, and cloud.

- **Mastercard** announced investments and patents in blockchains.

- **NASDAQ** identified 'blockchain' as a high-growth opportunity and mentioned investments in blockchain technologies.

- **Oracle** listed 'blockchain' as part of its Software as a Service (SaaS).

The following *companies cited blockchains as a risk factor* that could adversely affect their companies: **Accenture**; **American Express; Eastman Kodak; Goldman Sachs; Northern Trust; State Street**, and **Visa.** American Express, Goldman Sachs, Northern Trust, and Visa cited blockchains as one of many technologies that could adversely affect their core businesses. Accenture acknowledged blockchain as a potential risk if client demand waned. Eastman Kodak wrote in their 2018 10-K report, *"Kodak cannot predict whether, or the extent to which, the trading price of the Company's common stock will continue to be affected by blockchain or cryptocurrency markets and any volatility in such markets."* State Street warned that FinTech technologies, including blockchains, may impose "additional costs on us, involve dependencies on third parties and may expose us to increased operational and model risk." Note that Accenture (as well as several other companies) discussed blockchains with both positive and adverse statements in their 10-Ks.

Another interesting finding is the decline in blockchain and distributed ledger mentions within the last year. The peak year for blockchain/distributed ledger mentions was 2017, when 112 companies used these terms (see Figure 2.11). The sizeable drop in mentions of these words in 2018 10-K reports corresponds to the precipitous drop in the value of cryptocurrencies, which fell to $134 billion, down nearly 90 percent, by the start of 2019. The dual decline seems more than coincidental even though enterprise blockchain applications are very different applications than cryptocurrency applications.

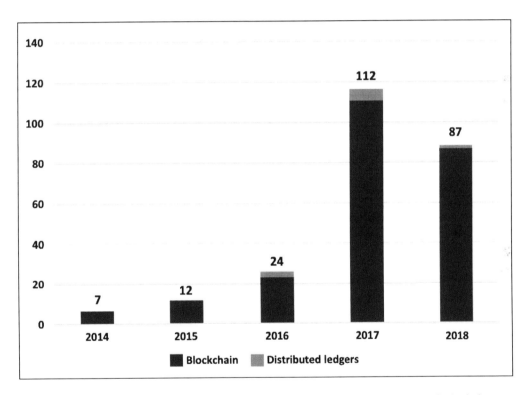

Figure 2.11: Number of 10-K reports that included the terms 'blockchain' or 'distributed ledger'

2.6. Blockchain's technology hype cycle

Taking the entire blockchain landscape into consideration, how mature is the blockchain market as we enter 2020? To answer this question, we'll look at Gartner's assessment of where blockchains are placed on its well-known hype cycle. Gartner's technology hype cycle comprises five phases that map the level of expectations about the innovation over time (see Figure 2.12). During the **technology trigger phase**, early proof-of-concepts capture media attention and interest, but there are no real applications. During the **peak of inflated expectations phase**, a few early successes garner even more attention. Senior executives start to take notice, new entrants jump into the market, and the technology may be viewed as a silver bullet, i.e. something that promises to instantly solve a long-standing problem. Many organizations start testing the technology, but enter the **trough of disillusionment phase** when instant success is not achieved. Organizations regroup. They learn to apply sound project management, change management, and what we call 'action principles' to deliver successful applications. In other words, it's hard work to get value from a new innovation. As time passes, upgraded versions of the technology are released, the market producers consolidate, and organizational consumers learn how to gain value from the innovations. Gartner calls this the **slope of enlightenment phase**. The last phase, called the **plateau of productivity phase**, sees market maturity, widespread adoption, and integration into the enterprises' standard technology portfolios.

Every year, Gartner updates its map of current emerging technologies through the five phases. In 2015, blockchains were not yet on Gartner's map. However, by July of 2016, Gartner placed blockchains as past the 'technology trigger phase' and was indeed approaching the apex of the 'peak of inflated expectations phase'. A year later in July 2017, Gartner placed blockchains as nearly finished with that phase; blockchains were headed for the 'trough of disillusionment'. A year later, the market hadn't budged. Finally, by September of 2019, Gartner placed blockchain technologies as near the bottom of the trough. Gartner estimated that more than 90 percent of enterprise blockchain platform implementations will fail or need to be replaced. This is due to a fragmented blockchain market and 'unrealistic expectations'.[136] Gartner predicted that blockchains would not reach of the 'plateau of productivity' until after 2022.

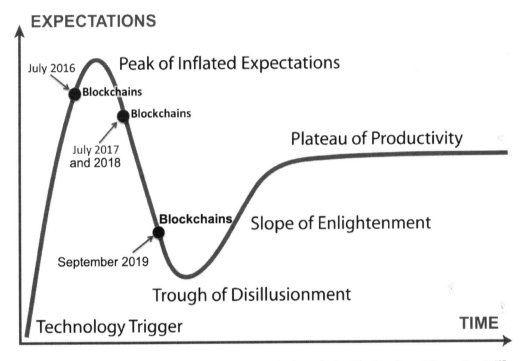

Figure 2.12: Gartner's Mapping of Blockchains via its Technology Hype Cycle[137]

We make three points about the hype cycle depicted in Figure 2.12. First, it is a useful tool for discussing overall global trends, but industries and specific organizations within industries adopt technologies at different rates. For example, companies like EY, IBM, Microsoft, and Walmart had already reached the slope of enlightenment by 2019. Second, the pace of adoption is not deterministic; individuals and organizations do not just sit around and wait for the future, they actively create it. Third, blockchains comprise a variety of technologies and sub-markets, and some are more mature than others. In 2019, Gartner decomposed the blockchain market into 37 different technologies, and placed these on the hype cycle.[iv] It shows that exchanges and cryptocurrencies are more mature than stablecoins and fiat digital currencies (like China plans to do). It also shows that financial services and governments are ahead of advertising and customer service industries.

2.7. Conclusion: The landscape shifts rapidly

The global blockchain landscape shifts rapidly and unpredictably—there will be big winners and big losers that we cannot foresee today. This chapter has been tempered with phrases such as 'as of the beginning of 2020' and 'so far' to reflect that fact. While the value of markets will fluctuate widely and individual players will come and go, the *categories* of key players will remain relevant. Startups, traditional enterprises, blockchain working groups, standard-making bodies and regulators will continue to shape and transform the blockchain foundations for the 'Internet of Value'. In the next chapter, we answer the questions:

- What exactly are blockchain applications?
- What value do they promise and how do they work?

[iv] The link to view Gartner's 2019 Hype Cycle for Blockchain Business is: https://www.gartner.com/en/newsroom/press-releases/2019-09-12-gartner-2019-hype-cycle-for-blockchain-business-shows

Citations

[1] Quote from Prisco, G. (2015). 'Nasdaq to Push Forward with Blockchain Applications', *Bitcoin Magazine*, https://bitcoinmagazine.com/articles/nasdaq-push-forward-blockchain-applications-1432680278/

[2] Quote from Lacity, M., Zach, S., Paul, C. (2019). *Blockchain Governance Models: Insights for Enterprises*, Blockchain Center of Excellence, University of Arkansas.

[3] Chaum, D. (1982). *Computer Systems Established, Maintained and Trusted by Mutually Suspicious Groups*, University of California, Berkeley.

[4] Popper, N. (2015). *Digital Gold: Bitcoin and the Inside History of the Misfits and Millionaires Trying to Reinvent Money*, Harper, New York.

[5] Burniske, C. and Tatar, J. (2017). *Cryptoassets: The Innovative Investor's Guide to Bitcoin and Beyond,* McGraw Hill, United States.

[6] https://en.bitcoinwiki.org/wiki/Namecoin
https://en.bitcoinwiki.org/wiki/Litecoin

[7] Monero uses the CryptoNote protocol developed by Nicolas van Saberhagen, that defined an algorithm with increased data obfuscation compared to Bitcoin. With Monero, a recipient's address is only used once, so that the sender cannot trace subsequent transactions on the ledger. When the recipient spends money out of that address (thus becoming a "sender" address in a subsequent transaction), the address gets hidden within a group signature https://cryptonote.org/whitepaper.pdf; https://en.wikipedia.org/wiki/Monero_(cryptocurrency).

[8] https://z.cash/technology/

[9] Cuen, L. (August 30, 2019). *Why Tether volume is at all-time highs*. https://www.coindesk.com/why-tether-volume-surged-to-all-time-highs-in-august

[10] USD Coin. https://www.coinbase.com/usdc

[11] Gemini Coin https://gemini.com/

[12] JP Morgan Press Release (February 14 2019). *JP Morgan Creates Digital Coin for Payments.* https://www.jpmorgan.com/global/news/digital-coin-payments

[13] Shieber, J. (2019). 'In a big reversal, Libra reportedly could peg its cryptocurrencies to national currencies', *TechCrunch,* https://techcrunch.com/2019/10/20/in-a-big-reversal-libra-reportedly-could-peg-its-cryptocurrencies-to-national-currencies/

[14] (October 23, 2019). *Mark Zuckerberg grilled by US Congress over Libra* https://www.dw.com/en/mark-zuckerberg-grilled-by-us-congress-over-libra/a-50957685

[15] Perez, E. (October 2, 2019). 'Stablecoins Backed by Precious Metals', *CoinTelegraph*. https://cointelegraph.com/news/stablecoins-backed-by-precious-metals-how-do-they-work

[16] Petro news (2020). *CoinTelegraph*, https://cointelegraph.com/tags/petro

[17] Makerdao. *A better money*. https://makerdao.com/en/

[18] This website tracks the trading price of cryptocurrencies in US$dollars and the total number of coins in circulation to calculate a market cap: https://coinmarketcap.com/all/views/all/

[19] Most cryptocurrencies are created as hard forks from existing open source code, most commonly from Bitcoin. Litecoin, Zcash, and Dash, are Bitcoin hard forks. Monero and NEM, both among the top ten cryptocurrencies by market capitalization as of July 2017, have different code bases. Monero uses Proof-of-Work based on the CryptoNote protocol, which masks the origin, destination, and actual transaction amount (see https://moneroblocks.info/); NEM is based on new code. https://www.nem.io/

[20] As the price volatility is extremely high, see https://coinmarketcap.com/all/views/all/ for today's values.

[21] Jeffries, A. (November 27th 2013). *Bitcoin hits $1,000 for the first time,* https://www.theverge.com/2013/11/27/5151396/bitcoin-hits-1000

[22] Russell, J. (May 20th 2017). *Bitcoin just surged past $2,000 for the first time*, https://techcrunch.com/2017/05/20/btc2k/

[23] Cheng, E. (November 28th 2017). *Bitcoin surpasses $10,000 for the first time*, https://www.cnbc.com/2017/11/28/bitcoin-surpasses-10000-for-the-first-time.html

[24] Cheng, E. (December 6th 2017). *Bitcoin tops record $19,000, then plunges in wild 2-day ride*, https://www.cnbc.com/2017/12/06/bitcoin-tops-13000-surging-1000-in-less-than-24-hours.html

[25] https://coinmarketcap.com/

[26] To put these numbers in context, price volatility indices that calculate the standard deviation of a price from its mean during a certain time period may be used to compare historical price fluctuations. Using the price volatility index of a 30-day window, Bitcoin's 2017 year end index was 7.14 percent and Ethereum's was 5.26 percent. For comparison, the volatility of gold averages around 1.2 percent and the volatility major fiat currencies averages between 0.5 and 1.0 percent. *'The Bitcoin Volatility Index'*, tracked at https://www.buybitcoinworldwide.com/volatility-index/

27 Vigna, P. (November 4, 2019). 'Large Bitcoin Player Manipulated Price Sharply Higher, Study Says', *The Wall Street Journal*, https://www.wsj.com/articles/large-bitcoin-player-manipulated-price-sharply-higher-study-says-11572863400

28 Griffin, J. and Shams, A. (2019). *Is Bitcoin Really Un-tethered?*, https://ssrn.com/abstract=3195066 or http://dx.doi.org/10.2139/ssrn.3195066

29 Willams-Grut, O. (Jan 17, 2018). Here are all the theories explaining the crpto market crash, https://www.insider.com/bitcoin-cryptocurrency-market-crash-explained-causes-2018-1

30 Alois, JD. (August 13, 2019). 'Research: Since 2014 $32.3 Billion Has Gone Into Blockchain Investments with Record Amount in 2018. During First Half of 2019, Blockchain Deals Have Dropped', *CrowdFund Insider*, https://www.crowdfundinsider.com/2019/08/150513-research-since-2014-32-3-billion-has-gone-into-blockchain-investments-with-record-amount-in-2018-during-first-half-of-2019-blockchain-deals-have-dropped/

31 Orcutt, M. (April 2, 2019). 'Venture capitalists are still throwing hundreds of millions at blockchains', *Technology Review*. https://www.technologyreview.com/s/613247/venture-capitalists-are-still-throwing-hundreds-of-millions-at-blockchains/

32 CB Insights (October 27, 2017). *Blockchain in Review: Investment Trends and Opportunities*, CB Insights webinar; http://support.citrixonline.com/en_US/Webinar See also: Levi, A. (May 21, 2017), "Corporate Trends in Blockchain," CB Insights webinar presentation.

33 Orcutt, M. (April 2, 2019). 'Venture capitalists are still throwing hundreds of millions at blockchains', *Technology Review*. https://www.technologyreview.com/s/613247/venture-capitalists-are-still-throwing-hundreds-of-millions-at-blockchains/

34 Digital Currency Group, http://dcg.co/portfolio/

35 Griffith, E. (May 5, 2017). 'Why Startups are Trading IPOs for ICOS', *Fortune Magazine*, http://fortune.com/2017/05/05/ico-initial-coin-offering/

36 Higgins, S. (July 13th 2017). '$232 Million: Tezos Blockchain Project Finishes Record-Setting Token Sale', *Coindesk*, https://www.coindesk.com/232-million-tezos-blockchain-record-setting-token-sale/

37 https://www.icodata.io/stats/2018

38 FortuneJack (September 12, 2018). *How to Identify and Avoid ICO Scams*. https://fortunejack.com/blog/article/how-to-identify-and-avoid-ico-scams

39 FinanceMonthly (2018). https://www.finance-monthly.com/2018/10/the-10-biggest-ico-scams-swindled-687-4-million/

Kharpal, A. (November 21st 2017). 'Cryptocurrency start-up Confido disappears with $375,000 from an ICO, and nobody can find the founders', *CNBC News*, https://www.cnbc.com/2017/11/21/confido-ico-exit-scam-founders-run-away-with-375k.html

[40] Biggs, J. (April 13, 2018). 'Exit scammers run off with $660 million in ICO earnings', *Tech-Crunch*, https://techcrunch.com/2018/04/13/exit-scammers-run-off-with-660-million-in-ico-earnings/

[41] Patel, D. (December 7th 2017). 'Six red flags of an ICO scam', *Techncrunch*, https://techcrunch.com/2017/12/07/6-red-flags-of-an-ico-scam/

[42] https://www.icodata.io/stats/2019.

[43] https://www.icodata.io/stats/2019.

[44] Shin, L. (December 4th 2017). '$15 Million ICO Halted By SEC For Being Alleged Scam', *Forbes Magazine*, https://www.forbes.com/sites/laurashin/2017/12/04/15-million-ico-halted-by-sec-for-being-alleged-scam/ - 1728c7141569

[45] Shin, L. (December 4th 2017). '$15 Million ICO Halted By SEC For Being Alleged Scam', *Forbes Magazine*, https://www.forbes.com/sites/laurashin/2017/12/04/15-million-ico-halted-by-sec-for-being-alleged-scam/ - 1728c7141569

[46] US Securities and Exchange Commission (2020). Spotlight on Initial Coin Offerings (ICOs) https://www.sec.gov/ICO

[47] Williams, R. (April 23, 2019). *ICO Regulations—Which are the Countries with Restrictions?*, https://www.cryptonewsz.com/ico-regulations-which-are-the-countries-with-restrictions/16264/

[48] Fries, T. (2019). STOs v. ICOs: 'What's the Difference?', *The Tokenist*, https://thetokenist.io/stos-v-icos-whats-the-difference/

[49] For example, Polymath created the ST-20 standard; Harbor the R-Token standard; and the Ethereum community the ERC1400, ERC1410 and ERC1404 standards. Chester, J. (2019), "How to Run A Successful Security Token Offering in Compliance with New SEC Guidance," *Forbes*, https://www.forbes.com/sites/jonathanchester/2019/04/15/how-to-run-a-successful-security-token-offering-in-compliance-with-new-sec-guidance/#53987fde238a

[50] Winslet, T (2019). 'Top 3 Initial Exchange Offerings (IEOs) to Watch in the Crypto Market', *The Daily Hodl*, https://dailyhodl.com/2019/04/11/top-3-initial-exchange-offerings-ieos-to-watch-in-the-crypto-market/

[51] Trustnodes (June 28, 2019). *IEOs, Tokens Raise $3.3 billion*, https://www.trustnodes.com/2019/06/28/ieos-tokens-raise-3-3-billion

[52] Blockchain Council (April 10 2019). *Top 10 countries leading blockchain technology in the world.* https://www.blockchain-council.org/blockchain/top-10-countries-leading-blockchain-technology-in-the-world/

[53] *Blockchain Startup*s, https://angel.co/blockchains

[54] LongHash (February 2020). *Blockchain Companies in China*, https://www.longhash.com/en/livecharts/company-status

[55] Hill, E. (January 28, 2020). 'More than 700 new blockchain companies launch in China in January alone', *Yahoo Finance*, https://finance.yahoo.com/news/more-700-blockchain-companies-launch-090011333.html

[56] Crunchbase (2020). *European Union Blockchain Companies.* https://www.crunchbase.com/hub/european-union-blockchain-companies#section-overview

[57] Whittemore, N., and Collins, C. (2019), 'A History of Crypto Exchanges', *Nomics*, https://blog.nomics.com/essays/crypto-exchanges-history/

[58] *Mt. Gox CEO Mark Karpeles pleads not guilty to embezzlement*, July 11th 2015, http://www.aljazeera.com/news/2015/08/japan-arrests-mtgox-bitcoin-head-missing-387m-150801054245349.html

[59] Coinmarket tracks cryptocurrency exchanges on its website at https://coin.market/exchanges

[60] https://www.rise.global/blockchain-100

[61] Gupta, A. and Mondal, T. (2017). *HfS Blueprint Report: Enterprise Blockchain Service*, https://www.hfsresearch.com/blueprint-reports/hfs-blueprint-enterprise-blockchain-services

[62] Grand View Research (December 2016). Blockchain Technology Market Analysis, http://www.grandviewresearch.com/industry-analysis/blockchain-technology-market/

Grand View Research (2019). Blockchain Technology Market Size, Share, & Trends Analysis Report By Type, By Component, By Application, By Enterprise Size, By End Use, By Region, And Segment Forecasts, 2019 - 2025

https://www.grandviewresearch.com/industry-analysis/blockchain-technology-market

[63] Grand View Research (2016) Blockchain Technology Market Analysis, http://www.grandviewresearch.com/industry-analysis/blockchain-technology-market/

Grand View Research (2019) Blockchain Technology Market Size, Share, & Trends Analysis Report By Type, By Component, By Application, By Enterprise Size, By End Use, By Region, And

Segment Forecasts, 2019 - 2025

https://www.grandviewresearch.com/industry-analysis/blockchain-technology-market

[64] IDC (March 4, 2019). *Worldwide Blockchain Spending Forecast to Reach $2.9 Billion in 2019, According to New IDC Spending Guide*, https://www.idc.com/getdoc.jsp?containerId=prUS44898819

[65] Gartner (2019). 2019 CIO Agenda: *Blockchain's Emergence Depends on Use Cases.* G00401994.

[66] Deloitte (2019). Deloitte's 2019 Global Blockchain Survey: *Blockchains get down to business.*

[67] Del Castillo, M. (April 16 2019). *Blockchain 50: Billion Dollar Babies.* https://www.forbes.com/sites/michaeldelcastillo/2019/04/16/blockchain-50-billion-dollar-babies/#777c8eb657cc

[68] Marr, B. (January 22, 2020). 'The 5 Biggest Blockchain And Distributed Ledger Trends Everyone Should Be Watching In 2020', *Forbes,* https://www.forbes.com/sites/bernardmarr/2020/01/22/the-5-biggest-blockchain-and-distributed-ledger-trends-everyone-should-be-watching-in-2020/#17056e9d56f0

[69] Lacity, M. (2018). *A Manager's Guide to Blockchains for Business*. SB Publishing. Stratford-upon-Avon, UK

Del Castillo, M. (July 3, 2018). 'Big Blockchain: The 50 Largest Public Companies Exploring Blockchain', *Forbes*, https://www.forbes.com/sites/michaeldelcastillo/2018/07/03/big-blockchain-the-50-largest-public-companies-exploring-blockchain/#36a19a72b5b2

[70] Deloitte (2019). Deloitte's 2019 Global Blockchain Survey: *Blockchains get down to business.*

[71] ESI Intelligence (2019). https://esg-intelligence.com/blockchain-articles/2019/06/19/top-four-enterprise-blockchain-consortia-trends-2019/

ESL Intelligence (2020), List of all Blockchain Consortia, https://esg-intelligence.com/access-enterprise-blockchain-intelligence/list-of-all-blockchain-consortia/

[72] https://www.r3.com/

[73] The Linux Foundation (January 22nd 2016). The Hyperledger Project Charter, available at https://www.hyperledger.org/about/charter

[74] Hyperledger Project Charter https://www.hyperledger.org/about/charter

[75] Connell, J. (June 2017). *On Byzantine Fault Tolerance in Blockchain Systems*, https://cryptoinsider.com/byzantine-fault-tolerance-blockchain-systems/

[76] https://www.hyperledger.org/projects

[77] https://www.hyperledger.org/projects

[78] NS Insurance (August 1, 2019). *B3i releases property catastrophe excess of loss product*, Cat XoL v1.0 https://www.nsinsurance.com/news/b3i-releases-property-catastrophe-excess-of-loss-product-cat-xol-v1-0/

[79] *Enterprise Ethereum Alliance Becomes World's Largest Open-source Blockchain Initiative*, posted July 17th 2017 on https://entethalliance.org/enterprise-ethereum-alliance-becomes-worlds-largest-open-source-blockchain-initiative/

[80] https://entethalliance.org/

[81] *Welcome EEA Members*, https://entethalliance.atlassian.net/wiki/display/EEA/Welcome+EEA+Members

[82] https://tokentaxonomy.org/resources/technical-documents/

[83] Stanley, A. (October 1, 2018). 'Hyperledger And Enterprise Ethereum Alliance Join Forces In Enterprise Blockchain Boost', *Forbes*, https://www.forbes.com/sites/astanley/2018/10/01/hyperledger-and-enterprise-ethereum-alliance-join-forces-in-enterprise-blockchain-boost/#979c5be4aa23

[84] https://identity.foundation/

[85] BiTA Std 120-2019: Location Component Specification https://static1.squarespace.com/static/5aa97ac8372b96325bb9ad66/t/5c7e8882f9619a98a55ec24d/1551796355748/BiTAS+Location+Component+Specification+v4.pdf

[86] https://www.oocblockchain.com/use-cases

[87] https://www.lexico.com/en/definition/coopetition

[88] Lucasxhy (September 11, 2018). *Cross-Chain-Interoperability*, https://medium.com/@lucx946/cross-chain- interoperability-3566695a1a72

[89] https://en.wikipedia.org/wiki/Standards_organization

[90] GS1 (2017). EPCIS and CBV Implementation Guideline, Release 1.2., Ratified, Feb 2017, https://www.gs1.org/docs/epc/EPCIS_Guideline.pdf

[91] Mainelli, M. (January 3, 2017). *Which way for blockchain standards in 2017?* Coindesk, https://www.coindesk.com/which-way-for-blockchain-standards-in-2017

[92] GS1 (2018). *Bridging Blockchains Interoperability is essential to the future of data sharing.* https://www.gs1.org/sites/default/files/bridging_blockchains_-_interoperability_is_essential_to_the_future_of_da.pdf

[93] GS1 (2018). *Bridging Blockchains Interoperability is essential to the future of data sharing.* https://www.gs1.org/sites/default/files/bridging_blockchains_-_interoperability_is_essential_to_the_future_of_da.pdf

[94] https://blockchain.ieee.org/

[95] *Standards Catalogue: ISO/TC 307 Blockchain and DLT,* https://www.iso.org/committee/6266604/x/catalogue/p/0/u/1/w/0/d/0

[96] https://www.nist.gov/publications/blockchain-technology-overview.

[97] Coleman, L. (August 8 2018). *China to Draft for Three Domestic Blockchain Standards in 2018,* CNN, https://www.ccn.com/china-to-drafts-for-three-domestic-blockchain-standards-in-2018

[98] Lacity, M., Zach, S., Paul, C. (2019). *Towards Blockchain 3.0 Interoperability: Business and Technical Considerations* (01st ed., vol. 2019). Blockchain Center of Excellence.

[99] https://www.iso.org/stages-and-resources-for-standards-development.html

[100] Tapscott, D., and Tapscott, A. (2016). *Blockchain Revolution*, Penguin Random House, NYC, 56.

[101] Gautam, A. (March 5th, 2019). *Which Countries Have the Best Cryptocurrency Regulations?* https://hackernoon.com/which-countries-have-the-best-cryptocurrency-regulations-f3a45341b34

[102] IRS (2019). *Frequently Asked Questions on Virtual Currency Transactions.* https://www.irs.gov/individuals/international-taxpayers/frequently-asked-questions-on-virtual-currency-transactions

[103] Source: http://www.gao.gov/modules/ereport/handler.php?1=1&path=/ereport/GAO-16-375SP/data_center/General_government/5._Financial_Regulatory_Structure

[104] SEC (May 9, 2019). *How we Howey.* https://www.sec.gov/news/speech/peirce-how-we-howey-050919

[105] Mark Vilardo, special counsel, Office of Chief Counsel, Division of Corporation Finance, United States Securities and Exchange Commission discussed rulings during the Evolving Regulation of Crypto, October 25, 2019, School of Law, University of Arkansas.

[106] National Conference of State Legislaltors (July 23 2019). *Blockchain 2019 Legislation,* https://www.ncsl.org/research/financial-services-and-commerce/blockchain-2019-legislation.aspx

[107] *Banking on Bitcoin*. Movie directed by Christopher Cannucciari, released November 22nd 2016.

[108] https://en.wikipedia.org/wiki/Legality_of_bitcoin_by_country

[109] Allison, I. (November 14 2019). *Wyoming's New Crypto Banking Law Could Defang New York's BitLicense*, Coindesk, https://www.coindesk.com/wyomings-new-crypto-banking-law-could-defang-new-yorks-bitlicense

[110] Mejdrich, K. (November 19 2019). 'Wyoming—yes, Wyoming—races to fill crypto-banking void, *Politico,* https://www.politico.com/news/2019/11/21/wyoming-cryptocurrency-banking-072727

[111] De, N. (February 12, 2020). *US Financial Crimes Watchdog Preparing 'Significant' Crypto Rules, Warns Treasury Secretary Mnuchin,* Coindesk, https://www.coindesk.com/us-financial-crimes-watchdog-preparing-significant-crypto-rules-warns-treasury-secretary-mnuchin

[112] The SAFT Project: https://saftproject.com/

[113] https://en.wikipedia.org/wiki/Legality_of_bitcoin_by_country_or_territory

[114] *China 'Blockchain Day' could become reality after Xi Jinping's endorsement of technology* https://www.scmp.com/economy/china-economy/article/3035368/china-blockchain-day-could-become-reality-after-xi-jinpings

[115] Horsley, S. (January 13, 2020). *China To Test Digital Currency. Could It End Up Challenging The Dollar Globally?* National Public Radio (NPR), https://www.npr.org/2020/01/13/795988512/china-to-test-digital-currency-could-it-end-up-challenging-the-dollar-globally

[116] Gov.uk (December 19 2018). Check if you need to pay tax when you receive cryptoassets, https://www.gov.uk/guidance/check-if-you-need-to-pay-tax-when-you-receive-cryptoassets

Gov.uk(December 19 2018). Check if you need to pay tax when you sell cryptoassets, https://www.gov.uk/guidance/check-if-you-need-to-pay-tax-when-you-sell-cryptoassets

[117] Government Office for Science. (2015). Distributed Ledger Technology: *Beyond Blockchain,* https://assets.publishing.service.gov.uk/government/uploads/system/uploads/attachment_data/file/492972/gs-16-1-distributed-ledger-technology.pdf

Naqvi, N. (2020). *National Blockchain Roadmap.* https://www.linkedin.com/posts/britishblockchain_uk-policymakers-government-activity-6634732895456100352-rq-q

[118] *Global Regulations on Cryptocurrencies (August-September 2017),* available at https://www.cyberius.com/global-regulations-on-cryptocurrencies-aug-sep-2017/

[119] *Majandus (in Estonian)* (July 25, 2016). *There are no intrinsic barriers to legitimizing the use of Bitcoin.* Retrieved 15 March 2017. https://majandus24.postimees.ee/3776225/analuus-olemuslikke-takistusi-bitcoini-kasutamise-seadustamiseks-pole

[120] Ummelas, O. (June 1, 2018). 'Estonia Scales Down Plan to Create National Cryptocurrency'. *Bloomberg*. Retrieved 7 October 2018. Comply Advantage https://complyadvantage.com/knowledgebase/crypto-regulations/cryptocurrency-regulations-estonia/

[121] https://en.wikipedia.org/wiki/Legality_of_bitcoin_by_country_or_territory

[122] https://en.wikipedia.org/wiki/Legality_of_bitcoin_by_country_or_territory

[123] US Library of Congress. Regulation of Cryptocurrency Around the World https://www.loc.gov/law/help/cryptocurrency/world-survey.php This website tracks major bitcoin regulations by jurisdiction: https://en.wikipedia.org/wiki/Legality_of_bitcoin_by_country_or_territory

[124] Anderson, B. (January 9th 2020). *The Most In-Demand Hard and Soft Skills of 2020*, https://business.linkedin.com/talent-solutions/blog/trends-and-research/2020/most-in-demand-hard-and-soft-skills

[125] Petrone, P. (January 1, 2019). *The Skills Companies Need Most in 2019 – And How to Learn Them.* https://learning.linkedin.com/blog/top-skills/the-skills-companies-need-most-in-2019--and-how-to-learn-them

[126] Sharma, R. (Hune 25, 2019). 'The Blockchain Job Market is Booming'. *Investopedia*. https://www.investopedia.com/news/blockchain-job-market-booming/

[127] Blockchain Council (October 31 2019). *5 Skill Sets a Blockchaon Developer Must Have,* https://www.blockchain-council.org/blockchain/5-skill-sets-a-blockchain-developer-must-have/

[128] Upwork (2019). *50 most in-demand blockchain-related skills,* https://www.upwork.com/hiring/top-blockchain-skills/

[129] China's patent office is the National Intellectual Property Administration (CNIPA)

[130] Lacity, M., Steelman, Z. R., Yates, J., Wei, J. (2019). *US and China Battle for Blockchain Dominance.* https://cointelegraph.com/news/us-and-china-battle-for-blockchain-dominance

[131] Santacreu, A.M. (2018) *What Does China's Rise in Patents Mean? A Look at Quality vs. Quantity*, Economic Research Federal Reserve, No. 14 Bank of Saint Louis, https://research.stlouisfed.org/publications/economic-synopses/2018/05/04/what-does-chinas-rise-in-patents-mean-a-look-at-quality-vs-quantity

[132] Quote from Lacity, M., Steelman, Z. R., Yates, J., Wei, J. (2019). *US and China Battle for Block-*

chain Dominance. https://cointelegraph.com/news/us-and-china-battle-for-blockchain-dominance

[133] EPO (December 5 2018). *EPO holds first major conference on blockchain.* https://www.epo.org/news-issues/news/2018/20181205.html

[134] Statista (2020). Largest blockchain patent owners in Europe as of July 2019, by number of filings at the European Patent Office. https://www.statista.com/statistics/1028046/blockchain-patent-owners-epo-authority/

[135] Lacity, M., Allee, K., Zhu, Y. (2019). *Blockchain in Business: What do Companies' 10-K Reports Say About DTL?*. https://cointelegraph.com/news/blockchain-in-business-what-do-companies-10-k-reports-say-about-dlt

[136] De Meijer (September 27, 2019). *Gartner and Blockchain: The Good and the bad*, https://www.finextra.com/blogposting/17938/gartner-and-blockchain-the-good-the-bad-and-the-

[137] Figure was created from Gartner's generic hype cycle and 2015, 2016, and 2017 versions:

https://upload.wikimedia.org/wikipedia/commons/thumb/9/94/Gartner_Hype_Cycle.svg/1200px-Gartner_Hype_Cycle.svg.png
http://na2.www.gartner.com/imagesrv/newsroom/images/emerging-tech-hc-2016.png;
https://blogs.gartner.com/smarterwithgartner/files/2017/08/Emerging-Technology-Hype-Cycle-for-2017_Infographic_R6A.jpg

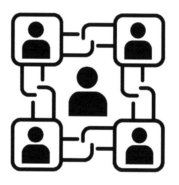

Chapter 3

The Blockchain Application Framework

"There are very few fundamental shifts in global infrastructure that can happen in our lifetimes. The financial infrastructure is one of them, and the Blockchain is changing the way we think about the transfer of value."

Adam Draper, Founder of the Boost VC Accelerator[1]

"We don't trust what we don't understand."

Darren Shelton, Morgan Shipping[2]

3.1. Introduction

As the quote above from Adam Draper suggests, blockchains are changing the way we think about value. But as the quote from Darren Shelton suggests, we won't trust blockchains until we understand them. That is the main learning objective for this chapter—to help readers learn how blockchains work.

In Chapter 1, we covered the pivot from an **'Internet of Information'** to an **'Internet of Value'** at a high level. We explained that Bitcoin moved us towards an 'Internet of Value' for one type of application, namely, peer-to-peer payments. Bitcoin achieved this by tackling some very old—and new—problems with algorithms and behavioral incentives. Specifically, we learned that Bitcoin shifted (1) from government-issued currencies to a cryptocurrency; (2) from trusted third parties (TTPs) to automated and community-driven, counter-party risk mitigation; and (3) from party-level record keeping to shared record keeping.

Thousands of blockchain innovations are being developed, some with significant departures from Bitcoin's architecture. For example, enterprise blockchain applications often have digital assets to represent goods and services, but few have abandoned fiat currencies for cryptocurrencies[(i)]. Consequently, many people now call the space 'distributed ledger technologies'. Still others contend that if the space is called 'distributed ledger technologies', it fails to capture the richness of blockchains.[3] The debates over nomenclature become more comprehensible after first understanding the components of a blockchain application.

In this chapter, we develop a framework to classify any type of blockchain application. To appreciate the framework, we first need a deeper understanding of how partners trade before and after a shared blockchain application. Each approach has advantages and disadvantages, which will inform the *business impetus* for the adoption (or non-adoption) of blockchain applications. Presuming the blockchain approach promises enough business benefits, we proceed with an explanation of each component of a blockchain application, including protocols, code bases, use cases, and application interfaces. We then illustrate the framework by mapping Bitcoin to it. By the end of this chapter, readers will be able to map any blockchain application to the framework and understand the trade-offs of different choices among its component parts. We will have succeeded if, by the end of the chapter, readers can comprehend the meaning the following definition of a blockchain application:

*A blockchain application is a peer-to-peer system for validating, time-stamping, and permanently storing transactions on a shared **distributed ledger**. **Digital assets**, native to each blockchain application, exist only in digital form and come with rights of use. **Cryptography** and **consensus** algorithms are used to validate transactions, to update the ledger, and to keep*

[(i)] *Fiat money* is government-issued currency that is not backed by a physical commodity with intrinsic value, such as gold or silver.

*the ledger and network secure. Most blockchains also use **smart contracts** that apply rules to automatically execute transactions based upon pre-agreed conditions.*

3.2. Trade before and after a blockchain

Let's use a simple scenario to compare how parties transact before and after a blockchain application so we can better understand blockchain's potential business value. Suppose four enterprises transact with each other (see left side of Figure 3.1). The four trading partners mitigate counter-party risks by engaging a trusted third party to provide truth attestations; that is, to verify information about the parties, assets, and transactions. The trusted third parties **provide vital services to facilitate trade**; that is why our four trading parties rely upon them. The TTP provides **clear control and accountability**. The trading parties have an identifiable institution to address questions, concerns, or complaints. Additionally, trading partners **can alter agreements** as new information becomes available, or as circumstances change. However, the TTP can command significant fees for such services. Let's assume the four trading parties pay, on average, five percent of the value of each transaction to the TTP for these services. As a benchmark, in more complex scenarios, like remittances and global supply chains, **transaction costs can be high**—between eight and 22 percent of the value of the transaction.[4]

In our simple scenario in Figure 3.1, each party maintains its own systems to record debits, credits, and other data on their private ledgers (represented by different patterned database icons). Each party benefits from **controlling their own software and ledgers**; each enterprise can swiftly and unilaterally execute decisions within the boundaries of the firm. Each firm can modify its records and alter its software as it sees fit. Issues that arise, such as the discovery of a software bug or an attack on the network, can be dealt with immediately. Records can be modified when errors are discovered. However, the very essence of trade is *inter-organizational*; the setup that functions well within the boundaries of the firm often functions very poorly across firm boundaries. Among the four trading partners and one TTP in our scenario, there are five **versions of the truth,** which need to be reconciled. Even after reconciliation, nothing prevents a party from re-writing history after-the-fact. Because **each party can modify its own records**, partners cannot be confident they are dealing with the same historical record of transactions through time, thus hindering the ability to uniformly trace the origin of

Before blockchains:
Every party has their own
ledger and relies on a trusted
third party to establish trust ...

After a blockchain:
Every party runs the same software, has an
identical copy of a shared ledger and transacts
directly; trust is established through cryptography
and computer algorithms...

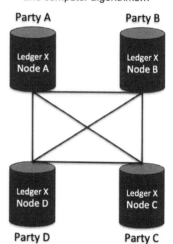

Party A	Party B
Ledger A	Ledger B

Trusted 3rd Party — Ledger E

Ledger D	Ledger C
Party D	Party C

Party A	Party B
Ledger X Node A	Ledger X Node B
Ledger X Node D	Ledger X Node C
Party D	Party C

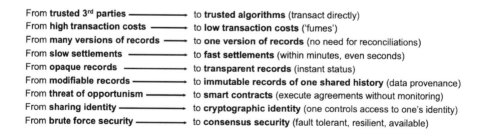

From **trusted 3rd parties** ⟶ to **trusted algorithms** (transact directly)
From **high transaction costs** ⟶ to **low transaction costs** ('fumes')
From **many versions of records** ⟶ to **one version of records** (no need for reconciliations)
From **slow settlements** ⟶ to **fast settlements** (within minutes, even seconds)
From **opaque records** ⟶ to **transparent records** (instant status)
From **modifiable records** ⟶ to **immutable records of one shared history** (data provenance)
From **threat of opportunism** ⟶ to **smart contracts** (execute agreements without monitoring)
From **sharing identity** ⟶ to **cryptographic identity** (one controls access to one's identity)
From **brute force security** ⟶ to **consensus security** (fault tolerant, resilient, available)

Figure 3.1: Trade before and after a shared blockchain application

an assett and every change to its status over time (called 'data provenance'). **Reconciliations, in turn, slow settlement times**. Let's conservatively assume it takes 24 hours to settle transactions in our simple ecosystem. In a more realistic scenario such as trade finance, the knotwork of players involved—customers, suppliers, banks, customs, transporters, and warehouses—may take weeks to settle transactions.[5]

Moreover, each party has **low transaction visibility**; each party can only see the transactions coming in and out of its own organization—the rest are opaque. Each party has to work with the trusted third party to assess the status of a transaction. In more complex scenarios, some parties spend days or weeks tracking down the status of a transaction. Consider cross-border payments; when a manufacturer in one country sends payment to a supplier in another country, the manufacturer and the supplier's financial institutions, national payment systems, and corresponding banks, process the transaction. Parties to an exchange have no access to the status of the transaction, the fees being charged, or even which institution controls a transaction as it works its way through the knot of interlocking relationships. The threat of 'vendor opportunism'—the idea that vendors may pursue their self-interests with guile; may withhold information; or may not comply with the terms and conditions of the agreement—always exists.[6] Therefore, trading partners **spend a lot of resources monitoring agreements** to make sure that trading partners are behaving as promised.

Returning to our scenario, what about each party's customers? Their customers routinely turn over much of their personal data—including national identification numbers; home addresses; credit card numbers; birth dates; employment records; utility bills and more—simply to verify their identities to the institutions that sit in the middle of their transactions. **The risks of information leakage and identity theft are high**, as any partner might use the data for something other than the original transaction.[7]

In our little ecosystem, each party spends significant resources protecting their IT perimeters against cybersecurity attacks. Think of it as **brute force cybersecurity defense**. In reality, large enterprises successfully fend off thousands of cybersecurity threats each day. However, a single security breach can cost an organization billions of dollars to remedy. High profile attacks include Heartland Payment Systems in 2009, which cost the company $2.8 billion to remedy; Citibank in 2011, which cost $19.4 million; and JP Morgan Chase in 2014, which cost $1 billion.[8] Think also about the security breaches at Equifax, Target, Sony, and Netflix—the list goes on.

In short, before a shared blockchain application, each party maintains its own records and relies on trusted third parties to provide truth attestations. The trusted third parties add significant value, and parties like having control over their own data, but the entire setup prompts disputes; requires onerous reconciliations; commands high transaction fees; provides little transaction transparency; is slow to settlement transactions; and creates cybersecurity vulnerabilities. Blockchain applications aim to overcome these limitations.

Returning to our scenario, the right side of Figure 3.1 shows how the same four parties could transact if they decide to share a blockchain application. Each party would agree to operate an independent computer node in the network. Each independent node would run the same software and maintain an identical copy of the digital ledger. The nodes would constantly chatter with each other to make sure no party tampered with the records. If anyone cheats, the other nodes will ignore or banish it.

One notes that after a shared blockchain application, there is no need for a trusted third party; instead, the blockchain application uses cryptography and computer algorithms to perform truth attestations. This allows **trading partners to transact directly**. While the parties will have to figure out a way to pay for and to govern the shared software, the overall **transaction costs should be lower** by eliminating the TTP. For now, we will assume the four players still rely on fiat currencies, but their blockchain application will have some form of native digital asset, such as a token to represent physical items.

Transactions are only added to the ledger if they are valid; it's a confirm-before-commit process instead of post-then-confirm-later process. As such, parties can rely on **one version of the truth**, so there is **no need for reconciliations**, enabling **faster settlement times.** The transactions can settle in sub-second to sixty minutes, depending on which consensus algorithm is used in the blockchain application. With one **transparent**, shared version of the truth, parties of an exchange can instantly determine the status of a transaction by reading the ledger. Furthermore, transactions on the shared distributed ledger are **immutable**, thus every party can be confident they are always dealing with the same historical data, guaranteeing consistent **data provenance**. Rather than solely rely on paper contracts, verbal agreements or handshakes, parties can rely on **smart contracts** that automatically execute the terms of agreements without oversight. No more monitoring and worrying that trading partners are not fulfilling their obligations. Moreover, consumers and institutions **control their own identity** with cryptographic digital signatures, reducing the risks of information leakage and identity theft. Furthermore, blockchain applications promise **heightened security**. Blockchain applications still function properly even if a high percentage of nodes are faulty—or even malicious—enabling fault tolerance, resiliency and 100 percent availability. In theory, the only way to break a blockchain application is to commandeer more than 50 percent of the nodes. Distributed software offers quite a bounty of business value!

However, there are downsides to distributed trading systems. Without a trusted third party, the risk profile will be altered—to whom does one complain or seek remediations from in cases of fraud or malicious acts? Smart contracts are only reliable if the terms and conditions can be explained, but in a world filled with uncertainty and ambiguity, coded agreements are not always possible. Parties will need to agree to unambiguous interpretations of data and event standards. Shared software and data require shared governance, and it is challenging to coordinate changes among many partners. Some of these downsides can be alleviated with good governance models and sound action principles, which are discussed at length in subsequent chapters. Table 3.1 summarizes the advantages and disadvantages of centralized and distributed trading systems.

	Centralized Trading Systems with TTPs	**Distributed Trading Systems with a blockchain application**
Description	Trusted third parties facilitate trust in trading relationships; each party centrally owns its own systems of records (software and data, including ledgers) within the boundaries of the firm	Software is shared by trading partners; cryptography and consensus algorithms facilitate trust
Advantages	• Trusted third parties absorb counter-party risks • Trusted third parties are accountable • Each firm controls its internal systems to modify records and to alter software as each sees fit • Trading partners can adapt terms of an agreement to meet changing circumstances	• Trading partners transact directly without needing a trusted third party • Low transaction costs • With shared data, there is no need for reconciliations • Fast transaction settlement times • Instant status of transactions • Data provenance • Execute agreements without oversight • Control over one's identity reduces information leakage and identity theft • Cybersecurity is fault tolerant, resilient, and always available
Disadvantages	• High transaction costs • Disputes over information between trading partners require reconciliation • Slow transaction settlement times • Lack of transparency across trading partners • Trading partners may alter records after the fact, making data provenance unreliable • Trading partners may not act in good faith • Each firm spends a lot of resources on cybersecurity	• Without a trusted third party, the risk profile changes • No single point of accountability. Who does one seek remediations from in cases of fraud or malicious acts? • Records cannot be modified unless the majority of nodes agree • Software cannot be updated unless the majority of nodes agree • Smart contracts are not easily modifiable if circumstances change

Table 3.1: Trade before and after a blockchain application

Table 3.1 suggests the *business impetus* for the adoption of blockchain applications. If advantages outweigh the disadvantages, we have a very good reason to keep learning. Next, we present the blockchain application framework.

3.3. The blockchain application framework

A blockchain application comprises protocols, code bases, use cases, and application interfaces (see Figure 3.2). As one becomes more familiar with blockchain technologies, one appreciates that protocols are the real innovations in the space. **Protocols** specify rights of access and the rules for how transactions in a blockchain application authenticate asset ownership and how transactions are structured; addressed; transmitted; routed; validated; sequenced; secured; and added to the permanent record. *A blockchain protocol is often called a 'trust protocol'. However, the word 'trust' is narrowly defined to mean: 'trust that the records on the distributed ledger agree across copies.'* Trust here has nothing to do with the faith or confidence that trading partners are benevolent or will play by the rules. In fact, it is more accurate to say that we can assume many actors will indeed be malevolent. 'Trust' equates to trust that the computer algorithms will reject faulty transactions, ignore faulty nodes on the network, and never modify the valid transactions once they have been added to the ledger. For a given blockchain application, protocols serve as the blueprints to ensure the correctness and ongoing integrity of records. In general, blockchain protocols define the rules for the distributed ledger; participation and validation; native digital assets; cryptography; consensus (to make sure everyone has the identical copy of the ledger); and smart contracts. Once rules are established, protocols are programmed into **code bases**, like Ethereum; EOS; Hyperledger Fabric; Corda; Quorum; Chain; or MultiChain. From there, a code base can be adapted for a particular **use case**, like tracking items in a supply chain or for cross-border payments. Finally, all blockchain applications have **interfaces** where users access the system. We'll begin with distributed ledger protocols.

3.3.1. Distributed ledgers

Protocols define the structure of the distributed ledger. The most common structure is a *chain of block*s—hence the name 'blockchain' (see Figure 3.3). With a blockchain structure, recently approved transactions are sequenced and collected into a block. Each block comprises a header and a payload of transactions. The block header includes a

117

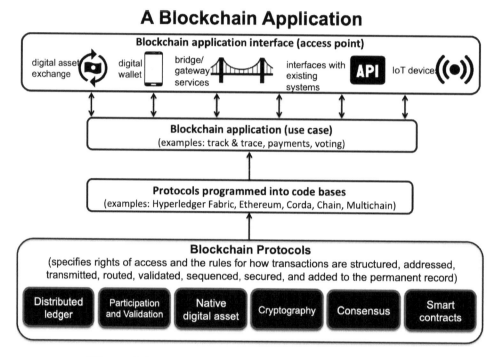

Figure 3.2: Components of a blockchain application

pointer to the previous block of transactions, forming a chain of sequenced blocks over time, all the way back to the first block, called the 'genesis block'. Bitcoin, Ethereum, Quorum and Hyperledger Fabric structure their digital ledgers as blockchains.

Another common structure is a ***continuous stream of transactions***, one after the other, through a process of continual ledger close. A completely new ledger is created every few seconds in such a way that the most current version could be reconstructed from all the prior versions. Ripple and Stellar use this structure. Their ledgers are more complex than Bitcoin's ledger because they maintain account settings, balances, trustlines and different types of transactions like sell offers, payments, and cancel offers. The account balances are updated with the most recent set of validated transactions. Figure 3.4 shows how a ledger gets updated.

Distributed ledger structured as a chain of blocks:

Distributed ledger structured as a
continuous ledger with account
balances and current transactions:

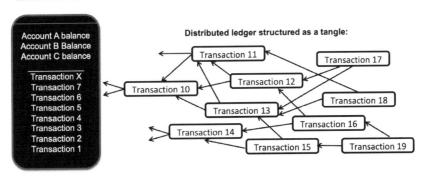

Figure 3.3: Examples of three distributed ledger structures

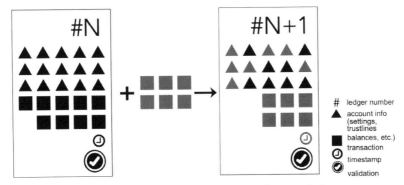

Figure 3.4: Ledger structure for a continuous ledger process

Ledger #N+1 updates the account balances with all the recently approved
transactions since ledger #N

Source: https://casinocoin.org/build/concept-consensus.html

119

IOTA structures its distributed ledger as a ***tangle*** of transactions.[9] Each new transaction has to use its computing resources to validate two other transactions. Serguei Popov, the author of the IOTA white paper explains: *"The main idea of the tangle is the following: To issue a transaction, users must work to approve other transactions. Therefore, users who issue a transaction are contributing to the network's security. It is assumed that the nodes check if the approved transactions are not conflicting. If a node finds that a transaction is in conflict with the tangle history, the node will not approve the conflicting transaction."*[10] Figure 3.5 is an example of Tangle's ledger. Each circle represents a transaction. If readers go to the URL, they can click on any transaction to learn its history.

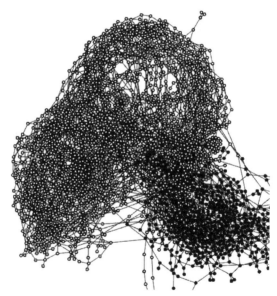

Figure 3.5: Iota's tangle structure

Each circle represents a transaction

Source: http://tangle.glumb.de/

Different structures have tradeoffs between security and speed of transaction settlement. In general, the chain of blocks is the most secure; the tangle promises to be the quickest.

3.3.2. Rights of participation and validation

Rights of participation define who is allowed to submit transactions to the blockchain network. Rights of validation define who is allowed to run validator nodes in the blockchain network. The rights of participation and validation may vary by stakeholder type.

At a very high level, rights of participation are either open to the public or private; rights of validation are either permissionless (anyone may operate a validator node) or permissioned (an individual or institution needs permission or must be selected/ voted upon to run a validator node). However, there are nuances; EOS, for example, distinguishes between node validators—which anyone may run—and block producers, which must be voted upon by the community. Permissionless blockchains need strong incentives to attract independent, 'well-behaved' validator nodes. Bitcoin and Ethereum incentivize good behavior by awarding cryptocurrencies to miners. Many permissioned blockchains have participants take turns validating the next set of transactions to the digital ledger. Plotting these two dimensions yields four types of blockchain networks (see Table 3.2):

		Who can operate a validator node?	
		Permissionless *(Anyone)*	**Permissioned** *(Requires permission, selection, or election)*
Who can submit transactions?	**Public** *(Anyone)*	**Public-permissionless** • Bitcoin • Ethereum • Monero • EOS (node validators)	**Public-permissioned** • Ripple • EOS (block producers)
	Private *(requires keys to access)*	**(Virtual) Private-permissionless** • EY Ops Chain Public Edition (under development)	**Private-permissioned** • MediLedger • IBM Food Trust • TradeLens

Table 3.2: Types of blockchain networks

121

1. **Public-permissionless**

2. **Public-permissioned**

3. **Private-permissioned**

4. **(Virtual) Private-permissionless**

Next, we examine the four types of blockchains in more detail ...

1. Public-permissionless blockchains

With public-permissionless blockchains anyone can participate, and anyone can run validator nodes. Bitcoin, Ethereum, Monero, and EOS are popular public-permissionless blockchains. Anyone with access to the Internet can observe a public blockchain to see all the transactions that have taken place over time (see Table 3.3 for websites to observe Bitcoin, Ethereum, and Monero blockchains). To transact on public-permissionless blockchains, users need some sort of application interface (such as a digital wallet). Anyone may run a validator node by downloading the source code and turning on the mining function. (Although Bitcoin miners need specialized Application-Specific Integrated Circuit (ASIC) hardware to mine competitively).

Blockchain	Native Digital Asset (Cryptocurrency Symbol)	Website to observe all transactions	Instructions to download code to operate a node
Bitcoin	Bitcoins (BTC)	https://btc.com/	https://www.bitcoinmining.com/
Ethereum	Ether (ETH)	https://etherscan.io/	https://eth.wiki/en/fundamentals/mining
Monero	Monero (XRM)	https://moneroblocks.info/	https://web.getmonero.org/get-started/mining/

Table 3.3: Public-permissionless blockchains

122

2. Public-permissioned blockchains

With public-permissioned blockchains, anyone can transact, but node validators are selected or elected. Ripple and EOS are examples (see Table 3.4).

Blockchain	Native Digital Asset (Cryptocurrency Symbol)	Website to observe all transactions	List of Validator Nodes
Ripple	Ripple (XRP)	https://xrpcharts.ripple.com/#/transactions	https://xrpcharts.ripple.com/#/validators
EOS	(EOS)	https://bloks.io/#transactions	https://bloks.io/#producers

Table 3.4: Public-permissioned blockchains

Ripple

Ripple is a decentralized, real-time settlement system. Anyone can transact on the Ripple network by using a digital wallet or engaging a gateway partner, which are mostly financial institutions. Institutional customers use an Application Programming Interface (API)—a piece of software that connects two software applications—to connect to the Ripple network via a Ripple Gateway. When institutions join the Ripple network, they can select which nodes they want to perform validation checks, which is called a Unique Node List (UNL), or they can accept the default list maintained by Ripple. Ripple maintains its own validator nodes around the world and also has CGI and MIT as transaction validators.[11] Without the incentives of mining, Ripple asks institutions to run a validator node when they join the system to help secure the network.

EOS

EOS was developed to keep all of the advantages of a public blockchain platform—open, secure, decentralized—but without the latency, scalability, and resource intensity. Anyone can transact on EOS and operate a validator node if they meet minimal criteria.[12] However, only 21 'block producers' can add blocks. The owners of EOS cast votes for block producers in proportion to their stake.[13] The validator nodes with the most votes become a 'delegate'. The algorithm takes turns selecting a leader from among the panel of delegates for a current time period. After the time period elapses, another round of voting occurs to select the next panel of delegates.[14] Delegates are rewarded with transaction fees. Blocks are produced about every 500 milliseconds, with each of the 21 producers getting a turn. On the day of writing this, nine block producers were located in China; three in Singapore; and one or two in the Cayman Islands, BVI, Hong Kong, Japan, Ukraine, and the United States.

3. Private-permissioned blockchains

Private-permissioned blockchains require authorization to participate and to operate validator nodes. Private-permissioned blockchains rely upon a front-end gatekeeper to enforce the rights of access (see Figure 3.6). Unlike a trusted third-party that sits in the middle of transactions, the gatekeeper is like a security guard that checks a badge

Figure 3.6:

A private-permissioned blockchain with a gatekeeper to enforce the rights of access

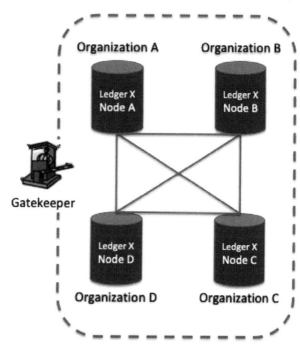

before allowing entry. It has no ability to alter the ledger or to stop smart contracts from executing.[ii] The gatekeeping function may be governed collaboratively by the trading partners or by a single enterprise, such as a regulatory authority that issues licenses for participation: *"existing participants could decide future entrants; a regulatory authority could issue licenses for participation; or a consortium could make the decisions instead."*[15] Once participants are past the gatekeeping function, they enter the distributed blockchain application.

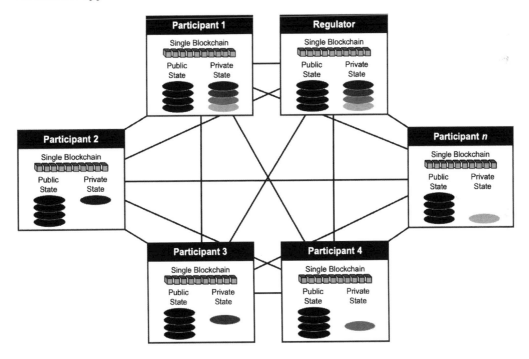

Figure 3.7: Quorum has public and private states stored on a single blockchain

Source: Crosman 2017[16]

[ii] This is true, provided that the organization that serves as the gatekeeper operates fewer than 50 percent of the nodes. If a gatekeeper does operate 50 percent or more of the nodes, there is little point in using a blockchain except under specific circumstances, such as an intra-organizational blockchain across divisions.

Many private-permissioned blockchains also allow participants to select validator nodes and to create private channels with their own private ledgers. There is typically 'public' data, that all approved network participants can view, and 'private' data that only the parties to the transaction can submit and view. Quorum—the permissioned version of Ethereum—is an example (see Figure 3.7). In other protocols, like Hyperledger Fabric, there are no 'public' views, only channels for private views that must be configured and approved for each participant in the network.

Private-permissioned blockchains are the most common enterprise blockchain solutions because they provide assurances of confidentiality, fast settlement times, resource efficiency, and regulatory compliance. MediLedger, the IBM Food Trust and TradeLens serve as examples of private-permissioned blockchains.

MediLedger

Founded by Chronicled in 2017, MediLedger is a block-enabled platform for the pharmaceutical sector, designed to comply with drug regulations enacted in the United States, Europe, Asia and South America. Its first projects focused on compliance with the US Drug Supply Chain Security Act of 2013. The act requires that all participants in the US pharmaceutical sector track and trace sellable units for certain classes of pharmaceuticals from manufacturers to pharmacy on one interoperable electronic system. Qualified participants (such as licensed manufacturers and pharmacies) may join the network.[17] Any qualified participant may operate a node, but it is likely that smaller players will engage a cloud provider or service provider to operate a node on their behalf. The validator's identity is known, thereby staking the organization's reputation on preserving the network. Its working group members include McKesson; Pfizer; AmerisourceBergen; Cardinal Health; Genentech; Gilead; and Amgen.[18]

IBM Food Trust

The IBM Food Trust is a blockchain platform for global food supply. It was commercially available in October of 2018. It aims to improve food safety, food freshness, and supply chain efficiency, while reducing food fraud and food waste. The IBM Food Trust platform relies on 'trust anchors' for validation. Trust anchors receive a full copy of the encrypted ledger but can only view the transaction if data owners grant access.[19] Initially, trust anchors were operated in IBM's cloud, but as the network grows, more participants will run trust nodes and possibly on other cloud environments.[20]

As of 2018, the platform had over four million transactions on more than 350 stock keeping units (SKUs), and more than 50 members adding data to the system.[21] Major enterprise adopters include Walmart; Carrefour; Smithfield; Topco; Golden State Foods; and Nestlé.

TradeLens

Developed by Maersk and IBM, TradeLens is an industry platform—released in 2018, after years of development—used to track shipping containers in the global supply chain.[22, 23] TradeLens also relies on 'trust anchors'. Trust anchors participate in consensus to validate transactions, host data, and assume a critical role of securing the network. So far, Maersk (via IBM's cloud environment) operates nodes; Hapag-Lloyd and Ocean Network Express (ONE) announced they will each operate a blockchain node.[24] As of April 2019, TradeLens had 60 members and over 100 ecosystem partners, including carriers, ports, terminals operators, 3PLS, and freight forwarders. According to Bridget van Kralingen, Senior VP for Blockchain at IBM, TradeLens had tracked 500 million events on 20 million containers by April 2019. TradeLens was adding between 25,000 to 30,000 documents a day.[25]

4. (Virtual) Private-permissionless blockchains

For a long time, virtual private-permissionless blockchains were deemed to be either theoretical or nonsensical.[26] Theoretically, people described that a private-permissionless blockchain could exist, say, by deploying a smart contract on a permissionless network that restricts access and use to specific public keys.[27] In 2019, Ernst & Young (EY) took a major step to making it a reality; it launched Nightfall on Github.[28] Nightfall is a set of protocols that provides private transactions on public Ethereum. In essence, EY's idea is a 'virtual private blockchain', similar to a virtual private network (VPN) that is connected to the public Internet, but data remains private from anyone not authorized to see the transaction. Authorized users, for example an organization's auditor or tax authority, will be able to decipher the data only with the right encrypted key.

Paul Brody, head of EY's Blockchain Technology, said:

> *"Blockchain technology holds tremendous promise to bring in a new era of transparency, accountability and efficiency in business. I am working to make sure that happens and, in particular, to ensure that open, decentralized and truly public blockchains are successful."*[29]

While Table 3.2 creates a helpful framework for categorizing blockchain networks, there are also hybrid blockchains. EY's WineChain serves as an example. EY developed WineChain to restore trust in the wine supply chain. Each wine bottle gets a QR code (see Glossary) that is tokenized and posted to public Ethereum. This way, customers can scan the wine with their phone and get verification that the wine is legitimate. Wine producers; brokers; importers; wholesalers; distributors; and retailers rely on Quorum (a private-permissioned blockchain), to track the bottle as it moves through the supply chain (see Figure 3.8).[30]

3.3.3. Native digital assets

A protocol defines the uses of a blockchain application's native digital asset—an asset that exists only in digital form and comes with rights of use. Over 5,000 native digital assets were being traded as of January 2020.[31] Native digital assets can serve multiple functions in blockchains. Five common uses are:

1. As a **cryptocurrency**, a native digital asset serves the same functions as fiat money, namely as a medium of exchange for payment of debts; as a common measure of value; and as a store of value that should retain its worth over time.

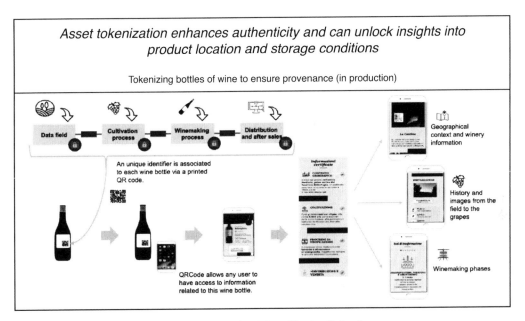

Figure 3.8: EY's WineChain Solution

Source: EY, with permission

2. Native digital assets can also be used as a **crypto-token** to represent anything of value. For example, EY uses a token to represent a specific bottle of wine. Crypto-tokens can be used to represent *fungible* (non-unique) assets, such as loyalty rewards and airline frequent flyer miles, in which one token is interchangeable with another. Crypto-tokens can be used to represent *non-fungible* (unique) assets where the token represents a particular asset in the real world, creating what one can consider to be the digital twin. For example, a unique token could be created to represent a particular diamond; a particular medical device; a particular plot of land; or a particular work of art. Crypto-tokens create new ways to track assets through supply chains.

3. Blockchains rely on participants to operate nodes to validate transactions and to constantly re-check the integrity of the ledger's records. For some blockchains, native digital assets are a way to **compensate participants for securing the network.**

4. Native digital assets can be used to **discourage people from over-using a shared resource** by requiring a small fee to submit transactions. Ethereum, for example, uses its native digital asset 'ether' to pay for specific actions on the blockchain network.

5. Additionally, native digital assets serve as a **counter-measure to Denial of Service (DoS) attacks**, as a malicious actor trying to spam millions of transactions would run out of funding.[32]

To achieve the full vision of an 'Internet of Value', we need standards for native digital assets. The Enterprise Ethereum Alliance (EEA), a consortium of enterprises aiming to develop standards for enterprise use of Ethereum,[33] is leading the Token Taxonomy Framework initiative and, so far, have specified the following common token behaviors:

- *Transferable* to other people, such as money or land titles, or *non-transferable* to other people, such as identity or a vote;

- *Whole* or *divisible,* and if divisible, the number of decimal places are specified;

- *Singleton,* such as a unique token for non-fungible assets like art, or *non-singleton* for fungible assets;

- *Mintable,* to create new tokens, or *non-mintable* where the total token supply is fixed;

- *Burnable,* to remove tokens from the supply, or *non-burnable*; and

- *Role support,* to allow or prevent certain actions.

The public Ethereum has two token standards that are widely used: the ERC-20 Token Standard for fungible tokens, and the ERC-721 Token Standard for non-fungible tokens. In June of 2019, the ERC-1155 Token Standard was issued that allows for the creation of both fungible and non-fungible tokens within a single smart contract.[34]

3.3.4. Cryptography

Blockchains rely heavily on cryptography—the science of securing data in the presence of third party adversaries. There's a lot of imposing mathematics that secure blockchains, but here we will cover hexadecimal numbering system, hashes, and digital signatures.

Many blockchains rely on cryptography that is expressed in hexadecimals, otherwise known as base 16. For those accustomed to the digital world (base 10), it takes a moment to realize that many blockchain data fields like addresses, transaction IDs, and block IDs are actually large numbers expressed in hexadecimal, which contain letters A, B, C, D, E and F (see Table 3.5).

Decimal Base 10	Hexadecimal Base 16	Decimal Base 10	Hexadecimal Base 16
0	0	16	10
1	1	17	11
2	2	18	12
3	3	19	13
4	4	20	14
5	5	21	15
6	6	22	16
7	7	23	17
8	8	24	18
9	9	25	19
10	A	26	1A
11	B	27	1B
12	C	28	1C
13	D	29	1D
14	E	30	1E
15	F	31	1F

Table 3.5: Decimal to hexadecimal conversion

The main advantage of a hexadecimal numbering system is that it is more compact; it requires fewer digits to express large numbers. In the blockchain world, the numbers are quite large! For example, this is a Bitcoin transaction ID, which is a *number* expressed in hexadecimal:

950ecd628c3630b0d7dec443eee2444d1dbb68a9a249c542d5d36e38df4e06ff

That number, converted to the decimal system is:

67420767812655468082789583782332908473009847828119132972854950135256499226367[35]

The Bitcoin ID above is actually created by taking inputs to the transaction—including the sender's account address, receiver's account address, miner's fee, and transaction amounts—and putting it through a hashing algorithm.

Hashing Algorithms

A hash is a mathematical algorithm for transforming one input into a different output. Given a specific input, the identical output will always be reproduced. A good hashing algorithm makes it practically impossible to determine the input value based on the output value, which is why hashes are called 'one way' functions. Blockchains use hashes in many places to add layers of security. Public keys are hashed into addresses; addresses and amounts within a transaction are hashed to create a unique and secure transaction ID; transaction IDs within a block are hashed together multiple times to produce a Merkle Root (see Glossary) that resides in a block header; and all the data in the block header is hashed to create a unique and secure block ID. SHA-256 is an example of a hashing algorithm.

SHA-256

SHA-256 is a secure, one-way hash function commonly used in blockchains. It was designed by the US National Security Agency. It takes any-sized input value and produces a 32 byte (i.e. 256 bit[(iii)]) output value using hexadecimal notation. The output

---

[(iii)] A bit is a binary digit that can have a value of '1' or '0'. For example, the decimal number '256' is expressed as '100000000' in binary.

looks nonsensical, but the same input will always produce the exact same output. Figure 3.9 shows three examples. The first example transformed the name 'MaryLacity' into a 32 byte output. The second example, 'Marylacity', merely changed a capital 'L' to a small 'l', yet the output is completely different from the first example. The third example shows how a large block of text can still be transformed to a unique 32 byte output.[iv]   It's quite remarkable!

Example	Input (m)	SHA-256 Output H(m) in hex (base 16)
1	MaryLacity	681794341783bb9b8e0c310ec316643bb3d1000766bdb5b32c63d3ffb7bad161
2	Marylacity	de850a9d2f7d47163333ba3455cb94ea0209324470944df4c3d97dde99b5ad02
3	Dr. Mary Lacity is Curators' Professor of Information Systems and an International Business Fellow at the University of Missouri-St. Louis. She is also a Senior Editor of MIS Quarterly Executive and on the Editorial Boards for Journal of Information Technology, MIS Quarterly Executive, IEEE Transactions on Engineering Management, Journal of Strategic Information Systems, and Strategic Outsourcing: An International Journal.	9c819a612575844b8ea04017efc56ef5d4aea8aa83934dc72d679eb6b65e92b9

Figure 3.9: Three examples of the SHA-256 hash function

Source: http://www.xorbin.com/tools/sha256-hash-calculator

As a cryptographically secure one-way hash function, SHA-256 takes any size input and produces a unique 32 byte output.

Digital Signatures

A digital signature is the most important cryptographic feature to understand because consumers are ultimately responsible for their own digital signatures. If consumers don't protect them, they risk losing their digital asset. Here's how a digital signature works:

[iv] Astute readers may count what seems to be 64 characters, but hex uses two spaces to represent one character. '681794341783bb9b8e0c310ec316643bb3d1000766bdb5b32c63d3ffb7bad161' is best read as '68 17 94 34 17 83 bb 9b 8e 0c 31 0e c3 16 64 3b b3 d1 00 07 66 bd b5 b3 2c 63 d3 ff b7 ba d1 61'

When a consumer buys a native digital asset, let's say a bitcoin, the system generates a unique pair of numbers that are mathematically related, called a private-public key pair. The public key is the address we see stored on the blockchain (well actually, it's a hashed version of the public key). The private key is stored off the blockchain, most typically in a digital wallet. To move value out of the address stored on the blockchain, one needs to verify he or she owns the address by using his or her private key, stored off the blockchain. Computer algorithms verify that the private key is indeed the mathematical mate to the public key. Both keys are needed to digitally sign the transaction (see Figure 3.10). Thus, a blockchain uses digital signatures to verify asset ownership and thus does not need to rely on a trusted third party to provide this function.

Blockchain applications commonly use **Elliptic Curve Cryptography (ECC)** to generate the keys. Interested readers may consult the Glossary to learn more.

Figure 3.10: Proof of digital asset ownership using private-public key pairs.

3.3.5. Consensus Protocols

As the name implies, consensus protocols are the rules that make sure all the nodes in a blockchain network agree—that nodes are using the same exact copy of the digital ledger. A consensus protocol assures *"a common, unambiguous ordering of transactions and blocks and guarantees the integrity and consistency of the blockchain across geographically distributed nodes."*[36] Many consensus protocols have been proposed, including Proof-of-Work; Proof-of-Stake; Proof-of-Activity (which combines Proof-of-Stake with Proof-of-Work); Proof-of-Authority; Proof-of-Burn; Proof-of-Capacity; Proof-of-Elapsed Time; Proof-of-Listening; and Proof-of-Luck—the list goes on.[37, 38]

Although consensus protocols vary in their validation procedures, in general, all consensus protocols seek to verify legitimate transactions, reject unverifiable transactions, ignore faulty nodes on the network, and prevent modifications to the ledger. The process of validation begins when a new transaction is broadcast to the network. Computer algorithms on the other nodes verify legitimate ownership of the asset (based on the owner's digital signature with his or her private key) and check that the asset has not been given away before by scanning the digital ledger, thus preventing double spending. Which node gets to collect verified transactions, sequence them and add them to the official ledger depends on the network's specific consensus protocol.

Three common *classes* of consensus protocols are 'proof-of-work' (used by Bitcoin, Ethereum, and Monero), 'proof-of-stake' (used by NXT and possibly Ethereum in the future), and 'Practical Byzantine Fault Tolerance (PBFT)' (used by Ripple, Stellar, Hyperledger Fabric, Corda and Tendermint). Within the class of consensus, it's important to note that different blockchain applications using the same 'class' of protocol may vary from the descriptions below. For example, versions of PBFT include Redundant Byzantine Fault Tolerance (RBFT);[39] Delegated Byzantine Fault Tolerance;[40] and Federated Byzantine Agreement [41]— to name but a few.

Proof-of-Work (PoW)

Proof-of-Work (PoW) is a consensus protocol created by Cynthia Dwork and Moni Naor in 1993 to prevent junk email.[42] Satoshi Nakamoto adopted the 'proof-of-work' consensus protocol for Bitcoin in the 2008 white paper.[43] Ethereum also uses Proof-of-Work (for now). Nakamoto needed a way to find independent verifiers to validate transactions and add blocks to the blockchain without relying on trusted third parties. Nakamoto proposed to reward other nodes in the network with newly issued bitcoins when they validate all recently submitted transactions and create the next block. So that validator nodes take the task seriously, Nakamoto proposed a competition among computer nodes in the blockchain network to be the first to collect recently verified transactions into a block and then to find an acceptable block identification number (known as the blockhash) for the next block in the blockchain. It's not easy to find an acceptable number—it takes a lot of computing power to perform the brute force guesses to find a hash number that is less than the current mining 'difficulty' (see Glossary for details). The difficulty is part of the proof that the miner's computer did a significant amount of work to earn the block reward. The Proof-of-Work protocol creates a highly secure ledger, as an attacker would need to gain control of more than 50 percent of the nodes, rewrite history and find all new hashes that adhere to the protocol before other nodes notice. The cons of the protocol include slower transaction settlement times and higher electricity consumption compared to other protocols.

Proof-of-Stake (PoS)

Proof-of-Stake (PoS) is a consensus protocol created by Sunny King and Scott Nadal, in a 2012 white paper.[44] Instead of 'mining' for coins, the protocol selects a member to 'forge' new currency as a reward for validating the transactions and creating the next block. (In other versions of the protocol, there is no 'forging' of new coins; the selected member node is awarded only transaction fees paid by senders.) The member node is selected in a semi-random way. It's called a 'proof-of-stake' because the members with the highest 'stake' (e.g. have the largest account balances; holding the coins the longest period of time) are giving priority in the selection algorithm. Participants in the blockchain can estimate with some certainty which member will likely be the next 'forger'. A Proof-of-Stake process uses much less energy than a Proof-of-Work process. It creates a highly secure ledger, as an attacker would need to gain control of more than 50 percent of the cryptocurrency to rewrite the ledger. However, critics claim it is less secure than proof-of-work because people with small stakes have little to lose by voting for multiple blockchain histories, which leads to consensus never resolving.[45] Peercoin and Nxt use Proof-of-Stake. Figure 3.11 compares Proof-of-Work with Proof-of-Stake.

Figure 3.11: Proof-of-Work *vs.* Proof-of-Stake

Source: https://blockgeeks.com/wp-content/uploads/2019/05/proofofworkvsproofofstake-1.jpg

Practical Byzantine Fault Tolerance (PBFT)

Practical Byzantine Fault Tolerance (PBFT) is a consensus protocol created by Miguel Castro and Barbara Liskov in 1999.[46] With PBFT, nodes need permission to serve as validator nodes, forming a member list. Each round, a node from the member list is selected as leader (see Figure 3.12). A client node sends a request to the leader node to validate a transaction. The leader node multicasts the request to all the other authorized nodes. The authorized nodes execute the request independently and then send to each other and reply to the client. The client waits for a certain percentage of replies to confirm validation, typically waiting for 2/3 of the nodes to agree. The leader node then changes for next round.

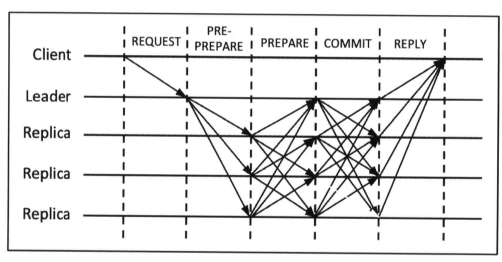

Figure 3.12: Practical Byzantine Fault Tolerance (PBFT) consensus process

Source: Castro & Liskov (1999) https://theintelligenceofinformation.files.wordpress.com/2017/02/hotdep_ img_1.jpg

Consensus protocols have tradeoffs been number of transactions processed per second; settlement speed; resource consumption in terms of electricity consumed; security; and anonymity vs. confidentiality (see Figure 3.13).

	PoW	PoS	PBFT
Trust of a node comes from:	PoW makes it financially impractical to alter ledger	Node has something to lose if it misbehaves	The reputation of known participants operating 'trust nodes' is on the line
Advantages:	• Most secure ledger • Most decentralized • Most anonymous	• Faster settlement than PoW • More TPS than PoW • Fewer resources than PoW	• Highest TPS • Fastest settlement times • Lowest resource consumption • Confidentiality
Disadvantages:	• High resource consumption (electricity burned to operate mining equipment) • Slowest settlement times • Fewest Transactions Per Second (TPS)	• Nothing at stake if someone continues to vote on multiple versions, making consensus impossible	• Most centralized • Anonymity lost • Settlement affected by number of nodes

Figure 3.13: Advantages and disadvantages of Proof-of-Work (PoW), Proof-of-Stake (PoS) and Practical Byzantine Fault Tolerance (PBFT)

3.3.6. Smart Contracts

A smart contract—a concept developed by Nick Szabo in 1994—is *"a piece of software that stores rules for negotiating the terms of a contract, automatically verifies the contract and then executes the terms."*[47]   Anything that can be coded with clearly specified rules, can be coded into a smart contract, which is secured and permanently stored on a blockchain. Ethereum was the first major blockchain to include full smart contracting capabilities, thus escalating blockchains from peer-to-peer payment systems to platforms that can execute machine-to-machine agreements. As of January 2020, over 1,000,000 contracts were running on Ethereum, but many of these are simple little contracts such as 'hello world'.[48]

Smart contracts' magic (and danger) is that, once deployed, they execute automatically and cannot be stopped. Therefore, parties must agree to all the terms of the contract before deploying it. Smart contracts are commonly used to automatically move value around accounts based on agreed upon conditions. As we shall see, use cases abound: lotteries; voting; crowdsourcing; asset sharing (lookout Uber, Airbnb, and Spotify); asset tracking; identity management; bidding; rating; gaming; and gambling. In general, smart contracts can be classified as either deterministic or non-deterministic.

A deterministic smart contract

A deterministic smart contract means that the contract, once deployed on the blockchain, can execute autonomously without the need for any outside information. A lottery is a good example. A smart contract for a lottery could define the time period when people could send value to the smart contract account to buy lottery tickets. The smart contract could specify how the winning lottery number would be selected, perhaps by taking the hash of a randomly selected block and awarding the account that is closest to that number as the winner. The smart contract could automatically transfer the money to the winning account. If the lottery was regulated, the smart contract could be coded to deduct taxes.

A non-deterministic smart contract

A non-deterministic smart contract means that outside information is needed to execute the contract. Horse race betting is an example. Like a lottery, a smart contract for horse race betting could be coded to define when people could send value to the smart contract account to place their bets. The rules for adjusting odds could also be mechanized in the contract. However, smart contracts for horse racing cannot run autonomously; they need outsiders (called '*oracles*') to inform the smart contract of the winning animal. Unlike trusted third parties, an oracle in this scenario does not control the funds, the smart contract does.

Autonomous execution of organizations

One special kind of smart contact is called a Decentralized Autonomous Organization (DAO). This is expalined by Henning Diedrich, author of Ethereum: Blockchains, Digital Assets, Smart Contracts, DAOs:[49]

> *"The idea of a DAO is to create a completely independent entity that is exclusively governed by the rules that you program into it and 'lives' on the chain. This is more than using the blockchain to manage a company: instead, the code is the entire company. And it cannot be stopped."*

The concept of a DAO is intriguing. As the name implies, the idea is to create a new organization that runs automatically based on codified rules encrypted in a smart contract. It runs without anyone controlling it, and it cannot be modified or rescinded once it is launched. ***Think of a Decentralized Autonomous Organization as a completely digital 'company' with no managers or employees.*** The 'owners' are the ones who transferred cryptocurrencies to the DAO's accounts during an initial funding period. Their investments are subject to the rules of the contract, such as limiting when accounts can be liquidated. How well did this idea work in practice? Well the coders of one particular DAO created such havoc, it resulted in a huge battle within the Ethereum open source community, resulting in a 'hard fork'. The story, covered in Chapter 5, is an important reminder of the challenges of shared governance over distributed systems.

So far, we have covered protocols for the distributed ledger; participation and validation; native digital assets; cryptography; consensus (to make sure everyone has the identical copy of the ledger); and smart contracts. All these rules must be specified and agreed upon before protocols are programmed into code bases.

3.3.7. Code bases

Open source communities, consortia, or even private companies and individuals, can program protocols into *code bases*. A code base is the set of programming instructions based on the agreed upon rules, i.e. the protocols. Many code bases are managed by an open community who decides what changes can be made to the code base. Open source code bases also allow people to download the code and play with the code in a test environment called a 'sandbox'.

Of course, Bitcoin was the first blockchain code base, but most businesses initially adopt open-source code bases for permissioned code bases, although many are experimenting with public Ethereum. HfS Research found that the top code bases for enterprises were Ethereum, Hyperledger Fabric, R3 Corda, Ripple and Quorum.[50] MultiChain has also gained momentum by partnering with companies like Accenture, Cognizant, and Mphasis to help build blockchain applications.

GitHub (bought by Microsoft in 2018) is a version-controlled repository hosting service that manages many open source blockchain code bases. Code bases are released in stages, such as alpha; beta; release candidate; and general availability. Upgrades are released and tracked using version control. From a manager's perspective, the immaturity of the code bases may be a concern, as software vulnerabilities may takes months or years to be fully identified (see Table 3.6).

Code base	Released
Bitcoin Core	Initial release: 2009
Ethereum	General availability: 2015
Chain	Initial release: 2016
Quorum	Beta: 2017
Corda	Beta: 2017
Hyperledger Fabric	Beta: 2017
Multichain	Pre-beta 2017

Table 3.6: Code base release dates

The number of lines of code serves as a proxy as to the complexity of the code base. For example, Google has 2 billion lines of source code; Facebook has 62 million lines of code;[51] and Microsoft Windows has about 50 million lines of code.[52] In contrast, Bitcoin Core has about 77,000 lines of code (version written in C); Ethereum has about 100,000. However, the number of lines of code numbers vary by client. For example, Ethereum protocols have been coded in various computer languages like Go; Rust; C++; Python; Java; Ruby; etc.

3.3.8. The blockchain application use case

Code bases can be used to develop *blockchain use cases,* i.e. applications. Figure 3.14 provides examples of use cases across industries collected from press announcements and Google alerts.

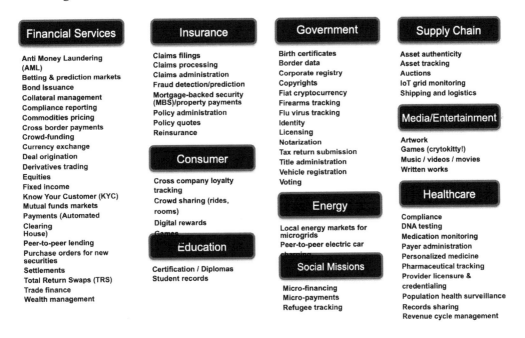

Figure 3.14: Blockchain use cases

Sources: various press announcements, Google alerts

143

Firms from the financial services industry were the first to take serious notice of blockchain's opportunities and threats, and therefore have explored more use cases than other industries. Insurance, healthcare, supply chain and governments are quickly catching up.

As noted in prior chapters, thousands of blockchain applications have been built, but many of these were still in sandboxes, or in test environments, as of the beginning of 2019. These 'test' applications—also called Proof-of-Concepts (POCs)—have occurred across industries and geographies. Moving blockchain applications from the isolation of innovation labs into full-scale live productions will take time, due to the inescapable issue of 'technology embeddedness'.[53] Technology is never neutral, but rather technologies are developed and deployed in a dynamic legal; political; organizational; regulatory; social; economic; and physical world. It is technology embeddedness that makes predictions about the future of enterprise blockchains so speculative. These technology embeddedness challenges are discussed in Chapter 6.

3.3.9. The blockchain application interface ('access point')

To access permissionless blockchain applications, users need a digital wallet they download themselves, or go through an exchange like Coinbase, Kraken, or Binance. To access permissioned blockchains, enterprise users typically interface through gateway services, or build their own interfaces to existing systems using Application Programming Interfaces (APIs). Increasingly, devices—like sensors or your Amazon 'Alexa', that gather information from the environment—are connected to blockchains. These devices are known as the 'Internet-of-Things' (IoT)[v], and they are an input, feeding data to a blockchain. For example, IoT sensors can measure the temperature in a truck and send that data to a smart contract; the smart contract might be programmed to alert trading partners when temperature excursions exceed agreed upon levels.

---

[v] The Internet of Things (IoT) is a system of interrelated computing devices, mechanical and digital machines, objects, animals or people that are provided with unique identifiers and the ability to transfer data over a network without requiring human-to-human or human-to-computer interaction.

Interfaces are blockchains' main points of vulnerability. Nearly all of the hacks we hear about occur at the access points. We've already introduced the notion of a digital signature that comprises private-public key pairs. Hackers don't waste their time trying to calculate the private key because it's theoretically impossible to figure out the private key if one only has the public key (at least until Quantum computers are mainstream—see Chapter 8). Hackers find it much more lucrative to *steal* the private keys.

Many consumers do not realize just how vulnerable they are to theft or loss of their private keys. Many people keep their private keys in digital wallets stored on their mobile devices, again, not realizing that if the phone breaks or is lost or is hacked, they lose their private keys. As a general rule, private keys cannot be recovered—there is no help desk to call to retrieve them like when one forgets a password, and no credit card company to report and recover damages from fraud. That said, new services are emerging that may help with recovery of private keys, but it is still early days and therefore difficult to find a provider with a strong historical track record. The safest places to store private keys are on a storage drive that is not connected to the Internet and, quite ironically, on a piece of paper that is locked in a fireproof safe.

Other people trust their centralized exchanges to store and protect their keys. However, hackers most commonly target exchanges because they can steal large numbers of private keys. One of the largest heists occurred in August of 2014, when 850,000 bitcoins—then worth $450 million—were stolen from the wallets managed by Mt. Gox, the largest Bitcoin exchange at the time. It's important to understand that such heists have not breached the blockchain itself. These heists happen outside the blockchain, that is, in the vulnerable access points to a blockchain.

Many exchanges now comply with regulations, including Know Your Customer (KYC) and Anti-Money Laundering (AML) requirements. For example, Coinbase had money transmitter licenses from 45 US States and a New York State Virtual Currency License by 2019. Coinbase also has commercial criminal insurance that is greater than the value of digital currency maintained in online storage (98 percent of the private keys are stored offline). Increased compliance means a loss of user anonymity, a consequence counter to the Cypherpunk values of the initial Bitcoin adopters.

Having explained all parts of a blockchain application, the next question is usually: *"How does a blockchain's distributed ledger differ from a traditional distributed database?"*

3.4. Blockchain's distributed ledger vs. traditional distributed databases

"In short: the difference is decentralized control."

Shaan Ray, blockchain pundit[54]

"Blockchain are really developing, not only as a place to secure data, but also through the smart contract. Blockchains are an interesting way to create links between companies without going through the formal process that you normally would with databases."

Founder of a blockchain consortium[55]

"Blockchains are not just Distributed Ledger Technology... Blockchains are about guarantee of execution."

Henning Diedrich, author of *Ethereum: Blockchains, Digital Assets, Smart Contracts, DAOs*[56]

'Distributed databases' is an umbrella term that encompasses many different architectural designs where data is stored in multiple places, and where agreement is maintained through computer algorithms that lock and time stamp records. Given that definition, we see that ***blockchains are distributed database systems, just of a special kind***. Whereas traditional distributed databases are centrally controlled so that a single organization can decide to alter records or access rules, blockchains are distributed—no one entity has the power to roll back or alter history. When is the distributed control of blockchains preferable to the centralized control of traditional databases? Some pundits argue that the answer depends on the 'trust boundary' (see Figure 3.15).

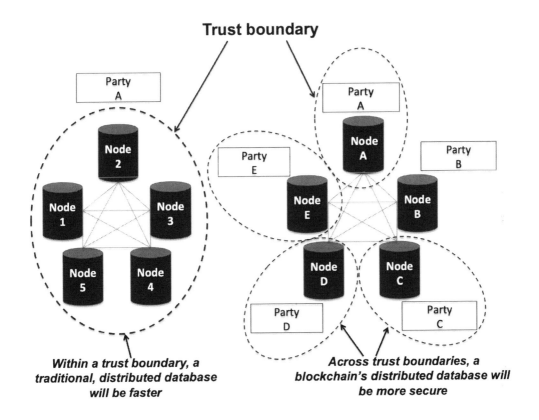

Figure 3.15: The 'trust boundary' as the distinguishing difference

Source: Adapted from Richard Gendal Brown[57]

Those with this view recognize that all the nodes in a traditional distributed database environment trust each other, and therefore fewer verifications are required.[58] Trust is not presumed among nodes in a blockchain distributed ledger, so every event must be checked and rechecked, which is one reason why traditional distributed databases are magnitudes faster than blockchains.[59] Other experts also point to the inclusion of smart contracts as a distinguishing feature and advantage of blockchains over distributed database systems.

Hopefully by now, readers are comfortable with the notions of blockchains' protocols, code bases, use cases and application interfaces. We've learned that blockchains are appropriate for contexts where trading partners do not want any one entity in charge of validating and maintaining their shared records. Armed with the knowledge of these concepts, we revisit Bitcoin and see how it is indeed just one type of blockchain application. We are now ready to map Bitcoin to the blockchain application framework introduced in Figure 3.2.

3.5. Mapping bitcoin to the blockchain application framework

Like all blockchain applications, Bitcoin has its own protocols, code base, use case, and access points, which are mapped to the blockchain application framework depicted in Figure 3.16.

Beginning at the bottom of the figure, Bitcoin's ***distributed ledger*** is structured as a chain of blocks. Bitcoin participation access is open to the ***public*** and anyone can operate a validator node, i.e. it is ***permissionless.*** Bitcoin's ***native digital asset*** is a bitcoin. Bitcoin uses digital signatures (and other sophisticated ***cryptographic*** techniques) to authenticate asset ownership and to secure transactions. Bitcoin uses Proof-of-Work as its mechanism to ensure ***consensus*** across nodes in the network. Bitcoin does not have what is called a 'Turing Complete'[60] (see Glossary) ***smart contracting*** component—this innovation came later, with Ethereum—but Bitcoin does have a scripting language that is intentionally restricted to increase security.

Moving up the framework diagram in Figure 3.16, the ***code base*** is called Bitcoin Core, and is maintained and supported by an open source community. Anyone may download the code base from GitHub (https://github.com/). As of 2020, there were about 10,000 reachable nodes running the full Bitcoin source code, which means any of them could be competing for mining rewards.

Bitcoin's ***use case*** is a payment application system; it is used to settle and store transfers of value on the distributed ledger.

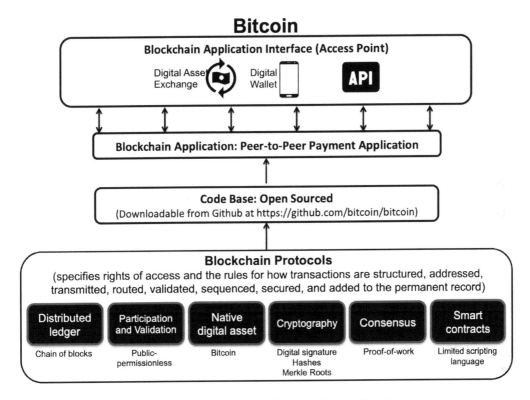

Figure 3.16: Bitcoin mapped to the blockchain application framework

The **_interface_** to Bitcoin requires wallet software that stores the user's private keys off the blockchain. Wallet software makes it easy for users to transfer bitcoins (see Figure 3.17). Software developers can also access Bitcoin with over 125 APIs. For example, the API 'getBalance' triggers a remote call that returns the balance in a digital wallet.[61]

To get a better understanding of Bitcoin's transparency, immutability and anonymity, one may visit https://blockchain.com/explorer to see the most recent blocks (see Figure 3.18). One can also search the entire history of the blockchain by block number (called block 'height'), transaction ID or address (i.e. a hashed version of the public key).

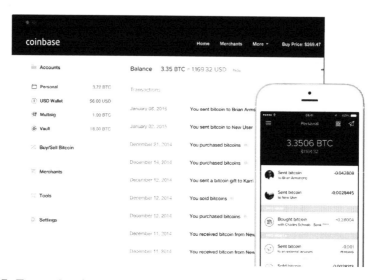

Figure 3.17: Example of a web-based and mobile digital wallet interface to Bitcoin

Source: https://www.coinbase.com/assets/home/global3-f9646244d66dd7c26191f091585db0f4feda2af3c
ad7cfe63b0de080d1cd36c5.png

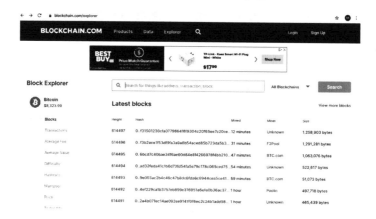

Figure 3.18: A screenshot of a website to view Bitcoin's blockchain

Block 61497 was the 'latest block' on January 25, 2020 at 10:07am

Source: https://blockchain.com/explorer

Readers should now also be able to interpret the data stored for a Bitcoin transaction (see Figure 3.19). The transaction in the figure, which occurred on February 25 of 2016, shows a transfer of value from the sender's address on the left to the receiver's address on the right. The sender also provided a small transaction fee for the miner of .005 bitcoins. The 'hash' is a unique transaction identifier calculated from the inputs.

Figure 3.19: An example of a transaction stored on Bitcoin's public ledger

Source: https://blockchain.com/explorer

3.6. Conclusion

In this chapter, we have learned that a blockchain application comprises protocols, code bases, use cases, and application interfaces. We've invested some time understanding the differences between public/private and permissioned/permissionless protocols, and we took a closer look at the protocols associated with distributed ledgers; native digital assets; cryptography; consensus; and smart contracts. Hopefully, readers can now comprehend the definition that opened this chapter:

A blockchain application is a peer-to-peer system for validating, time-stamping, and permanently storing transactions on a shared ***distributed ledger***. ***Digital assets***, native to each blockchain application, exist only in digital form and come with rights of use. ***Cryptography*** and ***consensus*** algorithms are used to validate transactions, to update the ledger, and to keep the ledger and network secure. Most blockchains also use ***smart contracts*** that apply rules to automatically execute transactions based upon pre-agreed conditions.

From a business perspective, managers need to see more examples of blockchain applications—the topic of the next chapter.

Citations:

[1] https://www.brainyquote.com/authors/adam-draper-quotes.

[2] Welcome speech by Darren Shelton, Blockchain in Oil and Gas Conference, September 18, 2019, Houston, Texas.

[3] Diedrich, H. (2016), *Ethereum: blockchains, digital assets, smart contracts, decentralized autonomous organizations*, Wildfire publishing.

[4] The World Bank estimated that sending remittances cost an average of 7.99 percent of the amount sent; *Navigating the world of cross-border payments*, http://www.iqpc.com/media/1003982/57107.pdf. The administrative costs for tracking containers in the global supply chain was roughly 22 percent of the retail costs according to Anderson, J., & Van Wincoop, E. (2004). Trade Costs: *Journal of Economic Literature, 42*(3), 691-751. Retrieved from http://www.jstor.org/stable/3217249.

[5] For example, the European Central Bank reported that the average time to settle cross-border credit transfers was 4.8 working days in 1999. McKinsey found little progress by 2015, as the average settlement times were still between three to five business days. European Central Bank (September 1999), *Improving Cross-border Retail Payment Services: The Eurosystem's view*, https://www.ecb.europa.eu/pub/pdf/other/retailpsen.pdf. McKinsey (2015), *Global Payments 2015: A Healthy Industry Confront Disruption*, https://www.mckinsey.com/industries/financial-services/our-insights/global-payments-2015-a-healthy-industry-confronts-disruption

[6] Williamson, O., (1991), 'Comparative economic organization: the analysis of discrete structural alternatives', *Administrative Science Quarterly*, 36 (2), 269–296.

[7] Catalini, C., and Gans, J. (2016), 'Some Simple Economics of the Blockchain', *MIT Sloan School of Management Working Paper* 5191-16.

[8] Ross, A. *11 data breaches that stung US consumers*, posted on bankrate.com: http://www.bankrate.com/finance/banking/us-data-breaches-1.aspx.

[9] Popov, S. (2017), *The Tangle*, IOTA whitepaper, https://iota.org/IOTA_Whitepaper.pdf.

[10] Popov, S. (2017), *The Tangle*, IOTA whitepaper, https://iota.org/IOTA_Whitepaper.pdf.

[11] Bauerle, N. (2017), *What is the Difference Between Public and Permissioned Blockchains?* https://www.coindesk.com/information/what-is-the-difference-between-open-and-permissioned-blockchains/.

[12] To operate an EOS validator node, an individual or organization must have a public website URL; at least one social media account, and ID on Steemit; sufficient hardware; plans to scale hardware; plans

to benefit the community; telegram and testnet nodes a roadmap; and a dividend position. Source: Ben Sigman (May 8, 2018). EOS Block Producer FAQ, https://medium.com/@bensig/eos-block-producer-faq-8ba0299c2896.

[13] To view the 21 EOS validator nodes and block producers, see https://bloks.io/vote.

[14] Delegated Proof of Stake, https://lisk.io/academy/blockchain-basics/how-does-blockchain-work/delegated-proof-of-stake.

[15] Jayachandran, P. (May 31, 2017), *The difference between public and private blockchain*, https://www.ibm.com/blogs/blockchain/2017/05/the-difference-between-public-and-private-blockchain/

[16] Crosman, P. (April 28, 2017). 'JPMorgan defection underscores tough blockchain choices', *American Banker*, https://www.americanbanker.com/news/jpmorgan-defection-underscores-tough-blockchain-choices

[17] POA Network, *Proof of Authority: Consensus Model with Identity at Stake*, https://medium.com/poa-network/proof-of-authority-consensus-model-with-identity-at-stake-d5bd15463256.

[18] https://www.mediledger.com/.

[19] *What are Key Responsibilities for a Trust Anchor?* https://www.ibm.com/blockchain/solutions/food-trust/food-industry-technology#1797811.

[20] IBM Press Release (October 23, 2018), *IBM and Microsoft Announce Partnership Between Cloud Offerings*, https://www.pbsnow.com/ibm-news/ibm-and-microsoft-announce-partnership-between-cloud-offerings/.

[21] IBM Food Trust Fact Sheet December 2018, https://newsroom.ibm.com/download/IBM+Food+Trust+-+Ecosystem+Fact+Sheet+Dec+2018.pdf.

[22] TradeLens Overview (October 2, 2018), https://shipbrokers.fi/wp-content/uploads/2018/10/jeppe-kobbero-tradelens-presentation.pdf.

[23] Jensen, T. (December 12, 2018), *Blockchain Strategize Digital Infrastructuring: Blockchain technology bridging the Document Platforms towards real business value in Maritime Supply Chains*, Pre-ICIS Workshop, San Francisco.

[24] Maersk Press Release (July 2, 2019), *TradeLens Blockchain-Enabled Digital Shipping Platform Continues Expansion with Addition of Major Ocean Carriers Hapag-Lloyd and Ocean Network Express*,

https://www.globenewswire.com/news-release/2019/07/02/1877150/0/en/TradeLens-Blockchain-Enabled-Digital-Shipping-Platform-Continues-Expansion-With-Addition-of-Major-Ocean-Carriers-Hapag-Lloyd-and-Ocean-Network- Express.html.

[25] Bridget van Kralingen & Mike White at Blockchain Revolution Global 2019, https://youtu.be/7crOWQnz9tw.

[26] Some authors only consider three types of blockchains, for example, Pedersen, A., Risius, M., and Beck, R. (2019), 'A Ten-Step Decision Path to Determine When to Use Blockchain Technologies', *MIS Quarterly Executive*, 18(2), Article 3.

[27] Daniels, A. (October 18, 2018). 'The Rise of Private Permissionless Blockchains', *Medium*, https://medium.com/ltonetwork/the-rise-of-private-permissionless-blockchains-part-1-4c39bea2e2be.

[28] Nightfall, https://github.com/EYBlockchain/nightfall.

[29] https://www.ey.com/en_us/people/paul-brody.

[30] *Restoring trust in the wine industry, from grape to glass*, EY, https://www.ey.com/en_us/global-review/2018/restoring-trust-in-the-wine-industry.

[31] https://coinmarketcap.com/all/views/all/.

[32] Beck, A. (2002), *Hashcash-A Denial of Service Counter-Measure*, white paper, http://www.hashcash.org/papers/hashcash.pdf.

[33] Enterprise Ethereum Alliance, https://entethalliance.org/.

[34] The Ethereum token standards are available on Github:

https://github.com/ethereum/EIPs/blob/master/EIPS/eip-20.md

https://github.com/ethereum/EIPs/blob/master/EIPS/eip-721.md

https://github.com/ethereum/EIPs/blob/master/EIPS/eip-1155.md

[35] This website converts large numbers: https://www.mobilefish.com/services/big_number/big_number.php.

[36] Baliga, A. (April 2017), *Understanding Blockchain Consensus Models*, https://www.persistent.com/wp-content/uploads/2017/04/WP-Understanding-Blockchain-Consensus-Models.pdf.

[37] Proof-of-Elapsed-Time (PoET) was created by the Hyperledger Sawtooth project, https://www.hyperledger.org/projects

[38] Chan, R. (May 2, 2016), *Consensus mechanisms used in blockchains*, posted on https://www.linkedin.com/pulse/consensus-mechanisms-used-blockchain-ronald-chan

[39] Hyperledger Foundation, *Hyperledger Architecture, Volume 1*, https://www.hyperledger.org/wp-content/uploads/2017/08/HyperLedger_Arch_WG_Paper_1_Consensus.pdf.

[40] Connell, J. (June 2017), *On Byzantine Fault Tolerance in Blockchain Systems*, https://cryptoinsider.com/byzantine-fault-tolerance-blockchain-systems/.

[41] Maziières, D. (2016), *The Stellar Consensus Protocol: A Federated Model for Internet-level Consensus*, white paper, https://www.stellar.org/papers/stellar-consensus-protocol.pdf.

[42] Dwork, C., and Naor, M. (1993), *Pricing via processing: Combatting Junk Mail*, http://www.hashcash.org/papers/pvp.pdf.

[43] Nakamoto, S. (2008), *Bitcoin: A Peer-to-Peer Electronic Cash System*, https://bitcoin.org/bitcoin.pdf.

[44] King, S., and Nadal, S. (2012), PPCoin: Peer-to-Peer Crypto-Currency with Proof-of-Stake, https://peercoin.net/assets/paper/peercoin-paper.pdf.

[45] *Distributed Consensus from Proof of Stake is Impossible, posted by Andrew Poelstra on* https://www.smithandcrown.com/open-research/distributed-consensus-from-proof-of-stake-is-impossible/.

[46] *Practical Byzantine Fault Tolerance*, Proceedings of the Third Symposium on Operating Systems Design and Implementation, New Orleans, USA, February 1999, http://pmg.csail.mit.edu/papers/osdi99.pdf.

[47] 'The Future of Blockchains: Smart Contracts', *Technode*, http://technode.com/2016/11/14/the-future-of-blockchain-technology-smart-contracts/.

[48] This website tracks contract accounts running on Ethereum: https://etherscan.io/contractsVerified.

[49] Diedrich, H. (2016), *Ethereum: blockchains, digital assets, smart contracts, decentralized autonomous organizations*, Wildfire Publishing.

[50] Fersht, P. (2018), *The top 5 enterprise blockchain platforms you need to know about*, https://www.horsesforsources.com/top-5-blockchain-platforms_031618.

[51] Source: http://www.visualcapitalist.com/millions-lines-of-code/.

[52] https://code.org/loc.

[53] Lacity, M. and Willcocks, L. (2018), Robotic Process and Cognitive Automation*: The Next Phase*, SB Publishing, Stratford-upon-Avon, UK.

[54] Shaan Ray (November 5, 2017), *Blockchain versus traditional databases*, Hackernoon, https://hackernoon.com/blockchains-versus-traditional-databases-c1a728159f79.

[55] Personal Interview with Mary Lacity in 2018.

[56] Diedrich, H. (2016), *Ethereum: blockchains, digital assets, smart contracts, decentralized autonomous organizations*, Wildfire Publishing.

[57] Brown, R. (November 8, 2016), *On distributed databases and distributed ledgers*, posted on https://gendal.me/2016/11/08/on-distributed-databases-and-distributed-ledgers/.

[58] Brown, R. (November 8, 2016), *On distributed databases and distributed ledgers*, posted on https://gendal.me/2016/11/08/on-distributed-databases-and-distributed-ledgers/.

[59] Diedrich, H. (2016), *Ethereum: blockchains, digital assets, smart contracts, decentralized autonomous organizations*, Wildfire Publishing.

[60] In layman's terms, 'Turing complete' means a programming language has a comprehensive instruction set; Bitcoin's scripting tool is not 'Turing complete' because it has no way to program logic loops—among other missing features. (See https://en.bitcoin.it/wiki/Script for Bitcoins command set).

[61] This site explains Bitcoin's APIs: https://bitcoin.org/en/developer-reference#bitcoin-core-apis.

PART II

Business Application Examples

Chapter 4

Business Applications for Financial Services

"In the international trade finance case, it's a very old legacy process with a lot of paper documents. It was perceived that there could be value and the banks would be able to introduce a more efficient process through this technology."

Lead Digital Architect for a large global bank[1]

"Initially, the payment people paid attention to cryptocurrency and it was appropriate for them to watch over this new phenomenon. Sometime in the mid 2015 timeframe, the entire financial services industry—ourselves included—became enlightened that this was far more broadly applicable than cryptocurrency."

Blockchain Architect for a large global bank[2]

4.1. Overview of the cases

Enterprises in the financial services sector have been among the first traditional organizations to recognize the threats and opportunities afforded by cryptocurrencies. Traditional enterprises, including banks like Barclays, Santander, State Street, and Wells Fargo that have been in continuous operation for hundreds of years, are among the early explorers of blockchain technologies. Industry consortia like R3, founded in 2014, were started to help incumbent enterprises create standards, write code bases, and bring blockchain financial services applications to life. Over 250 FinTechs have entered the space—such as Axoni, BitPesa, and Digital Asset Holdings.[3] These enterprises have developed proof-of-concepts (POCs) for a dizzying array of financial services: Anti Money Laundering (AML); betting & prediction markets; bond issuance; collateral management; compliance reporting; commodities pricing; cross-border payments; crowd-funding; currency exchange; deal origination; derivatives trading; equities; fixed income; Know Your Customer (KYC); mutual funds markets; payments; peer-to-peer lending; purchase orders for new securities; settlements; Total Return Swaps (TRS); trade finance; and trade reporting. Many POCs never evolved beyond the sandbox.

In this chapter, we provide four examples of deployed financial services blockchain-based applications developed by Ripple, Stellar, WeTrade and Santander (see Table 4.1). Interestingly, the first two are examples of global payments applications for currency exchanges and remittances. In a way, global payments are the poster child of enterprise blockchain applications, enabling peer-to-peer trading; rapid settlement times; low transaction costs; guarantee of execution; and heightened security for the trade of fiat currencies (in addition to cryptocurrencies) that comply with all regulations. We'll see that **Ripple** and **Stellar** do have native digital assets—which grab much of the attention, because both cryptocurrencies are typically among the top ten cryptocurrencies by market capitalization—but our focus is on enterprise uses. Ripple and Stellar serve as examples of new enterprises that have already deployed operational applications; Ripple was launched in 2012 and Stellar was launched in 2015.

WeTrade was founded by a consortium of banks that pooled money to develop a blockchain platform to automate trade finance services, primarily for small-to-mid-sized customers, and then a joint venture to launch the service into production in 2018. The global bank, **Santander,** is involved in many blockchain-enabled financial services, but we highlight its bond issuance and settlement on a public blockchain in this chapter. But first, we need to understand better, the pain points in today's financial services in order to appreciate the aims of these blockchain applications. Let's first begin by understanding how global payments work before blockchains.

Enterprise	Enterprise Type	Blockchain Application	Status as of 2020
Ripple	Private startup	Global payments; targets institutions	Ripple provides an open-sourced network that enterprise adopters access through gateways. The network has been running 'without incidence' since 2014.
Stellar	Non-profit	Global payments; targets the underserved	Stellar provides an open-sourced network upon which enterprise adopters build applications. The network has been running since 2015.
WeTrade	First a consortium, then a Joint Venture	Trade finance	WeTrade launched in 2017 and reached full operations by July 2018; It had been adopted by 17 European banks.
Santander	Traditional Enterprise	Santander is involved in many blockchain-enabled financial services, but we highlight its bond issuance and settlement	Santander launched a one year, $20 million dollar bond on Ethereum in 2019.

Table 4.1: Blockchain application examples for financial services

4.2. Global payments before blockchains

"Around 2 billion people don't use formal financial services and more than 50 percent of adults in the poorest households are unbanked. Financial inclusion is a key enabler to reducing poverty and boosting prosperity."

Jim Yong Kim, President of the World Bank[4]

According to McKinsey, the world sends more than $135 trillion dollars across borders each year.[5] Third-party intermediaries collect about $2.2 trillion in revenue to facilitate these transactions. Money may move around the world in several ways using a variety of services, but we'll focus on a simplified version of the process. In today's global financial systems, each country has its own national payment system and uses its own sovereign currency.[6] A bank must be licensed to use its country's national payment system. International transactions often rely on the cooperation between banks in different countries, creating a messy web of correspondent bank relationships (see Figure 4.1 for a simplified depiction).[7] With a cross-border payment in today's global financial system, the sending and receiving parties' financial institutions, national payment systems, and corresponding banks process the transaction. Parties to an exchange have no access to the status of the transaction or even which institution controls a transaction as it works its way through the system. Fees accumulate with each step in the process. Trading partners do not always know the fees in advance, which can become quite substantial. Sending remittances cost an average of 7.99 percent of the amount sent, and takes several business days to settle.[8,9]

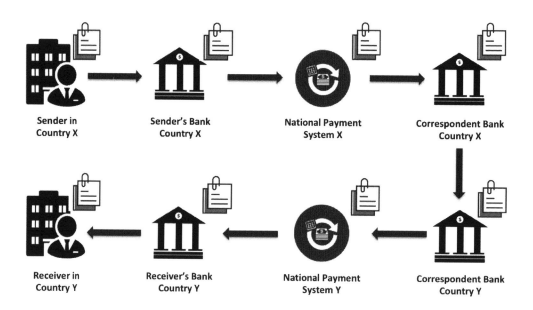

Figure 4.1: A simplified example of cross-border payments before blockchains

Because of the high transaction costs, financial intuitions cannot offer reasonably priced services for low-income people. On average, American banks incur costs of $349 a year per checking account and recover only $268 in transaction fees.[10] In short, banks lose money on checking accounts, so they have few financial incentives to service low-income people. Consequently, up to a quarter of the world's population doesn't have access to financial services—they rely solely on cash. According to research by McKinsey, everyone will benefit from larger financial inclusion.[11] If 1.6 billion more people are included, McKinsey estimated they would generate:

- $3.7 trillion to GDP by 2025

- $2.1 trillion in new credit

- $4.2 trillion in new deposits

- 95 million new jobs

Experts generally agree that banks and governments need to be part of the solution.[12] The poor cannot simply adopt cryptocurrencies to solve all of their financial needs. They need access to fiat currencies for credit and payments. The Financial Services for the Poor Program, funded by the Bill & Melinda Gates Foundation, defined the minimum requirements for a globally inclusive mobile payments platform: The platform must run on inexpensive mobiles phones;[13] it must support national currencies; governments must set regulations to deter fraud, money laundering and cyberterrorism; transactions must settle quickly for small merchants, and it must be interoperable with other systems.[14] So far, there are about 150 mobile payment platforms (like bKash and M-pesa), but they operate in islands.[15,16] So how might blockchains help?

Alin Dragos, a member of the MIT Digital Currency Initiative, believes banks can increase financial inclusion if they adopt blockchains to radically reduce their back office costs. He estimates banks could get their average costs per account down to $100 per year. A more ambitious bank might build a blockchain centric bank, which might reduce costs to $50 a year.[17] Additionally, blockchains for identities could help the more than 230 million undocumented migrants worldwide gain access to financial services and employment.[18]

So, there are plenty of problems to tackle in the global payments arena. As one of the first blockchain applications for business, many people recognized that blockchain applications for cross-border payments could alleviate many of the pain points.[19] Bitcoin provided the baseline model, but its anonymity, low scalability, and massive resource consumption could not meet the needs of trading partners in the highly regulated world of financial services. Ripple and Stellar each built global payments applications that overcome Bitcoin's limitations while still delivering rapid settlement times and low transaction costs. They are each interesting in that they target different markets. Ripple targets institutional customers; Stellar aims to expand access to financial services for those excluded today. After their stories are told, we'll move to other financial services contexts, namely trade finance and bond issuances and settlements.

4.3. Ripple

"Banks join Ripple's global settlement network to send cross-border payments in real time. Ripple eliminates time delays and ensures certainty of settlement, resulting in new revenue opportunities and lower transaction costs for banks and their customers."

Ripple website[20]

"Digital currencies were born out of the necessity for a monetary form that was not controlled by a central bank and cannot be manipulated by politics… Ripple is the first currency exchange that allows trading in all currencies or any unit that has value like frequent flier miles, virtual currencies, and mobile minutes."

Elliott Branson, author of
Ripple: The Ultimate Guide to Understanding Ripple Currency[21]

Ripple was founded by Chris Larsen and Jeb McCaleb in 2012 to build upon Ryan Fugger's idea for a decentralized, real-time settlement system. Headquartered in San Francisco, Brad Garlinghouse is its current CEO.[22] Ripple received Angel funding in 2013, Series A funding in 2015 and Series B funding in 2016. Investors include Accenture; Andreessen Horowitz; CME Ventures; Google Ventures; SBI Group; Santander InnoVentures; Standard Chartered; and Tetagon.[23] By 2019, more than 300 financial institutions joined RippleNet and Ripple employed 534 people.[24]

Ripple aimed to overcome Bitcoin's relatively slow settlement times, inability to trade other currencies, and massive electricity consumption, while still being inexpensive, transparent, private, and secure. According to Ripple's website, its network handles 1,500 transactions per second (TPS), settles payments in four seconds, operates 24x7, and can scale to 50,000 TPS. It also claims a seven-year track record of its distributed ledger closing without incident.[25]

Ripple's target customers are primarily institutional enterprises like banks, corporates, payment providers and exchanges. As of 2018, Ripple offered three integrated services that ran on its RippleNet platform: *xCurrent* to process payments; *xRapid* to source liquidity; and *xVia* to send payments. For banking customers, Ripple envisions that banks will capture new revenue by booking new corporate and consumer clients, reduce their transaction costs, and provide one integration point and a consistent experience for rules, standards and governance.[26] For corporates, Ripple promises on-demand payment with tracking and delivery confirmation and richer data transfers such as appending invoices to payment transfers.[27]

Germany's online bank, Fidor, was Ripple's first institutional customer, which announced the partnership in early 2014. As of 2019, Ripple's customers include such powerhouses as American Express, MoneyGram, Santander, and SBI.[28] In 2018 Santander launched a service called One Pay FX—which runs on RippleNet—in Brazil, Poland, Spain, and the United Kingdom.[29] With an app, customers can send global remittances with four or five clicks.[30] Another corporate customer, SBI Remit, enables Thai nationals living in Japan to send money directly to their Siam Commercial Bank accounts in Thailand. Prior to this service, Thai nationals living in Japan had to hire agents and use cash for transfers. After the service, which took just three months to deploy, transfers settle in three seconds.[31] *Fortune Magazine* covered a story about American Express using Ripple for its US-based corporate customers to send funds to their UK-based accounts at Santander Bank. According to this article, some customers were actually using the service in November 2017.[32]

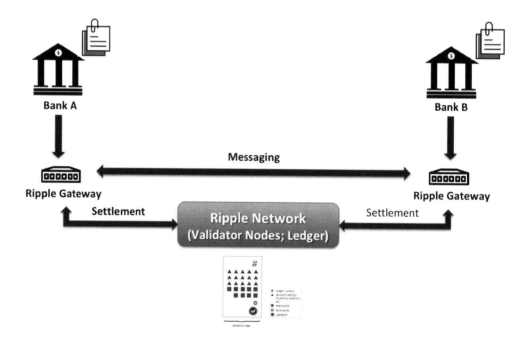

Figure 4.2: A high-level depiction of two banks using Ripple

Institutional customers use an API to connect to the Ripple network via a Ripple Gateway (see Figure 4.2). Gateways can establish trust lines up to certain amounts with other gateways. Two gateways that trust each other can transact directly. However, if the sending gateway does not have a direct trust line with the receiving gateway, the network protocol will find a path of trust, thus transactions will 'ripple' through the network. One may think of this path as appropriating other people's trust. If Sally wants to send money to Sam without really trusting Sam, Sally could send money to someone she trusts, say John; John then sends the money to someone he trusts, say Sue; Sue sends the money to Sam, whom she trusts. If no path of trust can be found, the value can be transferred using Ripple's native digital asset called 'Ripple' (symbol XRP). In this way, XRP can be used as a bridge currency if no paths of trust exist between trading partners. The protocol searches for the best possible exchange rates and makes the currency exchanges in seconds, costing just a few cents worth of fees.[33]

So what's happening with the ledger? Ripple's ledger stores issuances, i.e. digital balances that represent currency or assets of value held by an issuer. Here's how it works:

> *"When a customer sends money into the XRP Ledger, a gateway takes custody of those assets outside of Ripple and sends issuances in the XRP Ledger to the customer's address. When a customer sends money out of the XRP Ledger, she makes an XRP Ledger payment to the gateway, and the gateway credits the customer in its own system of record, or in some other account. Like issuances, XRP can be freely sent and exchanged among XRP Ledger addresses. Unlike issuances, however, XRP is not tied to an accounting relationship—XRP can be sent directly from any XRP Ledger address to any other, without going through a gateway or liquidity provider."[34]*

Figure 4.3 maps Ripple to the blockchain application framework which was developed in Chapter 3. Beginning with the protocols, Ripple defined a new distributed ledger protocol, called the Ripple Transaction Protocol (RTXP).[35] The protocol is sometimes referred to as 'semi-permissioned' in that XRPs can be sent to anyone (permissionless), but also features trust lines where transactions can only ripple through the network on approved paths.

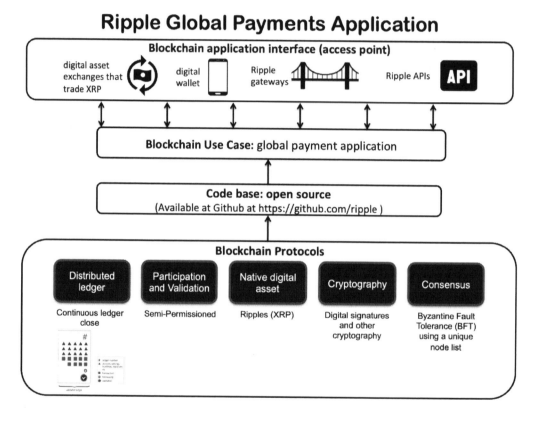

Figure 4.3: Ripple mapped to the blockchain application framework

Distributed Ledger

Ripple does not structure transactions as a chain of blocks. It structures the ledger as a long list of sequenced transactions and account settings/balances that gets closed every few seconds.[36] The ledger also stores buy and sell offers for different currencies.

Every version of the ledger has a unique ID and time stamp. Like Bitcoin, Ripple transactions are permanently stored, irreversibly, on Ripple's distributed ledger. On March 22, 2020, Ripple was on the 54,290,062th version of the ledger (See Figure 4.4).

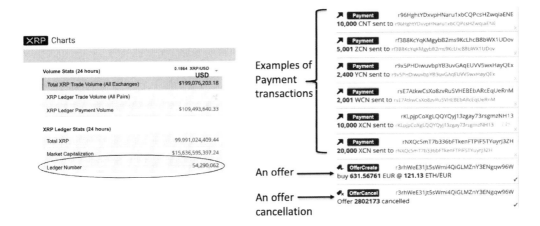

Figure 4.4: Live Ripple ledger on March 22, 2020

The Ripple ledger can be viewed on https://xrpcharts.ripple.com/#/transactions

Native Cryptocurrency

Ripple's native cryptocurrency, called 'ripples' (XRP), serves several purposes. As noted above, XRP can be used as a bridge currency if no path of trust can be found between trading partners. XRP is also a way to pay gateways, as each may establish fees in the form of XRP for using the gateway. If trading partners transact directly without using gateways, senders of ripple transactions pay a small amount of ripples so that attackers won't spam the system with millions of transactions, as the attackers would run out of XRP.[37] Designed to be a scarce asset, the XRP money supply is exactly 100 billion ripples and was issued at the launch of the protocol, rather than released through the process of mining as Bitcoin does.[38] Ripple is a deflationary currency—once ripples have been used to pay for transactions, they are destroyed. Participants are not required to use ripples; they can transact directly with other currencies.[39]

Consensus Protocol

Ripple uses a Byzantine Fault Tolerance (BFT) consensus protocol. In this consensus system, transactions for which the majority of nodes on the network agree upon get recorded in the ledger.[40] (See Chapter 3 for a longer explanation). A Ripple transaction is considered 'safe' after it has been validated by 80 percent of the nodes.[41]

When institutions or consumers join the Ripple network, they can select which nodes they want to perform validation checks from among the 130 plus nodes registered (as of March 2020) or they can accept the default list of about 33 nodes maintained by Ripple, which is called a Unique Node List (UNL). (See https://xrpcharts.ripple.com/#/validators for a list of registered nodes). Ripple advises users to pick validator nodes across continents and across industries where collusion is unlikely, such as selecting merchants; financial firms; non-profits; political parties; and religious groups from North America, South America, Europe, Asia, and Australia (see Figure 4.5).[42]

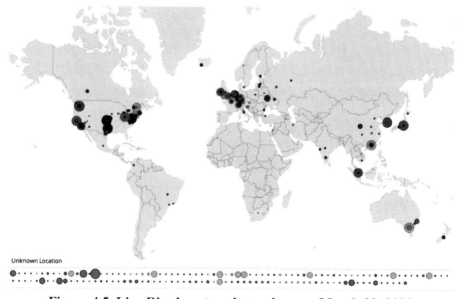

Figure 4.5. Live Ripple network topology on March 23, 2020

The location of Ripple nodes can be viewed on https://xrpcharts.ripple.com/#/topology

Without the incentives of mining, Ripple asks intuitions to run a validator node when they join the system to help secure the network. The costs of performing the validator role are near zero dollars.[43] It only takes a few seconds for transactions to settle, and uses much less electricity than Bitcoin—about as much electricity as it costs to run an email server.[44]

Smart Contracts

In July 2014, Ripple Labs proposed a project to add smart contracts to Ripple. Just a year later, Ripple abandoned the project, saying it was not needed.[45]

Code Base

Ripple's code base is open source and may be downloaded from Github.[46]

Application Interface

Users may transact directly with the Ripple network using a Ripple wallet, but it requires a minimum balance of 20 XRPs.[47] Most customers use Ripple gateways operated by cryptocurrency exchanges or financial institutions.[48] Ripple has bridge protocols that allow payments to and from external networks. For example, Ripple has a Bitcoin bridge protocol that allows users to send ripples to bitcoin addresses.[49]

Issues with Ripple

Like all new startups, Ripple has faced some challenges around trust, hacks, and regulatory compliance. Regarding trust, some people worried that Ripple's owners had too much control over the money stock and network nodes. Ripple's owners retained 20 billion ripples at launch and gifted the rest to Ripple—charged with distribution to gateways, market makers, and charitable organizations.[50] The worry was this: What prevents owners from cashing in and thus devaluing the currency? After years of concern, Ripple's owners promised, in May 2017, to put 55 billion ripples into escrow and release about 1 billion into the market each month.[51]

Blockchains, in principle, are not supposed to rely on trusted third-party institutions. In practice, network participants typically accept Ripple's default list of nodes rather than pick their own nodes, thus giving Ripple centralized power. David Mazières of the Stellar Foundation wrote:

> *"Generally, membership in Byzantine agreement systems is set by a central authority or closed negotiation. Prior attempts to decentralize admission have given up some of the benefits. One approach, taken by Ripple, is to publish a 'starter' membership list that participants can edit for themselves, hoping people's edits are either inconsequential or reproduced by an overwhelming fraction of participants. Unfortunately, because divergent lists invalidate safety guarantees, users are reluctant to edit the list in practice and a great deal of power ends up concentrated in the maintainer of the starter list."* [52]

In 2015, Ripple was fined $700,000 by the US Department of the Treasury for violating the Bank Secrecy Act of 1970, specifically charging that Ripple willfully failed to implement an Anti-Money Laundering (AML) program and failed to report suspicious activity.[53] Ripple agreed to enhance its protocol to meet current banking regulations.[54]

Like many new blockchains, very early on, Ripple was hacked backed in October 2014. Due to a weakness in the code, a hacker was able to send 1000 bitcoins from an address that had only .0001 bitcoins in funding.[55] Ripple reported fixing the bug a few days later and since then, the network has operated without incident.

In summary, Ripple is an important blockchain application—it's running, it's working, and its adoption rate by institutional customers is increasing. The next example focuses on solving the problem of financial exclusion.

4.4. Stellar

"Stellar Development Foundation and Stellar seek to unlock the world's economic potential by making money more fluid, markets more open, and people more empowered."

Stellar Development Foundation[56]

"Our goal is to make global payments as open as the Internet, so that anyone can send money around the world easily, regardless of what financial institutions they are using. Payments should move like email and should all be interoperable."

Jed McCaleb, Cofounder and CTO of Stellar Development Foundation[57]

Jed McCaleb and Joyce Kim co-founded the Stellar Development Foundation (SDF)—a US-based, non-profit organization—in 2014. Stellar's mission is to expand financial access and literacy worldwide.[58] The white paper for the Stellar protocol was released in April of 2015 and the network went live in November of that year.[59,60] By the end of 2017, SDF had secured $3 million in funding from Plug and Play, Innovating Capital, and Stripe.[61] As of March 2020, SDF has about 60 employees.[62]

Stellar enables the creation and trade of all forms of digital assets, including currencies, cryptocurrencies, commodities, stocks, and bonds.[63] Stellar's network for global payments settles transactions in three to five seconds at a very low transaction fee of one lumen (Stellar's native digital asset) for 100,000 transactions. On March 26, 2020, one lumen cost just $.04 (four cents)! Stellar can process over 1,000 operations per second.

SDF does not have direct contact with users. Instead, SDF aims to have other institutions develop business models and use the Stellar code base to develop applications for services such as remittances, micropayments, mobile branches, mobile money, and other services for the under-banked. Stellar does not charge institutions or individuals any fees to use the Stellar network, beyond the modest per-transaction fee. Its network is based on open source code that is supported by the foundation, but adopters are free to develop commercial applications, modify or distribute the source code.

One of its first adopters was the Parkway Project, which involved Oradian, an Africa-focused FinTech, which aimed to bring financial services to 300,000 unbanked people in rural Nigeria, 90 percent of whom are women.[64] The project was halted for a while when the Nigerian Central Bank stopped all remittance companies from operating in Nigeria except Western Union and MoneyGram. Eventually, Cowrie, a FinTech based in Nigeria, was successful in developing a service on the Stellar network. The **Cowrie Exchange** is anchored to the Nigeria Inter-Bank Settlement System Plc (NIBSS). Cowrie serves as the issuer of the stable coin, NGNT, that is pegged to Nigeria's fiat currency—Nigeria Naira—allowing people to send payments to and from Nigeria and the European Union.[65] Its customers include Tempo, SatoshiPay, and Coinqvest, which also have their own services built on the Stellar Network.

Tempo adopted Stellar for cross-border payments for customers to pay utility bills.[66] As of 2018, Tempo has helped customers from Europe—mostly based in France and Germany—to transfer payments to Coins.ph, their company based in the Philippines.[67] Jed McCaleb said: *"Tempo is pretty awesome; there's real money flowing across the live network."*[68]

SatoshiPay allows web publishers to charge viewers a very small amount of crypto. A publisher posts the Stellar Wallet widget as a payment option on their website, and users just click on it and the micropayment gets processed and settled on the Stellar ledger.

Coinqvest has an application for customers to pay merchants using digital currencies (Euros, Naira, and US Dollars) or cryptocurrencies (lumens, bitcoins, ether, litecoins, or ripples).[69]

Saldo is another adopter. It uses the Stellar Network to help US migrant workers to pay utility bills for their families in Mexico. The application serves a vital need because utility providers require monthly payments, but a typical utility bill is less money than the transaction fee to send the payment across borders.[70]

IBM is Stellar's most notable institutional adopter so far. In October of 2017, IBM and KlickEx—a Polynesian-based payments system for low value electronic foreign exchange—announced it would use Stellar for cross-border payments. Jed McCaleb said: *"IBM is using Hyperledger Fabric for some parts of the project, and they're using Stellar to do the cross-border payments."*[71] More recently, **IBM World Wire** allows existing financial institutions to connect to the network using World Wire API, send a payment through a Stellar anchor, and settle the transaction on the Stellar network.[72] According to Jesse Lund, Vice President of IBM, *"Stellar provides a bridge for us from these purely private network and this completely open wild west network."*[73] IBM essentially built a sub-network to enforce rules, but uses the Stellar network to provide an open audit trail.

Institutional users that connect to the Stellar network as anchors, are responsible for being licensed and for complying with regulations.[74] Jed McCaleb explained, *"The Stellar foundation is never in the flow of funds; we don't have customers. We provide the software and financial institutions deploy it. The burden of regulatory compliance lays on the anchor—the financial institutions—using the network because they still have the relationship with the person who's sending the money and the person who's receiving the money."*[75]

The Stellar Foundation does not have the capacity to help institutions develop applications using the Stellar network, although there is a strong demand for such services. To meet this need, Jed McCaleb founded Lightyear.io in May 2017 (now called Inter/Stellar). He explained: *"When we talk to financial institutions, they want somebody to provide service and support, and they want someone to help them with integration. SDF is not set up to do that. Pretty quickly, we realized that there's a need for a for-profit institute. So essentially you can think of SDF as the Linux and Lightyear as the RedHat."*

As far as network statistics, the Stellar Network had over 4.5 million accounts; over 6,100 accounts were active daily, and the ledger was closing every 5.4 seconds on March 23 of 2020.[76]

Figure 4.6 maps Stellar to the blockchain application framework developed in Chapter 3. As noted above, McCaleb was also cofounder of Ripple, which he left to start Stellar.[77] Due to the common history, Stellar's protocol was based on the Ripple protocol, so they are similar in terms of its distributed ledger process. Both networks also make use of APIs to connect organizations to the networks, but Stellar uses the term 'anchors' whereas Ripple calls them trust lines between 'gateways'. Stellar, as we shall see, uses a different consensus algorithm than Ripple and aims to be more decentralized.

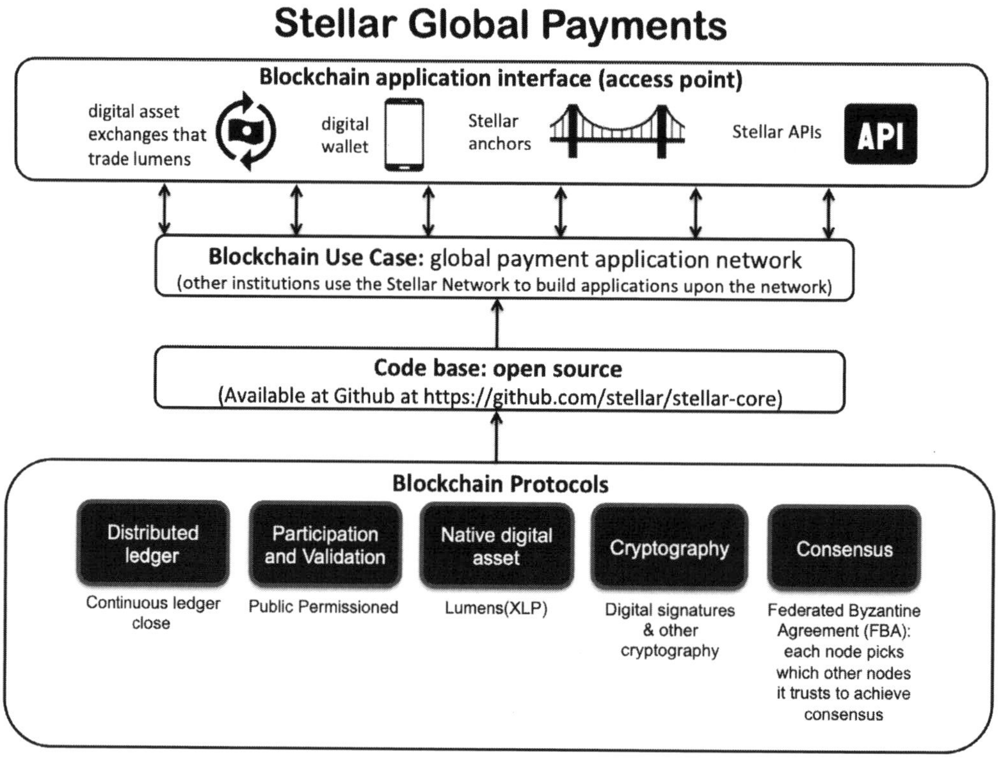

Stellar Global Payments

Blockchain application interface (access point)

digital asset exchanges that trade lumens

digital wallet

Stellar anchors

Stellar APIs

API

Blockchain Use Case: global payment application network
(other institutions use the Stellar Network to build applications upon the network)

Code base: open source
(Available at Github at https://github.com/stellar/stellar-core)

Blockchain Protocols

Distributed ledger	Participation and Validation	Native digital asset	Cryptography	Consensus
Continuous ledger close	Public Permissioned	Lumens(XLP)	Digital signatures & other cryptography	Federated Byzantine Agreement (FBA): each node picks which other nodes it trusts to achieve consensus

Figure 4.6: Stellar mapped to the blockchain application framework

Distributed Ledger

Like Ripple, Stellar structures the ledger as a long list of sequenced transactions and account balances that get closed every few seconds. The ledger also stores the current order books, which records the buy and sell offers for different currencies. Stellar's transactions are permanently stored on the distributed ledger and are irreversible. However, Stellar users may freeze funds on the ledger so that they cannot be spent in instances of disputed or mistaken transactions.[78] On March 23, 2020, Stellar was on its 28,825,068th ledger version (see Figure 4.7).

Figure 4.7: Example of a Stellar ledger, showing the header and the first two transactions

Source: https://stellar.expert/explorer/public/ledger/28825068

Native Cryptocurrency

Stellar's native digital asset, lumens (XLM), serves several purposes. First, lumens are used to fund the operations of the SDF. Stellar released 100 billion lumens in 2014, retaining five percent for the foundation to operate, and holding the rest in reserve. XLM is an inflationary currency—new lumens are added to the network at the rate of one percent of the money supply each year.[79] The foundation aimed to distribute lumens to a broad range of individuals and organizations, including 50 percent to individuals; 25 percent for non-profits aiming to reach underserved populations; and 20 percent to bitcoin holders.[80] To reach individuals, the foundation releases lumens for auctions on exchanges like Kraken. People and institutions may also apply to the SDF for lumens to fund projects. In order to provide additional stability to the system, employees of the foundation are not allowed to buy lumens at auctions, and Stellar's owners agreed not sell any of the lumens for at least five years.[81,82] In November of 2019, the SDF decided to burn 50 billion lumen that were in reserve because it was having a hard time getting them distributed into the market.[83] As of March 2020, the total money supply was 50 billion lumens, of which over 20 billion lumens had been distributed.[84]

Second, lumens can be used as a bridge currency within the Stellar network if no direct markets exist between trading partners. Jed McCaleb offered this example:

> *"If you imagine somebody wants to send money from Thailand to Brazil, there's probably not a good liquid market between those two currencies. So you would go to some bridge currency in the middle. Maybe you would go Thai baht to US dollars, US dollars to Brazilian real. But you could also go to the lumens in the middle, or bitcoins. You can go through multiple hops to get the best rates."* [85]

Finally, lumens are used to prevent Denial of Service (DoS) attacks. Each Stellar transaction requires a minor fee of 0.00001 lumens. *"This fee prevents users with malicious intentions from flooding the network (otherwise known as a DoS attack). Lumens work as a security token, mitigating DoS attacks that attempt to generate large numbers of transactions or consume large amounts of space in the ledger."* [86]

Consensus Protocol

Stellar's protocol is called the Stellar Consensus Protocol (SCP).[87] Its main distinction from Ripple is a new model for consensus called Federated Byzantine Agreement (FBA). FBA distinguishes between a network-level *quorum* of nodes that need to agree, and a *quorum slice* that a particular node chooses to rely upon to validate transactions. This protocol ensures that the Stellar network remains permissionless in that anyone may join, but empowers each participant operating a node to decide which other nodes it will trust to validate transactions and add them to the ledger.[88]

As of March 2020, the Stellar network had 34 full validator nodes, operated by the SDF, IBM Worldwire, SatoshiPay, Coinqvest, and many others.[89,90] Nodes are distributed globally, in such countries as the US, United Kingdom, Germany, and Singapore.[91] When asked how quorum slice selection works in practice, Jed McCaleb explained that people select a diverse set of nodes where collusion behind the scenes would be highly unlikely. He said:

> *"Nodes are advertised on each company's website. It would be very unlikely for IBM, Tempo and a university to collude, so while there is no magical answer, people can make sound judgments."*

Smart Contract

Stellar does not contain a Turing complete smart contracting feature.[92]

Code Base

Stellar's code base is open source and may be downloaded from Github, (https://github.com/stellar/stellar-core).

Application Interface

Users may transact directly with the Stellar network using a digital wallet, but it requires a minimum balance of 20 XLMs to ensure that accounts are authentic.[93] Stellar does not own or operate any digital wallets, but maintains a list of organizations that do (see https://www.stellar.org/lumens/wallets/). Users may also access the Stellar network through anchor institutions who built services on top of the network. Anchors take deposits from their customers and issue credits to addresses stored on the distributed ledger. According to McCaleb, SDF's goals for 2020 are:

> *"We are still super focused on making the network useful for people. We are not just building this for the technology; we want Stellar to materially improve people's lives. We are releasing a Latin American-focused consumer wallet this spring and we are going to do a lot to grow its adoption and usefulness."*[94]

In summary, Stellar is an important blockchain network—it's running, it's working, and its adoption rate is increasing. The next case provides an example of a consortium of banks that built and launched a platform for trade finance.

4.5. WeTrade

> *"Blockchain is not easy. You need many players progressing at the same pace and it's not just about the technology. The business side, sales and marketing, legal, compliance, and operations are all very important too. One of the key objectives is to get all the participants acting at the same pace on the network."*

> **Ciaran McGowen, CEO at WeTrade**[95]

WeTrade is a trade finance platform that began development in 2017 and reached full operations by July 2018. The WeTrade platform was developed first by a consortium of European banks and then formalized as a Dublin-based Joint Venture (JV) among CaixaBank; Deutsche Bank; Erste Group; HSBC; KBC; Natixis; Nordea; Rabobank; Santander; Société Générale; UBS; and UniCredit.[96] WeTrade partners contributed about €15 million (about $16 million) in financing. IBM Blockchain Services is the technology provider. As of March 2020, the platform is being used across trading partners in 17 companies and 19 countries.[97]

The context

Trade finance is a process which helps to reduce counter-party risks for the financing of trade between a buyer and a seller, often internationally. Exporters/sellers need to mitigate payment risks and want to get paid as early as possible by importers/purchasers. Importers/purchasers want to make sure goods were shipped and often want extended credit on their payment. Trusted third parties like banks step in to reduce the financial risks of exporters and importers. The exporter's bank may loan money to the exporter based on the contract. If exporters want to mitigate their risks further, they may even sell their receivables at a discount. The importer's bank may provide a letter of credit that will ensure the exporter of getting paid upon proof that the goods were shipped, such as a bill of lading. Many banks struggle with establishing trade finance services, particularly to scale. According to Roberto Mancone, a co-founder and COO of WeTrade at the time:

> *"The traditional trade finance model run by banks had not evolved for decades. Both banks and companies were constrained. Banks were not able to scale their platform to make it available to all clients."*[98]

The solution

WeTrade, founded by seven European banks in March 2017, came together to reduce the pain points common to many banks. Initially, the seven banks formed a consortium, with each bank putting in $200,000, an amount below capital investment levels that do not require layers of approvals. The banks did not merely want to do a POC—they were committed to developing a live platform in 12 months. To move things forward, they did not require unanimous decisions, but rather required a 51 percent or 67 percent majority depending on the complexity of the decision. To prevent anti-trust violations, the banks were prohibited from discussing go-to-market strategies. While the consortium was focused on the technical implementation, the partners also were working in parallel to develop a legal entity. The joint venture came in February of 2018, when all of the consortium's intellectual property was transferred to it. The banks, which had now grown to 12 members, became shareholders in the JV, but each bank would still need a license to operate the software. Banks could also license the software without becoming investors. Roberto Mancone became the COO of the JV. He said:

> *"We needed a legal entity before the platform went live, one with a proper board, a clear strategy, and standard rules of governance."*[99]

While still a consortium, WeTrade brought in IBM because it wanted to build a platform that would not only work for the initial participating banks, but for hundreds of banks.[100] WeTrade is built on the IBM Blockchain Platform using HyperLedger Fabric, a permissioned blockchain. Each bank operates a node. Functionally, WeTrade helps customers to find trusted trade partners, request financing, automate and secure payment, and track the trade journey end-to-end. The participating banks verify the buyers and sellers. A typical process works as follows: Alice, the seller, wants to sell goods to Bob, the buyer. Provided that Alice's and Bob's banks are licensed to use WeTrade, they can use the platform to facilitate the trade. Alice logs in to WeTrade through her bank's portal, creates a trade proposal for Bob that specifies terms and conditions, such as payment schedules. Bob gets pinged to review the proposal. If Bob agrees, Bob's bank then reviews the proposal. If Bob's bank agrees, the smart contract is launched. All parties privy to the contract can observe the paper trail of the trade. Once Bob signals receipt of the goods, Bob's bank automatically pays Alice. Figure 4.8 provides a product overview.

According to Mancone, the most difficult challenge in realizing WeTrade was getting traditional competitors to agree. The joint venture allowed the competitors to share the risks and rewards and to establish a set of rules as if they were one company. By 2019, transactions were growing by 38 percent per month.[101]

Mancone left WeTrade in April of 2019, in part, because the platform does not reinvent trade financing; it primarily automates and improves traditional processes. He said:

"We are building solutions that are perceived as valuable by the providers of the solutions, not the users."[102]

He viewed WeTrade as an important and courageous first step, but ultimately concluded:

"I can see how this technology can change the business model, but to do that you need the stakeholders to come from different industries, not the same industry. That way it will be the final consumer (company or corporate) that reaps the rewards, rather than a group of incumbents."[103]

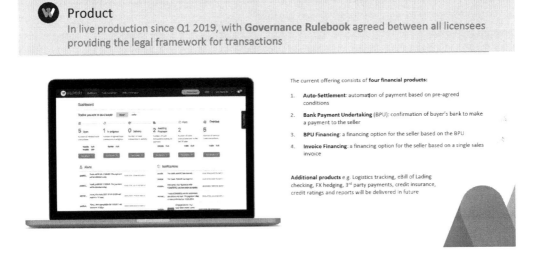

Product

In live production since Q1 2019, with **Governance Rulebook** agreed between all licensees providing the legal framework for transactions

The current offering consists of **four financial products:**

1. **Auto-Settlement**: automation of payment based on pre-agreed conditions
2. **Bank Payment Undertaking** (BPU): confirmation of buyer's bank to make a payment to the seller
3. **BPU Financing**: a financing option for the seller based on the BPU
4. **Invoice Financing**: a financing option for the seller based on a single sales invoice

Additional products e.g. Logistics tracking, eBill of Lading checking, FX hedging, 3rd party payments, credit insurance, credit ratings and reports will be delivered in future

Figure 4.8 WeTrade product overview

Source: Permission from WeTrade

Ciaran McGowan, WeTrade's current CEO, said that he was focusing on improving value for customers:

> *"The [client] feedback has been very positive, in that it's an innovative and intuitive solution. But it can be improved: our clients would like much more. For example, in terms of the efficiency of the end-user, they would like integration with their ERP system rather than having to duplicate entries. They are also very keen to have logistics services as part of the offering. The other feedback we're getting is the search facility for pairing companies— they want more customers on there in terms of opportunities.*[104] *So that's driving our priority number one, which is expanding the WeTrade network and going global."*[105]

As of March 2020, banks were participating from Austria; Belgium; Czech Republic; Denmark; Finland; Germany; Greece; Ireland; Italy; Liechtenstein; Luxembourg; Netherlands; Norway; Spain; Sweden; Switzerland; and the United Kingdom.[106] Fees to use the platform for banks begin at $55,000, largely to cover the cost of cloud hosting for the application. As of 2020, 55 percent of transactions were automatic payments; 27 percent were for bank payment undertaking (BPU); and 18 percent were for BPU financing. Customers are primarily small and medium-sized businesses (SMEs), which bear the brunt of late payments worldwide.[107] WeTrade's main network scaling challenge is that both the exporter and buyer need to bank with one of the licensed adopters.[108]

Competition

At the beginning of 2018, there were five active trade finance consortia (See Figure 4.9). **Marco Polo** launched its network in 2017 and has risen as a major player along with **WeTrade**. The Hong Kong Trade Finance Platform (HKTFP)—a venture led by the Hong Kong Monetary Authority (HKMA) and 20 banks—became a separate company called **eTradeConnect.** To help with interoperability across various platforms, eTradeConnect signed an MOU with WeTrade in October of 2018.[109] The Batavia consortium disbanded when three banks from Batavia joined WeTrade.[110]

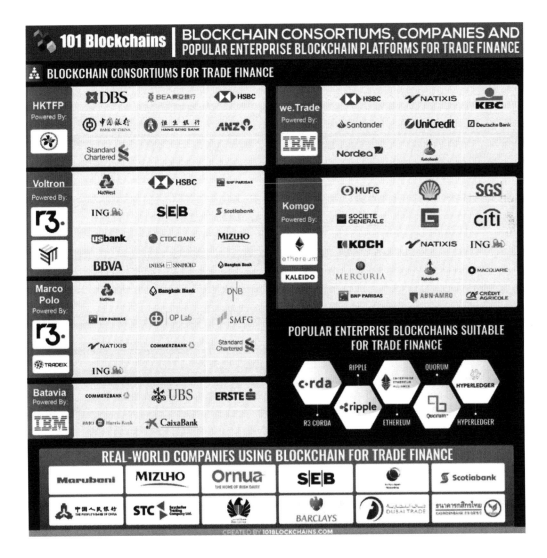

Figure 4.9. Active trade finance consortia in 2019

Source:https://fintechnews.ch/wp-content/uploads/2019/06/trade-finance-blockchain-consortia-101blockchains.com_.jpg

At Voltron, Standard Charter Bank became the first bank to complete an international letter of credit on its platform in 2019.[111] In January of 2020, the Voltron consortium launched a separate legal entity in Singapore called **Contour**, after live pilots in 14 countries with more than 50 banks. Its primary service is to streamline the Letter of Credit from 5–10 days to under 24 hours.[112] **Komgo** created a JV in August of 2018 and has since launched its platform, claiming 12 banks and 100 corporate clients with its first two services for digital letters of credit and KYC. Shareholders include ABN Amro; BNP Paribas; Citi; Crédit Agricole; Gunvor; ING; Koch Supply & Trading; Macquarie; Mercuria; MUFG Bank; Natixis; Rabobank; Shell; SGS; and Société Générale.[113]

How many trade finance platforms will the world ultimately embrace? There will likely be continued consolidation and cooperation for interoperability across trade finance platforms in the future.

4.6. Santander

> *"Banco Santander was one of the first global financial institutions that really wanted to understand the implications of blockchain technologies on the financial industry. We were one of the first banks to take the concept seriously and allocate resources to figure it out."*

**John Whelan, Managing Director,
Digital Investment Bank, Santander**[114]

Santander is a wholly owned subsidiary of the Spanish conglomerate, Santander Group. Santander has a long history stretching back to 1857, when it was founded in Spain.[115] Like many global banks, Santander aggressively explores emerging technologies to help achieve its mission *"to provide easy-to-use banking products and services"*.[116] Santander was one of the first major banks to recognize the potential impact of Bitcoin to the financial services industry. It's been active in the space since 2014. So far, Santander's major blockchain explorations include:

- **Impact Studies.** In 2014, Santander was one of the first banks to commission a study of Bitcoin and its potential uses in the financial industry.[117]

- **Blockchain Lab.** In 2016, Santander was also one of the first banks to create a Blockchain Lab to experiment with blockchain technologies. Santander explores use cases based on three questions: Is the current process slow? Costly? Error-prone? In the blockchain space, the bank is primarily exploring private networks that are operated by an organization or consortium, but it has also experimented with public blockchains.[118]

- **Venture capital investment.** Santander's UK-based venture capital arm, called Innoventures, as noted above, provided funding for Ripple. It's also provided funding for Digital Asset Holdings, the private blockchain platform that was founded by Blythe Masters, the inventor of the credit default swap; Elliptic, a startup aiming to establish a global standard for blockchain monitoring; and Securitize, a platform for security token issuance and life cycle management.[119]

- **Santander One Pay FX.** In 2018, Santander used a Ripple-enabled mobile app for cross border payments between Spain, United Kingdom, Brazil, and Poland for its retail customers.[120] One Pay FX does not use the public Ripple network or XRP, rather, it uses a new enterprise platform that applied Ripple's technology.

- **Enterprise Ethereum Alliance** (EEA). Santander is a member of the EEA. In 2018, Julio Faura, chairman of the EEA, and founding EEA member from Santander Bank, said:

  "The Alliance's mission from day one has been to build the framework that could be used to meet all the needs of its members. The public release of the Enterprise Ethereum Architecture Stack enables enterprise members to collaborate and collectively contribute to, and benefit from, the global Ethereum effort and the EEA's forthcoming specification."[122]

- **WeTrade**. In 2018, Santander, as noted above, became a founding member of WeTrade.[121]

- **Hyperledger Project.** Santander is an active member of the Hyperledger Project. For example, it is working on Hyperledger Avalon, a trusted compute service framework which aims to make sure computations are done correctly and secretly by using zero-knowledge proofs, multi-party compute, and trusted execution environments.[123]

- **Smart Payments.** In 2019, Santander and other Spanish banks (Bankia, BBVA and CaixaBank) and Iberpay, which manages Spain's national payment system, began a six-month POC to test smart payments on a private blockchain. Grant Thornton's Blockchain Lab served as the technology partner. Each partner operates a node.[124]

- **Utility Settlement Coin (USC).** Santander and 13 other major banks (The Bank of New York Mellon; Barclays; Canadian Imperial Bank of Commerce; Commerzbank; Credit Suisse; ING Group; KBC Bank; Lloyds Banking Group; Mitsubishi UFJ Financial Group; Nasdaq; Sumitomo Mitsui Banking Corporation; State Street Corporation and UBS) had been working quietly on the issuance of blockchain-based currencies in the commercial and central banking sector worldwide for several years. On June 3, 2019, the banks publicly announced the project when they created a new company, called *Fnality International*. Fnality is headquartered in London and it raised $63.2 million in funding from participating banks. USC aims to be a token that is fully backed and guaranteed at all times by a central bank's national fiat currency.[125] Fnality plans to begin with the tokenization of the Euro, US dollar, British pound, Canadian dollar, and the Japanese yen.[126] Within each jurisdiction, USCs will ensure that settlement is achieved in compliance with local settlement finality laws and regulations.[127] *Clearmatics*, Fnality's technology partner, is building a solution on a private version of Ethereum called Autonity.[128]

- **Digital Bond Issuance.** In 2019, Santander completed a complete end-to-end bond issuance on the public Ethereum blockchain network.[129] We'll now take a closer look at this unique and important application.

4.6.1. Santander's Digital Bond Issuance

The context

Santander wanted to learn what it takes to launch a real financial instrument on a public blockchain. For Santander, a pilot is a significant undertaking because it involves real money, meaning that the solution must comply with all internal security requirements and with all regulations and it must be approved by the new products committee. It selected a bond issuance because it's a low volume financial instrument with clearly defined rules. Santander could also use its separate legal entities to serve as the independent parties typically involved in a bond issuance and settlement.[130]

The solution

Santander's Digital Bond Issuance was for a standard, one-year $20 million bond that paid a 1.98 percent fixed rate, payable over four quarters. It was launched in September 2019 on Ethereum, the public blockchain, which was used as the register and clearing house.[131] Banco Santander S.A. served as the *issuer* of the bond; Santander Securities Services Treasury as the *investor*; Santander Corporate Investment Bank served as the *dealer* which connects issuers with investors; and Santander Securities served as the *custodian* bank.[132] Based on legal advice from the global law firm Allen & Overy, Santander issued the digital bond under English law because English law requires a register of record, but it does not specify the type of register.[133] Under English law, a register of record could be a piece of paper, a spreadsheet, a central securities depository, or, yes, even a blockchain. (Santander could not use Spanish law because it requires that the register of record is a central securities depository.)

In order to execute the digital bond, the issuer and investor had to be onboarded to the blockchain issuance platform to comply with KYC and AML. The blockchain issuance platform maintains a whitelist of trustworthy participants that also controls ownership limits. Bond tokens were created in the form of 100 units at $200,000 per unit.[134] Figure 4.10 depicts the workflow, which can be followed on etherscan.io.

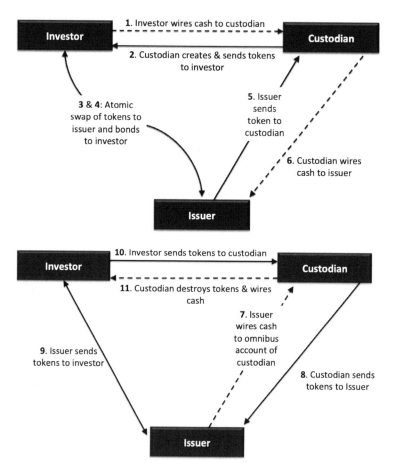

Figure 4.10: Digital blockchain bond issuance and settlement workflow

Cash flows are steps 1, 6, 7, and 11;
Tokens flows are in steps 2, 3, 5, 8, 9, and 10; bonds are step 4

- In step 1, the ***investor*** sent $20 million of real cash from their cash account to a custody account at the custodian bank.
- In step 2, the ***custodian*** verified that the real cash was in fact received and created digital cash tokens that the custodian then sent back to the investor. (This was the tokenization step). The investor was then ready to invest their digital cash tokens in the bond.
- Steps 3 and 4 happen concurrently: the investor committed the 20 million digital cash tokens to be invested in the $20 million bond; the ***issuer*** authorized the transaction to proceed. An atomic swap was done where the bond was delivered to the investor and the issuer received the $20 million in digital cash tokens. Both the bond and the commitment are controlled by a smart contract running on Ethereum. Essentially, the smart contract serves as the escrow account. In the future, the issuer may have many investment options for these digital tokens. In today's world, the issuer can't do much with them so, at this stage in blockchain maturity, the issuer converted them back to US dollars.
- In step 5, the ***issuer*** sent the digital cash tokens to the custodian bank.
- In step 6, the ***custodian*** destroyed the tokens (called de-tokenization) and wired $20 million in real cash to the issuer's account.

As far as quarterly payments from the issuer to the investor, steps 7 to 11 are controlled by the smart contract.

- In step 7, the ***issuer*** sends the quarterly payment in real cash from their cash account to a custody account at the custodian.
- In step 8, the ***custodian*** verifies that the real cash is in fact received, creates digital cash tokens, and sends the tokens back to the issuer.
- In step 9, the ***issuer*** sends the digital cash tokens to the smart contract, which distributes the token to the investor.
- In step 10, the ***investor*** sends the tokens to the custodian bank.
- In step 11, the ***custodian*** bank destroys the tokens and wires real cash to the investor's account.[135]

Proof of transactions are viewable on Ethereum (see Figure 4.11).[136]

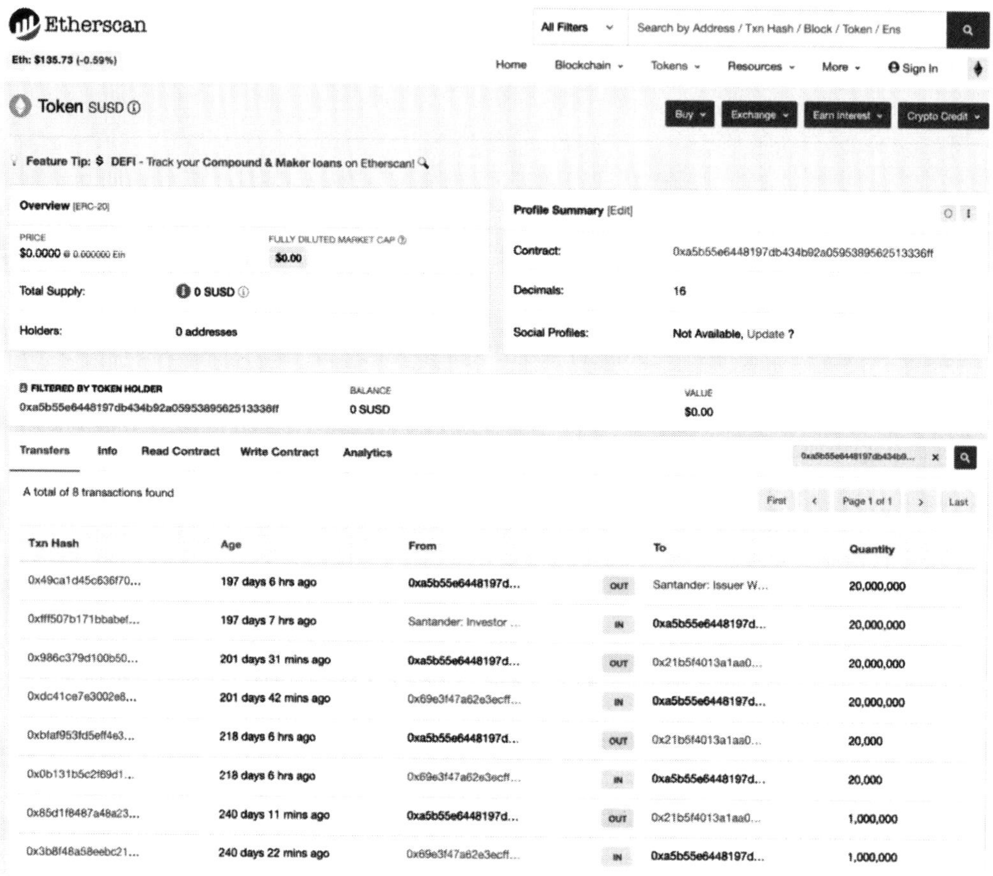

Figure 4.11: Ethereum's records of Santander's ERC-20 token (SUSD) as of March 25, 2020

Source: https://etherscan.io/token/0xa5b55e6448197db434b92a0595389562513336ff?a=0xa5b55e6448 197db434b92a0595389562513336ff

The application is mapped in Figure 4.12.

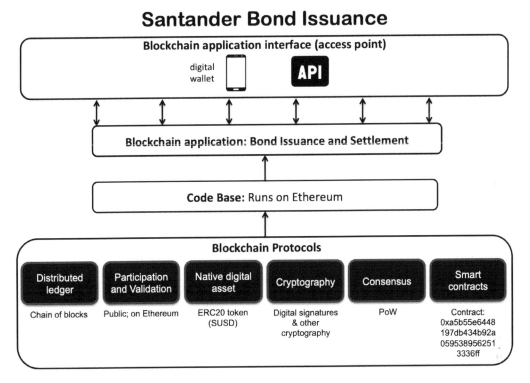

Figure 4.12: Santander bond mapped to the blockchain application framework

In reflecting upon all of Santander's blockchain initiatives—many of which potentially will disrupt the bank's traditional revenue streams—John Whelan, Managing Director, Digital Investment Bank said:

"My own sense is that we have no choice. The technology allows this to be built. If we do not build it, somebody else will. So, I think the banks realize that our competitors are not just other banks, but our competitors are also big tech, whether it's Facebook, Google, Alibaba or TenCent. In many respects, money and value are just ones and zeros in a machine and that's an engineering problem, not a financial problem." [137]

4.7. Conclusion

Ripple, Stellar, WeTrade, and Santander represent a variety of organizations exploring blockchain applications to solve problems in today's financial systems. They are important examples of live production systems used by enterprises. There are many other live examples and more platforms for financial services. In the next chapter, we'll explore blockchains applications in supply chains.

Citations:

[1] Personal interview with Mary Lacity

[2] Personal interview with Mary Lacity

[3] CBInsights (2017), The FinTech 250, https://www.cbinsights.com/research-fintech250

[4] The World Bank, *Financial Inclusion*, posted on http://www.worldbank.org/en/topic/financialinclusion/overview

[5] McKinsey (2016), *Global Payments 2016: Strong Fundamentals Despite Uncertain Times*, https://www.mckinsey.com/industries/financial-services/our-insights/a-mixed-year-for-the-global-payments-industry

[6] Again, the actual process depends on which services are used. Many banks use SWIFT (Society for the Worldwide Interbank Financial Telecommunication), an international payment network; members of the European Union might use SEPA (Single Euro Payments Area) to manage bank transfers of money. SEPA *"enables customers to make cashless euro payments to anyone located anywhere in the area, using a single bank account and a single set of payment instruments; SEPA guarantees that euro payments are received within a guaranteed time, and banks are not allowed to make any deductions of the amount transferred."* SEPA is also used by Iceland, Liechtenstein, Norway, Switzerland, Monaco and San Marino. https://en.wikipedia.org/wiki/Single_Euro_Payments_Area

[7] http://paymentsviews.com/2014/05/15/there-is-no-such-thing-as-an-international-wire/

[8] *Navigating the world of cross-border payments*, http://www.iqpc.com/media/1003982/57107.pdf

[9] McKinsey (2015), *Global Payments 2015: A Healthy Industry Confront Disruption*, http://www.mckinsey.com/~/media/mckinsey/dotcom/client_service/financial services/latest thinking/payments/global_payments_2015_a_healthy_industry_confronts_disruption.ashx

[10] American Bankers Association (2016), *Fees and Pricing of Banking Products*, http://www.texasbankers.com/docs/FeesandPricingofBankingProducts.pdf

[11] McKinsey (2016), *Digital Finance for All*, http://www.mckinsey.com/~/media/McKinsey/Global Themes/Employment and Growth/How digital finance could boost growth in emerging economies/MG-Digital-Finance-For-All-Full-report-September-2016.ashx

[12] Peric, K. (April 18th 2017), *Fighting Poverty with Digital Payments*, presented at MIT Blockchain for Business Conference. http://events.technologyreview.com/video/watch/kosta-peric-bill-and-melinda-gates-foundation-fighting-poverty/

[13] Most of the 150 person-to-person, mobile payment platforms in Africa and Asia can operate on a $5 phone and only need a basic 2G calls and SMS. Source: Peric, K. (April 18th 2017), *Fighting Poverty with Digital Payments*, presented at MIT Blockchain for Business Conference. http://events.technologyreview.com/video/watch/kosta-peric-bill-and-melinda-gates-foundation-fighting-poverty/

[14] Peric, K. (April 18th 2017), *Fighting Poverty with Digital Payments*, presented at MIT Blockchain for Business Conference. http://events.technologyreview.com/video/watch/kosta-peric-bill-and-melinda-gates-foundation-fighting-poverty/

[15] bKash, a mobile payment platform launched in 2011 in Bangladesh, had over 17 million users by 2015. Source: Young, Y. (January 20th 2016), *Bill Gates Invests in Mobile Payment Network bKash; Used by 10 percent of Bangladeshis*, https://btcmanager.com/bill-gates-invests-in-mobile-payment-network-bkash-used-by-10-of-bangladeshis/

[16] Vodofone launched M-Pesa in 2007 is a mobile payment platform that operates in Kenya, Tanzania, Afghanistan, South Africa, Indian and Eastern Europe. https://www.mpesa.in/portal/

[17] Dragos, A. (June 27th 2017), *Blockchain technology promises to drastically reduce the costs to offer a checking account*, https://medium.com/mit-media-lab-digital-currency-initiative/blockchains-and-financial-inclusion-f767a2347e3d

[18] *Blockchain and Financial Inclusion for Citizens in Poverty*, July 11th 2016, https://letstalkpayments.com/blockchain-and-financial-inclusion-for-citizens-in-poverty/

[19] Arshadi, N. (2017), *Application of Blockchain to the Payment System: A Less Costly and More Secure Alternative to ACH*, working paper.

[20] https://ripple.com/network/financial-institutions/

[21] Branson, R. (2015), *Ripple: The Ultimate Guide to Understanding Ripple Currency*, Elliot Branson Publications.

[22] https://ripple.com/

[23] https://ripple.com/

[24] https://en.wikipedia.org/wiki/Ripple_(company)

[25] https://ripple.com/xrp/

[26] https://ripple.com/use-cases/

[27] https://ripple.com/use-cases/corporates/

[28] https://ripple.com/network/financial-institutions/

[29] Santander website, *One Pay FX: blockchain for streamlining international transfers*, https://www.santander.com/en/stories/one-pay-fx-blockchain-for-streamlining-international-transfers

[30] Ripple Case study (October 1, 2018), *Swell 2018: How Banco Santander Launched a Payment App for Millions*, https://ripple.com/insights/swell-2018-how-banco-santander-launched-a-payment-app-for-millions/

[31] Ripple case study: https://ripple.com/customer-case-study/sbi-remit/

[32] Reuters (November 16th 2017), *American Express Is Getting Into Blockchain-Based Payments With Ripple*, http://fortune.com/2017/11/16/amex-payments-ripple-blockchain/

[33] Branson, R. (2015), *Ripple: The Ultimate Guide to Understanding Ripple Currency*, Elliot Branson Publications

[34] https://ripple.com/build/gateway-guide/

[35] Schwartz, D., Youngs, N., and Britto, A. (2014), *The Ripple Protocol Consensus Algorithm*, https://ripple.com/files/ripple_consensus_whitepaper.pdf

[36] https://ripple.com/build/ledger-format/

[37] Branson, R. (2015), *Ripple: The Ultimate Guide to Understanding Ripple Currency*, Elliot Branson Publications.

[38] Branson, R. (2015), *Ripple: The Ultimate Guide to Understanding Ripple Currency*, Elliot Branson Publications.

[39] *Technical FAQ: Ripple Consensus Ledger*, https://ripple.com/technical-faq-ripple-consensus-ledger/

40   *Ripple Review*, http://www.toptenreviews.com/money/investing/best-cryptocurrencies/ripple-review/

41   Bob Way at Ripple.com, as reported in Seibold, S., and Samman, G. (2016), *Consensus: Immutable Agreement for the Internet of Value*, KPMG White paper.

42   *Selecting Validators*, https://wiki.ripple.com/Consensus

43   *Technical FAQ: Ripple Consensus Ledger*, https://ripple.com/technical-faq-ripple-consensus-ledger/

44   *Technical FAQ: Ripple Consensus Ledger*, https://ripple.com/technical-faq-ripple-consensus-ledger/

45   Maxim, J. (June 24th 2015), *Ripple Discontinues Smart Contract Platform Codius, Citing Small Market*, https://bitcoinmagazine.com/articles/ripple-discontinues-smart-contract-platform-codius-citing-small-market-1435182153/

46   https://github.com/ripple

47   Agarwal, H. (December 31st 2017), *Ripple (XRP) Wallet—Best Wallets For Ripple*, https://coinsutra.com/best-ripple-xrp-wallets/

48   https://ripple.com/build/gateway-guide/

49   Branson, R. (2015), *Ripple: The Ultimate Guide to Understanding Ripple Currency*, Elliot Branson Publications.

50   Branson, R. (2015), *Ripple: The Ultimate Guide to Understanding Ripple Currency*, Elliot Branson Publications.

51   Levy, A. (May 26th 2017), *Bitcoin rival Ripple is suddenly sitting on billions of dollars worth of cryptocurrency*, CNBC News, http://www.cnbc.com/2017/05/26/bitcoin-rival-ripple-is-sitting-on-many-billions-of-dollars-of-xrp.html

52   Maziières, D. (2016), *The Stellar Consensus Protocol: A Federated Model for Internet-level Consensus*, White Paper, https://www.stellar.org/papers/stellar-consensus-protocol.pdf

53   Press release by the United States Department of the Treasury on May 5th 2016: https://www.fincen.gov/sites/default/files/shared/20150505.pdf

54   Todd, S. and McKendry, I. (2015), 'What Ripple's Fincen Fine Means for the Digital Currency Industry', *American Banker*, https://www.americanbanker.com/news/what-ripples-fincen-fine-means-for-the-digital-currency-industry

55   *Stellar and Ripple Hacked: Justcoin to the Rescue*, October 14th 2014, https://cointelegraph.com/news/stellar-and-ripple-hacked-justcoin-to-the-rescue

[56] https://www.stellar.org/foundation

[57] Personal interview with Mary Lacity in 2017

[58] https://www.stellar.org/about/mandate/

[59] Maziières, D. (2016), *The Stellar Consensus Protocol: A Federated Model for Internet-level Consensus*, White Paper, https://www.stellar.org/papers/stellar-consensus-protocol.pdf

[60] https://en.wikipedia.org/wiki/Stellar_(payment_network)

[61] Stellar Funding, https://www.crunchbase.com/organization/stellar

[62] Email exchange with Jed McCaleb, March 25, 2020.

[63] Stellar Develop Foundation (2020), *Cowrie's cross-border payment services for Nigeria powered by Stellar*, https://www.youtube.com/watch?v=sDj8THW1UWg&feature=youtu.be

[64] ShapShak, T. (2016), 'Instant Money Transfer Service Stellar Launches for Nigeria's Rural Women', *Forbes Magazine*, https://www.forbes.com/sites/tobyshapshak/2016/02/02/stellar-launches-mobile-money-service-for-nigerias-rural-woman/#49d71f577183

[65] Stellar Develop Foundation (2020), *Cowrie's cross-border payment services for Nigeria powered by Stellar*, https://www.youtube.com/watch?v=sDj8THW1UWg&feature=youtu.be

[66] *Business Solutions Powered by Stellar*, https://www.stellar.org/how-it-works/powered-by-stellar

[67] https://coins.ph/blog/conveniently-send-money-from-europe-to-the-philippines-with-tempo/

[68] Personal interview with Mary Lacity

[69] https://www.coinqvest.com/en/integrations

[70] Stellar Case Study. Saldo. https://www.stellar.org/case-studies/saldo

[71] Personal interview with Mary Lacity

[72] https://www.ibm.com/downloads/cas/YW3W2JPZ

[73] Stellar Case Study. IBM World Wire, https://youtu.be/GtQY8Jfa4NA

[74] https://www.stellar.org/how-it-works/stellar-basics/

[75] Personal interview with Mary Lacity

[76]   https://stellar.expert/explorer/public/network-activity
https://stellar.expert/explorer/public/ledger/28825068

[77]   Bello, K. (May 2016), *Ripple vs Stellar Lumens*, https://www.youtube.com/watch?v=aeONeHlF9y4

[78]   https://www.stellar.org/how-it-works/stellar-basics/

[79]   *Difference between Ripple and Stellar*, https://galactictalk.org/d/242-difference-between-ripple-and-stellar

[80]   https://www.stellar.org/lumens/

[81]   https://www.stellar.org/about/mandate/

[82]   https://www.stellar.org/lumens/

[83]   Dale, B. (November 5th, 2019), *Stellar's Foundation Just Destroyed Half the Supply of Its Lumens Cryptocurrency*, Coindesk, https://www.coindesk.com/stellars-foundation-just-destroyed-half-the-supply-of-its-lumens-cryptocurrency

[84]   See https://dashboard.stellar.org/ for current distribution numbers

[85]   Personal interview with Mary Lacity

[86]   https://www.stellar.org/lumens/

[87]   Maziières, D. (2016), *The Stellar Consensus Protocol: A Federated Model for Internet-level Consensus*, White Paper, https://www.stellar.org/papers/stellar-consensus-protocol.pdf

[88]   https://medium.com/a-stellar-journey/on-worldwide-consensus-359e9eb3e949

[89]   https://stellarbeat.io/nodes

[90]   To view organizations operating nodes, see https://stellarbeat.io/organizations

[91]   To view live nodes, see https://dashboard.stellar.org/

[92]   Benoliel, M. (December 4th 2017), *Why Stellar could be the next big ICO platform*, https://hackernoon.com/why-stellar-could-be-the-next-big-ico-platform-f48fc3cb9a6c

[93]   https://www.stellar.org/lumens/

[94]   Email exchange with Jed McCaleb, March 25, 2020.

[95] Email exchange with Mary Lacity, March 22, 2020.

[96] IBM. Helping companies trade seamlessly with IBM Blockchain.

[97] Morris, N. (2020), *Automated trade payments prove popular for we.trade blockchain.* Ledger Insights, https://www.ledgerinsights.com/wetrade-blockchain-trade-finance-automated-payments/

[98] IBM, *Helping companies trade seamlessly with IBM Blockchain.* https://www.ibm.com/blockchain/use-cases/success-stories/#section-7

[99] Interview with Mary Lacity, March 24, 2020

[100] IBM Blockchain Video. *Valuable Visionaries: Roberto Mancone*, view-source:https://www.ibm.com/blockchain/use-cases/success-stories/#section-7

[101] WeTrade Press Release (August 8[th,] 2020*). we.trade transactions grow at 38 percent per month throughout 2019.* https://cms.we-trade.com/app/uploads/we.trade_press_release_38percentgrowth_2019.08.08.pdf

[102] Quote from PYMNTS (April 30, 2019). B2B PAYMENTS *we.trade Co-founder Quits, Reveals Blockchain Doubts*, https://www.pymnts.com/news/b2b-payments/2019/wetrade-cofounder-quits-blockchain-doubt/

[103] Quote from PYMNTS (April 30, 2019). B2B PAYMENTS *we.trade Co-founder Quits, Reveals Blockchain Doubts*, https://www.pymnts.com/news/b2b-payments/2019/wetrade-cofounder-quits-blockchain-doubt/

[104] Vanci, M. (December 17, 2019), 'Five Spanish banks will test payments with a private blockchain', *Criptonoticias,* https://www.criptonoticias.com/negocios/servicios-financieros/cinco-bancos-espanoles-probaran-pagos-blockchain-privada/

[105] Quote from Was, S. (September 2019), *Exclusive interview: New we.trade manager talks expansion plans, TradeLens partnership and platform roadmap*, Global Trade Review. https://www.gtreview.com/news/fintech/exclusive-interview-new-we-trade-manager-talks-expansion-plans-tradelens-partnership-and-platform-roadmap/

[106] WeTrade website. Country pull down menu, https://we-trade.com/request-access

[107] Morris, N. (2020), *Automated trade payments prove popular for we.trade blockchain.* Ledger Insights, https://www.ledgerinsights.com/wetrade-blockchain-trade-finance-automated-payments/

[108] Morris, N. (2018), *Trade finance blockchain race is about to start*, https://www.ledgerinsights.com/wetrade-trade-finance-blockchain-race/

[109] Hong Kong Monetary Authority Press Release (October 18, 2018). https://www.hkma.gov.hk/eng/

news-and-media/press-releases/2018/10/20181031-4/

[110] Wass, S. (March 10 2018), *we.trade and Batavia merge blockchain platforms for trade finance*, Global Trade Review, https://www.gtreview.com/news/fintech/we-trade-and-batavia-merge-blockchain-platforms-for-trade-finance/

[111] Palmer, D. (August 7, 2019), 'Standard Chartered Completes First Transaction on Blockchain Trade Platform Voltron', *Coindesk,* https://www.coindesk.com/standard-chartered-completes-first-transaction-on-oil-industry-blockchain-voltron

[112] FinExtra (January 28, 2020), *Bank-backed blockchain trade finance platform Contour launches*, https://www.finextra.com/newsarticle/35179/bank-backed-blockchain-trade-finance-platform-contour-launches

[113] Wass, S. (September 1, 2019), *Komgo blockchain platform for commodity trade finance goes live*, Global Trade Review, https://www.gtreview.com/news/fintech/komgo-blockchain-platform-for-commodity-trade-finance-goes-live/

[114] Presentation by John Whelan, Managing Director, Digital Investment Bank, Santander, to the Blockchain Center of Excellence, University of Arkansas, December 3[rd, 2019.]

[115] https://en.wikipedia.org/wiki/Santander_Bank

[116] Santander website https://www.santanderbank.com/us/about/about-us/leadership

[117] Presentation by John Whelan, Managing Director, Digital Investment Bank, Santander, to the Blockchain Center of Excellence, University of Arkansas, December 3[rd, 2019.]

[118] Presentation by John Whelan, Managing Director, Digital Investment Bank, Santander, to the Blockchain Center of Excellence, University of Arkansas, December 3[rd, 2019.]

[119] https://santanderinnoventures.com/portfolio-companies/

[120] Delventhal, S. (April 13, 2018), *Santander Launches Blockchain Payments Service*, Investopedia, https://www.investopedia.com/news/santander-launches-blockchain-payments-service/

[121] https://we-trade.com/banking-partners

[122] Enterprise Ethereum Alliance Press Release (May 2, 2018), *Enterprise Ethereum Alliance Advances Web 3.0 Era with Public Release of the Enterprise Ethereum Architecture Stack.* https://entethalliance.org/enterprise-ethereum-alliance-advances-web-3-0-era-public-release-enterprise-ethereum-architecture-stack/

[123] HyperLedger Avalon (October 3, 2019), *Introducing Hyperledger Avalon*, https://www.hyperledger.org/blog/2019/10/03/introducing-hyperledger-avalon

[124] LedgerInsights (December 23rd, 2019), *Santander, BBVA in Spanish blockchain smart payments trial*, https://www.ledgerinsights.com/enterprise-blockchain-news-roundup-23dec/

[125] Huillet, M. (June 3, 2019). 'Major Utility Settlement Coin project raises $63 million for commercial realization', *CoinTelegraph,* https://cointelegraph.com/news/major-utility-settlement-coin-project-raises-63-mln-for-commercial-realization

[126] Allison, I. (June 13, 2019), '14 Banks, 5 Tokens: Inside Fnality's Expansive Vision for Interbank Blockchains', *Coindesk,* https://www.coindesk.com/fnality-utility-settlement-coin-central-bank-token-blockchain

[127] Huillet, M. (June 3, 2019), 'Major Utility Settlement Coin project raises $63 million for commercial realization', *CoinTelegraph,* https://cointelegraph.com/news/major-utility-settlement-coin-project-raises-63-mln-for-commercial-realization

[128] llison, I. (June 13, 2019), '14 Banks, 5 Tokens: Inside Fnality's Expansive Vision for Interbank Blockchains', *Coindesk,* https://www.coindesk.com/fnality-utility-settlement-coin-central-bank-token-blockchain

[129] Palmer, D. (December 10th, 2019), 'Santander Exec Claims Blockchain Success as Bank Redeems Ethereum-Issued Bond', *Coindesk,* https://www.coindesk.com/santander-exec-claims-blockchain-success-as-bank-redeems-ethereum-issued-bond

[130] Presentation by John Whelan, Managing Director, Digital Investment Bank, Santander, to the Blockchain Center of Excellence, University of Arkansas, December 3rd, 2019.

[131] Palmer, D. (December 10th, 2019), 'Santander Exec Claims Blockchain Success as Bank Redeems Ethereum-Issued Bond', *Coindesk,* https://www.coindesk.com/santander-exec-claims-blockchain-success-as-bank-redeems-ethereum-issued-bond

[132] Santander press release (September 12, 2019), *Santander launches the first end-to-end blockchain bond,* https://www.santander.com/en/press-room/press-releases/santander-launches-the-first-end-to-end-blockchain-bond percentC2 percentA0

[133] Huillet, M. (September 12, 2019). https://cointelegraph.com/news/santander-issues-20-million-end-to-end-blockchain-bond-on-ethereum, *CoinTelegraph,* https://cointelegraph.com/news/santander-issues-20-million-end-to-end-blockchain-bond-on-ethereum

[134] Smart Contract viewable on Ethereum: https://etherscan.io/address/0xa5b55e6448197db434b92a0595389562513336ff

[135] Presentation by John Whelan, Managing Director, Digital Investment Bank, Santander, to the Blockchain Center of Excellence, University of Arkansas, December 3rd, 2019.

[136] Ethereum Transactions related to the digital bond are viewable:

Santander Issuer Waller: https://etherscan.io/address/0x12959b84d507df134ec59c1fc4044b03f33a9947#tokentxns.

Santander Investment Wallet: https://etherscan.io/address/0xe08193b5afcfea60fceb22f065e88e76718c6ee3

ERC20 Token (SUSD): https://etherscan.io/token/0xa5b55e6448197db434b92a0595389562513336ff?a=0xa5b55e6448197db434b92a0595389562513336ff

[137] Presentation by John Whelan, Managing Director, Digital Investment Bank, Santander, to the Blockchain Center of Excellence, University of Arkansas, December 3rd, 2019.

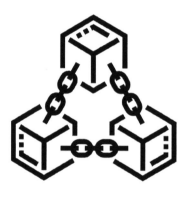

Chapter 5

Business Applications for Supply Chains

"The advent of new technologies—most notably blockchain—has the potential to radically transform how transactions are recorded, stored and used throughout supply networks. The result: a transparent supply chain that, if the hype holds true, will usher in unprecedented levels of visibility, accountability, efficiencies, collaboration, and trust."

Remko Van Hoek, Brian Fugate, Marat Davletshin, and Matthew Waller, Integrating Blockchain into Supply Chain Management.[1]

"Consumers increasingly want to know that the ethical claims companies make about their products are real. Distributed ledgers provide easy ways to certify that the backstories of the things we buy are genuine. Transparency comes with blockchain-based time-stamping of a date and location—on ethical diamonds, for instance—that corresponds to a product number."

Blockgeeks [2]

5.1. Overview of the cases

Today's global supply chains are a complex web of trading partners and trusted third-parties. Before a blockchain solution, each party maintains its own centralized systems and subsequently partners face significant challenges trying to synchronize the data about the flow of physical goods and services, with the actual flow of goods and services (see Figure 5.1).

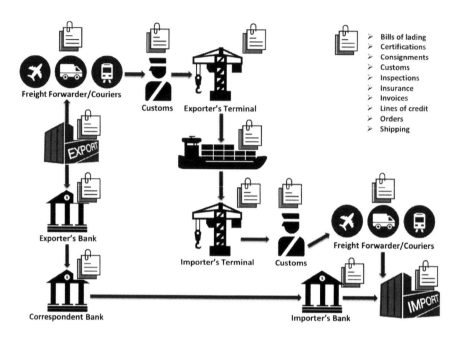

Bills of lading
Certifications
Consignments
Customs
Inspections
Insurance
Invoices
Lines of credit
Orders
Shipping

Figure 5.1: Global supply chains before a blockchain application

While manufacturers; exporters; couriers; freight forwarders; customs; inspectors; exporters; shippers, and importers, move physical goods through the global supply chain, they are also creating data about those movements with bills of lading; certifications; consignments; customs forms; inspections data; insurance forms; invoices; lines of credit; purchase orders; shipping manifestos; and receiving documents.

While manufacturers, exporters, couriers, freight forwarders, customs, inspectors, exporters, shippers, and importers are moving physical goods, they are also creating data about those movements with bills of lading; certifications; consignments; customs forms inspections data; insurance forms; invoices; lines of credit; purchase orders; shipping manifestos; and receiving documents, to name just a few. As a consequence of so many players with their own centralized systems, and so much paperwork: assets get lost; shipping containers get delayed in ports because of missing paperwork; inconsistent records across trading partners trigger disputes; and counterfeit products slip through supply chains, to highlight some of the many challenges. Consequently, consumers often have no way of confidently knowing the actual sources of the products they purchase.

Enterprise(s)	Enterprise Type	Blockchain Application	Status as of 2020
The IBM Food Trust	Traditional enterprises	Food tracing from farm-to-fork and from bait-to-plate	The IBM Food Trust processed 24 million transactions with 250 partners by Q1 2020
TradeLens	Traditional enterprises	Tracks shipping containers in the global supply chain	By Q1 2020, 175 organizations, including 100 ports and terminals, used the platform; over 1 billion transport events on 20 million containers have been recorded and 8 million documents had been loaded
MediLedger	Startup	Authenticates and tracks pharmaceuticals	Product Verification is its first service; MediLedger also completed an FDA pilot with 26 supply chain partners in 2020
EY WineChain	Traditional enterprises	Authenticates and tracks wine bottles	As of 2020,15 million bottles were being tracked across 100 wineries
OpenSC, VeChain, Provenance, and other food tracing solutions	Startups and traditional enterprises	Food tracing from farm-to-fork and from bait-to-plate	Solutions are in production with networks and services expanding
Everledger	Startup	Diamond tracking	Everledger has tracked diamonds since 2017 and is now offering solutions for gemstones, luxury goods, art, wine, e-recycling and antiquities
VeriTX	Traditional manufacturer to startup	Trading platform for 3-D printed and traditionally manufactured parts	Actively working with partners to move the platform to market in 2020

Table 5.1: Blockchain application examples for supply chains

Blockchain-enabled supply chains are already in production to address many of the challenges. Supply chain partners often have an easier time deploying blockchain solutions compared to financial services because many supply chain solutions track items, not money (yet). The compliance burden is therefore less onerous. In Chapter 3, we've already introduced the IBM Food Trust, TradeLens, MediLedger, and WineChain as supply chain examples. In this chapter, we'll dig deeper into the IBM Food Trust and explore other live blockchain solutions for food, diamonds, and parts (see Table 5.1).

5.2. Challenges and solutions for food safety

The food supply chain has been particularly challenging to coordinate because of its scale. The global food and grocery retail market will exceed $12 trillion in 2020.[3] While much of the world's food supply is safe, there is significant room for improvement. The World Health Organization reports that 600 million people get food poisoning, and 420,000 die, each year from consuming contaminated foods.[4] Besides food contamination, the world food supply suffers significant amounts of food waste, food mislabeling, and food fraud, such as claiming horsemeat as lamb and claiming non-organically grown vegetables as organic.[5] Human rights and environmental problems, such as slave labor and unauthorized use of pesticides, remain grave concerns. For example, the International Labor Organization estimates that 3.5 million people are forced to work in agriculture, fishing, and forestry.[6] Each country has its share of food safety challenges, but here we focus on the US and China as the largest food producers and consumers.

The US food industry is a $6 trillion business.[7] The US Centers for Disease Control and Prevention (CDC) estimates that 48 million Americans get sick from food; 128,000 Americans are hospitalized; and 3,000 die of foodborne diseases, each year.[8] The US Department of Agriculture (USDA) had 61 active food recalls in January 2020, primarily for beef; pork; poultry; seafood; and salads. For example, The Pride of Florida recalled nearly 70,000 pounds of raw beef products that may be contaminated with *E. coli*. Other recalls were prompted by mislabeling, some by circumventing import inspections, some by misbranding, and some because of undeclared allergens.

Food waste is also a large problem; $162 billion of food is wasted every year in the US, largely due to the inability to estimate demand and to track supplies.[9] The FDA and USDA need the cooperation of everyone in the food supply chain to improve food safety. Frank Yiannas, the FDA Deputy Commissioner for Food Policy and Response announced in early 2020:

> *"Very soon, we will release a blueprint for FDA's New Era of Smarter Food Safety...While prevention will remain our priority, we will also pursue ways to empower consumers with actionable real-time information, including direct to consumer outreach and notifications."*[10]

China's food market is worth $527 billion, of which meat products are the largest segment.[11] China has had a number of food safety crises. For example, in 2008, milk and infant formula were adulterated with a toxic substance (melamine) to boost the protein content that causes bladder and kidney stones, resulting in 300,000 infant illnesses and 54,000 hospitalizations.[12] In 2013, some local Chinese pork dealers lifted 15,000 dead pigs from a river, processed and sold them.[13] In 2020, Chinese fishmongers continued to add diesel fuel to dying fish to make them thrash.[14] Beyond these headlines, the use of pesticides, dangerous chemical additives, and unsanitary conditions remain challenges. To help improve food safety, the Chinese government consolidated food safety regulation with the creation of the State Food and Drug Administration of China (SFDA) in 2003. However, in 2007, the head of the CFDA was executed for taking bribes. Today, about ten government departments and ministries are responsible for food safety, including the Ministry of Health; the State Food and Drug Administration; the Ministry of Agriculture; the State Administration for Industry and Commerce; the General Administration of Quality Supervision; Inspection and Quarantine; the Ministry of Commerce; the Ministry of Science and Technology; and the National Institute of Nutrition and Food Safety.[15]

All stakeholders, including farmers, distributors, suppliers, retailers, consumers, government, and academics need to be involved in food safety. While there is no single-pronged solution, sharing information across supply change partners is an important part of any food safety solution. As we have pointed out many times, without a blockchain solution, every party in the food supply chain manages its own systems of records (software and data) within the boundaries of the firm or relies on a trusted-third party to manage their systems on their behalf. Each party can only see data coming in and out of their own systems, which is why is can take weeks to trace a food recall from a retail store back to the originating farm or fishery. Improving food safety requires much better tracking of information as food passes through the entire supply chain; known as 'farm to fork' and 'bait to plate' traceability. Blockchain-enabled solutions offer the ability to share data with ecosystem partners in a secure way. In the food industry, a number of blockchain-based solutions have been developed. We'll begin with the most well-established solution.

5.2.1. The IBM Food Trust

While we've covered the **IBM Food Trust** at a high level in Chapter 3, here we take a closer look at the solution. IBM and Walmart—the world's largest retailer which earned $514 billion in revenue in 2019—began conducting food traceability pilot programs for mangos and pork back in 2016. The solution, based on HyperLedger Fabric, reduced traceability for mangos from seven days to under three seconds.[16] In 2017, other supply chain partners joined the network, including Dole, McCormack, McLane, Driscoll's, Unilever, Golden State Foods, Nestle, and Kroger. As of 2020, 250 members had joined.

IBM offers three services on the platform: Trace, Certifications, and Fresh Insights (see Figure 5.2). *Trace* helps participants follow products through the supply chain by tracking product identification, product labels, and purchase order numbers. Trace can also be used to follow how ingredients were transformed from raw materials to finished products. *Certifications* monitor current, expiring, and expired certificates. *Fresh Insights* monitor at risk inventory by tracking events such as time since harvest and dwell times at each location in the supply chain. IBM has a tiered pricing model based on size of business, starting at $100 per month.

Figure 5.2: Overview of the IBM Food Trust solution

Source: https://www.slideshare.net/bluecrux/build-a-supply-chain-40-ecosystem-using-blockchain/10

Data items are based on GS1 standards.[17]   IBM runs the platform in its cloud, but it cannot interpret any of the data. The IBM Food Trust platform relies on 'trust anchors' for validation using a Practical Byzantine Fault Tolerance (PBFT) consensus mechanism (see Chapter 3 or glossary). Trust anchors receive a full copy of the encrypted ledger but can only view the hashes of the transaction unless data owners grant access. Trust anchors are responsible for the following:[18]

- **Resource ownership**: Run accounts in tamper-resistant Z Secure Service Containers that ensure encryption of data, both in flight and at rest.

- **Verification**:   Providing verification that events were submitted by an individual, with the corresponding hash.

- **Endorsement**: Trust Anchors can be added as endorsers to incoming transactions, providing an additional level of trust for the submitting company, such as private-label brands.

- **Data extractions**: In the event of an investigation, a member of the IBM Food Trust can use their decryption key and ask the Trust Anchors to extract the relevant data from the shared ledger and endorse its authenticity.

As the network grows, more participants will run trust nodes and possibly on other cloud environments.19   As of first quarter 2020, the platform has processed over 24 million transactions and tracks over 19,000 SKUs.[20] The IBM Food Trust continues to expand both its network and services, particularly for cold chain and for consumer applications. Ramesh Gopinath, Vice President of Blockchain Solutions for IBM, discussed the plans for 2020:

> *"Food Trust was originally developed to make food recalls surgical and help members of the supply chain make food systems more sustainable. As we build out the solution, all of our modules will continue to be laser focused on solving specific frictions in the supply chain. IoT integration is one area of growth, by using sensor data we can further automate food traceability and make it even easier to monitor cold chain conditions, ensure food freshness and reduce waste. There is also enormous interest in integrating the platform with consumer facing applications that let consumers see exactly where their food came from, learn about the products, how to prepare them, and more."* [21]

5.2.2. Other blockchain-based food traceability solutions

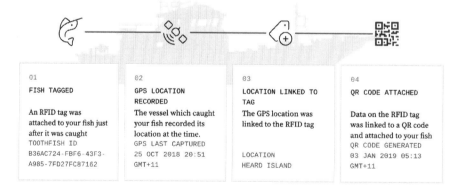

01	02	03	04
FISH TAGGED	GPS LOCATION RECORDED	LOCATION LINKED TO TAG	QR CODE ATTACHED
An RFID tag was attached to your fish just after it was caught	The vessel which caught your fish recorded its location at the time.	The GPS location was linked to the RFID tag	Data on the RFID tag was linked to a QR code and attached to your fish
TOOTHFISH ID B36AC724-FBF6-43F3-A985-7FD27FC87162	GPS LAST CAPTURED 25 OCT 2018 20:51 GMT+11	LOCATION HEARD ISLAND	QR CODE GENERATED 03 JAN 2019 05:13 GMT+11

Figure 5.3: Example of tracing a Patagonian Tooth Fish
Source: https://opensc.org/product-example

Besides the IBM Food Trust, there are other food solutions using blockchain technologies. For example, **OpenSC**, cofounded by the World Wildlife Fund and Boston Consulting Group, helps Austral Fisheries to trace fish from 'bait to plate'.[22] Freshly caught fish are tagged with an RFID device and registered on the blockchain. The Global Positioning System (GPS) is linked to the RFID tag, so every time the fish is scanned, the event is captured in the blockchain to trace its journey (see Figure 5.3). When the fish is processed, data from the tag creates a unique QR code that is attached to the package.

Many other solutions also use QR codes adhered to animals or packages as the public key identifier. As another example, Grass Roots Farmer' Cooperative, based in Little Rock, Arkansas, uses the **Provenance** platform to trace poultry, pork, and beef (see Figure 5.4).

Figure 5.4: Grass Roots blockchain solution

Source: https://mediad.publicbroadcasting.net/p/shared/npr/styles/medium/nprshared/201710/558623705.png

Grass Roots uses a QR code, blockchain technology, and a mobile app for consumers to trace poultry through the supply chain back to the farm

Other examples: Minnesota-based Cargill traced 200,000 turkeys from 70 farms to retail stores.[23] Some food giants have developed their own solutions, like France-based Carrefour did to trace milk and US-based Bumble Bee Foods did for fish (with SAP).[24]

VeChain, based in Singapore, is a public blockchain that is 'inspired' by Ethereum, but it uses centralized governance that makes updates easier. It uses a Proof-of-Authority consensus mechanism where 101 Authority Masternode Operators are known and verified. These include academic institutions, enterprise users, and business and technical partners. It uses a dual-token native digital asset, VET and VTHO. VET serves as a value-transfer medium for business activities and VTHO serves to fund transaction processing. The latter is similar to how Ethereum charges 'gas prices' to process a transaction. In VeChain, 30 percent of the transaction gas price (in VTHO) is awarded to the Authority Node Operator and 70 percent is destroyed. The design aims to prevent transaction fees (VTHO) from being directly exposed to the volatility of the price of VET. According to the VeChain white paper:

> *"VTHO is generated automatically via holding VETs. In other words, whoever holds VET gets VTHO and are able to use the VeChainThor blockchain for free as long as the operations performed consume less than the VTHO generated. VTHO can be transferred and traded to allow users to acquire extra VTHO for performing a larger scale of operations such as running a blockchain application."[25]*

VeChain can be explored on https://vechainstats.com/.

In 2019, Walmart launched the Walmart China Blockchain Traceability Platform, with the help of **PwC** (PricewaterhouseCoopers) and **VeChain.** By year end, it aimed to have over 100 products across 10 categories such as meat, rice, and fresh produce traced. Information is traced on a public blockchain called VeChainThor, where consumers can learn about the products, including the source, routing, and inspections from farm to retail store on the website[26]

In addition to blockchain-based solutions for food traceability, other supply chain solutions trace other types of goods. Next we examine solutions for tracing diamonds.

5.3. Everledger

Everledger tracks diamonds from mines to retail stores. Founded in 2015 by Leanne Kemp, she aimed to help stop 'blood diamonds'—diamonds mined to finance conflicts in such places as Sierra Leone, Liberia, Angola, and the Ivory Coast—by better tracking the warranties associated with fair trade practices established by the United Nations. The United Nations created the World Diamond Congress to define the standards, which it subsequently passed in 2003. Known as the 'Kimberly Process Certification', the process requires sellers of rough and polished diamonds to insert a warranty declaration on invoices that reads:

> *"The diamonds herein invoiced have been purchased from legitimate sources not involved in funding conflict and in compliance with United Nations resolutions. The seller hereby guarantees that these diamonds are conflict free, based on personal knowledge and/or written guarantees provided by the supplier of these diamonds."*[27]

Everledger tracks diamonds by creating a unique digital twin version of the physical diamond by specifying 40 meta data points using high resolution photographs (see Figure 5.5). Everledger worked with IBM to build the blockchain application on Hyperledger Fabric. Over 1 million diamonds were represented on the ledger as of March 2017.[28] Everledger has since expanded its business model to track and trace other valuable assets such as gemstones, luxury goods, art, wine, e-recycling and antiquities.[29]

Although Everledger was first to market with tracking diamonds, other players have since entered the market. In May of 2018, De Beers tracked 100 high-value diamonds from the mine to the retailer using a blockchain, which eventually led to a spinoff called **Tracr**. In January 2019, Russia's Ministry of Education and Science introduced its own blockchain solution for responsible diamond trade, which was developed by a Russian startup called **Bitcarat.com**.[30] Canadian-based Lucara Diamond uses **Clara**, another blockchain-based tracker.[31] It's solution tracks diamonds from 'mine to finger'.[32]

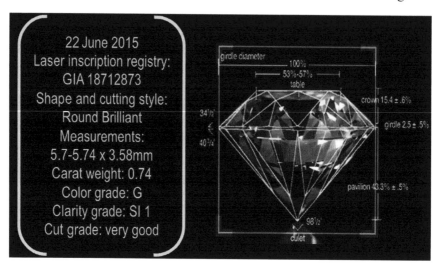

Figure 5.5: Everledger's digital identifier for a fair trade diamond

Source: https://www.youtube.com/watch?v=GAdjL-nultl

5.4. VeriTX

"Coasian economics says firms exist because you have trust inside the company. Blockchain has allowed us to take trust outside of the four walls of the firm and distribute it, so we have distributed trust."

James Allen Regenor, Founder and CEO of VeriTX.[33]

Colonel James Allen Regenor, USAF (ret) founded VeriTX in 2019. VeriTX was incorporated in Delaware, with its head office in East Aurora, New York. VeriTX's mission is to enable the fourth modality of logistics, which Regenor calls digital, following the first three modalities of land, sea, and air. The company built a business-to-business platform for the buying and selling of digital assets (like printing specs) and physical assets, powered by blockchain technology. The platform has been built and tested with many POCs with global strategic partners, and it will launch into production in 2020. The 2020 timeline is possible because VeriTX actually has a longer history dating back to when Colonel Regenor joined Moog in 2013 after retiring from 31 years of military service in the US Air Force. The VeriTX journey begins thereafter with Moog's acquisition of a 3D print business in Detroit, Michigan, in Nov 2015.

Moog Inc. is a $3.2 billion US precision manufacturer and provider of integrated control systems. The company operates three divisions: Aircraft, Space and Defense, and Industrial Systems. Its biggest markets are defense and commercial aircraft.[34] Regenor was hired in Aircraft partly for his scenario-based planning skills to help Moog envision future business directions. One such scenario went as follows:

> *"Imagine a scenario where lives depend upon a mission being flown off the deck of an aircraft carrier far out at sea. The only available aircraft has just been grounded with a failed critical part. There is no part inventory on the carrier. But we do have a 3-D printer and a stock of powder aboard. A technical data package is available for the part, and a replacement is quickly printed. You are the responsible person who needs to get this part quickly fitted to the aircraft and to sign the plane off as safe and ready to fly. How would you know if the newly printed additive manufacturing part you are holding in your hand is good for use?"[35]*

Essentially, Regenor imagined a completely decentralized manufacturing process in which military and commercial customers could print parts where they need them, when they need them. The potential business value was enormous, such as significantly less downtime, lower inventory costs, lower customs fees, and lower shipping and transportation costs.[36] The challenges to realize such a decentralized manufacturing process—particularly in such a highly regulated context—were equally as enormous. What if the 3-D printing instructions had been tampered with by a cyber-terrorist? Or what if the instructions were counterfeit? Military and commercial users would need a way to guarantee that the part that came off the printer was authentic and that the part was ready for use. Furthermore, the newly printed part would need to be tracked over its entire lifetime, so it would need an embedded unique ID when it came off the printer. Military and commercial users would need a decentralized network with the highest security. Technically, Regenor and his team quickly realized that blockchain technologies might be the ideal technical solution: a decentralized blockchain application for decentralized additive manufacturing.[37]

Regenor became Moog's Business Unit Director of Additive Manufacturing & Innovation in April of 2016 and then Director of Transformative Technologies in 2017 to bring the vision to fruition. His team began building a platform-based business model for the entire lifecycle of 3-D printed parts—from part design to part decommissioning.

The main components of the VeriTX design are described below.

Unique, embedded IDs on 3D printed parts

Regenor and his team created a two-layer authentication protocol to ensure the integrity of the parts in the supply chain. First, each part is printed with an embedded unique hash 'watermark' that can be viewed with a camera on a smart phone app. Second, the hash is permanently stored on the blockchain at time of origin. Additionally, the blockchain application will also store the part's every movement and every transfer of ownership, thus enabling the part to be tracked and traced through the supply chain.[38]

Blockchain platform

The VeriTX platform was designed to integrate 3-D printing, blockchain, and artificial intelligence technologies (see Figure 5.6).

Regenor and his team began working with blockchain partners to build the solution because no single blockchain standard has yet emerged. It is possible, for example, that VeriTX will need to connect to multiple blockchains. Nuco, a Toronto-based blockchain startup founded by three Deloitte blockchains leads in 2016, was one of its early partners. Nuco was building an interoperable blockchain network called Aion, which could serve as a hub.[39] Regenor said: *"Aion will allow us to move data between the multiple blockchains that could be present in our supply chain. We think this is a very important step, and we're glad to be participating in it."*[40] Regenor and his team also worked with a major ERP supplier because the platform would need to connect not only with other blockchains, but also to legacy ERP systems, particularly for Moog's enterprise customers.

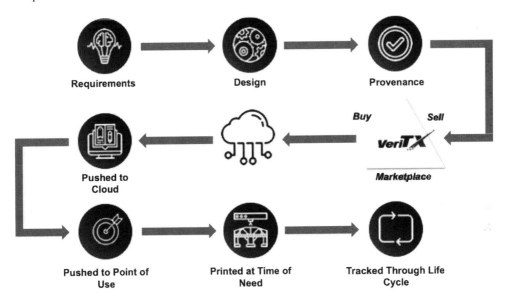

Figure 5.6: VeriTX's blockchain end-to-end solution

Source: James Regenor, with permission

Proof-of-concepts

Regenor and his team conducted a number of POCs in partnership with industrial customers and technology providers. On February 7th 2018, Moog and Singapore Technology Aerospace (STA) announced the completion of a demonstration of the first digital end-to-end manufacturing of a 3-D printed part in the aerospace vertical on a blockchain. In the demonstration, STA bought a digital part from Moog using Microsoft's Azure blockchain application and printed the part on premises at their facility. When STA downloaded the file, the settlement happened instantaneously; the payment used a token that moved value between Moog and STA.

In another POC, Moog, Nuco, and one of Moog's largest aerospace customers tested the use of blockchain for parts provenance using traditionally manufactured parts because the pathway for certification of 3-D printed aerospace parts is still being developed by the certification agencies. Regenor started exploring other technologies to uniquely identify traditionally manufactured parts. Moog did a POC with Alitheon, a company that uses simple mobile phone cameras and proprietary software to transform 54,000 unique surface characteristics of individual objects into a unique digital ID—no tags are appended, the object serves as its own identifier! (See Figure 5.7.) Alitheon's software can scan the object at any time with a mobile phone, and if the object was previously recorded on the blockchain, the software authenticates the object and provides a match confidence score.[41] For the POC, Moog sent 20 metal parts to Alitheon for scanning, which Alitheon then sent back to Moog. Moog scanned them upon receipt, matched them with Moog's ID, and then brutalized the materials by dropping them on concrete floors, grinding them with handheld motors, and grit blasting the parts. Moog sent these worn parts back to Alitheon, which was still able to identify the unique parts, even when only 3,700 unique surface features remained on the original parts.[42]

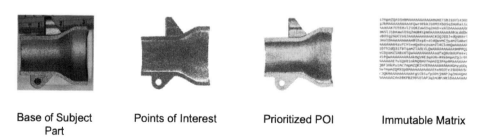

| Base of Subject Part | Points of Interest | Prioritized POI | Immutable Matrix |

Figure 5.7: Creating unique IDs from 54,000 unique surface areas for metal parts

Source: https://www.moog.com/news/blog-new/VeriPart-linking-digital-to-physical.html

In 2019, Regenor and his team did a much-publicized live test of producing a 3D replacement for a business-class seat part for an inbound aircraft. The Boeing 777-300 aircraft left from Auckland New Zealand, and while it was in flight, it radioed Air New Zealand maintenance facility in Auckland to report the part broken. Although the part is not critical, it would deem the seat unsellable. The maintenance facility ordered the digital part from its supplier, Singapore-based ST Engineering (STE). STE pushed the order to Moog to print the part in Los Angeles. Using a mobile printer, Regenor printed the part and it was replaced 30 minutes after the Boeing 777-300 landed in Los Angeles by the maintenance crew.[43] Regenor explained:

> *"We proved that we could whittle a 43 day lead time down to an hour. Digital logistics fundamentally changes supply chains."*[44]

In 2019, Moog completed a large POC with the National Center for Manufacturing Sciences; Microsoft; Marine Corps Fabrication; AMRDEC; Fleet Readiness Center; Naval Undersea Warfare Center; and Tinker Air Force Base. Each site printed two parts, one made of polymer and one made of metal. The POC confirmed that:

> *"it could ensure that the digital asset wasn't manipulated, the source is valid, only the permitted quantity was made, and the intellectual property ownership was protected".*[45]

In addition to POCs, Regenor and his team were seeking IP protection on new inventions; working to define standards with competitors and trading partners; working with government legislators and regulators to define regulations for military acquisition of 3-D parts; and defining a new viable business model to generate revenues and a marketing strategy to attract adoption. Here again, we have an example of why it takes longer than expected for enterprises to get blockchain applications out of innovation labs and into live production. The technical hurdles are jumpable … the ecosystem obstacles are more like a steeplechase. Let's examine what Regenor and his team were doing on each front.

Working on standards and digital data

Regenor and his team began working with a nonprofit organization that conducts research and manages several US national laboratories, and other partners on an industry consortium for additive manufacturing in the aerospace industry. Regenor said:

> *"When they started with standards for aircrafts, the standards were based on wood, glue and fabric. Since then, they've helped develop standards for forgings and castings of metals, plastics, composites and everything else."*[46]

The consortium is building a digital library for general properties of 3-D printed materials. This step is needed so that manufacturers can pivot from 'point approvals' to 'design allowables'. Regenor explained:

> *"Currently, when you make a part, you have to take it to the military or the FAA (Federal Aviation Authority) and seek approval for a particular part made from a particular pattern on a particular machine. It's extremely narrow. With additive manufacturing, we need to get approval for a family of parts from a family of patterns on a family of machines. In order to get there, you have to create the data, so that is what we have been doing."*[47]

Regenor foresees that the data will become part of an open digital catalogue. While some competitors are building proprietary data catalogues that will have to be built on proprietary machines, Regenor believes that real customer value is generated from open architectures. Regenor was also working with the American Standards Association (ASA) on standards for 3-D printed parts, called, 'America Makes & ANSI Additive Manufacturing Standardization Collaborative (AMSC)'.[48] The AMSC published a Version 2.0 roadmap for additive manufacturing in June of 2018.[49]

Working with legislators and regulators

For the vision to become a reality, Regenor and his team needed the US government to create 3-D printing regulations for Department of Defense (DoD) acquisitions. Regenor described how he first approached getting regulations updated:

"In the Federal Acquisition Regulations for electronic parts, it says that there has to be provenance. So, I sat down with my pen and everywhere it said 'electronic', I put in the words 'additive manufacturing'. I went back to our lobbyist and said, 'Hey, let's put this in front of committee. Let's get this added to the Federal Acquisition Regulations.' So, we decided to use federal regulation to help create market space."[50]

Next, Regenor informed the US House Armed Services Committee about the threat of counterfeiting for additive manufactured parts. Regenor explained:

"With 3-D printing, you have to worry about complex parts being counterfeit. Anybody can print something that looks like the part they are holding in their hand. It won't have the same material properties or the same characteristics, but the guy pulling it off the shelf will not know the difference."[51]

Legislators understood the concern; the National Defense Authorization Act of 2018 included funds for additive manufacturing technology development and required briefings on blockchain technologies from agencies.[52]

Working to protect IP

While at Moog, Regenor had several internal and external lawyers working on protecting its intellectual property. VeriPart's first extension for a registered trademark was granted on January 15, 2018.[53] Moog has also filed several patent applications. The patent for 'secure and traceable manufactured parts' describes 3-D parts provenance, from initial requirements through the entire product life cycle using blockchain.[54] The patent describes three integrities: data integrity, process integrity, and performance integrity. In December 2017, Moog extended the patent into the space domain.[55] Regenor explained:

"If you are on a space station, space factory, spaceship, or space colony, you'll need 3-D printed parts."[56]

Moog also applied for a patent pertaining to the neural network part of the platform.

Working on the business model

Initially, Regenor had a very simple strategy: How do you create value for customers in an ecosystem enabled by blockchain? To attract customers to the platform, Regenor foresaw following Apple's strategy when it launched iTunes. Apple initially offered a seed catalogue of music to attract customers, then updated the catalogue each week to keep customers coming back. Similarly, Regenor planned to seed the digital catalogue for general properties of 3-D printed materials. This catalogue would allow customers to move from 'point approvals' to 'design allowables'. Customers will initially go to the platform to access the digital catalogue, but as the ecosystem grows, other parties will be able to offer more services on top of the platform.

Initially, the business plan included the creation of a joint venture with at least five equal partners (of which Moog would be one) to manage the platform and a separate consortium would govern each industry vertical. Regenor planned to first build the platform for the aerospace industry, and then expand to automotive, medical and other industries that use 3-D printed parts.

Trying to launch a new business within a traditional business proved to be a slow process. Ultimately, Regenor decided to depart Moog in May of 2018 to accelerate moving from POCs to live production. He also said:

> *"To be successful, we need VeriTX to be a neutral third-party platform."*

Regenor stayed on as a consultant with Moog as he launched VeriTX. While Regenor was named on the patents (along with other Moog employees), Moog owns the patents, so VeriTX licenses the patents from Moog. In late 2019, Moog became a strategic partner with VeriTX.

Moving Forward

Regenor, first while working with Moog, and then by launching VeriTX, has made a lot of progress on realizing the vision of building a blockchain-enabled platform that enables part providence for additive and traditional manufacturing. The technology is ready; the POCs have proved the technical and business viability; VeriTX has strategic partners in place (see Figure 5.8); it has a digital catalog. The last piece is the final round of funding. Regenor anticipates a 2020 launch:

"People say the Internet took 10 years, so blockchain will take ten years. But blockchain is built on the Internet, so we'll leverage the Internet protocols and fold those into blockchain so we can have an exponential acceleration rather than a linear acceleration."

Figure 5.8: VeriTX's strategic partners as of 2020

Source: https://www.veritx.co/

5.5. Conclusion

The IBM Food Trust; TradeLens; MediLedger; EY WineChain; OpenSC; VeChain; Provenance; Everledger; Tracr; Bitcarat.com; Clara; and VeriTX show how ecosystem platforms can help to improve supply chains. They improve supply chain visibility, authenticate products, remove friction points in trade, reduce administrative costs, and reduce time wasted on paperwork. For those interested in a deeper examination of blockchains in supply chains, *Integrating Blockchain into Supply Chain Management* by Remko Van Hoek, Brian Fugate, Marat Davletshin, and Matthew Waller is recommended.[57]

In the next chapter, we explore uses of blockchain solutions for the energy sector.

Citations:

[1] Van Hoek, R., Fugate, B., Davletshin, M., and Waller, M. (2019). *Integrating Blockchain into Supply Chain Management*, Kogan Page, London.

[2] https://blockgeeks.com/guides/what-is-blockchain-technology/

[3] ReportBuyer Press Release (Aug 27, 2018), *The global food and grocery retail market size is expected to reach USD 12.24 trillion by 2020*, https://www.prnewswire.com/news-releases/the-global-food-and-grocery-retail-market-size-is-expected-to-reach-usd-12-24-trillion-by-2020--300702659.html

[4] World Health Organization (2020). Food Safety, https://www.who.int/news-room/fact-sheets/detail/food-safety

[5] Spink, J., Embark, P., Savelli, C., and Bradshaw, A. (2019), *Global perspectives on food fraud: results from a WHO survey of members of the International Food Safety Authorities Network (INFOSAN)*. *npj Sci Food* **3,** 12. https://www.nature.com/articles/s41538-019-0044-x

[6] Grossman, E. (October 25, 2016), *Did slaves produce your food?* https://civileats.com/2016/10/25/did-slaves-produce-your-food-forced-labor/

[7] Statista (2020). *Total retail and food services sales in the United States from 1992 to 2018*; https://www.statista.com/statistics/197569/annual-retail-and-food-services-sales/

[8] CDC (2020), Burden of Foodborne Illness: Findings, https://www.cdc.gov/foodborneburden/2011-foodborne-estimates.html

[9] Food Waste: Rescuing US Cuisine. https://www.rescuingleftovercuisine.org/challenge?gclid=Cj-0KCQiA4NTxBRDxARIsAHyp6gBqhPgXvYsvwoDJHRewOeXi5nv1sK8f1oMw5BP0AtNnseRDNRYk vqgaAgu5EALw_wcB

[10] Yiannas, F. (January 26, 2020), *FDA's Frank Yiannas on Food Safety*. https://www.linkedin.com/posts/frank-yiannas-3b106015_fda-activity-6627357552072015872--eaC

[11] Statista (2020). Food in China. https://www.statista.com/outlook/40000000/117/food/china

[12] Huang, Y. (July 16, 2014), *The 2008 Milk Scandal Revisited*, https://www.forbes.com/sites/yanzhong-huang/2014/07/16/the-2008-milk-scandal-revisited/#1d10db394105

[13] Crouch, E. *(March 26, 2013)' 'Illegal pig dealers in Zhejiang linked to Shanghai hog wash'. Shanghaiist.* http://shanghaiist.com/2013/03/26/illegal_pig-dealers_in_zhejiang_linked_to_shanghai_river_hogs/

[14] Zuo, M. (January 10, 2020), 'Chinese city clamps down after customer is duped into buying fish tainted with diesel', *South China Morning Post*, https://www.scmp.com/news/china/society/article/3045601/chinese-city-clamps-down-after-customer-tricked-buying-fish

[15] Food Safety in China. https://en.wikipedia.org/wiki/Food_safety_in_China#Food_safety_incidents

[16] Kamath, R. (2018), 'Food Traceability on Blockchain: Walmart's Pork and Mango Pilots with IBM', *The Journal of The British Blockchain Association*, 1(1), 1-12.

[17] https://www.ibm.com/blockchain/solutions/food-trust

[18] *What are Key Responsibilities for a Trust Anchor?* https://www.ibm.com/block-chain/solutions/food-trust/food-industry-technology#1797811

[19] IBM Press Release (October 23 2018), *IBM and Microsoft Announce Partnership Between Cloud Offerings*, https://www.pbsnow.com/ibm-news/ibm-and-microsoft-announce-partnership-between-cloud-offerings/

[20] Email exchange with Ramesh Gopinath, Vice President, Blockchain Solutions, IBM, March 31, 2020

[21] Email exchange with Ramesh Gopinath, Vice President, Blockchain Solutions, IBM, March 31, 2020

[22] https://opensc.org/case-studies.html

[23] Grass Roots Farmer's Cooperative (February 10, 2019), *From Pasture to Plate – Trace The Journey of Your Food*. https://www.grassrootscoop.com/blog/from-pasture-to-plate-trace-the-journey-of-your-food/

Bloch, S., and Fassler, J. (Novemeber 23, 2018), *Why Car "blockchain-based" turkeys obscure more than they reveal*, The Counter, https://thecounter.org/cargill-blockchain-traceable-turkey-contract-farming-reality-thanksgiving/

[24] O'Neil, S. (July 7, 2019), 'Blockchain for Food, How the Industry Makes Use of the Technology'. *CoinTelegraph*, https://cointelegraph.com/news/blockchain-for-the-food-how-industry-makes-use-of-the-technology

[25] VeChain white paper https://www.vechain.org/whitepaper/

[26] Palmer, D. (June 25, 2019), *Walmart China Teams with VeChain, PwC on Blockchain Food Safety Platform*, Coindesk, https://www.coindesk.com/walmart-china-teams-with-vechain-on-blockchain-food-safety-platform
Mitra, R. (August 28, 2019), *VeChain partners with Walmart, BYD, DNG VL and BMW. FXStreet*, https://www.fxstreet.com/cryptocurrencies/news/vechain-partners-with-walmart-byd-dng-vl-and-bmw-201908280048

Consumer view: https://traceability.walmartmobile.cn/walmart/p/10000919067888862973

[27] https://en.wikipedia.org/wiki/Kimberley_Process_Certification_Scheme

[28] Presentation by Everledger's CEO at IBM Interconnect: https://ibmgo.com/interconnect2017/?cm_mc_uid=19734726856314943335282&cm_mc_sid_50200000=1494367094&cm_mc_sid_52640000=1494367094 (About an hour and 15 minutes into the video)

[29] https://www.everledger.io/industry-solutions/

[30] https://bitcarat.com/

[31] O'Neal, S. (February 6, 2019), 'Diamonds are blockchain's best friend', *CoinTelegraph*, https://cointelegraph.com/news/diamonds-are-blockchains-best-friend-how-dlt-helps-tracking-gems-and-prevents-fraud

[32] https://www.lucaradiamond.com/clara/

[33] Regenor, J. (April 18th 2017), *Industry Impact: Aerospace Supply Chain*, presentation at the Blockchain for Business Conference at MIT, Cambridge Massachusetts

[34] Moog 2016 Annual Report, http://www.moog.com/content/dam/moog/literature/Corporate/Investors/Annual_Report/2016/2016-Annual-Report.pdf

[35] Small, G., *Additive Manufacturing Reshaping Logistics*, http://www.moog.com/news/blog-new/IntroducingVeripart_Issue3.html

[36] Small, G., *Additive Manufacturing Reshaping Logistics*, http://www.moog.com/news/blog-new/IntroducingVeripart_Issue3.html

[37] Regenor, J. (April 18th 2017), *Industry Impact: Aerospace Supply Chain*, presentation at the Blockchain for Business Conference at MIT, Cambridge Massachusetts

[38] Regenor, J., op. cit., April 18, 2017.

[39] *Moog announces partnership with Aion,* Aion Foundation, October 5, 2017, available at https://blog.aion.network/moogaionpartnership-6d37ce15b2fd.

[40] Galang, J. *Nuco raises $27 million to build interoperable blockchain network,* BetaKit, October 10, 2017, available at https://betakit.com/nuco-raises-27-million-to-build-interoperable-blockchain-network/.

[41] Alitheon website. https://www.alitheon.com

[42] Moog Press Release (2019), *VeriPart™ – Linking Digital to Physical*, https://www.moog.com/news/blog-new/VeriPart-linking-digital-to-physical.html.

[43] Davies, S. (July 17, 2019), 'Moog's connecting flight to distributed manufacturing', *TCT Magazine*, https://www.tctmagazine.com/3d-printing-news/moogs-connecting-flight-to-distributed-manufacturing/

[44] James Regenor, presentation to the Blockchain Center of Excellence, December 3, 2019.

[45] National Center for Manufacturing Sciences Press Release (March 27, 2019), *Project Success: Blockchain Huge Success Story with Five Demonstrations*, https://www.ncms.org/project-success-blockchain-huge-success-story-with-five-demonstrations/

[46] Personal interview with Mary Lacity.

[47] Personal interview with Mary Lacity.

[48] *America Makes & ANSI Additive Manufacturing Standardization Collaborative (AMSC)*, https://www.ansi.org/standards_activities/standards_boards_panels/amsc/

[49] *Standardization Roadmap for Additive Manufacturing* https://www.ansi.org/news_publications/news_story?menuid=7&articleid=fc19f3c2-de56-4d96-9d42-cc0c7a0c8c37

[50] Regenor, J. (April 18th 2017), *Industry Impact: Aerospace Supply Chain*, presentation at the Blockchain for Business Conference at MIT, Cambridge Massachusetts

[51] Personal interview with Mary Lacity

[52] *National Defense Authorization Act for Fiscal Year 2018*, https://www.congress.gov/bill/115th-congress/house-bill/2810/text - toc-HBA0AA81CFC4F410E95EF87129909DC2A

[53] https://www.battelle.org/homepage

[54] *Patent for Secure and Traceable Manufactured Parts, Patent number 20180012311*, https://patents.justia.com/patent/20180012311

[55] *Patent for Outer Space Digital Logistics System. Patent number 20180136633*, https://patents.justia.com/patent/20180136633

[56] Personal interview with Mary Lacity.

[57] Van Hoek, R., Fugate, B., Davletshin, M., and Waller, M. (2019), *Integrating Blockchain into Supply Chain Management*, Kogan Page, London.

Chapter 6

Business Applications for Energy

"Although blockchain seems to be generating the most buzz in financial services, the networked infrastructure of the energy industry makes it particularly suited for blockchain technology applications. Also, with the rise of the Internet of Tthings, the entire energy industry may soon find its operations transformed into a vast global network of connected devices—all feeding digital data into blockchain-enabled platforms that can capture and share information in real time."

Deloitte, *Blockchain: A true disrupter for the energy industry*[1]

"Every day I get to 'Think' and work on everything from digitizing electric grids so they can accommodate renewable energy and enable mass adoption of electric cars, helping major cities reduce congestion and pollution, to developing new micro-finance programs that help tiny businesses get started in markets such as Brazil, India, Africa."

Ginni Rometty, CEO of IBM.[2]

6.1. Overview of the cases

The global energy sector, comprising oil and gas, electric utilities, and renewable energies generates about $90 trillion each year.[3] While energy literally powers our lives, the industry stresses our natural resources. By their very nature, energy problems are global

231

problems, requiring many partners across firm and country boundaries to cooperate. Blockchain technologies are well suited to transform the generation, distribution and consumption of energy. The World Economic Forum, in collaboration with PwC and Stanford Woods Institute for the Environment, reported blockchain-based solutions were being developed to address: climate change; biodiversity and conservation; healthy oceans; water security; clean air; and weather and disaster resilience.[4] By 2018, over 60 blockchain use cases were being explored.[5]

In this chapter, we focus on blockchain solutions for electric energy. The world over, large electric utilities are the primary suppliers of electricity. These large, centrally-managed organizations have been operating with the same business models for 100 years or more and they are markedly energy inefficient. According to Lawrence Livermore National Laboratory, only 32 percent of electric energy generated in the US is actually 'useable energy', called 'exergy'.[6] That means most of the electric energy generated by utilities is wasted through the processes of conversion, transportation and consumption.[7]

Consumers are increasingly concerned about the waste, expense, and lack of control over their power supply. Consequently, many households have installed solar panels on their properties. US solar power installations doubled from 2015 to 2016, and more than 2 million US households and commercial properties had solar power by 2019.[8,9]

Consumer adoption of solar panels is prompted by many factors besides lower electric bills; consumers want energy independence, increased property values and reduced carbon footprints. Pertaining to this last point, Energysage—a company that helps consumers find solar solutions—claims:

> *"a typical residential solar panel system will eliminate three to four tons of carbon emissions each year—the equivalent of planting over 100 trees annually."*[10]

However, US consumers with solar panels are still connected to, and reliant upon, their major electric utility providers. Any excess capacity generated from a household solar panel is put right back into the traditional electric grid and the utility provider credits the consumer's bill; the 'prosumers' – households that produce excess energy – have no market to sell excess capacity to besides the utility provider. That is, until now. Lawrence Orsini, founder and CEO of **LO3 Energy**, aimed to create a way for neighbors to buy and sell excess electric capacity directly from each other. His company, along with partners, built a technology platform to create peer-to-peer markets for the sharing economy (see Table 6.1).

According to a report by EY, of the 3.5 million electric charging stations in the world, fewer than 500,000 are available to the public, and most of those are in China.[11] EY, along with a number of other companies, are using blockchain technology to create markets for charge station owners and electric car drivers. Here we focus on one such company, based in Germany, called **Share&Charge**. It built an open network platform for electric car charging stations and electric car owners (see Table 6.1).

Enterprise(s)	Enterprise Type	Blockchain Application	Status as of 2020
LO3 Energy	Private startup	Peer-to-peer marketplace for electricity generated from neighbor's solar panels	The Brooklyn Microgrid, LO3's first project, was running in a shadow market of 60 prosumers and around 500 consumers by year-end 2017. It took a few years to obtain permission from NY regulators to operate the Brooklyn Microgrid in a regulatory sandbox, which happened in December of 2019. LO3 Energy has many other projects worldwide and launched Pando in 2019, an end-to-end transactive energy platform and marketplace.
Share & Charge	Innogy spinoff	Peer-to-peer marketplace for charging electric cars	Over 1,000 blockchain-enabled charging stations installed around Germany in 2017. As of 2019, the Open Charging Network (OCN) is open for public testing.

Table 6.1: Blockchain application examples for energy

6.2. LO3 Energy

"With the Microgrid, there is no need for a utility company to act as an intermediary, leaving residents in control of their own power."

LO3 Energy News story[12]

"We're really providing choice. More choice for the community, more choice for what types of energy they can buy, who they can buy it from, what they can do with the money that they were spending on energy."

Lawrence Orsini, Founder and CEO of LO3 Energy[13]

"The grid of the future runs on data."

Don Tapscott, Founder of the Blockchain Research Institute[14]

Lawrence Orsini spent years in the energy sector before founding LO3 Energy in 2012 in Brooklyn New York. He worked for PECI, a non-profit based in Portland Oregon that helps utilities, governments and other clients to become more energy efficient.[15] He was also Director of New Products at CLEAResults, an Austin Texas-based company that helps utilities, businesses, and consumers to become more energy efficient.[16] This position brought him to New York City.

Orsini envisioned a future of energy production and consumption that is sustainable, local, reliable, efficient, and self-governing. He wanted to build the platform where prosumers sell excess energy capacity from their solar panels directly to neighbors using a mobile app. His idea became even more pertinent in the aftermath of Hurricane Sandy, which hit New York City in October of 2012. It was the largest hurricane on record at the time—a whopping 1,100 miles in diameter. As Hurricane Sandy flooded the streets of New York City, power went out to over 800,000 residences and businesses and stayed off for days.[17] Even residents with solar panels could not use their own power because the photovoltaic panels (PV) that connected them to the utility grid were shut off. The pain and aftermath of Hurricane Sandy awakened consumers and made them receptive to LO3 Energy's value proposition.

Orsini has experienced many successes. By 2019, LO3 Energy had raised over $5.8 million in two funding rounds. Centrica; Braemar Energy Ventures; Siemens; Sumitomo Corporation; and Shell Ventures are investors.[18] LO3 Energy has been lauded with numerous awards, such as the Bloomberg New Energy Finance (BNEF) Pioneers Winner in 2018 and the Global Corporate Venturing's Digital Energy Investment of the Year in 2019.[19] LO3 has been featured by CNN, Forbes, Reuters, and many more outlets.[20] The technology is ready. Consumers are ready. However, widespread commercialization needs more regulators and existing utilities to embrace disruption, which has been slow to come. First, we look at LO3's technology and then we explore its first major pilot, called the Brooklyn Microgrid.

6.2.1. Exergy—a transactive energy platform

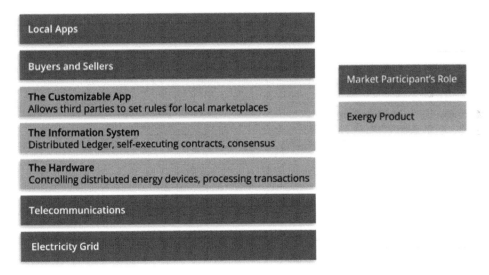

Figure 6.1: Exergy's transactive energy stack

Source: LO3 Energy (2018) Exergy Business White Paper

To accomplish Orsini's vision, LO3 Energy built both the hardware and software, with partners, to create what is called a 'transactive energy platform' they branded as 'Exergy' (see Figure 6.1). The platform comprises hardware such as smart meters, switches, and controllers. The software is based on a proprietary blockchain-based application with a customizable, mobile user interface.

The IoT smart meters are installed on the prosumers' properties to measure production and consumption of electricity (See Figure 6.2 for sample hardware). The hardware feeds data to the blockchain-based application every second. Only the prosumers need the specialized hardware installed; consumers interact with the platform through a mobile or desktop app. LO3 is working with Siemens to build the physical grid that will separate from the main utility grid so that locally-generated power can be re-routed to critical locations in time of need.[21] Most importantly, Exergy's hardware is 'device agnostic' so that other suppliers can operate Exergy-compliant hardware.[22]

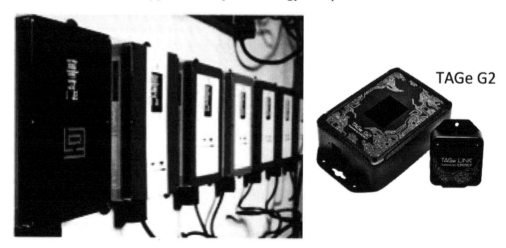

Figure 6.2: Examples of LO3 hardware

Sources: Left – https://www.power-technology.com/wp-content/uploads/sites/7/2017/09/Transactive-Grid-element.jpg. Right – http://manda-borealis.com/work/

LO3 launched a digital exergy token through a private sale in 2017 to accredited private investors. In the future, Exergy will launch a public digital token and it will be managed by the Exergy Foundation, a 501(c)3 not-for-profit. The token is needed to capture the data about the current state of the grid, the time and location of production, and multi-party consumption requirements. Orsini explained:

"It's not an ICO, it's a token event. The token is really a permission to the network, so without a token, you can't incorporate data to the network. Without data in the network, you have no value to the network, so there's no reason for your participation".[23]

Exergy's digital ledger records information collected from the smart meters about the state of the grid, the time and location of production, the consumption requirements, and the buy and sell offers of market participants. Orsini explained the suitability of a blockchain for the platform as follows:

"The architecture is very well aligned with our decentralized infrastructure. So the ledger needs to be on the grid; it needs to be distributed amongst the grid. If you're going to run a physical microgrid, or even a virtual microgrid, and you're incorporating a resiliency plan, then you can't have cloud hosting— because when the grid goes down, you have no communication."[24]

The consumer application connects neighbors to the blockchain to allow peer-to-peer transactions; neighbors use the app to place and execute buy and sell orders. Essentially, prosumers are selling their excess capacity credits to neighbors rather than back to the utility. The consumer application is a white-label product that other companies can rebrand. As LO3 continues to build and improve upon the platform, it is conducting live tests throughout the world. Here, we focus on its first project, called the Brooklyn Microgrid project.

6.2.2. The Brooklyn Microgrid Project

"The next time a superstorm comes through and knocks out all of the power, Brooklyn Microgrid will make sure the power stays on in critical areas so you have a safe place to charge your phone, get food or send out emails to let people know you are okay."

Neighbor featured on Brooklyn Microgrid Introduction[25]

In 2016, LO3 tested the microgrid concept in one residential neighborhood on President Street in Brooklyn New York (see Figure 6.3). It chose this street for the proof-of-concept (POC) because it had a high concentration of solar adopters on one side of the street and a high concentration of neighbors interested in green energy on the other side. Orsini said:

"It was an obvious choice. These are neighbors across the street from each other, they had good relationships." [26]

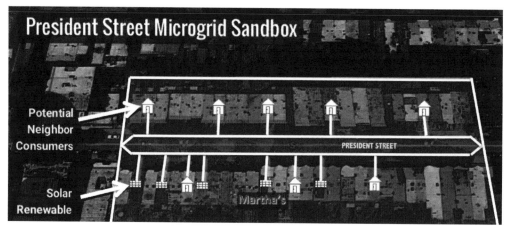

Figure 6.3: Site of proof-of-concept test on President Street in Brooklyn New York

Source: Microgrid media[27]

The POC proved that the smart meters could successfully count the electrons generated from solar panels, could record data on the prototype blockchain (initially built on Ethereum) and could make data accessible to prosumers and consumers.[28] This test also proved that consumers were willing to pay a little bit more for electricity produced by their neighbors. Orsini explained:

"What we are doing is enabling consumer choice. Many consumers don't want cheap, they want theirs. Just like many consumers are willing to pay

more for locally produced food, many are willing to pay more for locally produced electrons—and we empower them to do that. If they're looking for cheap, then they will have access to cheap as well. Our model has everything to do with providing choice." [29]

After the successful POC, LO3 was ready to scout for a location to expand the Brooklyn Microgrid project to a full-scale, live test of the business model and platform. The search was on for a location that would test the business model across social strata. After six months of searching, LO3 decided on Brooklyn's Gowanus and Park Slope neighborhoods (see Figure 6.4).

Figure 6.4: Gowanus and Park Slope neighborhoods of Brooklyn, New York
Source: Googlemaps[31]

Orsini explained:

> *"This neighborhood was the right place to do it. So, from a social strata perspective, we've got some of the poorest of the poor in New York living here in Brooklyn, all the way up to some of the most expensive properties in the city, right along the park. Mayor De Blasio (mayor of New York City) and Chuck Schumer (US Senator from New York State) live in Park Slope. From the business perspective, the strata covers manufacturing, light industrial, and local retail all the way up to the highest-end retail businesses. So, that's why we chose this location."*[30]

By December 2017, LO3 had installed 60 smart meters in the neighborhood and 500 consumers had downloaded the mobile application (see Figure 6.5).

Figure 6.5: Example of mobile app interface for Brooklyn Microgrid project.
Consumers can set the maximum daily rates and buy energy from neighbors,
clean energy, or brown energy sources.

Sources: Left: https://www.sacramento.energy/video-gallery
Right: Author's mobile app screenshot on February 24, 2018

The grid operates in a shadow market until all the regulatory requirements are met. Since inception, LO3 Energy has worked very closely with New York regulators and policy makers. LO3 has also met with the US Federal Energy Regulatory Commission. In 2017, Orsini said:

> *"We have a very good relationship with the regulators. The regulators in New York are pretty excited about and engaged in what we're doing, particularly for the transactive energy platform."*[32]

Despite Orsini's optimism, New York's utility regulations proved to be a stubborn obstacle. To build momentum, Adrienne Smith, Brooklyn Microgrid's executive director, launched a campaign on Change.org in 2019 to authorize Brooklyn Microgrid to operate as a commercial entity.[33] Smith said:

> *"All we need is [New York] Governor Cuomo to say 'Yes' to our campaign request and the network is already installed and ready to go."*[34]

On December 30, 2019, the Brooklyn Microgrid was granted permission for a yearlong regulatory sandbox pilot program.[35]

The same regulatory permission process will need to be repeated as communities adopt the Exergy platform in other US jurisdictions and beyond to other countries. Orsini had already met with regulators from Australia and Europe, but as a business model, it would be untenable for LO3 to lead the efforts for subsequent adoptions.[36] Therefore, going forward beyond the Brooklyn Microgrid project, LO3 Energy will sell its transactive energy platform, Exergy, directly to other communities or institutions interested in adoption, but it will not own the projects. Local adopters are in the best position to rally neighbors, educate users and secure local regulatory permissions. Several other community-based projects are underway, including projects in Sacramento California,[37] Vermont,[38] South Australia,[39] Germany,[40] Japan,[41] and across Europe.[42] Orsini said that hundreds of interested communities have approached LO3 about participation.[43]

Initially, LO3 Energy's business model sought to remove the monopoly power of incumbent utility providers by offering consumers a choice as to where they can buy and sell electricity credits. The business model evolved to welcome utilities. Orsini said in 2019, *"The whole intent of LO3 is to enable consumer choice, so people can decide with their dollars what the future looks like, who they're buying energy from, where it comes from and how it's produced. But that doesn't sideline utilities—in fact, they are a huge part of this."*[44] To that end, LO3 Energy released Pando in 2019, a software solution that brings utility providers into the community. Pando connects utilities and retailers to their customers, who are in turn, connected to their communities (see Figure 6.6).

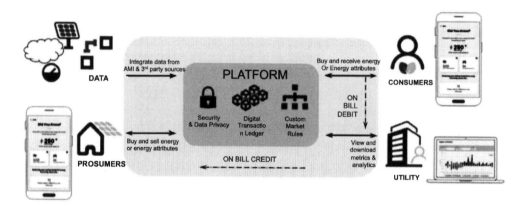

Figure 6.6: Pando: Bringing utility providers into the solution
Source: https://i2.wp.com/lo3energy.com/wp-content/uploads/2020/02/Pando1.
jpg?w=1280&ssl=1

According to LO3 Energy's website, Pando offers a marketplace for utilities that provides:

- **Flexible Trading:** Pando allows utilities to configure the marketplace to trade energy or energy attributes and enable consumers to source renewables from their local community.

- **Powerful Metrics:** Pando analyzes the market with customer and trade analytics, trading dynamics, offer subscriptions, and other configurable analytics from consumers in an easy-to-use portal.

- **Personal Energy Management:** Pando leads customers on a new energy journey, starting with valuable energy tools on a branded mobile application, to learn about their energy profile and renewable engagement opportunities.

- **Highly Extensible:** Pando securely integrates to third-party software such as billing systems and energy devices to streamline the customer experience.

- **Simple Deployment**: Pando can be launched in 90 days with a team of experts who partner with utilities through every implementation stage from design collaboration, to test and turn up, and ongoing support.

- **Secure and Scalable:** Pando uses blockchain technology to ensure personal and system data security and scalability.[45]

Orsini is well on his way to realizing his vision for energy production and consumption that is sustainable, local, reliable, efficient, and self-governing. LO3 energy is ahead of other players in the space because Orsini and his team knew that they needed to do more than just build a great platform—they needed to prove they could get the platform legally and socially embedded into a real community, which they did with the Brooklyn Microgrid. To scale globally, they also needed to show that its platform could attract other partners, particularly incumbent utilities, to build new business models on top of it.

Competition

Other blockchain-based energy solutions have been announced, such as Co-Tricity; GridSingularity; Grid; PowerLedger; Daisee; OmegaGrid, and many others.[46] Some of these projects have continued to progress, such as PowerLedger, which had 23 projects in eight countries in 2020.[47] Other projects, however, have already succumbed to what Orsini calls 'the valley of death'. He argued that many startups had confused the market with 'blockchain-first' strategies that ultimately failed. In contrast, LO3 Energy intends to overcome the 'valley of death' because Exergy was developed as an 'energy-first' solution. Orsini said:

> *"LO3 is not a blockchain company getting into energy. We are an energy company specifically created to bring blockchain into the industry."*[48]

The next case addresses a business model innovation for electric car charging.

6.3. Share&Charge

> *"The idea is to solve the lack of public charging infrastructure in Germany by integrating private charging stations. We are enabling people with our app to share their charging stations."*
>
> **Dietrich Sümmermann, Innogy Innovation Hub
> and Co-founder of Share&Charge**[49]

Innogy, a subsidiary of the Germany-based electric utility RWE, was established in 2016 to focus on renewable energy solutions. Innogy's Innovation Hub aims to create or collaborate with start-ups to bring new energy solutions based on 'ethical machines' to market.[50] One of its projects is 'Share&Charge', a startup venture to create a peer-to-peer marketplace for electric car charging. Innogy wanted to expand Germany's infrastructure by enabling 60,000 private charging stations to join Germany's 6,500 public charging stations.

Owners of charging stations and drivers of electric cars use a Share&Charge wallet (see Figure 6.7). Owners of a charging station can set their own flat rate, time-based, or kilowatt hour-based fees. The fees can also be discounted for family, friends, or charities. Using a mobile app, drivers can search for nearby charging stations, charge their electric cars at any of the authorized stations and pay for the charges using Share&Charge's native digital asset, an ERC20 token, initially called a 'Mobility Token'.[51]

Figure 6.7: Share&Charge mobile app

Source: https://shareandcharge.com/wp-content/uploads/2018/08/perspective-app-mockup-1200x788.png

Working with the partners TÜV Rheinland and MotionWerk, Share&Charge first installed over 1,000 blockchain-enabled electric charging stations around Germany in 2017 (see Figure 6.8).[52] The initial application was built on the public Ethereum using three smart contracts: MobilityToken[53], ChargingPoles[54], and LibManager[55]. MobilityToken was the token contract that held balances and enforced rules; each token was backed by a real Euro and complied with German regulations. ChargingPoles registered all of the charging pole stations and executed the operations at the charging stations, such as the start and stop meter functions. LibManager was a library of contracts that allowed Share&Charge to update smart contracts or fix programming errors.[56] Since this initial application, Share&Charge has launched its own blockchain network, called the Open Charging Network (OCN). Energy Web Chain (EWC), which is based on Ethereum, uses a Proof-of-Authority consensus protocol. EWC is open source.[57] As of 2019, the OCN is open for public testing.

Figure 6.8: First generation Innogy charging station with embedded Ethereum node

*Source: https://cdn-images-1.medium.com/max/1600/1*aZuXOx0TiiXEry3QoZMDjw.jpeg*

As far as building it network of partners, Share&Charge launched its 'Oslo2Rome' pilot in six European countries, which proved the solution could work across borders.[58] By 2018, Share&Charge had welcomed partners in France, Finland, Germany, the Netherlands, Switzerland, and the United Kingdom.[59] Also in 2018, Share&Charge launched a non-profit foundation to help further develop the Open Charging Network. Share&Charge tested an in-car wallet in 2019 in a Toyota.[60] The app directs drivers to a charging station based on the driver's preferences, such as 'close to a coffee shop' or 'near a playground', and can book a charging time to minimize congestion.[61] Share&Charge anticipates it will move from test to full production in the third quarter of 2020.

Competition

There are a number of traditional enterprises and platforms with similar aims as Share&Charge, such as P2P Electric Vehicle Charging; eMotorWorks; Oxygen Initiative; Easy Park; Chargemap; Aerovironment; and Charg, and some with expanded functionality.[62] For example, EY's OpsChain Tesseract platform is designed for shared vehicle ownership, of which charging would be one feature. The platform could enable radical new business models, like limiting the number of vehicles in a congested city by having cities and citizens co-own and share vehicles.[63]

6.4. Conclusion

LO3 Energy and Share&Charge are two powerful 'Internet of Value' examples for the energy sector. They are each providing a peer-to-peer platform to empower everyday prosumers and consumers to share their energy resources. Their adoption journeys are similar in that each launched a POC on public Ethereum that expanded consumer awareness. Their founders simultaneously built network effects by uniting with partners across country borders, worked with regulators, and built a more robust platform based on a faster and more scalable consensus mechanism than Ethereum's proof-of-work. In the next chapter, we explore the challenges of credentialing and an application solution called SmartResume.

Citations:

[1] Deloitte (2018). *Blockchain: A true disrupter for the energy industry*, https://www2.deloitte.com/content/dam/Deloitte/us/Documents/energy-resources/us-blockchain-disruptor-for-energy-industry.pdf

[2] https://www.brainyquote.com/topics/renewable-energy-quotes

[3] Investopedia, *What Percentage of the Global Economy Is the Oil and Gas Drilling Sector?* https://www.investopedia.com/ask/answers/030915/what-percentage-global-economy-comprised-oil-gas-drilling-sector.asp

Investopedia, *Utilities Sector: Industries Snapshot (NEE, GAS)*, https://www.investopedia.com/articles/investing/031116/utilities-sector-industries-snapshot-nee-gas.asp

Allied Market Research Renewable Energy Market Outlook–2025 https://www.alliedmarketresearch.com/renewable-energy-market

[4] World Economic Forum (2018), *Building Block(chain)s for a Better Planet*, http://www3.weforum.org/docs/WEF_Building-Blockchains.pdf

[5] World Economic Forum (2018), *Building Block(chain)s for a Better Planet*, http://www3.weforum.org/docs/WEF_Building-Blockchains.pdf

[6] Stark, A. (2015), *American energy use up slightly, carbon emissions almost unchanged,* https://www.llnl.gov/news/american-energy-use-slightly-carbon-emissions-almost-unchanged-0

[7] Conversion waste happens when converting natural gas, coal, nuclear, hydro, geothermal and wind to electricity. Transportation waste occurs when pushing electricity over long distances. About 5 percent of electric energy is lost in transit. Consumption waste occurs when consumer appliances lose electric energy to heat, for example. Source: Lempriere, M (April 11 2017), The Brooklyn microgrid: blockchain-enabled community power, http://www.power-technology.com/features/featurethe-brooklyn-microgrid-blockchain-enabled-community-power-5783564/

[8] Ferris, R. (February 15th 2017), *US solar installations nearly doubled in 2016, and broke some records*, CNBC, https://www.cnbc.com/2017/02/14/us-solar-installations-nearly-doubled-in-2016-and-broke-some-records.html

[9] Solar Energy Industries Association Press Release (May 9th, 2019), *United States Surpasses 2 Million Solar Installations*, https://www.seia.org/news/united-states-surpasses-2-million-solar-installations

[10] Energysage (2017), *Why go solar—Top 10 benefits of solar energy*, https://www.energysage.com/solar/why-go-solar/

[11] EY, *How to lead the charge on crowdfunded EV infrastructure*, https://www.ey.com/en_kr/automotive-transportation/how-to-lead-the-charge-on-crowdfunded-ev-infrastructure

[12] Lempriere, M. (April 11th 2017), *The Brooklyn microgrid: blockchain-enabled community power*, http://www.power-technology.com/features/featurethe-brooklyn-microgrid-blockchain-enabled-community-power-5783564/

[13] Orsini, L. (April 18th 2017), *Industry Impact: Peer-to-Peer Energy Transactions, presentation Principal and Founder*, LO3 Energy at the Business of Blockchain conference http://events.technologyreview.com/video/watch/lawrence-orsini-lo3-industry-impact/

[14] Don Tapscott (2018), *Why Data is the Key to Democratizing Energy*, https://www.youtube.com/watch?v=R53f9f8EsbQ

[15] http://www.peci.org/

[16] https://www.clearesult.com/

[17] Spurlock, C. (December 6th 2017), *Hurricane Sandy New York City Power Outage Map: Thousands Without Electricity In Metro Area*, Huffington Post, https://www.huffingtonpost.com/2012/10/31/hurricane-sandy-new-york-city-power-outage-map_n_2050380.html

[18] https://www.crunchbase.com/funding_round/lo3-energy-series-unknown--6ea0ed61#section-overview

[19] https://lo3energy.com/bnef-new-energy-pioneers-winner/

[20] https://lo3energy.com/press/

[21] Orsini, L. (April 18th 2017), *Industry Impact: Peer-to-Peer Energy Transactions, presentation Principal and Founder*, LO3 Energy at the Business of Blockchain conference http://events.technologyreview.com/video/watch/lawrence-orsini-lo3-industry-impact/

[22] LO3 Energy (2018), Exergy Business White Paper, https://exergy.energy/wp-content/uploads/2018/04/Exergy-BIZWhitepaper-v10.pdf

[23] Personal interview with Mary Lacity in 2017

[24] Personal interview with Mary Lacity in 2017

[25] https://vimeo.com/195896508

[26] Personal interview with Mary Lacity

[27] http://microgridmedia.com/its-like-the-early-days-of-the-internet-blockchain-based-brooklyn-microgrid-tests-p2p-energy-trading/

[28] http://microgridmedia.com/its-like-the-early-days-of-the-internet-blockchain-based-brooklyn-microgrid-tests-p2p-energy-trading/

[29] Personal interview with Mary Lacity

[30] Personal interview with Mary Lacity

[31] Googlemaps https://www.google.com/maps/@40.6844854,-73.98659,13z

[32] Personal Interview with Mary Lacity.

[33] *Local Renewable Energy Now*. https://www.change.org/p/john-b-rhodes-the-nys-public-service-commission-local-renewable-energy-now?signed=true

[34] Maloney, P. (October 18, 2019), *Brooklyn Microgrid Launches Campaign to Create Regulatory Sandbox*, https://microgridknowledge.com/brooklyn-microgrid-regulatory-sandbox/

[35] Maloney, P. (December 30, 2019), *Brooklyn Microgrid Moves Ahead with Pilot Regulatory Sandbox for Program*, https://microgridknowledge.com/brooklyn-microgrid-regulatory-sandbox-approved/

[36] Orsini, L. (April 18th 2017), *Industry Impact: Peer-to-Peer Energy Transactions, presentation Principal and Founder*, LO3 Energy at the Business of Blockchain conference, http://events.technologyreview.com/video/watch/lawrence-orsini-lo3-industry-impact/

[37] https://www.sacramento.energy/

[38] https://lo3energy.com/first-us-marketplace-for-locally-produced-clean-energy-launched-by-lo3-energy-and-green-mountain-power/

[39] Financial Review (October 2017), *LO3 to trial peer-to-peer energy sharing in South Australia*, http://www.afr.com/business/energy/lo3-energy-to-trial-peertopeer-energy-sharing-in-south-australia-20171010-gyxw3s#ixzz53VrCB6MY

[40] LO3 Energy Press Release (November 17th 2017), *US start-up LO3 Energy begins two German projects*, https://lo3energy.com/us-start-lo3-energy-begins-two-german-projects/

[41] https://lo3energy.com/eldesign-forest-energy-and-lo3-energy-launch-first-local-solar-energy-trading-market/

[42] De, N. (December 13th 2017), *Blockchain Startup LO3 Partners With Power Exchange*, Coindesk, https://www.coindesk.com/blockchain-startup-lo3-partners-power-exchange/

[43] Personal interview with Mary Lacity

[44] Orsini, L. (September 25, 2019), *Why blockchain can turn Distributed Energy Resources from a big threat to massive opportunity for utilities*, https://energycentral.com/c/pip/why-blockchain-can-turn-distributed-energy-resources-big-threat-massive?utm_medium=eNL&utm_campaign=pulse&utm_content=0&utm_source=2019_09_30

[45] https://lo3energy.com/pando/

[46] Falls, A. (Oct 18 2016), *State Change #31-Martin Lundfall*, Cotricity, https://media.consensys.net/state-change-31-martin-lundfall-co-tricity-cd08ae5a40de

EWF (Oct 2018), *The Energy Web Chain* ; https://www.energyweb.org/

Reed, A. (Feb 2018), *P2P Energy Trading on the Blockchain* https://medium.com/wolverineblockchain/p2p-energy-trading-on-the-blockchain-db61fa2c8caf

Daisee Project Details https://hackaday.io/project/10879-2016-internets-of-energy-call-me-daisee/details

[47] https://www.powerledger.io/

[48] Orsini, L. (September 17, 2019), *How to escape the Valley of Death*, https://lo3energy.com/how-to-escape-the-valley-of-death/

[49] Video from Innogy, https://youtu.be/uJx79G2Zmyo

[50] https://innovationhub.innogy.com/

[51] Jentzsch, S. (April 30, 2017), *Share&Charge Smart Contracts: the Technical Angle*, https://blog.slock.it/share-charge-smart-contracts-the-technical-angle-58b93ce80f15

[52] https://shareandcharge.com/en/

[53] https://etherscan.io/token/0x8262a2a5c61A45Aa074cbeeDE42c808D15ea3ceD

[54] https://etherscan.io/address/0x61c810e21659032084a4448d8d2f498789f81cb5

[55] https://etherscan.io/address/0xf4d9d65481352C3Afd0750B46FbE0462eb29206d

[56] Jentzsch, S. (April 30, 2017), *Share&Charge Smart Contracts: the Technical Angle*, https://blog.slock.it/share-charge-smart-contracts-the-technical-angle-58b93ce80f15

[57] https://shareandcharge.com/wp-content/uploads/2020/03/OCN-1.0-Documentation.pdf

[58] Share&Charge Oslo2Rome Tour, November 27 to November 30, 2017. https://shareandcharge.com/oslo-2-rome/

[59] https://shareandcharge.com/uk-pilot/ Share&Charge Foundation. https://shareandcharge.com/wp-content/uploads/2019/12/ShareCharge-Partner-Program.pdf

[60] https://shareandcharge.com/in-car-wallet/

[61] https://shareandcharge.com/in-car-wallet/

[62] Zaheer, H. (April 25th, 2018), *P2P Vehicle Charging: Is blockchain a driver of EV adoption?* Power Technology Research. https://powertechresearch.com/p2p-vehicle-charging-is-blockchain-a-driver-of-ev-adoption/

[63] *EY, How to lead the charge on crowdfunded EV infrastructure,* https://www.ey.com/en_kr/automotive-transportation/how-to-lead-the-charge-on-crowdfunded-ev-infrastructure

Chapter 7

Business Applications for Credentials

"37 percent of 'bad hires' are the result of credential or skill misrepresentation."

PwC Research[1]

"The public is not ready to have self-sovereign identity to completely run credentials on a blockchain. There is value in blockchain, at least right now, of not putting personal data on a blockchain, but still having the benefits of knowing trusted institutions have done the certifications."

Dave Wengel, Founder and CEO of iDatafy[2]

7.1. Overview of identity and credentials

Thus far in this book, we have examined numerous blockchain platforms and applications that are marching us towards an 'Internet of Value'. However, as of 2020, the current state of blockchains is still missing universal components to realize the full vision. We are still missing the full power of individual self-sovereignty over our own identities and credentials and a truly user-friendly experience across blockchain platforms. Many organizations, consortia, and standards-making bodies are working on self-sovereign identity (SSI) and interoperability. In the future, individuals, organizations, and objects will be able to declare seamlessly their identities and credentials to any other individuals, organizations, or objects that require verification across blockchain solutions.

Until then, *issuers* own and control the claims they make about *subjects*, who could be individuals, organizations, or objects (such as vehicles, parts, or produce):

- Issuers control the claims they make about *individuals'* credentials, including *attributes* like birthdate, gender, height, and hair color; *entitlements* like citizenship, medical benefits, and membership rewards; and *certifications* like college degrees and technical training.

- Issuers control the claims they make about *organizations* pertaining to *attributes* like incorporation date, incorporation jurisdiction, industry type; *entitlements* like tax status and minority-owned business; and *certifications* like LEED certification level.

- Issuers control the claims they make about *objects* pertaining to *attributes* like physical dimensions and composition; *entitlements* like access rights for self-driving cars and drones; and *certifications* like fit-for-use, organic, energy-efficient, or sustainably produced.

When a *verifier*—which could be an individual, organization, or object—requests verification of a credential, they rely on the issuer's evidence for proof. For example, when HR manager Bob (verifier) wants Alice (subject) to prove she earned her college degree, Alice must contact her alma mater (issuer) and request an official transcript. For individuals, the consequences of issuers owning and controlling their credentials include threats to privacy; threats of surveillance capitalism where issuers use our data for profit; and threats of identity theft since issuers are often targets of hackers.[3] Even if all issuers were ethical and even if their cybersecurity was impenetrable, individuals still end up trying to manage relationships with hundreds of issuers through accounts and passwords.

After the 'Internet of Value', the locus of access and management will shift from issuers to subjects. Issuers will still provide (or rescind) the credentials, but those credentials will be stored on a shared registry (i.e. a digital ledger) were subjects have access to them and may decide whether to grant or deny access to verifiers (see Figure 7.1).

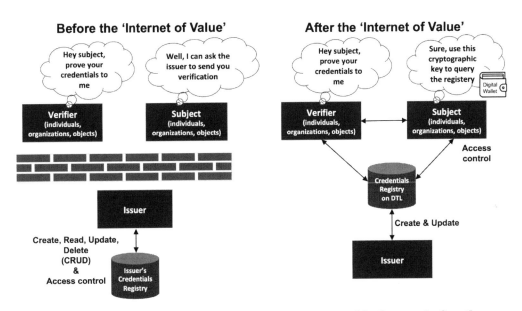

Figure 7.1: From centralized to decentralized control before and after the 'Internet of Value'

According to Alex Preukschat and Drummond Reed, authors of *Decentralized Digital Identity and Verifiable Credentials: Self-Sovereign Identity*, there are three adoption challenges to SSI as of 2020:

1. An interoperable ecosystem has not yet been established

2. People still need offline access when they do not have Internet or cell phone access

3. Individuals are not ready for decentralized key management

Concerning this last point, only a small proportion of the global population has the technical abilities to secure and manage their own private cryptographic keys. Therefore, for now, many individuals still will rely on a trusted third party to manage their private cryptographic keys for them.[4] For example, many of us allow exchanges to manage our cryptocurrency keys.

So, if SSI is still in the future, what blockchain-enabled solutions can be delivered today to give individuals access and management over their credentials without the risks of them mismanaging their keys? In this chapter, we present the case study of iDatafy's SmartResume, a digital resume where issuers create an individual's credentials, but individuals control access rights to their own resume; iDatafy serves as a neutral third party to protect cryptographic keys for users. The SmartResume platform is more than just a certified digital resume, it is a job acquisition platform that matches qualified job seekers with hiring organizations (see Table 7.1).

Enterprise	Enterprise Type(s)	Blockchain Application	Status as of 2020
iDatafy's Smart Resume	SME convened a consortium of credentialing and hiring organizations	Verified credentials, digital resume and job acquisition platform	Platform launched, primarily with Arkansas-based credentialing organizations, hiring organizations and individuals.

Table 7.1: Blockchain application example for credentials

Before presenting the SmartResume solution, we must first understand the talent acquisition challenges it's designed to overcome

7.2. Talent acquisition challenges

Despite all of the advanced Human Resource (HR) practices, investments, and technology innovations, we have yet to solve adequately this talent acquisition problem: *How can we create a trustworthy job market that efficiently matches qualified job seekers with hiring organizations?* Peter Cappelli, the George W. Taylor Professor of Management at the Wharton School and director of the Center for Human Resources, summed up the challenge nicely in a 2018 Harvard Business Review article:

"Businesses have never done as much hiring as they do today. They've never spent as much money doing it. And they've never done a worse job of it."[5]

Today's talent acquisition solutions include hundreds of job market and social media platforms like CareerBuilder, Indeed, LinkedIn, and Monster. According to one study, social media is now the most-used channel for recruitment efforts: 77 percent of recruiters used LinkedIn in 2018, followed by Facebook (63 percent) and Instagram (35 percent).[6] While such solutions do have the advantages of convenience and scale, they equally frustrate job seekers and recruiters. Distrust happens on both sides of the market. Specifically, recruiters doubt applicants' self-reported credentials and skills, while job seekers distrust that hiring companies and platforms keep their data private and select applicants in an unbiased manner. All of these misgivings are warranted.

Many applicants inflate their skills or make fraudulent claims on their resumes

Job sites and social media platforms do not verify credentials. Subsequently, fraud and inflated resumes remain problematic. A recent survey found that 75 percent of employers caught applicants lying on their resumes.[7] One of the most common frauds is claiming a university degree that was not earned. One high-profile example: the CEO of Yahoo was ousted after someone uncovered that he had not earned the computer science degree he claimed.[8] 'Diploma mills' are another problem in the US, because they award degrees with little or no academic study.[9] Consequently, hiring companies spend significant resources to investigate a job candidate's claims. Verification slows down the process and increases costs. On average, it costs companies $4,129 per hire, but costs can be as high as $40,000 per position for highly skilled workers.[10,11] Moreover, honest job applicants grow weary of the assumption of duplicity.

Hiring organizations and recruiters struggle with selection bias

Social media and many job site platforms reveal people's race; gender; age; religion; affiliations; and life-style choices; and recruiters may (in)advertently dismiss candidates based on this data rather than based on their qualifications. Some large companies have turned to artificial intelligence (AI) to modernize recruitment, but so far results did little to reduce biases. For example, Amazon's AI recruiting tool was designed to search for keywords based on past engineering candidates' resumes. Since most engineers were male in the past, the AI tool learned to prefer male applicants. Amazon abandoned the tool after the gender bias was revealed.[12] Social media, job site platforms, and AI tools are not the only sources of selection bias; relying on referrals from current employees creates a homogeneous applicant pool because people tend to refer people who are similar to them.[13]

Data privacy protection is another concern for all parties

Hiring organizations—particularly those 60 percent of companies that outsource recruiting—need to make sure applicant data is properly handled. In the US, for example, the Family Educational Rights and Privacy Act (FERPA) protects the privacy of student education records. Generally, schools must have written permission from the parent or eligible student before releasing any information about a student's education record.[14] Increasingly, data privacy regulations like the European Union's General Data Protection Regulation (GDPR) and California Consumer Privacy Act (CCPA) have increased data protection more broadly.[15,16] Despite these regulations, many job sites and recruiters routinely collect information on applicants like email addresses, phone numbers, age, ethnicity, photos, and other personal information.[17]

The scale of the job acquisition challenges is huge. According to the United States Department of Labor, there were 70 million job hires in the US in 2019.[18] On average, there were 250 applications for each corporate job listing, suggesting that hiring organizations processed at least 17 billion applications.[19] Furthermore, the process does not always end successfully; 6.4 million job openings went unfilled in 2019.[20] Isn't it time to re-invent job acquisition? iDatafy thinks so, and subsequently developed the SmartResume solution to restore trust in the job search process.

7.3. SmartResume

iDatafy, a company founded by David Wengel in Little Rock, Arkansas in 2011, created the SmartResume platform and career network to instill trust in the talent acquisition process. The platform prevents fraudulent claims by applicants, eliminates selection bias, and ensures data privacy compliance. The SmartResume platform is similar to LinkedIn or Upwork, but with *verified* credentials secured by blockchain technology. Wengel's vision is to make the SmartResume platform, *"the world's most trusted resume and certified career network."*

To launch the career network, iDatafy focused on its home base in Arkansas. It assembled a consortium of credentialing organizations, individuals, and hiring organizations to help develop the solution. The pilot project launched with the first credentialing organization, the Sam M. Walton College of Business at the University of Arkansas, in 2018. Within 18 months, the consortium included the University of Arkansas System at Fayetteville; Little Rock; Fort Smith; Community College at Morrilton; *e*Versity and Pulaski Technical. A number of other higher education institutions outside the UA System have signed on as well, with official announcements forthcoming.

Here we describe the consortium, platform, development journey, competition, and lessons learned.

7.3.1. SmartResume consortium

iDatafy convened a consortium of credentialing organizations, individuals, and hiring companies.

Credentialing organizations

Credentialing organizations are institutions that award credentials, such as colleges; universities; trade schools; professional associations; licensing bureaus; and government organizations. In the SmartResume platform, credentialing organizations create a SmartResume on behalf of an individual by certifying educational degrees; coursework;

honors; activities; awards; experiences; licenses; affiliations; research; skills; reference letters; or other certifications. The certifications appear on an individual's SmartResume as a tamperproof badge that is secured by blockchain technology (see Figure 7.2).

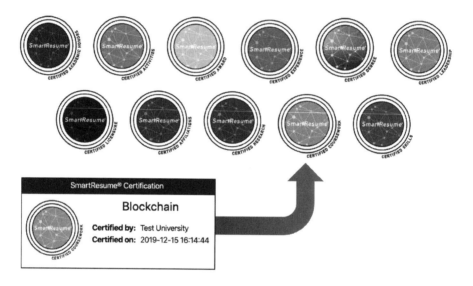

Figure 7.2: Example of SmartResume®'s certified badges
Each certification is secured on a tamper-proof ledger stored on a blockchain

As a key design decision, credentialing organizations choose the name and type of credential. This way, credentialing organizations gain value by promoting their brand. For example, the Walton College chose 'Leadership Walton' as one of its credentials. Leadership Walton is a professional development program for undergraduate business students, offering them a unique blend of academic, leadership, and career development opportunities specifically designed to guide them toward lifelong professional success.[21]

By putting credentialing organizations in control, the SmartResume platform prevents users from claiming credentials they did not earn, thus protecting the organization's brand. They also gain efficiencies by credentialing a person *once*, rather than re-affirming credentials every time a person changes employment. For educational institutions, an additional benefit of joining the SmartResume platform is that it serves as a meaningful way to connect with alumni. For workforce skill certifiers—such as organizations that train and certify truck drivers; steamfitters, pipefitters, sprinkler systems installers; and heating, ventilation, and air conditioning (HVAC) technicians—the platform provides better access for hiring companies to find qualified talent.

Individuals

Individuals like students, alumni, current job holders, and job seekers cannot launch their own SmartResumes. Rather, a credentialing organization must do so on the individual's behalf. However, individuals must opt in to the SmartResume platform; if an individual does not activate their SmartResume, it is not accessible by any third party. Individuals who activate their resumes can supplement their personal SmartResume with additional information, such as career objectives, hobbies, and interests. Hiring organizations can ascertain which credentials were verified by credentialing organizations by the presence of the blockchain badge and which entries were added by individuals. Each individual gets one SmartResume, which may contain verified credentials from many different organizations. Individuals are in control of their job matching preferences and may grant or deny full access rights to particular hiring organizations. Individuals do not have to pay to participate on the platform.

Hiring organizations

Hiring organizations include any institution searching for qualified employees. Hiring organizations (or outsourced recruiters) search for qualified candidates based only on their skills, as all demographic and personal information like name and gender are masked to prevent search bias. Figure 7.3 depicts a sample resume as it would appear to a hiring organization. If an organization is interested in connecting to an individual, the platform sends the individual an email request. Hiring organizations gain efficiencies by having a qualified applicant pool, and they no longer have to call each organization on a candidate's resume to verify credentials. Hiring companies pay to use the platform.

SmartResume®

A Resume You Can Trust.™

| Employers | Educator Institutions | Workforce Skill Certifiers | Individuals |

SmartResume JOB APPLICANT IDATIFIER™ A46B89BZM48X

EDUCATION

Bachelor of Science in Business Administration Finance
University of Arkansas, Fayetteville, AR
Expected Graduation Date: May 2020

Honors Program GPA 3.75/4.0
Dean's List - Fall 2017 and Spring 2018

EXPERIENCE

Investment and Insurance Compliance Assistant
Arvest Asset Management, Fayetteville, AR
January 2018 - Present

- Member of the AIC Arvest Insurance team for AAM, a brokerage firm branch or Arvest Bank
- Maintained licensure files for all Arvest Insurance Agents
- Assisted with new and renewed agent appointments with insurance companies
- Performed other managerial and secretarial duties such as faxing, scanning, telephone communication with agents and companies

Orientation Leader/Mentor, Office of First Year Experience
University of Arkansas, Fayetteville, AR, May 2017 - December 2017

- Assisted with the on-going planning, implementation, and evaluation of new student orientation
- Worked as a paraprofessional in presenting and distributing information to new students and guests
- Initiated and develop open communication and interaction with students and guests
- Served as a positive role model and ambassador on behalf of the University of Arkansas

Course Reserve Assistant, Mullins Library
University of Arkansas, Fayetteville, AR, September 2016 - May 2017

- Scanned for electronic reserves, gaining proficiency with Adobe software
- Prepared usage reports of electronic reserves
- Facilitated on-going communication with professors about individual needs for reserves
- Trained new employees on software and procedure

— — —>

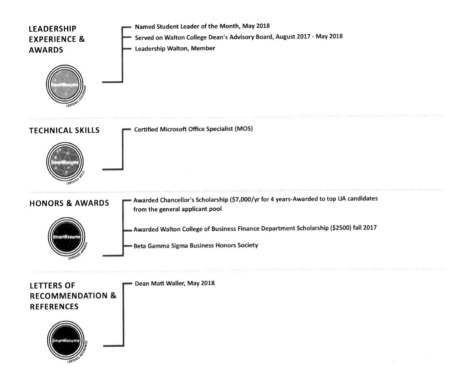

LEADERSHIP EXPERIENCE & AWARDS
- Named Student Leader of the Month, May 2018
- Served on Walton College Dean's Advisory Board, August 2017 - May 2018
- Leadership Walton, Member

TECHNICAL SKILLS
- Certified Microsoft Office Specialist (MOS)

HONORS & AWARDS
- Awarded Chancellor's Scholarship ($7,000/yr for 4 years-Awarded to top UA candidates from the general applicant pool
- Awarded Walton College of Business Finance Department Scholarship ($2500) fall 2017
- Beta Gamma Sigma Business Honors Society

LETTERS OF RECOMMENDATION & REFERENCES
- Dean Matt Waller, May 2018

**Figure 7.3: Opposite and above – An example of a SmartResume®
as viewed by a hiring organization**

7.3.2. The SmartResume Platform

The SmartResume platform is a hybrid platform that includes a web-based interface, traditional technologies, and a permissioned blockchain ledger. Andy Griebel, Chief Technology Officer (CTO), explained:

"We selected a hybrid solution. Blockchain technology provides the ability for multiple parties to verify and trust that credentials are valid. But it would be a mistake to build the entire solution on a blockchain because it would be sluggish."

From a user perspective, all of these components are seamless. People maneuver through the platform based on their roles, such as employers, educational institutions, workforce skill certifiers, and individuals. The user interface is constantly evolving and improving, but Figure 7.4 shows an example of an individual resume holder's view as of March 2020.

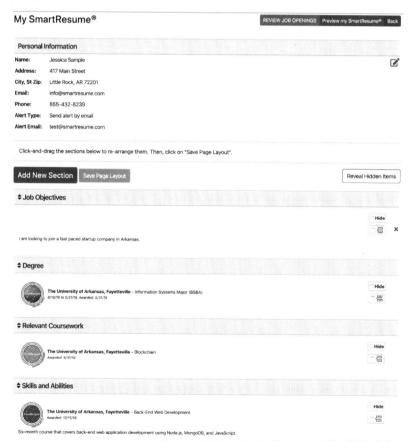

Figure 7.4: Screenshot for SmartResume® holders as of March 2020

Behind the user interface, iDatafy chose a hybrid solution to take advantage of the features for which blockchain technologies and traditional technologies are best suited.

Blockchain technology was selected to create a tamper-proof audit trail of verified credentials in a multi-party environment. Traditional databases were selected for high performance and scalability processes, such as searching for jobs and job candidates, enhancing SmartResumes with supplemental information, mapping credentials to Standard Occupation Codes, and protecting personal information.

iDatafy chose a permissioned blockchain where joining the network is by invitation-only and where only authorized members validate transactions. In 2018, iDatafy examined several permissioned blockchains, but ultimately selected Hyperledger Fabric. iDatafy felt it had the most maturity and momentum at the time. However, iDatafy could switch platforms if a superior technology emerges. Andy Griebel, iDatafy's CTO said:

"Our design is flexible; we could pivot to another platform if we needed to."

To comply with privacy regulations, no personal information is stored on the blockchain ledger. Instead, each SmartResume is associated with a unique Job Applicant Idatafier™. iDatafy only stores a minimum of information on the blockchain ledger associated with each credential, including the unique Job Applicant Idatafier™, credentialing organization, certification type, date, and timestamp.

Griebel offered this analogy about the value of a blockchain:

"Think of a blockchain as nothing more than a receipt that is validated by everybody who has touched it."

7.3.3. SmartResume's development journey

The first time Dave Wengel searched for "certified digital resumes", back in 2017, he was shocked to find zero results. Why hadn't anyone built a multi-credentialed resume? Wengel thinks it's because *"there's no value if you do not have a consortium."* He began to envision the solution and, based on his company's experiences, he knew building a consortium would be the key to success.

iDatafy's first product was ***LeadReview®***, a proprietary data consortium used to detect bad marketing leads. The solution was launched at the end of 2011 and has since processed more than 100 million queries. The company's second data consortium, **StudentReview®**, was developed in 2012 to detect student financial aid fraud in the US. The context was very similar to the job acquisition process in that the market for financial aid was subject to deception and mistrust. Many individuals with no intention of attending college were signing up for US Federal government financial student aid (called 'Pell grants') and would drop out immediately after receiving the money, enroll elsewhere, and repeat the deceit. In some cases, criminals organized into rings that recruited 'straw students' by promising them a share of the grant money. By 2011, criminals were swindling billions of dollars each year from the US federal government. iDatafy researched the problem and discovered that the individuals re-used the same contact information (like home addresses) to receive the checks. iDatafy created a consortium of higher education institutions to build and share a FERPA-compliant directory data about the students who habitually drop out and try to enroll in multiple schools. The StudentReview platform automatically analyzes the data and flags instances where contact information is duplicated. The system alerts colleges and universities when a new applicant has dropped out of other schools after receiving financial aid.[22]

The LeadReview, StudentReview, and SmartResume solutions are similar in that they aim to reestablish trust in markets. Each context also requires a consortium to build an ecosystem solution. To build a successful consortium, iDatafy developed a three-phased process called '**crawl, walk, run**'. We illustrate the process with the SmartResume consortium.

The Crawl Phase

Every consortium needs a first organizational adopter, preferably a prominent member of the target ecosystem that will help attract additional adopters through mimetic influences. For the SmartResume project, Wengel approached Matt Waller, Dean of the Sam M. Walton College of Business, University of Arkansas, to become the first consortium member. Wengel said:

"I had just attended the Walton College's first Blockchain for Business Conference in April of 2018, and I immediately connected the dots."

Wengel did not personally know Waller but sent him a note on the project after the conference. The Walton College was just about to launch the Blockchain Center of Excellence (BCoE), and Waller was looking for a blockchain project where the college could help lead in the development and implementation of an actual solution. Moreover, the SmartResume context of credentialing students seemed a perfect fit:

"If you think about it, colleges and universities have been issuing diplomas and transcripts for hundreds of years, but they have never actually issued certified resumes to their students, despite the colleges being in a position as a trusted authority to do so."

Matthew Waller, dean of the Sam M. Walton College of Business, University of Arkansas, and first adopter of SmartResume[23]

Waller convened meetings with leaders within and across the Walton College to determine the university's role in the initiative, including the campus CIO; the vice chancellor for economic development; the founding director of the BCoE; the chair of the information systems department (ISYS); and the associate vice provost from the registrar's office. While most of the leaders were supportive of the idea, they were initially concerned about adding another major IT project given the campus was in the middle of an enterprise resource planning (ERP) replacement. They did not want to build an interface to pull student records from a system that was about to be replaced. Wengel listened to the feedback and suggested a pilot with 20 students so that it would add very little to the university's workload. iDatafy would do the heavy lifting.

In fall 2018, iDatafy joined the BCoE's advisory board; was a sponsor of the BCoE's Blockchain Hackathon; and met many students studying blockchain technologies. Also in fall, small SmartResume pilot programs began. The Walton College recruited 10 ISYS students and 10 ISYS alumni to volunteer to be the first individuals to receive smart resumes. The university registrar launched the volunteers' SmartResumes on the platform by verifying credentials, doing so manually, one student at a time. The volunteers then activated their SmartResumes and provided iDatafy with feedback. iDatafy learned that there were many more skills and activities that should be certified in addition to degree programs, including the aforementioned Leadership Walton. Dean Waller agreed to manually verify Leadership Walton participation and other non-transcript accomplishments to appear on the students' SmartResumes.

Pilots with other early adopters continued throughout the fall. By November 2018, 93 SmartResumes had been created across four partner schools. Through feedback gained during the pilot programs, the platform was continually improved. For example, hiring organizations that recruit on many campuses wondered if there was a better way to find talent given that universities award similar degree programs, but name them differently. For instance, an information systems degree at one school might be called Computer Information Systems; Management Information Systems; Information Technology; Business Information Technology; Business Computing; or Information Systems Engineering at other schools. iDatafy responded by creating a map of a certifier's credentials to the Standard Occupational Codes (SOCs) created by the US Department of Labor. The crawl phase was successful. According to Wengel:

> *"All initial higher education partners agree that they want to scale SmartResume further based on successful pilot input from recipients and employers expressing a need for new way to find talent."* [24]

The Walk Phase

The walk phase involved adding more consortium members, improving the platform, and moving from manual data collection and verification to automated processes.

To grow the consortium after it had enough grass-roots members, iDatafy targeted the centralized University of Arkansas System. In early 2019, Wengel approached Johnny Key, Cabinet Secretary of the Arkansas Department of Education, and Michael Moore, Vice President for Academic Affairs for the University of Arkansas System and Chief Academic and Operating Officer for the University of Arkansas System eVersity, about the initiative. Moore saw the value:

"A couple of things were appealing to me from the University of Arkansas System and eVersity perspective. The platform provides an opportunity to elevate some of our students attending schools that might not get attention from big corporate partners. Also, it's free to use for our students."

Moore invited Wengel to present the SmartResume project at the July 2019 meeting of the 26 university Chief Academic Officers from across Arkansas. After follow-up meetings, iDatafy signed one Memorandum of Understanding (MoU) for all University of Arkansas System public institutions of higher learning. Companies that recruit Arkansas talent also began showing interest in the consortium. One non-profit organization, for example, created the first workforce skills centric SmartResume. The Arkansas Economic Development Commission agreed to certify its 'Future Fit' manufacturing job skills certifications on the platform.

The walk phase improved the platform's onboarding process by automating large data pulls and asking the credentialing organization to verify the batch. The batch is then automatically uploaded onto the platform where it creates an opt-in SmartResume for each individual in the batch. By December 2019, 5,371 current and former Walton College students' SmartResumes were created. In addition to degrees and major, credentials were verified with badges for Leadership Walton; the Chancellor's Award; Beta Gamma Sigma (an exclusive business honor society); the Supply Chain Management Award; financial management/investment relevant coursework (based on minors and areas of concentration); and varsity cross-country team membership. This granularity allows hiring organizations to target their recruiting efforts. About 25,000 SmartResumes had been created (but not necessarily activated) by March 2020. Wengel said:

"For us to create a hundred thousand Smart Resumés right now is easier than creating five Smart Resumes a year ago,"

The walk phase will be completed by mid-2020.

The Run Phase

Wengel explained:

> *"By this point we hope to scale our initiative and automate all data certification processes, issuances, and job matching. We anticipate scaling nationally."*

Plans for 2020 include:

- Establish a long-term governance plan and engage partner schools to operate trust nodes in the network.

- Rapidly expand employer network within and beyond Arkansas.

While iDatafy clearly has the lead in Arkansas, we next explore the global competitive landscape for certified virtual resumes.

7.3.4. Competition

Massachusetts Institute of Technology (**MIT**) was one of the first major universities to issue a diploma on a blockchain. In 2017, 111 students were given a Blockcerts Wallet app with access to a verified, tamper-proof digital diploma with its hash stored on the Bitcoin blockchain.[25] One of the major lessons from the experiment was that users found it difficult to manage their own private keys.[26] To scale the app for live production, MIT engaged the vendor, Learning Machine. As of 2020, all recent MIT graduates receive a digital diploma in addition to a physical diploma. Students opt in to activate the digital diploma by clicking on an official MIT invitation email sent to all recent graduates. Students download the Blockcerts mobile app and add MIT as an issuer. The app generates a unique public key, which users can share with hiring organizations. Hiring organizations use the public key to verify credentials on the web portal, https://credentials.mit.edu/. The service is free.[27] According to Mary Callahan, senior associate dean and registrar at MIT:

> *"From the beginning, one of our primary motivations has been to empower students to be the curators of their own credentials."*[28]

One downside of the MIT model is that it only verifies credentials from one institution, namely MIT. If everyone adopted this model, users would be given multiple public keys and hiring organizations would need to go to multiple portals to verify a single candidate. For this reason, **Blockcerts** has continued to build an open source community (MIT is not actively involved) where a user may have multiple issuers. The Blockcerts community has developed versions that run Ethereum, Sovrin and Hyperledger.[29] The software is published under MIT Free and Open Source Software (FOSS) license. Institutions that have built their own credentialing solutions using the open source software include McMaster Engineering in Canada, Georgia Tech in the US, and Universidad Carlos III in Madrid. Rather than build a solution, institutions can also hire companies like Learning Machine, which continues to help institutions implement Blockcerts.[30] Customers include the Southern New Hampshire University, Republic of Malta, Federation of State Medical Boards (FSMB), and National Training Agency's (NTA) Workforce Preparedness Program in the Bahamas. Blockcerts is planning to add photo IDs and transcripts soon.[31] Most of these, as Wengel notes, are verifying credentials, but not building smart resumes.

Our online research at the BCoE did not find any direct competitors, particularly within the Arkansas market. UK-based **APPII** was a company we found offering something similar to SmartResume, but for another market and with a different approach that is driven by individuals rather than by credentialing organizations. APPII provides a multi-credentialing service for a blockchain verified Curriculum Vitae (CV) (a CV is the UK term for resume).[32] Rather than build a career network consortium like iDatafy, APPII partnered with a job placement platform, TechnoJobs.[33] We also found other companies that store blockchain credentials on the Bitcoin network, including **Accredible** and **Credly**.[34] Canadian-based TerraHub Technologies created **Credential Wallet** for post-secondary credentials, and is working with PwC Canada.[35]

Large job posting platforms and large software companies are the most likely potential competitors (or perhaps partners) for iDatafy. They have global networks of hiring organizations and individuals but need to figure out how to verify credentials and to create individual resumes. Regarding the competition, Dave Wengel, founder and CEO, iDatafy said:

"Obviously, there are people out there doing blockchain diplomas, blockchain transcripts, and blockchain credential matching. No one has, to our knowledge, anywhere in the world, built a certified resume. Even if someone were to copy what we are doing, we know is how difficult it is to build a community"

7.4. Conclusion

The blockchain applications in Part II aimed to capture a wide-range of blockchain application use cases. But even with detailed examples, we are still missing important use cases across other industries, such as governments; insurance; healthcare; education; retail; media; and gaming. In particular, governments have huge opportunities to better manage identities, elections, registrations, and titles.

Technical and business maturity is needed to move more POCs from innovation labs to market. In general, technical challenges are the domain of protocols and code bases in our blockchain application framework, and business challenges are in the domain of use cases (see Figure 7.5). In the next chapter, we'll explore the technical challenges and emerging solutions. In Chapter 9, we'll address the business domain by specifying mindshifts, strategies and action principles to deploy live applications.

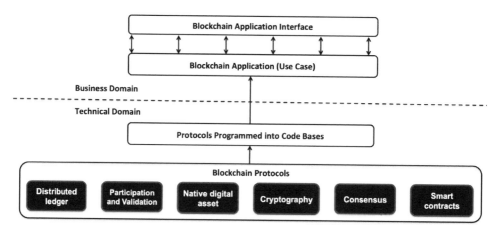

Figure 7.5: Business and technical domains of a blockchain application

Citations

[1] Ledger Insights (2019). PwC launches blockchain credentialing solution, https://www.ledgerinsights.com/pwc-blockchain-smart-credentials/

[2] Quote from Lacity, M. (2020), *Re-inventing Talent Acquisition: The SmartResume® Solution*, Blockchain Center of Excellence Case Study Series, BCoE 2020-01, University of Arkansas.

[3] Zuboff, S. (2019). *The Age of Surveillance Capitalism: The Fight for a Human Future at the New Frontier of Power*. New York: PublicAffairs.

[4] Preukschat, A. and Reed, D. (2020) *Decentralized Digital Identity and Verifiable Credentials: Self-Sovereign Identity*, Manning Publications, Version 2.

[5] Cappelli, P. (2019), 'Your Approach to Hiring is All Wrong', *Harvard Business Review*, https://hbr.org/2019/05/recruiting

[6] Jobvite (2018), *Recruiter National Survey*, https://www.jobvite.com/wp-content/uploads/2018/11/2018-Recruiter-Nation-Study.pdf

[7] CareerBuilder (2017), *75 percent of HR Managers Have Caught a Lie on a Resume*, http://press.careerbuilder.com/2017-09-14-75-of-HR-Managers-Have-Caught-a-Lie-on-a-Resume-According-to-a-New-CareerBuilder-Survey

[8] Pepitone, J. (May 14, 2012), 'Yahoo confirms CEO is out after resume scandal' *CNNMoney*. https://money.cnn.com/2012/05/13/technology/yahoo-ceo-out/

[9] In 2005, the US Department of Education launched the 'Database of Accredited Postsecondary Institutions and Programs' to combat the spread of fraudulent degrees.

[10] Turczynski, B. (January 9, 2020), *2020 HR Statistics: Job Search, Hiring, Recruiting & Interviews*, Zety, https://zety.com/blog/hr-statistics#job-search-statistics

[11] National Student Clearing House (2016), *The real cost of academic fraud*, https://nscverifications.org/wp-content/uploads/2016/06/CostOfAcademicFraud.pdf

[12] Hamilton, I. (October 10, 2018), *Amazon built an AI tool to hire people but had to shut it down because it was discriminating against women*, Business Insider, https://www.businessinsider.com/amazon-built-ai-to-hire-people-discriminated-against-women-2018-10

[13] Fatemi, F. (October 31, 2019), 'How AI is Uprooting Recruiting', *Forbes,* https://www.forbes.com/sites/falonfatemi/2019/10/31/how-ai-is-uprooting-recruiting/#43c6540f46ce

[14] Family Educational Rights and Privacy Act (FERPA). US Department of Education, https://www2.ed.gov/policy/gen/guid/fpco/ferpa/index.html

[15] European Union, *Complete guide to GDPR compliance*, https://gdpr.eu/

[16] *California Consumer Privacy Act (CCPA)*, https://oag.ca.gov/privacy/ccpa

[17] Smits, J. (2018), *Privacy in recruitment—Securing your candidate's data*, https://cammio.com/blog/privacy-in-recruitment/

[18] US Bureau of Labor Statistics (February 11, 2020), *Job Openings and Labor Turnover Summary*, Report USDL-20-0243. https://www.bls.gov/news.release/jolts.nr0.htm

[19] Turczynski, B. (January 9, 2020), *2020 HR Statistics: Job Search, Hiring, Recruiting & Interviews*, Zety, https://zety.com/blog/hr-statistics#job-search-statistics

[20] US Bureau of Labor Statistics (February 11, 2020), *Job Openings and Labor Turnover Summary*, Report USDL-20-0243. https://www.bls.gov/news.release/jolts.nr0.htm

[21] Leadership Walton. https://walton.uark.edu/career/leadership-walton.php

[22] Wengel, D. (2012), *A Proactive Stand Against Financial Aid Fraud*, iDatafy white paper.

[23] Quote from Adkison, M. (February 18, 2020), *U of A Partners with Blockchain Company for Innovative Resume-Building Program*, https://walton.uark.edu/insights/smart-resume.php

[24] Quote from Adkison, M. (February 18, 2020), *U of A Partners with Blockchain Company for Innovative Resume-Building Program*, https://walton.uark.edu/insights/smart-resume.php

[25] Jones, B. (October 19th, 2017), *MIT Has Started Issuing Diplomas Using Blockchain Technology*, Futurism, https://futurism.com/mit-has-started-issuing-diplomas-using-blockchain-technology

[26] MIT Media Lab (June 2, 2016), *What we learned from designing an academic certificates system on the blockchain*, Medium, https://medium.com/mit-media-lab/what-we-learned-from-designing-an-academic-certificates-system-on-the-blockchain-34ba5874f196#.4m4bmwcm0

[27] *Digital Diplomas*, MIT Registrar's Office, https://registrar.mit.edu/transcripts-records/digital-diplomas

[28] Sundararajan, S. (October 20, 2017), *100 Diplomas: MIT Issues Graduate Certificates on a Blockchain App*, Coindesk, https://www.coindesk.com/100-diplomas-mit-issues-graduate-certificates-on-a-blockchain-app

Drawdy, R. (January 21, 2019), *MIT Offers Digital Diplomas in the Blockchain*, Helix Education, https://www.helixeducation.com/resources/uncategorized/mit-offers-digital-diplomas-blockchain/

[29] https://www.blockcerts.org/

[30] Smolenski, N. (May 14, 2018), *Top 10 Reasons to Use Blockcerts*, https://medium.com/learning-machine-blog/top-10-reasons-to-use-blockcerts-ec7d29f2712c

[31] https://www.learningmachine.com/

[32] https://appii.io/

[33] Chaudhary, M. (November 29, 2017), *TechnoJobs and APPII Partners to Create Blockchain-verified Career Profile*, HR Technologist, https://www.hrtechnologist.com/news/recruitment-onboarding/techno-jobs-and-apii-partners-to-create-blockchain-verified-career-profile/

[34] https://help.accredible.com/what-are-blockchain-credentials

https://resources.credly.com/blockchain

[35] https://www.terrahub.ca/news/2018/8/3/industrial-blockchain-credential-wallet

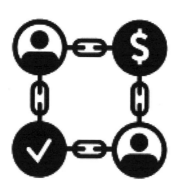

PART III

Road to Maturity

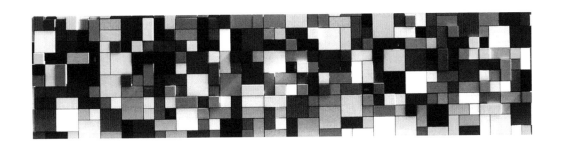

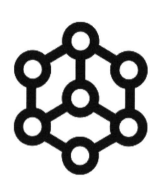

Chapter 8

Technical Challenges and Emerging Solutions

"There still remain those tech challenges, but those will probably be some of the more quickly resolved challenges, whereas a lot of the other ones such as regulatory challenges, challenges in collaboration, those are the ones that are probably going to take a lot longer for adoption."

John Burnett, Co-Founder of Omniex[1]

"I am less worried about the technology. Although the technology is not mature, it is less of a problem than standards and regulations."

Nilesh Vaidya, SVP Head of Banking &
Capital Market Solutions at Capgemini[2]

"I think that there is effective forward motion in the resolution and the ability to address some of the technical challenges that exist."

Eamonn Maguire, Global Lead, Blockchain Services, KPMG[3]

[4]

8.1. Introduction

Blockchain code is still considered nascent, with perhaps the exception of Bitcoin, which has been deployed since 2009. There are significant technical challenges pertaining to the massive resource consumption for certain protocols; security; performance and scalability; anonymity for public blockchains; confidentiality for private blockchains; and interoperability. This chapter examines all of these challenges and their emerging solutions.

Before adoption, enterprises need to ensure the technologies are 'enterprise ready' in that the software is secure enough and ready to handle the volume, speed, and confidentiality requirements for enterprise applications. Fortunately, people from around the world are collaborating to address these technical challenges for both permissionless and permissioned blockchains. As the quotes above attest, nearly all the blockchain experts we spoke to view the technical challenges as manageable; the open source communities as well as private enterprises just need more time to identify, debate, and develop technical solutions. Managers in traditional enterprises certainly need to be aware of the technical challenges and should monitor the emerging solutions, which vary significantly between permissionless and permissioned blockchains. Technical issues also point to the skills enterprises need to start building today.

8.2. Resource consumption

"It's worth the price; a single security breech costs an average of $3.8 million"

Don and Alex Tapscott, authors of Blockchain Revolution[5]

Computers that run blockchain nodes consume resources in the form of electricity. The computational intensity of a given blockchain's consensus protocol is the main driver of resource consumption. Recalling from Chapter 3, Bitcoin and Ethereum use the safest, yet computationally most resource-demanding protocol called a Proof-of-Work. Bitcoin's first miners, back in 2009, could successfully compete for a block reward using their desktop computers. As Bitcoin's price skyrocketed, miners shifted to specialized hardware and shared computational power through mining pools. Specifically, Bitcoin requires an Application-Specific Integrated Circuit (ASIC). Ethereum mining requires a Graphics Processing Unit (GPU). Proof-of-Work is admittedly a resource hog for both of these public networks. In order to compete, large mining centers have been established (see Figure 8.1 for an example).

Figure 8.1: Bitcoin mining site in Bowden, Sweden

Source: https://coinscage.com/wp-content/uploads/2017/05/bitcoin-mining-farm-1.jpg

Digiconomist, a site that tracks blockchain energy consumption, calculated that by 2020, each Bitcoin transaction required 646 kilowatts of electricity; Ethereum used 30 kilowatts of electricity per transaction. On an annual basis, those figures equate to the energy required to power 7.1 million US households for Bitcoin and 700,000 US households for Ethereum.[6] As the quote from Don and Alex Tapscott suggests, many people believe that this expense if worthwhile in order to secure the blockchains. However, people are finding ways to reduce electricity costs.

Mining pools are incentivized to erect data centers near a low cost source of electricity. For this reason, large mining pools have sprung up in China, which control over 80 percent of the mining power over Bitcoin during the past few years. Czech Republic, Iceland, and Georgia (the country) are other popular mining sites due to cheap electricity.[7] Within the US, the price of electricity varies greatly across the 50 States. Louisiana has the lowest average cost of electricity for mining one Bitcoin, at $3,224 per bitcoin in 2018. Hawaii and Alaska were the most expensive at $9,483 and $7,059 per bitcoin respectively.[8]

Innovative solutions aim to make mining more affordable. For example, *EZ Blockchain* developed a solution that converts the natural gas flaring waste from drilling and refining into electricity to power cryptocurrency mining. EZ Blockchain uses portable gas electric generators to power mobile data centers (see Figure 8.2). The business model helps drilling and refining companies reduce CO_2 emissions while generating money from cryptocurrency mining. As of 2020, EZ Blockchain has delivered 13 mobile mining units, primarily in North Dakota.[9]

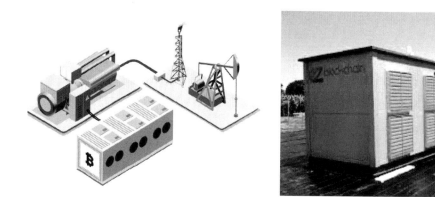

Figure 8.2: EZ Blockchain Mining

Source: https://www.ezblockchain.net/

Generators convert natural gas flaring to electricity to power portable data centers for mining cryptocurrencies.

Some public blockchains rely on less computationally intensive consensus algorithms compared to Proof-of-Work. For example, *Cardano* uses Proof-of-Stake and *EOS* uses Delegated Proof-of-Stake consensus protocols for public blockchains that consume much less energy. Permissioned blockchains rely on some form of Byzantine Fault Tolerance, which requires very little energy consumption—about as much energy as it takes to run an email server.

8.3. Security

"Centralized security doesn't work. We need secure, decentralized messaging so devices cannot be hacked."

Andre de Castro, CEO and Founder, Blockchain of Things[10]

"Blockchain presents a paradoxical situation when it comes to privacy and security. Blockchains are inherently secure with immutable transactions and hashing-based data-integrity. But most enterprises that I talk to have questions and concerns about confidentiality regarding who sees what. For real enterprise adoption of blockchain, we need to think about holistic security where it is not just a technical issue but a business challenge. In a lot of ways, it resembles the private versus public versus hybrid cloud debate."

Saurabh Gupta, Chief Strategy Officer, HfS Research[11]

One of blockchain's greatest selling points is heightened security over centralized systems that have single points of failure. In Chapter 3, we learned that blockchain applications still function properly even if a high percentage of nodes are faulty— or even malicious—promising unbeatable resiliency and 100 percent availability. If blockchains are so secure, why do we hear about so many heists and breaches? There are vulnerability points in today's blockchain technologies, particularly for digital wallets, code bases, smart contracts and the possibility of 51 percent attacks. Additionally, quantum computing poses a significant future security threat.

8.3.1. Digital wallet security

"Traditional companies will not want to use cryptocurrencies just to utilize blockchain's other features. Can you imagine trusting your IT department with a blockchain wallet full of private keys?"

Andre de Castro, CEO and Founder, Blockchain of Things[12]

Most heists on blockchains happen at the vulnerable access points of digital wallets where private keys are stored. As noted in Chapter 3, once a hacker steals a private key, he or she controls the asset and can easily transfer funds to another address. While users may store their digital wallets on their own devices, most users rely on centralized exchanges. Exchanges are a lucrative target for hackers because some exchanges control millions of private keys. We already covered one of the largest heists at *Mt. Gox*. But that was back in 2014. Jumping to 2019, there were twelve significant hacks of exchanges where $292 million worth of cryptocurrencies were stolen along with over 500,000 login credentials.[13] Among them was Singapore-based *Bittrue*, which was robbed of $5 million worth of Ripple and ADA (Cardano's coin). UK-based *Gatehub* lost $10 million worth of Ripple; and *Binance* lost $40 million worth of Bitcoin. Managers will naturally worry about the risk implications of these incidents, but risks can be mitigated. The largest crypto exchanges—Binance, *Coinbase* and *Gemini*—now have external or internal insurance to compensate users.

Lesson for managers: Enterprises will need to build or acquire new IT, cybersecurity, and cryptography skills to protect digital assets, particularly to protect private keys.

8.3.2. Code base security

Although much less frequent than the heists of private keys from digital wallets, many blockchains have had heists resulting from software weaknesses in the code base. These typically happen within the first year of launch when the code base is still very new.

The Bitcoin blockchain was hacked in August 2010 when someone exploited a software vulnerability to create 184 *billion* bitcoins, a highly suspicious act given the maximum money supply is only 21 *million* bitcoins.[14] A hacker of Ripple was able to transfer 1000 bitcoins from an address that had only .0001 bitcoins in 2014.[15] As software updates are implemented, new vulnerabilities could be introduced. For example, a serious bug in a Bitcoin Core update was discovered in 2018 that could have brought down the network with a denial-of-service attack, a type of malicious attack that floods a network with so many transactions that it disrupts service for legitimate users. Fortunately, the Bitcoin Core developers spotted it and fixed it before hackers could exploit it.[16] Although the source code was fixed quickly, these episodes offer an important warning.

> *Lesson for managers: enterprises will need software developers who understand how to build and test distributed applications.*

Since blockchain applications are distributed systems, enterprises will need to develop or attract talent capable of developing and testing decentralized applications ('DApps'). DApps offer benefits such as flexibility, transparency, and resiliency, but they are harder to test compared to traditional, centralized software. In particular, it's harder to identify computer programming logic errors (called 'bugs') in DApps. The enterprise will need software developers who can discover strange-sounding errors like mandelbugs, schrödinbugs, and heisenbugs (see Glossary).

8.3.3. Smart contract security

As defined in Chapter 3, a Decentralized Autonomous Organization (DAO) is an organization or company that is run entirely by rules encoded as computer programs in smart contracts that execute on a blockchain. Our interest here is about a particular DAO, confusingly named ***The DAO*** (as opposed to 'a' DAO). The DAO is perhaps blockchain's most ominous heist because its perpetrator(s) didn't steal private keys from a digital wallet stored off a blockchain or exploit a weakness in the code base. Rather, the perpetrator(s) exploited a weakness in a smart contract launched on the Ethereum blockchain. Here is the story…

Stephan Tual, Christoph Jentzsch and Simon Jentzsch proposed to launch a smart contract called 'The' DAO on Ethereum. They designed the DAO as an investment mechanism to fund Ethereum-related startups. Whoever invested in the DAO—by sending Ethereum's native digital asset (ether) to it during the fundraising round—could vote on investment ideas pitched to the DAO after launch. The DAO was deployed in May of 2016. Despite the concerns some people voiced—like Professor Emin Gün Sirer of Cornell University—about the weaknesses in the code, money poured in.[17] Because the votes on future projects were weighted by the size of the investment, people who wanted a powerful vote invested heavily.[18] The DAO raised $150 million worth of ether during its 28-day funding window, exceeding anyone's expectations, as this represented 15 percent of the ether money supply. In June of 2016, a hacker (or hackers) exploited a weakness in the smart contract's code to syphon $50 million in ether from the DAO's fund into another account they controlled. The Ethereum community was powerless to stop it, as smart contracts run autonomously. Vitalik Buterin, the co-founder of Ethereum, called for a complete stop in trading until the problem could be addressed. The price of ether fell immediately from $20 to $13.[19]

What should be done? Opposing views swarmed in: Vitalik Buterin wanted to 'freeze the account', which would require new code that had to be run by at least 50 percent of the nodes. Stephan Tual argued that the blocks should be unwound and that all the stolen ether should be returned to the investors' accounts.[20] Some members of the open source community insisted that ***nothing*** should be done. The blockchain was not breeched; the coders of the smart contract did a poor job, so they should suffer the loss. Chat rooms were ablaze with analogies to the US federal government bailing out the banks during the Global Financial Crisis of 2008 and accused the Ethereum Foundation of acting like a government. The decision was made to let miners vote, weighing their votes by their hashing power. The miners voted for a hard fork—a permanent divergence in the Ethereum blockchain. The blocks were rolled back and the stolen ether was returned. Those miners who refused to follow the fork proceeded mining with the original code, leaving us with *Ethereum* (fork followers) and *Ethereum Classic* (non-fork followers), where the thief can still cash out.

Other smart contract heists and vulnerabilities have come to light, such as with the smart contracts running Parity, POWH Coin, LastWinner and Fomo3D:

- *Parity* was launched by Gavin Wood, co-founder of Ethereum in 2017. Someone was able to exploit a weakness in the smart contract to steal $30 million worth of ether.[21]

- *POWH Coin* was deemed by many as a Ponzi scheme where new investors pay earlier investors.[22] But worse than the business model, *white hat hackers*—[22] ethical hackers who help to identify security defects—found a flaw in the smart contract that operated the *POWH Coin.* In 2018, *black hat hacker(s)*—criminals that exploit security defects for their own advantage—exploited an unsigned integer underflow opportunity, thereby enabling them to withdraw an infinite number of POWH's tokens. [23]

- *Last Winner* and *Fomo3D* are gambling smart contracts launched on Ethereum that share over 90 percent of code. In August 2018, AnChain identified five Ethereum addresses on Last Winner that exploited a flaw in the smart contract code to steal $4 million.[24]

    Lesson for managers: Enterprises will need to build or acquire new legal skills to assess risks and to establish the legality of agreements and new coding skills to build and aggressively test smart contracts before live deployment.

8.3.4. Fifty-one percent attack

"Mining pools are groups of cooperating miners who agree to share block rewards in proportion to their contributed mining hash power. While mining pools are desirable to the average miner, as they smooth out rewards and

make them more predictable, they unfortunately concentrate power to the mining pool's owner."

Jordan Tuwiner, Founder of Buy Bitcoin Worldwide[25]

"I'm not overly concerned about the Chinese miners acting in unison as a cartel. It's a big mistake to lump all of them under the same umbrella because they're all Chinese. Over the course of the last year, especially the last couple of months, we've seen all of those mining pools and solo miners act quite independently from each other."

Professor Emin Gün Sirer of Cornell University, 2017[26]

How likely can someone commandeer more than 50 percent of the nodes/hashing power? And where are the biggest threats? For large public blockchains, the threat comes from the concentration of power by mining pools. We'll specifically look at the threats of concentration of power for Bitcoin and Ethereum. For smaller-sized public blockchains, a single hacker may find it worthwhile to overtake the network if the hacker's electricity costs are lower than the amount of cryptocurrency he or she could steal through a double spend. We'll examine the 51 percent hacks that happened at Verge; ZenCash; Bitcoin Gold and Ethereum Classic. Private blockchains are not concerned with a 51 percent takeover; indeed, many private blockchains are operated under a 'benevolent dictator' governance model discussed in the next chapter.

Focusing on Bitcoin, the main threat of a 51 percent takeover comes from the concentration of power from China-based mining pools, which controlled over 80 percent of the mining power in 2020 (see Figure 8.3). ***Poolin, F2Pool, BTC.com***, and ***Antpool*** are among the largest China-based mining pools. In theory, the miners could possibly collude, or the Chinese government could seize control.[27] Concerning the latter threat, complete takeover by the Chinese government would crash the price, so a more likely threat is if the government quietly seized control of a few mining pools.[28]

The China-based company, ***Bitmain,*** poses another interesting threat. Bitmain is both the world's largest bitcoin mining hardware manufacturer with 70 percent market share and owner of Antpool, one of the largest mining pools. Antpool mined around 10 percent of all blocks as of this writing (see Figure 8.3). Being the largest provider and consumer of bitcoin mining hardware poses a serious conflict of interest. In April 2017, it was discovered that Bitmain built-in a 'backdoor' program within its Antminer hardware so that the company could easily seize control and shut down other miners competing with its mining pool. Here's how this could occur:

'The firmware checks-in with a central service randomly every one to 11 minutes. Each check-in transmits the Antminer serial number, a hardware identification number and IP address. Bitmain can use this check-in data to cross check against customer sales and delivery records making it personally identifiable. The remote service can then return 'false' which will stop the miner from mining.'[29]

Dubbed 'Antscape', Bitmain apologized and posted updates to the firmware.[30]

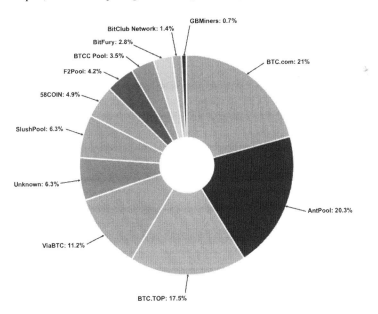

Figure 8.3: Bitcoin's largest winning mining pools on February 18, 2020

Source: https://blockchain.info/pools

Ethereum also tracks its top miners on https://www.etherchain.org/charts/miner. In February 2020, *Sparkpool, Ethermine, f2pool2*, and *Nanopool* were the top mining pools (see Figure 8.4). Sparkpool alone controlled more than 30 percent of the Ethereum network on this day.

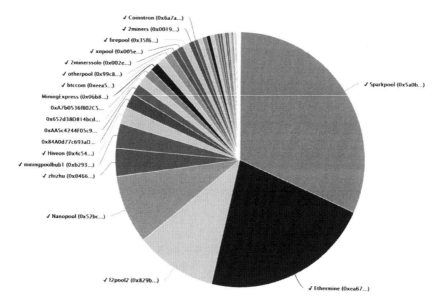

Figure 8.4: Ethereum's largest winning mining pools on February 18, 2020

Source: https://www.etherchain.org/charts/miner

Given that blockchains are supposed to be completely distributed applications, the dominance of a few key mining pools does pose a risk. The 2017 quote, above, from Professor Emin Gün Sirer, asserts that that the collusion concern is misguided because there is no evidence of collusion among Chinese mining pools. However, a 2018 study by Professor Sirer and his colleagues found that *"both Bitcoin and Ethereum mining are very centralized, with the top four miners in Bitcoin and the top three miners in Ethereum controlling more than 50 percent of the hash rate… The entire blockchain for both systems is determined by fewer than 20 mining entities."*[31]

Although Bitcoin and Ethereum have not suffered a 51 percent takeover, other blockchain networks have, including Verge; ZenCash; Bitcoin Gold and Ethereum Classic.

- At **Verge** (XVG), a privacy coin, a 51 percent takeover happened three times in 2018. In the first takeover, hackers stole $1 million worth of cryptocurrency. In the second takeover, they stole $1.8 million and prevented others from processing transactions. During the third takeover, over 142 million XVG were stolen.[32] Each time, developers sought to implement patches, but hackers were still able to spoof timestamps to double spend XVG.[33]

- **ZenCash** (ZEN) suffered a 51 percent attack in June of 2018 by a private miner with a large mining operation. By double-spending, the hacker swiped over $550,000 worth of its cryptocurrency. In this hack, the developers responded quickly with a patch.[34]

- **Bitcoin Gold** (BTG) experienced a 51 percent hack in January 2020. The hacker reorganized nearly 30 blocks to double spend $70,000 worth of the cryptocurrency.[35]

- Of all the 51 percent attacks, the one at **Ethereum Classic** is considered the most troubling. As noted above, Ethereum Classic was the 'non-fork' followers after the DAO attack on Ethereum in 2016. As early as 2018, white hats warned that a 51 percent takeover of Ethereum Classic could happen by spending as little as $2,216 in electricity.[36] In January of 2019, a hacker gained control of 51 percent of the network and stole over $1 million worth of the cryptocurrency. A few days later, the hacker voluntarily returned $100,000 to one of the exchanges it robbed, Gate.io. It's unclear why the hacker returned the money to this exchange, and not to others it stole from, like Coinbase.[37]

One takeaway from these events is that the communities rally around to save the networks.

8.3.5. Quantum computing

Blockchain's cryptography is deemed secure because today's digital computers don't have enough computational power to make feasible, the brute force guessing of a private key based on knowing only the public key. According to one source, today's digital computer would take billions of years to randomly guess a private key that matches a public key.[38] Looking far ahead, some people are concerned that the cryptography we deem to be secure today may become vulnerable in the future. Keeping in mind that permissionless blockchain records are immutable and *forever* public, there is indeed a risk that future technologies could break the cryptography that protects the blockchains of today. Quantum computing is one such risk.

Quantum computing will speed computers in such a way that brute force searches that are impractical today could be practical in the future.[39] How? Today's digital computers are based on binary digits, called 'bits', which represent the state of a computation with a '0' or a '1'. Today, we make digital computers faster by processing more bits per second, but each bit can still only represent one computation. Quantum computers will change this; they will be based on quantum bits, called 'qubits', which can simultaneously represent multiple states and therefore do multiple calculations at the same time. A 30-qubit computer could do one billion calculations simultaneously.[40]

According to Dr. Atefeh (Atty) Mashatan, Director of the Cybersecurity Research Lab at Ryerson University, there are two options:

> *"either replace the vulnerable components of existing platforms with quantum-resistant alternatives or go back to the drawing board and design new blockchains that are not quantum-vulnerable. The latter is much easier than the former."*

To quantum-patch an existing blockchain, cryptographic keys would need to be replaced with much larger key sizes, which will further hinder scalability. All of the balances from the old addresses would need to be transferred to new addresses stored in new quantum-resistant wallets. However, the patch would only work if the public key had not been previously broadcast. Dr. Mashatan explained:

> *"If a public key is broadcast and the associated wallet still contains some funds, an adversary who has access to an attack-capable quantum computer can find the corresponding private key and, consequently, impersonate the wallet owner and use the remaining funds."*[41]

8.4. Performance and scalability

> *"Everyone calculating everything does not scale. Not at all... Ethereum is many magnitudes slower than today's databases."*

> **Henning Diedrich, author of Ethereum: Blockchains, Digital Assets, Smart Contracts, DAOs**[42]

> *"Certainly there has been developments, and, in most cases, blockchains can address the requirements for scalability."*

> **Eamonn Maguire, Global Lead, Digital Ledger Services, KPMG**[43]

Although performance and scalability affect each other, they are conceptually distinctive. Performance is about the length of time it takes for a transaction to be processed in a system; scalability refers to the *throughput,* i.e. how many transactions can be processed per second. Performance and scalability issues are significantly greater for public, permissionless blockchains than for private, permissioned blockchains. We'll examine them separately.

8.4.1. Performance and scalability challenges of public blockchains

Because the *a priori* trust among trading partners is nil in a public blockchain, the computer networks need a lot of computational power to validate transactions and to constantly monitor the integrity of records. All this computation slows down performance and throughput. As we saw in the huge adoption surges of 2017, Bitcoin and Ethereum struggled to process transactions within the targeted windows.

Bitcoin is designed to settle transactions every ten minutes and was indeed settling close to that time as of February 2020. Bitcoin was handling between 3.3 and 7 transactions per second. Ethereum is designed to settle transactions in seven seconds, but the average was between 15 seconds and 5 minutes as of February 2020.[44] Settlement times are not fast enough for transactions requiring nearly instantaneous reaction times, such as IoT devices that monitor the status of critical systems, or for retail applications where a customer will certainly not wait around for a transaction to settle. Additionally, public blockchains like Bitcoin and Ethereum are considered too small in scale to handle the volumes that will be required for many enterprise applications. For example, PayPal was handling 193 transactions per second in 2017, SWIFT—the global provider of secure financial messaging services—was processing about 329 messages per second,[45] and Visa was handling 1,667 transactions per second (and claimed it could accommodate up to 56,000 transactions per second).[46]

Ethereum's scalability problem was really highlighted when one smart contract for the game *CryptoKitties* started using 10 percent of Ethereum's network capacity in November of 2017. Cryptokitties created a backlog of tens of thousands of transactions.[47] Ethereum's PoW consensus algorithm requires that every node processes the code in a smart contract, which is not only slow, but expensive.[48]

One consequence of public blockchains' lack of scalability is higher transaction costs. For most of Bitcoin's history, transaction fees were indeed very small, averaging about 11 cents (in US$) per transaction in June 2014, and 28 cents in December of 2016.[49] When the network is not congested, very small fees are enough to incentivize miners. For a specific example, we found a successful transaction on March 12th 2017, where a person offered just 45 cents worth of bitcoins to transfer over $8200 worth of bitcoins.[50] However, when the network is congested, miners cannot include all of the newly validated transactions in the next block, so the miners' algorithms select the transactions offering the highest fees. As Bitcoin traffic exploded in December of 2017, fees skyrocketed to as high as $55 per transaction.[51] During peak times in 2017, senders offering smaller fees sometimes waited days to be added to the blockchain, or worse, their orphaned transactions eventually dropped out and needed to be resent.[52]

Performance and scaling solutions for public blockchains

Open source communities and private enterprises have already implemented some innovations and continue to develop new solutions to improve public blockchains. Getting a globally diverse set of decentralized developers and miners to agree to upgrades is a considerable effort that can take years of negotiations and emergency meetings.[53] When the community cannot agree, splinter groups launch 'hard forks', which are permanent, divergent paths off of the original blockchain. This is why we now have not only the original Bitcoin, but Bitcoin XT; Bitcoin Classic; Bitcoin Gold; and Bitcoin Cash. Moreover, forks of forks happened when infighting continued. For example, Bitcoin Cash is a 2017 hard fork of Bitcoin, aiming to increase the size of blocks and to keep transaction fees low. The following year, the Bitcoin Cash community fought over two proposed upgrades, which prompted one faction to create a hard fork of Bitcoin Cash called Bitcoin SV (SV for 'Satoshi Vision'). Thus, the communities do not always agree on technical upgrades. Here, we highlight some of the major performance and scaling solutions for Bitcoin, called Segregated Witness and the Lightning Network. We also cover Catenis—as an example of an innovation by a startup—as well as innovations for Ethereum, including sharding, Proof-of-Stake, the Raiden Network, and Plasma (see Table 8.1).

For Bitcoin, *Segregated Witness*, called 'SegWit', has been the biggest protocol change in Bitcoin since its inception.[54] It improved Bitcoin in a number of ways. Firstly, SegWit squeezed more transactions into a block by moving digital signatures (called 'witnesses') from the sender's address to a new part of a Bitcoin block. By segregating the signatures, block sizes increased from 1 megabyte to, possibly, 4 megabytes, thus improving throughput. This innovation also solved *transaction malleability*—the possibility for a hacker to alter a digital signature before it is added to a block, which would change the transaction ID. The recipient would still receive the bitcoins, but the sender would not be able to find it by searching for the transaction ID (see Glossary).

Bitcoin	Ethereum
Segregated Witness: Separates digital signature from transactions to increase block size, fix transaction malleability and enable layer 2 solutions Implemented August 2017	**Proof-of-Stake:** block validators are selected based on their stake in the network, such as how many coins or how long coins have been owned. Uses less electricity than Proof-of-Work and creates blocks faster. Not yet available as of March 2020
Lighting Network: offchain payment channels to process intermediate transactions Available to SegWit adopters in 2017	**Raiden network:** offchain payment channels to process intermediate transactions Available as of 2018 **Plasma:** offchain payment channels to process intermediate transactions Not yet available as of March 2020
Catenis: instantaneous transactions between trusted IoT devices Available	**Sharding:** divide Ethereum into multiple chains called shards Not yet available as of March 2020

Table 8.1: Examples of performance and scalability solutions

Another consequence of moving the digital signatures, was that SegWit enabled the use of the *Lightning Network*. The Lighting Network tracks intermediate transfers of funds off-chain and only posts the value of the initial credit and the final account balance transfers to the blockchain. The solution helps unclutter the blockchain with intermediate transactions. Functionally, it's like opening up a bar tab. A person secures a bar tab with a credit card, orders several drinks (or sends a few drinks back), and then settles the final bill with one payment.

Not all of the Bitcoin miners welcomed SegWit. Some miners did not like the design, which moved the anchor for the signatures from being embedded in the Merkle Root to the first transaction in the block (called the coinbase transaction) used to reward the winning miner. Another issue was the deployment strategy: SegWit was released as a 'soft fork', which means than non-SegWit adopters could still mine Bitcoins. Some miners thought it would be cleaner (yet more difficult) to release as a 'hard fork' (see Glossary for '*Forks*'). Many emergency meetings occurred among the Bitcoin community as SegWit was being debated. SegWit had a rocky adoption, but was activated as a soft fork to the Bitcoin Core in August 2017.[55],[56] Two years later, a little less than half of Bitcoin transactions use SegWit, probably because people are slow to upgrade wallets. A faction of the mining community—representing about 2,000 nodes—decided to completely walk away from Bitcoin by creating a hard fork called ***Bitcoin Classic*** in May of 2016.[57]

Many other Bitcoin innovations have also been developed. For example, Andre de Castro, CEO and Founder, Blockchain of Things, developed ***Catenis,*** an enterprise application that sits on top of Bitcoin and allows nearly instantaneous transactions between an organization's IoT devices. De Castro made a very important distinction between transaction processing and settlement speeds in public blockchains like Bitcoin.[58] He said:

> *"Most people do not understand the difference between the speed of settlement and the speed of transactions. Bitcoin settles in ten minutes, but transaction speed is in milliseconds. If you own both the endpoints, you have no counter party risk and can execute immediately in the case of IoT. Now, what gets stored on the blockchain for an auditor to see, that doesn't need to happen right away. Auditors ask what happened six months ago."[59]*

The key is trust in the sending and receiving devices.

Turning our attention to Ethereum, a number of performance and scalability solutions are planned for 'Ethereum 2.0' also known as 'Serenity'.[60] The timing is difficult to predict, but Ethereum's roadmap calls for a phased solution that will start in 2020 (not in 2019 as previously planned). These solutions including sharding, Proof-of-Stake, and layer 2 processing for intermediate transactions (similar to the Lighting Network).

Sharding will involve segmenting the validation process so that not every Ethereum node validates every transaction. If adopted, each 'shard' in Ethereum would act like its own blockchain, but shards would be merged on the main chain by a sharding manger smart contract.[61]

Ethereum 2.0 will move from a Proof-of-Work to a **Proof-of-Stake** consensus protocol called Beacon Chain. Vitalik Buterin, Ethereum's co-founder, is an advocate for Ethereum moving to PoS. He said:

> *"Ethereum 1.0 is a couple of people's scrappy attempt to build a world computer; Ethereum 2.0 will actually be the world computer."*[62]

A new token, called ETH2, will be used for Beacon Chain, as a validator reward.

The **Raiden Network** is another protocol that runs as another layer on top of Ethereum. Heiko Hees, CEO and founder of Brainbot in Germany, launched the Raiden Network as a high-speed network for micropayments on Ethereum.[63] Described as similar to the Lightning Network, the basic idea is to switch from a model where all transactions hit the shared ledger on the blockchain (which is the bottleneck) to a model where users can privately exchange messages which sign the transfer of value. Raiden nodes connect to Ethereum nodes using an API. The processing of a million, confidential transactions per second is possible, because they are not added to the blockchain. Furthermore, transaction fees are reported to be 'tiny'.[64]

Plasma is another layer 2 option. With Plasma, there is only 1 transaction in a block that commits to a Merkle Root of the current owner of all the assets in the block. Plasma solves throughput (more transactions per second), but not settlement times. To improve settlement times, **payment channels** would work on top of Plasma. Within a Plasma block, instead of just listing the asset owned by someone, it's a channel with a ledger controlled with a multi-signature smart contract; people can exchange value in nanoseconds. However, to send payments across payment channels, Ethereum will need an interoperability solution.[65]

8.4.2. Performance and scalability of private blockchains

Private-permissioned blockchains solve the performance and scaling challenges by limiting the number of nodes needed to validate transactions and by allowing private messaging and channels among trading partners. Many permissioned blockchain protocols create divisions of labor, so some nodes might be validating transactions while other nodes might be sequencing their outputs, and still others may be adding sequenced blocks to the ledger. Subsequently, permissioned blockchain protocols like Corda, Quorum and Hyperledger Fabric can settle transactions within seconds.

As of 2020, the exact scalability of private blockchains is an unknown, as few have been adopted to scale. However, most private blockchains claim they are highly scalable. For example, IBM tested Hyperledger Fabric within its cloud data center and reported throughput of 3,000 transactions per second with latency of under a second.[66]

New innovations continue to boost performance. For example, *FastFabric* aims to increase Hyperledger Fabric transactions from 3,000 to 20,000 per second. Developed by professors at the University of Waterloo and University of Massachusetts, FastFabric improved throughput by separating the hardware for committer and endorser nodes; separating metadata from transaction data; introducing parallelism and caching; and moving world-state key-value stores to light-weight-in-memory stores.[67]

To benchmark the actual performance of different blockchains, the Hyperledger Project launched the Performance and Scalability Working Group in June 2017.[68] By 2019, the group published a working paper that usefully defines metrics for performance such as read latency; read throughput; transaction latency; and transaction throughput. This group will test different blockchains under conditions by varying the consensus protocol; geographic distribution of nodes; hardware environment (chip speed and memory); network model (firewalls and bottlenecks); number of nodes; software component dependencies; type of data store; and workload.[69]

8.5. Anonymity

Within many public blockchains, every transaction's sending address, receiving address and amount is transparent to anyone with access to the Internet. For example, Figure 8.5 illustrates an example of an actual Bitcoin transaction that took place on February 25, 2016 at 10:24:44 am. The public has no easy way to identify the trading partners, yet the world can observe when the transaction took place.[70]

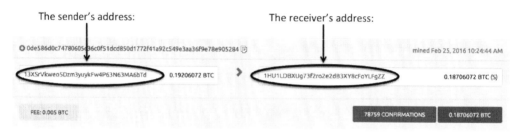

Figure 8.5: A Bitcoin transaction that occurred in Block 400000 on Feb 25, 2016

Although public blockchains are anonymous—in that no personal identities are revealed on the ledger—meta patterns can emerge where identities could be revealed. For example, many transactions are funded with multiple addresses, so patterns can emerge where one party can track another party's transactions. Figure 8.6 illustrates how this can occur. If Party A sends value to an address owned by Party B on one date, Party A can later determine additional addresses owned by Party B when Party B spends the coins. Consequently, it is more apt to describe Bitcoin (and Ethereum) as 'pseudo-anonymous'. This was something Satoshi Nakamoto acknowledged in his white paper. Nakamoto recommended that new addresses should be generated for new transactions:

> *"As an additional firewall, a new key pair should be used for each transaction to keep them from being linked to a common owner. Some linking is still unavoidable with multi-input transactions, which necessarily reveal that the same owner owned their inputs. The risk is that if the owner of a key is revealed, linking could reveal other transactions that belonged to the same owner."*[71]

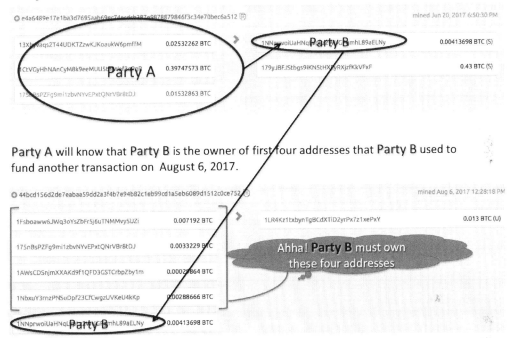

Figure 8.6: Meta patterns that can arise from a blockchain's transparency

Open source communities are working to address these issues. We examine two such solutions: zero knowledge proofs and CryptoNotes.

8.5.1. Zero-knowledge proofs

Zero-knowledge proofs (ZKPs) were developed by Shafi Goldwasser, Charles Rackoff, and Silvio Micali in 1985.[72] Zero-knowledge proofs are a method for one party to verify possession of a piece of information to other parties without revealing the information. In general, there are two types of zero-knowledge proofs: challenge-response and non-interactive.

As a simple example of a ***challenge-response ZKP***, suppose Alice wants to prove to Bob that she knows the exact number of jellybeans that fills a large jar without telling Bob the exact number (see Figure 8.7). What might Alice do to convince Bob she knows the amount? Alice could instruct Bob to take any number of jellybeans out of the jar after she leaves the room. Bob makes his choice. Alice re-enters the room and Bob exits the room. Alice recounts the beans and compares the current count with the previous count to calculate exactly how many jellybeans (if any) Bob removed. When Bob returns, Alice tells Bob exactly how many jellybeans he took. If Bob thinks Alice made a lucky guess, rounds of the same choice could be made over and over again. Eventually, Bob will be convinced that Alice possesses the knowledge of the exact number of jellybeans without her ever revealing the number. A challenge-response ZKP has some limitations: the challenge-response is coordinated for known parties; iterations can slow performance; and the results are probabilistic rather than deterministic, because Alice could get lucky by guessing the correct number.

Figure 8.7: Jellybean example for a challenge-response zero-knowledge proof

Most blockchain applications use another type of ZNP, called *a non-interactive zero-knowledge proof.* These ZKPs do not require iterations; someone can prove to the *public* that they know something.

Proving someone solved a Sudoku puzzle is a common example to illustrate a non-interactive ZNP.[73] A Sudoku puzzle has nine rows and nine columns. Within the puzzle, there are nine squares. Puzzles start with some cells filled in (see left side of Figure 8.8). To solve the puzzle, one must find a unique solution so that the numbers one through nine appear exactly once across each row, down each column, and within each square (see right side of Figure 8.8 for the solution). Suppose there is a contest to see who solved the puzzle first. Suppose Alice won. How might Alice convince everyone she solved the puzzle first without revealing the solution? Alice could construct an algorithm that takes the numbers from each *row* and randomly shuffles them; Takes the numbers from each *column* and randomly shuffles them; and takes the numbers within each *square* and randomly shuffles them. If the result shows 27 collections of nine numbers with each collection containing the numbers one through nine, Alice can prove she solved the puzzle without revealing the solution.

In blockchain applications, non-interactive ZKPs are used to guarantee that transactions are valid without revealing information about the sender, receiver, and/or transaction. Zcash, Quorum[75], EY's Nightfall, MediLedger, and many other blockchains use ZKPs. Zcash, for example, uses the cryptographic zero-knowledge proof 'zk-SNARK', which stands for 'Zero-Knowledge Succinct Non-Interactive Argument of Knowledge.'[76,77]

EY's Nightfall is a smart contract protocol that uses non-interactive ZKPs. Nightfall allows parties to exchange tokens on a public blockchain (Ethereum) in a way that protects their privacy by masking the sender, receiver, and amounts of the exchange while still preventing a double spend. Essentially, Nightfall is a confidential escrow service for ERC-20 (fungible) and ERC 720 (non-fungible) tokens.

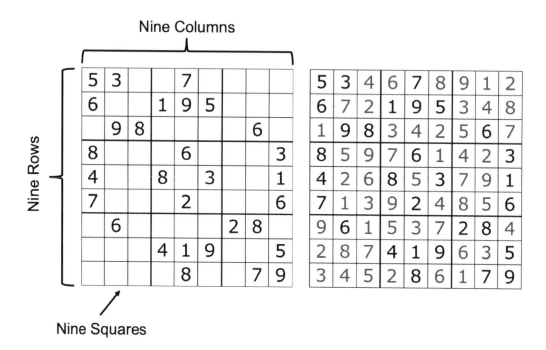

Figure 8.8: A Sudoku puzzle and its solution

Source: https://en.wikipedia.org/wiki/Sudoku [74]

On the left side of the figure, a Sudoku puzzle has some cells filled in. The challenge is to find the solution so that the numbers one through nine appear exactly once across each row, down each column, and within each square. The right side of the figure shows the solution.

Here we provide a high level overview; it is meant to convey the principles. Let's assume Alice wants to send Token T to Bob. At the start of the transaction, Alice's wallet currently has possession of the private key that controls the ownership of Token T recorded on the blockchain. To safely send the token to Bob in a way that prevents Alice from double spending it and ensures that only Bob can retrieve it (or that she can retrieve it before Bob does if the agreement goes sour), the following steps are executed:

1. Alice's wallet creates a token commitment by using her private key to put Token T in escrow controlled by a smart contract (called a shield contract) on the blockchain.

2. The shield contract takes control over the token.

3. Alice's software creates a token commitment for Bob using Bob's public key and a secret key only Alice knows.

4. Alice sends Bob's token commitment to the shield contract.

5. Alice's software also creates Alice's nullification of Alice's token commitment so she will no longer have control over the token *if* Bob retrieves it.

6. Alice's nullification is sent to the shield contract.

7. Offline, Alice sends the secret key, Bob's token commitment, and the token ID to Bob. This message happens *offchain*, so it's important this message is secured to prevent someone other than Bob from using it.

8. Bob can now take possession of Token T by proving to the shield contract he knows the secret key.

9. When Bob is ready, his software uses the secret key to nullify his token commitment and issues a PayToAddress command to move control of the token to Bob's wallet.

10. When the transaction is finished, the balance in the shield contract is zero and Bob has the private key that controls Token T in his wallet. Alice will no longer be able to retrieve it.

There seems to be a lot of steps here, but each step is necessary. Why doesn't Alice just send the money to Bob's wallet directly like Bitcoin does? The way Bitcoin works, recipients cannot prevent people from sending value to their addresses. In Bitcoin (and in many public blockchains), anyone can 'air drop' money into someone's wallet without their permission. Many individuals want—and certainly enterprises need—to control their receivables. Nightfall enables that; the recipient has to pro-actively retrieve the tokens from the shield contract.

According to Chen Zur, EY Partner/Principle and US Blockchain Practice Leader:

> *"With nightfall, there is no way for anyone to know that Alice and Bob did a transaction between them. All you know is that one of the wallets sent some tokens to another wallet, but there's no way to know what happened between them. And that's the first step. We are developing this further to also include contract rules for purchase agreements, such as terms and conditions, but what we have right now and what is in the public domain is the ability to move tokens between two wallets without anyone knowing what happened."*

As of 2020, EY has shown that running Nightfall on the public Ethereum is less expensive than using traditional private networks for high-value, low-volume transactions. A Canadian customer is using it to trace the provenance of high-value medical equipment.[78]

8.5.2. CryptoNote and Monero

CryptoNote is another protocol used in blockchains that offer more privacy than those used in Bitcoin and Ethereum. CryptoNote's transactions cannot be followed through the blockchain in a way that reveals who sent or received coins.[79] Monero is an example of a blockchain that uses the CryptoNote protocol. To understand how little information is revealed on Monero's public blockchain, see Figure 8.9.

Monero uses 'ring signatures' and a 'key image' to hide the sender's address; a 'stealth address' (also called a public key) to hide the recipient's address(es); and 'ring confidential transactions' to mask amounts. These innovations create complete anonymity, but do so in a way that prevents a double spend.

To understand how Monero works, we'll begin with the wallet. Every Monero wallet has two sets of private-public key pairs—one for viewing, one for spending:

- The *view key pair* is comprised of a private view key and public view key. An account owner needs the private view key to find transactions associated with his or her wallet address on the blockchain.

- The *spend key pair* is comprised of a private spend key and public spend key. The private spend key can only be used once, meaning that if someone wants to spend money from an address, one must spend all of it. As we will see, this architecture helps to prevent double spending.

A Monaro address is a concatenation of the *public spend key* and the *public view key*.

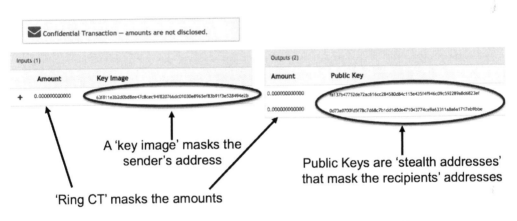

Figure 8.9: An example of a Monero transaction [80]

Let's walk through a transaction to see how the algorithms work. Suppose Alice wants to send four Monero to Bob. Her digital wallet will select an address or addresses that contains more than four Monero because Alice needs to offer the Monero miners a small transaction fee. The wallet selects an address with ten Monero in it. Again, the protocol requires that all ten Monero are consumed in the transaction. So, for this transaction, the wallet will send money to two addresses: Bob's address and a new address for Alice's change of 3.99 Monero (so the miner gets .01 Monero).

To create the input side of the transaction, Alice's wallet uses the unique private spend key stored only in her wallet that is associated with the public spend key. To create the output side of the transaction for Bob, Alice needs Bob's address (comprised of Bob's public spend key and a public view key). These will be used to create a new 'spend-one-time-only' public key for Bob. This public key serves as a 'stealth address' to mask Bob's real address. Alice will also get a new address for her change (see right side of Figure 8.9)

To process the transaction, Monero masks Alice's identity (or more specifically, masks her public spend key) by creating a 'ring signature' comprised of Alice's signature and a number of decoys selected from past Monero transactions stored in the blockchain. A 'key image' is derived from the output Alice sent, but it's impossible to know which address produced the key image to an outsider (see left side of Figure 8.9). To an outsider, any of the decoys could have used their private key to sign the transaction and create the key image, but really only Alice did. (Note: the more decoys requested, the more resources consumed, so higher fees will be needed to incentivize miners to include the transaction.)

To prevent a double spend, miners only need to make sure that the key image appears nowhere else in the blockchain. Thus, the key image is the main way Monero makes sure the private key was not used before to spend the amount.

So how does Bob's wallet find the money Alice sent if it's not visible on the blockchain? Bob's wallet scans the blockchain with his private view key to find the output. Since part of the new public spend address contains the public view key he sent to Alice, the private view key pair can find the transaction and lay claim to it. Once the output is detected, it is retrieved and put into Bob's wallet. Then, his wallet calculates a one-time private spend key that corresponds with the public spend key. Only he can spend it with his wallet's private spend key.

Finally, to mask the amounts, Monero uses 'ring confidential transactions' or 'RingCT'.

This protocol uses a 'range proof' to prove to miners that the inputs of a transaction are equal to the outputs, but miners do not know the value of either.

While zero knowledge proofs and CryptoNotes are effective at masking senders, receivers, and amounts, the blockchain protocol is not the only threat to anonymity. If wallets are transacting over the Internet, messages will contain other revealing information like an IP address. To achieve true anonymity, senders and receivers would need to use a network that masks IP addresses, like Tor or the Invisible Internet (IP2) protocol. For example, the illegal marketplace website, Silk Road, chose Bitcoin as its payment application and Tor as its network (see Glossary for the story of '*Silk Road*').

8.6. Confidentiality

"The issue is that some companies are afraid that information that's being collected for the blockchain will be used for other purposes. So let's say I'm a pharmacy. If I verified all the products I have on hand, I'm announcing my inventory. Companies are concerned that this added intelligence could be used for other purposes such as contract negotiations, etc."

Bob Celeste, CEO and Founder of the Center for Supply Chain Studies[81]

Moving from public, permissionless blockchains to private, permissioned blockchains, we obviously cannot allow anonymity among trading partners. Regulations require that enterprises know the identity of their customers, employees, and suppliers. However, enterprises are concerned about confidentiality. With one shared ledger, how do we allow some folks to view transactions while preventing other folks from viewing transactions when we are all sharing a blockchain application? Chapter 3 already presented **Quorum** as an example of a solution. With Quorum, participants can execute private and public smart contracts so that the ledger is segmented into a private state database and a public state database.[82] Within a single ledger, all nodes can view Quorum's public states, but only those nodes party to private contracts can view private states.

Hyperledger Fabric uses the concept of channels. Channels provide a data-partitioning capability, so that only those parties with permission to use the channel are able to see it.[83] Confidential transactions are encrypted with secret keys known only to their originators, validators, and authorized auditors. Smart contracts (called Chaincode in Fabric) specify a channel's parties and the rules by which assets can be created and modified on the channel's ledger (see Figure 8.10).[84]

MULTI-LEDGERING

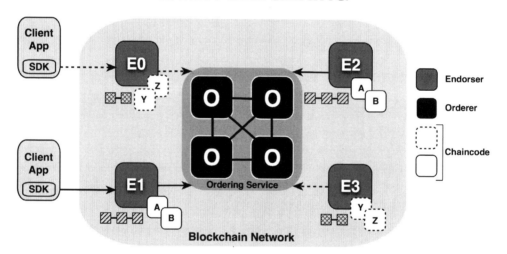

- PEERS **E0** AND **E3** CONNECT TO THE ▨ CHANNEL FOR CHAINCODES **Y** AND **Z**

- PEERS **E1** AND **E2** CONNECT TO THE ▧ CHANNEL FOR CHAINCODES **A** AND **B**

Figure 8.10: Channels in Hyperledger Fabric

Source: https://www.altoros.com/blog/wp-content/uploads/2017/04/hyperledger-fabric-v1-general-availability-multi-ledgering-

Fabric allows parties to use a software development toolkit (SDK) to code smart contracts—called chaincodes—to create separate ledgers for different agreements.

8.7. Interoperability

"Blockchains need to be integrated with different ERP systems. It really doesn't matter if you have great blockchain use cases if it doesn't add real value or if you can't make business decisions."

Rahul Shah, Strategy Manager, Axiom Technology Group[85]

"To build a chain of chains that acts as an intermediary for all the other chains, and implements a layer, through which the entire blockchain space can route their traffic to allow for better communication, is painfully slow and complex."

Lucasxhy, blockchain blogger[86]

Interoperability is the ability for one system to use another system. Among all of the technical challenges, interoperability is the most important one to solve to truly realize an 'Internet of Value'.[87] There is clearly a need for blockchain interoperability to seamlessly interconnect:

- multiple public blockchains (e.g. Bitcoin and Ethereum)

- multiple private blockchains (e.g. Hyperledger Fabric and R3)

- public and private blockchains (e.g. Ethereum and Hyperledger Fabric)

- blockchains with legacy systems (e.g. MediLeder and SAP; Ripple and SWIFT)

There are many blockchain interoperability projects (see Figure 8.11). Traditional companies like Accenture and IBM; startups like Aion, Cosmos, and Polkadot; and blockchain consortia like the Hyperledger Project, all have interoperability projects underway.

Figure 8.11: Blockchain interoperability projects

Interoperability requirements include:[88]

- **'All or none' atomicity:** An interoperability solution should ensure that *all* the actions associated with a cross-chain transaction execute, or *all* the actions should fail; no partial executions should be allowed. For example, if Alice records her assets on Chain A and she wants to send some value to Bob who records his assets on Chain B, an interoperability solution should ensure that (a) Alice's account is debited AND Bob's account is credited or (b) that NEITHER action occurs.

- **Universality:** An interoperability solution should be universal by not requiring a custom program to be built for each new chain.

- **No need for trusted third parties (TTPs):** An interoperability solution should not rely on centralized trusted third parties. If this criterion is required, it will eliminate the interoperability solutions that rely on notaries (explained below).

- **Source code availability:** An interoperability solution's source code should be available for audit so that other criteria can be assessed.

- **Developer and User Friendly:** An interoperability solution should be easy to use by developers and seamless to end-users.

All interoperability approaches 'get into' applications though Application Programming Interfaces (APIs) (see Glossary).

8.7.1. Three ways to connect blockchains

There are three common ways for connecting two or more blockchains:

1. **One-time asset pass** where an asset is 'destroyed' on chain A before being 'created' on chain B.

2. A **cross-chain oracle** where one chain needs to read data from another chain. One-way reads are also called 'one-way pegs'.

3. **Cross-chain transaction processing** where two or more blockchains want to coordinate operations so that a single asset can be used by more than one chain. These are also called 'two-way pegs'.

Among these three, cross-chain transaction processing is the Holy Grail of interoperability; the first two are relatively easy to accomplish.

One-time asset pass

Enterprises want the ability to switch blockchain solutions. To exit one blockchain application, an enterprise will want to export those assets to the new solution. Since digital ledgers are immutable, how is this done technically? One way is to 'burn' the asset on one blockchain and then recreate it on a different blockchain (see Figure 8.15). A proof-of-burn is an algorithm that sends value to a verifiably un-spendable address that permanently locks that value on chain. For Bitcoin, this is achieved by using the scripting language for the transaction in a way that would ensure the value could never be redeemed. For example, setting the 'txout' to only execute if $2 = 3$.[89] This, of course, does not address the other needs for switching blockchain solutions, such as grabbing all of the prior transactions that created the final state values.

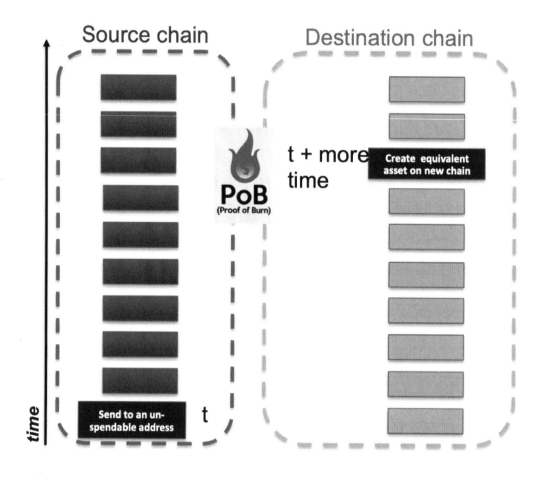

Figure 8.12. Proof-of-Burn is one way to 'destroy' assets on one blockchain and 'recreate' them on another

Cross-chain oracle

A cross-chain oracle is a one-way read of data from one chain by another chain. The term **oracle** refers to the external data needed from a source chain to perform some operation in a destination chain. **_BTC Relay_** was one of the first cross-chain oracles. BTC Relay allows users of applications developed on the Ethereum platform to pay with bitcoins. Developed by Joseph Chow, BTC Relay is an open-source smart contract that was deployed on the Ethereum blockchain in May of 2016.[90] The open source community conveyed much enthusiasm for it and was seen as an important application of Satoshi Nakamoto's **_Simple Payment Verification (SPV)_**.[91] (SPV proofs are explained below and in the Glossary.)

BTC Relay stores Bitcoin's blockchain headers inside of Ethereum, thus maintaining a mini-version of the entire Bitcoin blockchain. An application developer inside Ethereum can query BTC Relay to verify a transaction on the bitcoin network.[92] BTC Relay automatically executes with no trusted third parties. BTC Relay is quite fascinating in how it incentivizes people to keep adding new Bitcoin blocks to the smart contract, on average, every ten minutes. 'Relayers' who submit new Bitcoin block headers to BTC Relay contract get paid a small transaction fee when other developers query BTC Relay to verify a transaction.[93] BTC Relay is in essence a 'program' that reads from one chain to 'prove' existence and then is used as a 'true/false' or as a value in the Ethereum platform.

Despite the excitement of BTC Relay in 2016, there were no recent transactions in 2020.[94] This may be due to increase in competition (especially in the open source market) and alternative oracles being provided (e.g. _http://docs.oraclize.it/#home_) which do more than just peg bitcoin—they also provide other external resources that are 'authenticated' with proofs. With the emergence of cross-chain APIs that are built into the underlying foundation (e.g. Hyperledger and Ethereum integration), relays like this may not be needed as much in the future.

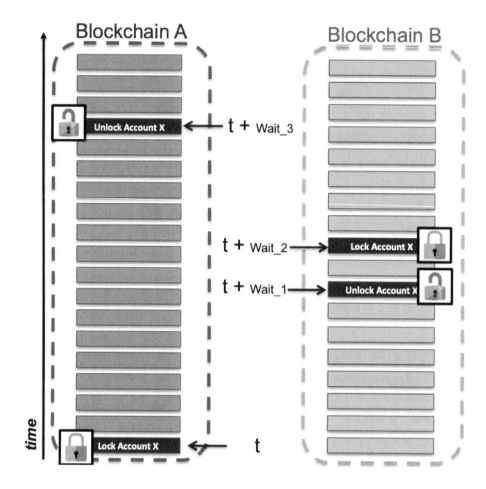

Figure 8.13: Blockchain time delays in cross-chain transactions

At time t, Chain A locks the address on Chain A and indicates an address on Chain B. That transaction requires some time for the Chain A nodes to reach consensus. After the wait, Chain B creates the equivalent number of assets on Chain B. (Assets are not moved across chains but are replaced with equivalent assets on Chain B). Chain B executes its transactions, locks the address, and indicates an address on Chain A. Some time must pass for the Chain B nodes to reach consensus. After a wait, Chain A unlocks the address and it is back in control of the asset.

Cross-chain transaction processing

For cross-chain transaction processing, a two-way peg is needed. With a two-way peg, an asset must be 'locked' in the source chain before actions on the destination chain are taken. When the destination chain is finished processing, it locks the asset in the destination chain so that the source chain can once again take control (see Figure 8.13).

We've covered three ways to connect blockchains. Next, we look at three examples of technical strategies for blockchain interoperability.

8.7.2. Technical strategies for interoperability

In 2016, the R3 blockchain consortium commissioned Vitalik Buterin, the inventor of Ethereum, to investigate strategies for blockchain interoperability.[95] He described three blockchain interoperability strategies:

1. **Notaries:** A single third party or multiple parties coordinate cross-chain operations.[96]

2. **Sidechains/relays**: A smart contract inside one blockchain automatically validates and reads events in another blockchain.

3. **Hash-locking**: Two or more blockchains coordinate operations using the same hash trigger. Operations can also be coordinated by adding a time-out feature to the shared hash feature, creating what are called Hash-Time Locked Contracts (**HTLCs**).

Notaries

Notaries are the simplest way to connect two or more blockchains. A notary has control of locks on both chains. A notary must operate full nodes (running the software and storing the entire ledger) for all of the chains to which it connects. This ensures that notaries are grabbing transactions as quickly as possible and have visibility to the entire set of transactions. Notaries may rely on just a single custodian or on multiple custodians. *A single notary* connects two or more blockchains using one trusted third party (see Figure 8.14).

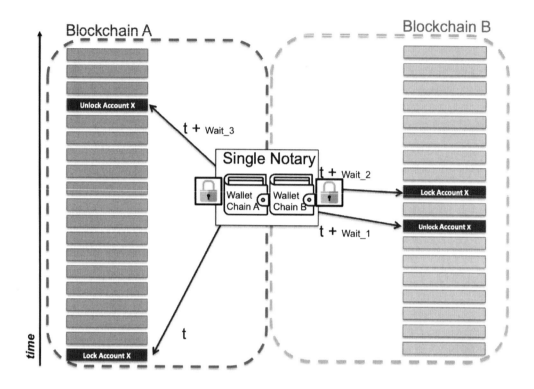

Figure 8.14: Single notary

Source: Figure adapted from Lerner (201)[97]

In this figure, a centralized exchange runs full nodes for both chains. It controls the wallets and locks for addresses stored on both chains. It is the simplest interoperability solution but relies on trusting one centralized party.

Exchanges are common examples of single notaries. Exchanges allow users to easily buy and sell cryptocurrencies and to exchange cryptocurrencies for fiat currencies; but that convenience comes at the acceptance and trust of centralized control, and with the risks of a single point of failure. Cyber-thieves target exchanges because of the large honeypot of value stored all in one place.

Accenture's Interoperability Node

In the permissioned space, Accenture's 'Interoperability Node' serves as a trusted notary. According to Accenture's white paper, a trusted interoperability node sits between the target distributed ledger systems (see Figure 8.15). Accenture is first creating interoperability nodes between R3 Corda, Digital Asset, Quorum, and Hyperledger Fabric. The process to create a node begins with the leaders of two blockchain applications. The leaders define acceptable business rules, policies, standards and governance. These understandings are used as inputs for Accenture to create the integration protocol in terms of agreed upon business logic. Accenture takes the integration protocol and configures an interoperability node that handles asset locking and prevents double spending.[98]

The service was tested in October 2018. Specifically, Accenture showed that information could be shared between R3 Corda and Digital Asset and between Hyperledger Fabric and Quorum.[99]

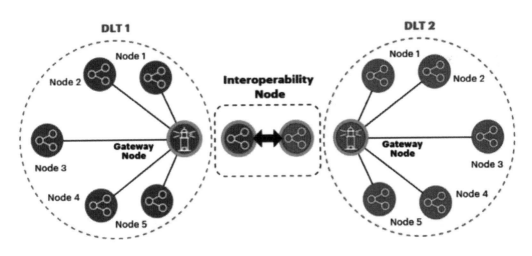

Figure 8.15: Accenture's interoperability node

Source: Treat el al. (2018)[100]

319

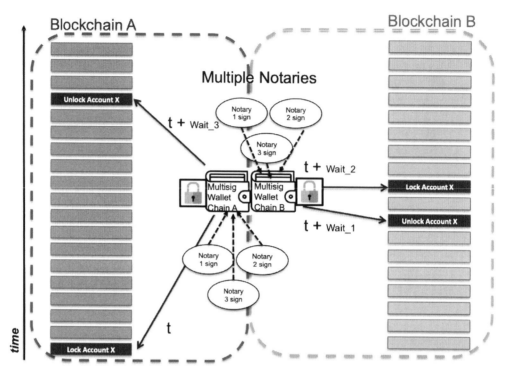

Figure 8.16: Multiple notaries

Source: Figure adapted from Lerner (2016)[105]

In this figure, an exchange runs full nodes for both blockchains. It holds the wallets and locks for addresses stored on both chains, but funds are only released when n of m signatures from federation members are signed. It is a simple interoperability solution, but relies on trusting the federation.

A multi-signature notary, or federation, relies on multiple, independent custodians (see Figure 8.16). Multi-signature addresses require multiple users to sign a transaction before it can be broadcast onto the blockchain network.[101] This method is more secure than a single notary, but trust remains centralized within the hands of a few entities. Typically, algorithms require that a majority of the notaries validate a transaction or event. More specifically, the federation requires that '*n* of *m*' members sign the transaction.

BitGo was the first multi-signature wallet, launched in August of 2013. The BitGo wallet required two out of three signatures, of which BitGo was one signatory. In 2015, the exchange Bitfinex adopted BitGo, providing all its customers with BitGo's multi-signature wallets. In 2016, Bitfinex was hacked and the perpetrator used the keys to steal $60 million from the exchange.[102] Since that fateful event, BitGo recovered and has reached many milestones, including providing multisignature wallets for 100 coins.[103] By 2020, BitGo serves as custodian to more than $2 billion in digital assets, which are insured by a $100 million policy with Lloyds.[104]

Sidechains/relays

Sidechains and relays provide the functions of a notary, but rely on automatically executing algorithms instead of on custodians. Back et al. (2014) first conceived of 'pegged sidechains' as a way for bitcoins and other ledger assets to be transferred between multiple, independent blockchains.[106] For these authors, a sidechain is a two-way peg to a parent chain (or main chain) that allows assets to be interchanged at a predetermined rate. But the term is relative to the asset, not to the network. For this reason, Vitalik Buterin laments the term 'sidechain' in his white paper on interoperability. He argued it is better to use the phrase, *"a relay of chain A exists on chain B"* or *"D is a cross-chain portable digital asset with home ledger A that can also be used on chain B."* [107]

According to Back et al. (2014), sidechains should:

- run in parallel to main chains
- allow free movement to/from the main chain
- be firewalled so theft in one chain cannot be replicated in the other chain
- allow for different consensus algorithms
- be fully independent from the main chain
- be fast and efficient[108]

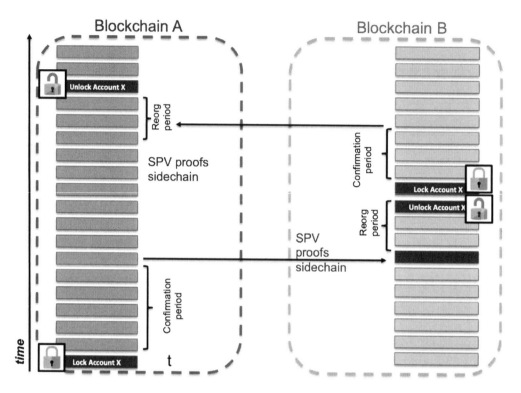

Figure 8.17: Cross-chain transactions using
Simple Payment Verification **(SPV) proofs**

Source: Figure adapted from Lerner (2016) [111]

SPV proofs run automatically and thus do not rely on TTPs. Chain A locks the asset and then must wait until the transaction has settled and more valid blocks have been created on top of it so that parties are confident that they are dealing with the longest, and thus most valid, chain. After the confirmation period, an SPV proof can be submitted to Chain B. Chain B now has to wait, a time called the 'reorg period'. It's possible, another party may submit an SPV proof that contradicts the previous SPV proof. Chain B will select the SPV with the longest chain. Once confident the SPV proof is valid, it unlocks the asset on Chain B, executes transactions, locks the asset, and waits for the transaction to settle before sending an SPV proof back to Chain A.

Liquid is an example of a federated sidechain to the Bitcoin blockchain. Developed by Blockstream, it allows members to settle Bitcoin transactions in seconds. According to its website, the federation of members include exchanges, traders, and financial institutions from nine countries across four continents.[109]

Many sidechains/relays use Satoshi Nakamoto's *Simple Payment Verification* (SPV). The idea is that someone can prove that their transaction is included in a valid block and that many other valid blocks were built on top of it. Nakamoto (2008) described SPV as a way to verify bitcoin transactions without running a full network node. Rather, one only needs to maintain a copy of the block headers and then find the security links—called a *Merkle tree* branch (see Glossary)—to the transaction, to prove it was verified and accepted by the network. SPV shows that 'tokens have been locked up on one chain so validators can safely unlock an equivalent value on the other chain.'[110] Figure 8.17 illustrates that SPV Proofs can be used to coordinate cross-chain transactions without relying on a notary but instead relying only on the algorithmic proofs.

Hash-Time Locked Contracts (HTLC)

HTLCs are a clever way to coordinate transactions across two blockchains by relying on the same data trigger, called a 'secret key', 'private key' or 'preimage'. Figure 8.18 shows how it works. Alice initiates a smart contract on one blockchain that locks value into an address with the hash of the secret key so that one of two things happen: The receiver, Bob, either retrieves the value in the address using the secret key (this is the 'hash lock') and his digital signature, or the contract, expires and returns the value to Alice (this is the 'time lock'). So how will Bob get the secret key in a safe manner? Bob creates a smart contract on his chain and locks value using the same hash of the secret key. Alice must reveal the secret key (and her digital signature) to unlock the value in Bob's contract. The instance that happens, Bob's smart contract learns the secret key and uses it to unlock the value on Alice's smart contract. It's a simple, yet brilliant, solution that eliminates counter-party risks.

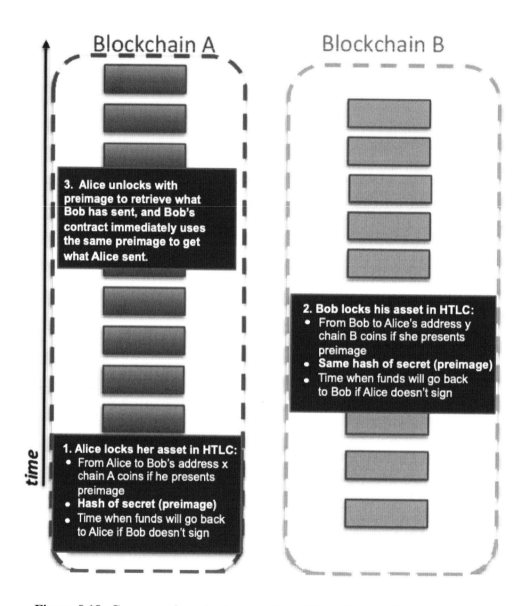

Figure 8.18: Conceptual rendering of a Hash-Time Locked Contract (HTLC)

Interledger Protocol

The Interledger Protocol (ILP) accommodates HTLCs. Two Ripple engineers published the ILP's white paper back in 2015. For a given payment, the ILP protocol sends many micropayments with confirmations between micropayments to minimize the risk that a node could steal or fail to send a payment through a network (see Figure 8.19). ILP uses 'cryptographic escrow' that 'conditionally locks funds to allow secure payments through untrusted connectors.'[112] For a given transaction, the ILP recognizes three types of participants: sender, routers, and receiver. Routers (also called 'connectors') are nodes that find a trust path between the sender and receiver. Nodes use the same hashlock for HTLCs across the paths.[113] (For a detailed example of how HTCLs flow through an end-to-end transaction, see https://interledger.org/rfcs/0022-hashed-timelock-agreements/.)

While HTLCs are used, they still require that the Interledger Module be updated and installed for each of the ledgers (blockchains) with which there is interaction. This means that as new platforms come online, if they do not follow a standard the protocol recognizes, one needs to be added.

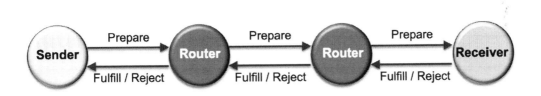

Figure 8.19: The Interledger Protocol

Source: https://interledger.org/overview.html

An aggregate payment is split into multiple micropayments. Each micropayment is routed over a network and a fulfillment confirmation must be received before sending the next micropayment.

Hyperledger Quilt

Quilt is an interoperability project under the Hyperledger Project umbrella that aims to implement the ILP protocol. According to its website:

> *"Hyperledger Quilt offers interoperability between ledger systems by implementing the Interledger Protocol (also known as ILP)."*

Launched in 2017, Hyperledger Quilt v1.0 was released in October of 2019.[114]

> ***Lesson for managers: Enterprises will need to build or acquire technical architecture skills that can understand how to connect blockchains and enterprise systems.***

Some blockchain architects earn salaries in the $200,000 to $400,000 range, so be prepared to pay.

8.8. Conclusion

We have thus outlined the major technical challenges and emerging solutions as of 2020. Many people are working to make blockchains more secure, more private, faster, scalable and interoperable. Managers need to be aware of the technical risks, but their focus of attention should be on the issues discussed in our final chapter on mindshifts, strategies, and action principles.

Citations

[1] Castillo, M. (January 3rd, 2017), *State Street's Blockchain Strategy: Big and Bold for 2017*, https://www.coindesk.com/state-streets-blockchain-strategy-big-and-bold-for-2017/

[2] Personal interview with Mary Lacity in 2017

[3] Personal interview with Mary Lacity in 2017

[4] Personal interview with Mary Lacity in 2017

[5] Tapscott, D. and Tapscott, A (2016), *Blockchain Revolution*, Penguin, New York City

[6] https://digiconomist.net/bitcoin-energy-consumption

https://digiconomist.net/ethereum-energy-consumption

[7] Tuwiner, J. (December 20, 2019), *Bitcoin Mining Pools*, https://www.buybitcoinworldwide.com/mining/pools/

[8] Sedgwick, K. (December 21st 2017), *These Are The Five Cheapest US States for Bitcoin Mining*, https://news.bitcoin.com/these-are-the-five-cheapest-us-states-for-bitcoin-mining/

Sharma, R. (February 21, 2018). *5 Best States for Bitcoin Mining (And the Worst)*. https://www.investopedia.com/news/five-best-states- bitcoin-mining-and-worst/

[9] https://www.ezblockchain.net/blog.html

[10] Personal interview with Mary Lacity and Kate Moloney in 2017

[11] Email interview with Mary Lacity in 2018

[12] Personal interview with Mary Lacity and Kate Moloney in 2017

[13] Thompson, P. (January 5, 2020). https://cointelegraph.com/news/most-significant-hacks-of-2019-new-record-of-twelve-in-one-year, *CoinTelegraph*, https://cointelegraph.com/news/most-significant-hacks-of-2019-new-record-of-twelve-in-one-year

[14] Shrem, C. (2019), *Bitcoin's Biggest Hack in History: 184.4 Billion Bitcoin from Thin Air*, Hackernoon, https://hackernoon.com/bitcoins-biggest-hack-in-history-184-4-ded46310d4ef

[15] *Stellar and Ripple Hacked: Justcoin to the Rescue*, Oct 14th, 2014, https://cointelegraph.com/news/stellar-and-ripple-hacked-justcoin-to-the-rescue

[16] Kaul, K. (September 23rd 2018). *'High Severity' Bug in Bitcoin Code Capable of Crashing the Cryptocurrency—Detected and Fixed*, LiveBitcoinNews, https://www.livebitcoinnews.com/high-severity-bug-in-bitcoin-code-capable-of-crashing-the-cryptocurrency-detected-and-fixed/

[17] Segal, D. (June 25th 2016), *Understanding the DAO attack*, http://www.coindesk.com/understanding-dao-hack-journalists/

[18] Diedrich, H. (2016), *Ethereum: blockchains, digital assets, smart contracts, decentralized autonomous organizations*, Wildfire publishing.

[19] Segal, D. (June 25th 2016), *Understanding the DAO attack*, http://www.coindesk.com/understanding-dao-hack-journalists/

[20] Segal, D. (June 25th 2016), *Understanding the DAO attack*, http://www.coindesk.com/understanding-dao-hack-journalists/

[21] Morisander (March 23, 2018). *The biggest smart contract hacks in history or how to endanger up to US $2.2 billion*, Medium, https://medium.com/solidified/the-biggest-smart-contract-hacks-in-history-or-how-to-endanger-up-to-us-2-2-billion-d5a72961d15d

[22] Karol (February 19, 2018). *PoWH Coin: What Happened To PoWHCoin Cryptocurrency?* https://bitcoinexchangeguide.com/powh-coin/

[23] Morisander (March 23, 2018). *The biggest smart contract hacks in history or how to endanger up to US $2.2 billion*, Medium, https://medium.com/solidified/the-biggest-smart-contract-hacks-in-history-or-how-to-endanger-up-to-us-2-2-billion-d5a72961d15d

[24] AnChain.AI (Aug 22, 2018). *Exposing An $18 Million USD Smart Contract Vulnerability*, Medium, https://medium.com/@AnChain.AI/largest-smart-contract-attacks-in-blockchain-history-exposed-part-1-93b975a374d0

[25] Tuwiner, J. (July 13th 2017), *Bitcoin Mining Pools*, https://www.buybitcoinworldwide.com/mining/pools/

[26] Emin Gün Sirer's presentation, *What Could Go Wrong? When Blockchains Fail*, Business of Blockchain conference, April 18th 2017, https://www.technologyreview.com/s/604219/blockchains-weak-spots-pose-a-hidden-danger-to-users/

[27] BitcoinChaser (September 21st 2017), *The Chinese Bitcoin Mining Takeover Conspiracy*, http://bitcoinchaser.com/chinese-bitcoin-mining-takeover-conspiracy/

[28] BitcoinChaser (September 21st 2017), *The Chinese Bitcoin Mining Takeover Conspiracy*, http://bitcoinchaser.com/chinese-bitcoin-mining-takeover-conspiracy/

[29] Crypto Mining Blog (April 27th 2017), *BitMain Up for Another Scandal with Antbleed Backdoor*, http://cryptomining-blog.com/8634-bitmain-up-for-another-scandal-with-antbleed-backdoor/

[30] Rowley, J. (April 27th 2017), *Tensions Persist as Traders Largely Shake Off The 'Antbleed' Bitcoin Backdoor Scandal*, https://news.crunchbase.com/news/tensions-persist-traders-largely-shake-off-antbleed-bitcoin-backdoor-scandal/

[31] Gencer, A.E., Basu, S., Eyal, I., cen Renesse, R., and Sirer, E.G, (January 15th 2018), *Decentralization in Bitcoin and Ethereum*, https://arxiv.org/pdf/1801.03998.pdf

[32] Avan-Nomayo, O. (May 29, 2018). *Strike Three? Verge suffers third suspected 51 percent attack*, Bitcoinist, https://bitcoinist.com/strike-three-verge-suffers-third-suspected-51-percent-attack/

[33] Hertig, A. (June 5, 2018). *Verge's Blockchain Attacks are Worth a Second Look*. Coindesk, https://www.coindesk.com/verges-blockchain-attacks-are-worth-a-sober-second-look

[34] Horizen (June 8, 2018). *ZenCash's Statement on Double Spend transaction*. https://blog.horizen.global/zencash-statement-on-double-spend-attack/

[35] Martin, J. (January 27, 2020). *Bitcoin Gold Blockchain Hit by 51 percent attack leading to $70K double spend*, CoinTelegraph, https://cointelegraph.com/news/bitcoin-gold-blockchain-hit-by-51-attack-leading-to-70k-double-spend

[36] Varsheney, N. (May 30, 2018). *Here's how much it costs to launch a 51 percent attack on PoW cryptocurrencies*, https://thenextweb.com/hardfork/2018/05/30/heres-how-much-it-costs-to-launch-a-51-attack-on-pow-cryptocurrencies/

[37] Zmudzinski, A. (January 13, 2019). *Ethereum Classic 51 percent hackers allegedly returned $100,000 to crypto exchange*, CoinTelegraph, https://cointelegraph.com/news/ethereum-classic-51-attackers-allegedly-returned-100-000-to-crypto-exchange

[38] Sharma, N. (November 5th 2017), *Is Quantum Computing an Existential Threat to Blockchain Technology?* https://singularityhub.com/2017/11/05/is-quantum-computing-an-existential-threat-to-blockchain-technology/ - sm.00009y4jmx95sdww11rov5gdjdlzo

[39] Schneier, B. (2015), *NSA Plans for a Post-Quantum World*, https://www.schneier.com/blog/archives/2015/08/nsa_plans_for_a.html

[40] Sharma, N. (November 5th 2017), *Is Quantum Computing an Existential Threat to Blockchain Technology?* https://singularityhub.com/2017/11/05/is-quantum-computing-an-existential-threat-to-blockchain-technology/ - sm.00009y4jmx95sdww11rov5gdjdlzo

[41] Email interview with Mary Lacity, February 20, 2020.

[42] Diedrich, H. (2016), *Ethereum: blockchains, digital assets, smart contracts, decentralized autonomous organizations*, Wildfire publishing.

[43] Personal interview with Mary Lacity in 2017

[44] https://etherscan.io/chart/blocktime

[45] SWIFT Fin Traffic & Figures, https://www.swift.com/about-us/swift-fin-traffic-figures

[46] *Bitcoin and Ethereum vs Visa and PayPal – Transactions per second*, Altcoin Today, April 22nd 2017, http://www.altcointoday.com/bitcoin-ethereum-vs-visa-paypal-transactions-per-second/

[47] BBC News (December 5th 2017), *CryptoKitties craze slows down transactions on Ethereum*, http://www.bbc.com/news/technology-42237162

Wong (December 4th 2017), *The Ethereum network is getting jammed up because people are rushing to buy cartoon cats on its blockchain*, https://qz.com/1145833/cryptokitties-is-causing-ethereum-network-congestion/?utm_source=MIT+Technology+Review&utm_campaign=d6185c2892-EMAIL_CAMPAIGN_2017_11_02&utm_medium=email&utm_term=0_997ed6f472-d6185c2892-156469793

[48] Sfox (May 24, 2019). *Ethereum 2.0: What the Next Three Years of Ethereum Will Look Like*, https://blog.sfox.com/ethereum-2-0-what-the-next-three-years-of-ethereum-will-look-like-b366a46f9704

[49] This website tracks average bitcoin transaction fee: https://bitinfocharts.com/comparison/bitcoin-transactionfees.html - 3m

[50] The second transaction on block 456958 shows a miner was paid by the sender .00036955 bitcoins to add this to the transaction to the block. On March 12, one bitcoin was worth $1232.99 , so miner received 45 cents that day to include this transaction https://blockexplorer.com/block/0000000000000000015c7bd17dc9a82f457a8aed35bc6606cca57cb5932deb7e

[51] To track average bitcoin transaction fee, see: https://bitinfocharts.com/comparison/bitcoin-transactionfees.html - 3m

[52] *Bitcoin's Transaction Backlog Hits All-Time High, Fees Skyrocket*, May 11thn 2017, http://www.trustnodes.com/2017/05/11/bitcoins-transaction-backlog-hits-all-time-high-fees-skyrocket

[53] Van Wirdum, A. (August 23, 2017). 'The Long Road To SegWit: How Bitcoin's Biggest Protocol Upgrade Became Reality', *Bitcoin Magazine*, https://bitcoinmagazine.com/articles/long-road-segwit-how-bitcoins-biggest-protocol-upgrade-became-reality

[54] For a technical explanation of segregated witness, see http://learnmeabitcoin.com/faq/segregated-witness

[55] Van Wirdum, A. (August 23, 2017). 'The Long Road To SegWit: How Bitcoin's Biggest Protocol Upgrade Became Reality', *Bitcoin Magazine*, https://bitcoinmagazine.com/articles/long-road-segwit-how-bitcoins-biggest-protocol-upgrade-became-reality

[56] *Bitcoin Magazine*. 'What is SegWit?' https://bitcoinmagazine.com/guides/what-is-segwit

[57] Reiff, N. (June 25, 2019). *A History of Bitcoin Hard Forks*, Investopedia, https://www.investopedia.com/tech/history-bitcoin-hard-forks/

[58] Catenis Enterprise, https://blockchainofthings.com/catenis-enterprise

[59] Personal interview with Mary Lacity and Kate Moloney in 2017

[60] Ethereum 2.0 Phases https://docs.ethhub.io/ethereum-roadmap/ethereum-2.0/eth-2.0-phases/

[61] *DistrictOx, Ethereum Sharding Explained*, https://education.district0x.io/general-topics/understanding-ethereum/ethereum-sharding-explained/

[62] Edgington, B. (August 28, 2018). *State of Ethereum Protocol #1*, Consensys, https://media.consensys.net/state-of-ethereum-protocol-1-d3211dd0f6

[63] Hertig, A. (May 31st 2016), *Will Ethereum Beat Bitcoin to Mainstream Microtransactions?*, https://www.coindesk.com/ethereum-bitcoin-mainstream-microtransactions/

[64] *The Raiden Network: High Speed Asset Transfers for Ethereum*, http://raiden.network/

[65] Robinson, Dan (2019). https://events.technologyreview.com/video/watch/dan-robinson-scaling-interoperability/

[66] IBM Research (February 2, 2018). *Hyperledger Fabric: A Distributed Operating System for Permissioned Blockchains*. https://www.ibm.com/blogs/research/2018/02/architecture-hyperledger-fabric/

[67] *What Is Hyperledger? How the Linux Foundation builds an open platform around the blockchain projects of Intel and IBM*, https://blockgeeks.com/guides/what-is-hyperledger/

Gorenflo, C., Lee, S. and Keshav, L. *FastFabric: Scaling Hyperledger Fabric to 20,000 Transactions per Second*. https://arxiv.org/pdf/1901.00910.pdf

[68] Castor, A. (June 14th 2017), *Hyperledger Takes on Blockchain Scaling with New Working Group*, https://www.coindesk.com/hyperledger-takes-on-blockchain-scaling-with-new-working-group/

[69] Hyperledger Blockchain Performance Metrics White Paper (2019). https://www.hyperledger.org/resources/publications/blockchain-performance-metrics

[70] To further protect privacy, users are advised to generate new addresses every time they receive bitcoins to prevent previous trading partners from detecting usage patterns.

[71] Nakamoto, S. (2008), *Bitcoin: A Peer-to-Peer Electronic Cash System*, p.6, https://bitcoin.org/bitcoin.pdf

[72] https://blockonomi.com/zero-knowledge-proofs/

[73] Lexie (December 7, 2017). *Zero-knowledge proofs explained Part 2: Non-interactive zero-knowledge proofs*. https://www.expressvpn.com/blog/zero-knowledge-proofs-explained-non-interactive-zero-knowledge-proofs/

Zhu, N. (April 8, 2019). *Understanding Zero-knowledge proofs through illustrated examples*, Medium, https://blog.goodaudience.com/understanding-zero-knowledge-proofs-through-simple-examples-df673f796d99

[74] https://upload.wikimedia.org/wikipedia/commons/thumb/e/e0/Sudoku_Puzzle_by_L2G-20050714_standardized_layout.svg/500px-Sudoku_Puzzle_by_L2G-20050714_standardized_layout.svg.png

[75] Allison, I. (May 22nd 2017), *Zero-knowledge proofs added to JP Morgan's Quorum*, http://www.ibtimes.co.uk/zero-knowledge-proofs-added-jp-morgans-quorum-blockchain-1622573

[76] *What are zk-SNARKs?*, https://z.cash/technology/zksnarks.html

[77] *What are zk-SNARKs?*, https://z.cash/technology/zksnarks.html

[78] EY (October 23, 2019). *Transforming the business lifecycle with Nightfall*, https://www.youtube.com/watch?v=SUtTy9RoXb0

[79] en.wikipedia.org

[80] https://moneroblocks.info/tx/898764c111ed490300fa58623c905ae335737a98ab28c49af34c8d9045915f82

[81] Personal interview with Mary Lacity in 2018

[82] Quorum White Paper, available at https://github.com/jpmorganchase/quorum-docs/blob/master/Quorum Whitepaper v0.1.pdf

[83] Cocco, S. and Singh, G. (March 20th 2017), *Top 6 technical advantages of Hyperledger Fabric for blockchain networks*, https://www.ibm.com/developerworks/cloud/library/cl-top-technical-advantages-of-hyperledger-fabric-for-blockchain-networks/index.html

[84] https://medium.com/chain-cloud-company-blog/hyperledger-vs-corda-pt-1-3723c4fa5028

[85] Personal interview with Mary Lacity and Kate Moloney in 2017

[86] Lucasxhy (September 11, 2018), *Cross-Chain-Interoperability*, https://medium.com/@lucx946/cross-chain- interoperability-3566695a1a72

[87] Ross, C. (December 5th 2016), *Blockchain Brings Us into The Future, But Only After It Drags Up the Past: Interoperability Becomes an Actual Issue Again*, http://www.horsesforsources.com/blog/christine-ferrusi-ross/the-interoperability-problems-blockchain-brings_120616

Ross, C. (April 18th 2017), *Simplify Blockchain by Refusing to Let Interoperability Issues Bog You Down*, posted on http://www.horsesforsources.com/Simplify-Blockchain-Refusing-Interoperability-Issues_041817

[88] The technical requirements come from several sources, particularly from Jin, H., Dai, X., Xiao, J. (2018), *Towards a Novel Architecture for Enabling Interoperability Amongst Multiple Blockchains*, IEEE 38th International Conference on Distributed Computer Systems, pp. 1203-1211. We also relied on:

Treat, D., Giordano, G., Schiatti, L., Borne-Pons, H. (Oct 22, 2018), *Connecting ecosystems: Blockchain integration*, Accenture White Paper, https://www.accenture.com/us-en/insights/blockchain/integration-ecosystems

Hardjono, T., Lipton, A., and Pentland, A. (2018), *Towards a Design Philosophy for Interoperable Blockchain Systems*, MIT Connection Science, https://arxiv.org/pdf/1805.05934.pdf

[89] https://en.bitcoin.it/wiki/Proof_of_burn

[90] Hallam, G. (May 2, 2016). *The BTC Relay is live! Bitcoin can now exist on the Ethereum blockchain*. Post to Reddit: https://www.reddit.com/r/Bitcoin/comments/4hhtwh/george_hallam_the_btc_relay_is_live_bitcoin_can/

[91] Nakamoto, S. (2008), Bitcoin: A Peer-to-Peer Electronic Cash System, https://bitcoin.org/bitcoin.pdf

[92] http://btcrelay.org/

[93] Ethereum, *Welcome to BTC Relay's Documentation!*, https://btc-relay.readthedocs.io/en/latest/index.htm

[94] BTC Relay's transactions can be viewed at https://etherscan.io/address/0x41f274c0023f83391de4e0733c609df5a124c3d4

[95] Buterin, V. (September 9, 2016). *Chain Interoperability*, https://static1.squarespace.com/static/55f73743e4b051cfcc0b02cf/t/5886800ecd0f68de303349b1/1485209617040/C hain+Interoperability.pdf

[96] For our interoperability discussion, notaries are trusted third parties. There are also projects in which smart contracts can serve as a notary, such as POEX.io that is used to 'time stamp' a document.

[97] Lerner, S. D. (April 2016). *Drivechains, sidechains, and hybrid 2-way peg designs*, https://uploads. strikinglycdn.com/files/27311e59-0832-49b5-ab0e- 2b0a73899561/Drivechains_Sidechains_and_ Hybrid_2-way_peg_Designs_R9.pdf

[98] Treat, D., Giordano, G., Schiatti, L., Borne-Pons, H. (Oct 22, 2018). *Connecting ecosystems: Blockchain integration*, Accenture White Paper, https://www.accenture.com/us-en/insights/blockchain/ integration-ecosystems

[99] https://newsroom.accenture.com/news/accenture-enables-interoperability-between-major-blockchain-platforms.htm

Accenture (October 22, 2018). *Connecting Ecosystems: Blockchain Integration*, https://www.accenture. com/us-en/insights/blockchain/integration-ecosystems

[100] Treat, D., Giordano, G., Schiatti, L., Borne-Pons, H. (Oct 22, 2018). *Connecting ecosystems: Blockchain integration*, Accenture White Paper, https://www.accenture.com/us-en/insights/blockchain/ integration-ecosystems

[101] https://en.wikipedia.org/wiki/Multisignature

[102] Higgins, S. (August 3, 2016), *The Bitfinex Bitcoin Hack: What We Know (And Don't Know)*. News Article, CoinDesk

[103] Press release (November 15, 2018). *BitGo First to Deliver Multi-Signature Security for Over 100 Coins and Tokens*, https://www.businesswire.com/news/home/20181115005640/en/BitGo-Deliver-Multi-Signature-Security-100- Coins-Tok

[104] https://www.bitgo.com/

Kharif, O. (February 19, 2019). *Crypto Startup Offers Insurance Against Quadriga Wallet Dilemma*, Bloomberg, https://www.bloomberg.com/news/articles/2019-02-19/crypto-startup-offers-insurance-against-quadriga-wallet-dilemma

[105] Lerner, S. D. (April 2016), *Drivechains, sidechains, and hybrid 2-way peg designs*, https://uploads. strikinglycdn.com/files/27311e59-0832-49b5-ab0e- 2b0a73899561/Drivechains_Sidechains_and_ Hybrid_2-way_peg_Designs_R9.pdf

[106] Back, A., Corallo, M., Dashjr, L., Friedenbach, M., Maxwell, G., Miller, A., Poelstra, A., Timón, J., and Wuille, P. (Oct 22 2014), *Enabling Blockchain Innovations with Pegged Sidechains*, https://blockstream. com/sidechains.pdf

[107] Buterin, V. (September 9, 2016), *Chain Interoperability*, https://static1.squarespace.com/ static/55f73743e4b051cfcc0b02cf/t/5886800ecd0f68de303349b1/1485209617040/C hain+Interoperability. pdf

[108] "Back, A., Friedenbach, M., Miller, A., Poelstra, A., Timon, J., and Wuille, P. (Oct 22m 2014). *Enabling Blockchain Innovations with Pegged Sidechains*, https://blockstream.com/sidechain

[109] https://blockstream.com/liquid-faq/

[110] *SPV, Simplified Payment Verification*, Bitcoin.Org glossary.

[111] Lerner, S. D. (April 2016), *Drivechains, sidechains, and hybrid 2-way peg designs*, https://uploads. strikinglycdn.com/files/27311e59-0832-49b5-ab0e- 2b0a73899561/Drivechains_Sidechains_and_ Hybrid_2-way_peg_Designs_R9.pdf

[112] Thomas, S., and Schwatz, E, (2015), *A Protocol for Interledger Payments*, https://interledger.org/ interledger.pdf

[113] *Hashed-Timelock Agreements (HTLAs)* https://interledger.org/rfcs/0022-hashed-timelock-agreements/

[114] https://www.hyperledger.org/projects/quilt

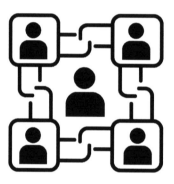

Chapter 9

Mindshifts, Strategies and Action Principles

"Blockchains will do for networks of enterprises and business ecosystems what Enterprise Resource Planning (ERP) did for the single company."

Paul Brody, Principal & Global Blockchain Leader at EY

"The only way we are going to get value for the whole industry is to think differently about working together. I've been calling blockchain a 'team sport' for a few years now. We have to work with our competitors on things that improve the entire industry, like safety, quality, and reducing barriers to trade across borders."

Dale Chrystie, Blockchain Strategist at FedEx,
Chair of BiTA Standards Council

"We have seen many successful blockchain pilots, but unless network participants feel comfortable using it to collaborate and share data at scale, the advantages of distributed ledgers won't materialize."

Marie Wieck, General Manager, IBM Blockchain[1]

9.1. Making enterprise blockchains a reality

Thus far in our journey, we've examined the blockchain landscape, the promised benefits of enterprise blockchains, actual examples of enterprise blockchains across industries, and the major technical challenges and emerging technical solutions. Now we turn to business issues. In this chapter, we examine what it takes for traditional enterprises to actually gain value from enterprise blockchains. It's not easy; enterprises face a daunting 'technology-embeddedness' challenge. Endemic to all technologies, live blockchain applications must be assimilated within complex institutional, political, regulatory, social, economic, and existing systems.[2] But while most technology solutions are adopted *inside* firm boundaries, blockchains are best-suited for inter-organizational contexts. It requires an unprecedented level of cooperation with competitors and other mind shifts that only an executive can champion efficaciously. It's no wonder that HfS Research found that only 131 out of 940 (14 percent) of blockchain initiatives had reached the production stage by Q1 2020.[3] But the good news is that we can learn important lessons from early adopters.

In this chapter, we present **action principles** for making blockchain-enabled solutions a reality (see Figure 9.1). Action principles are practices identified by our research that produced desirable results in real world implementations. Action principles are therefore grounded in data and are designed to assist other thoughtful agents as they embark on their own implementation journeys. Action principles are similar to best practices in that both seek to share knowledge from prior experiences. But whereas 'best practices' imply that mimicry is always recommended and will always produce similar results, action principles recognize that context matters. The usefulness of a practice depends on the objectives the organization is trying to achieve, whether the organization has the absorptive capacity to implement the practice effectively; and timing—there are better times than others to apply a specific practice. As social scientists, we view managers as thoughtful agents who scrutinize 'best practices' derived from other people's learnings to decide when and whether practices need to be modified, or perhaps discarded, within their organizations.[4]

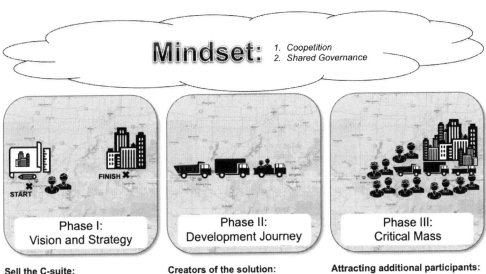

Figure 9.1: Action principles for making enterprise
blockchain-enabled solutions a reality

9.2. The blockchain mindset: coopetition and shared governance

Blockchain-based applications are primarily ecosystem solutions. Value comes from uplifting the entire ecosystem to remove friction and other pain points. It requires working with competitors, trading partners, open source communities, and regulators. Traditional enterprises need to think differently about competitive advantage and what 'winning' entails. Traditional enterprises also need to shift their mindsets when moving from internal, command-and-control, centralized applications to shared, distributed applications. Specifically, traditional enterprises need to shift to **coopetition** and **shared governance** mindsets.

9.2.1. Coopetition

"Companies are interested in pursuing these problems together. And in principle, we're tackling problems that are not a strategic advantage for them but that they all share."

Susanne Somerville, CEO of Chronicled and co-founder of MediLedger[5]

"Blockchains have competitors coming together in a platform, and that is different and counter-intuitive from how they have worked before. But the advantage of connecting one-to-many, of everyone seeing in real-time the information pertaining to the shipments they are involved in and visibility into the digital data documents, is a game-changer. Blockchain supports it and provides immutable trust."

Mike White, CEO of Maersk GTD[6]

Coopetition is a portmanteau of two words—'cooperation' and 'competition'. The concept has been around for over 100 years when realtors both cooperated and competed to create the first multiple listing real estate service.[7] However, coopetition has only recently been formalized in scholarly works, most notably by Giovanni Battista Dagnino and Giovanna Padula. In their 2002 paper, they conceptualized a 'coopetition strategy' as a new type of interfirm dynamic for value creation. They wrote:

"The coopetitive perspective stems from the acknowledgment that, within interfirm interdependence, both processes of value creation and value sharing take place, giving rise to a partially convergent interest (and goal) structure where both competitive and cooperative issues are simultaneously present and strictly interconnected. They give rise to a new kind of strategic interdependence among firms that we term coopetitive system of value creation."[8]

Coopetition among automotive manufacturers is a classic example. Companies such as BMW; Chrysler; Daimler; Fiat; Ford; Honda; GM; Porsche; Renault; Suzuki; Toyota; and Volkswagen have cooperated on R&D and car components to reduce costs, but have competed based on their own distribution channels and brands. Effective coopetition generates both economic value (lower costs, increased revenues, and risk mitigation) and knowledge value (best practices, standards, and technology development).[9] For the blockchain context, traditional enterprises will need to embrace the coopetition mindset:

✓ *Action Principle 1: Shift the mindset from competition to coopetition.*

For the blockchain context, coopetition entails complex relationships among three or more organizations that may operate at different levels (see Figure 9.2):

- *Macro-level coopetition* involves relationships among firms within and across industries.[10] The value of macro-level coopetition includes the creation of horizontal frameworks and standards across industries which serve to share learning, to reduce investment costs, and to accelerate adoption. The Hyperledger Project is an example of a macro-level blockchain initiative with participation across many industries and geographies.

- *Meso-level coopetition* involves relationships among firms within the same industry. Meso-level coopetition focuses on building solutions that uplift participants within an industry. WeTrade, IBM Food Trust, and TradeLens are examples.

- *Micro-level coopetition* involves relationships among organizations/divisions within a global firm. Many global firms operate independent legal entities that require formal transfers of value among them. Working together, they can reduce administrative costs for all and create possibilities for new products and services. Sandander's bond issuance and settlement on Ethereum is an example.

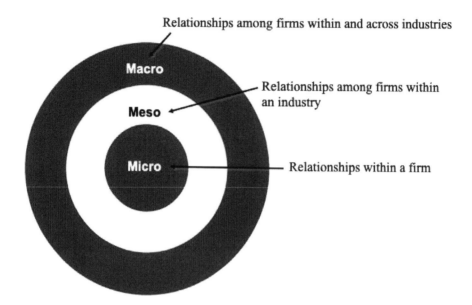

Figure 9.2: Three levels of coopetition

In the realm of blockchains, Dale Chrystie, Blockchain Strategist at FedEx and Chair of BiTA Standards Council, has been the most vocal advocate of coopetition, particularly at the macro-level. In 2020, Dale said:

> *"I have been talking about 'coopetition' around blockchain for more than a year, but the concept of 'coopetition' is so much bigger than blockchain. Coopetition isn't about people in one industry working on something together—it is about ALL industries working on something together."*

Effective coopetition requires that each participant commit to partnering behaviors (see Figure 9.3).[11] Each participant commits to **focusing on the future**, not where they may have conflicted in the past. Each participant **commits to a larger mission** rather than to its own advantage. Moreover, each participant stays committed to the greater mission even when they are outvoted on some issues.

Within any working group or consortium—particularly those that include competitors—there will be heated debates. During deliberations, participants do not say *"this is not my problem"* nor do they seek to assign fault or blame. Instead, participants treat a **problem for one as a problem for all** and rally to solve issues jointly. Whatever happens during deliberations, participants should subsequently **present a united front** to those outside of the group. Effective groups embrace a spirit of togetherness, and continually message the greater mission to the public.

Participation Pledge

1. I will focus on the future.
2. I am committed to our larger mission.
3. I will treat your problems as my problems.
4. I will present a united front.
5. My organization will devote time and resources.
6. My organization will be transparent about intentions.
7. My organization has authorized me to make decisions.

Figure 9.3: Example of a participant pledge

Each participating organization **commits time and resources to the endeavor**. Optimally, founding partners should commit equal resources to give equal voice. But in some contexts where smaller-sized or fringe players are needed for end-to-end processes, resource commitments can be commensurate with capabilities, size and potential realized benefits from the solution. Less powerful participants will want to know the answer to this question: *While you are cooperating here, where will you compete when this solution is delivered?* The more powerful partners need to be exceedingly **transparent in their intentions and behaviors** to convince less powerful partners to cooperate. The general consensus is that traditional competitors need to cooperate to build standards, to influence regulations, and to create platforms. Competition will then be based on products and services built on top of the platforms.

Most importantly, **each representative has sufficient credibility, clout and power within his/her organization** to make decisions on behalf of the enterprise.[12] Nothing slows down an effort faster than agreeing with ecosystem partners only to find no support back in one's own company.

9.2.2. Shared Governance

"Distributed ledgers present a dual challenge for companies, one that is arguably 20 percent technological and 80 percent governance."

Marie Wieck, General Manager, IBM Blockchain[13]

As I anticipated in 2019 when I left We.Trade in May 2019, enterprise blockchain projects driven by banks and insurances are too slow to pick up momentum based on governance issues among stakeholders and shareholders and lack of return on investment culture.

Roberto Mancone, A co-founder and former COO of WeTrade

Governance defines the decision-making rights pertaining to a blockchain-enabled solution. Enterprises need a better understanding of the scope of decisions to be made, the governance options, and how governance portfolios evolve over time. They need to embrace the following lesson:

✓ *Action Principle 2: Shift the mindset from command-and-control to shared governance.*

For an entire blockchain ecosystem, the scope of decision-making rights is complex. Participants need to agree on governance mechanisms for all of the following:

- **Mission:** What is the mission of the blockchain-based solution?

- **Data policies:** What data is collected? Who owns the data on the shared ledger? What is its exact format? Who can view the data? Who decides how data can be used? How is privacy ensured? How is erroneous data fixed on an immutable ledger? How is data retired?

- **Rights of participation:** Who can join us? Who can submit transactions? Who decides, or what is the process, to banish a participant?

- **Rights of validation:** Who is allowed to operate the validation nodes in the network? Are the individuals or institutions that operate nodes truly independent and unlikely to collude? Who decides, or what is the process, to banish a node?

- **Rights of overrides:** Who is authorized to roll back the ledger in the instance of egregious errors? (i.e. Who has the power to create a hard fork?)

- **Rights of ownership:** Who owns the software? How are licenses managed?

- **Compliance:** Who is in charge of ensuring regulatory compliance? Who is liable if a law is violated or a regulation is not followed?

- **Software update control:** Who decides what patches and functionality will be added and when? How are software changes coordinated across a distributed network of nodes?

- **Governance residence:** What governance, if any, is on chain so that majority-rule decisions are automatically adopted verses off-chain governance that requires human intervention?

- **Funding model:** Who pays what? Who decides the pricing model (including transaction fees)?[14]

Decision making rights might be held by benevolent dictatorships; oligarchies; stakeocracies; federations; representative meritocracies; meritocracies; and/or democracies. These governance structures have varying degrees of decentralization (see Figure 9.4) and have different advantages.

345

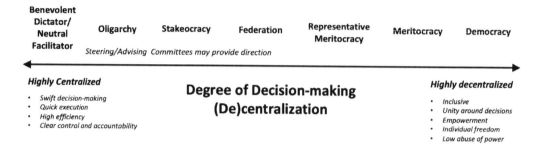

Figure 9.4: Blockchain governance models

The benefits of centralized decision-making include swift decisions, quick execution, high efficiency, and clear control and accountability

Users have an identifiable person, organization or group to address questions, concerns, or complaints. Issues that arise—such as the discovery of a software bug or an attack on the blockchain network—can be dealt with swiftly. Centralized governance, however, is viewed by many to be antithetical to the principles and purposes of blockchains, which aim to dissipate power across a network of participants.

The benefits of decentralized decision-making are inclusion; empowerment (every voice counts); unity around decisions; freedom to join and leave; and low abuse of power.

The main argument for centralized governance is to get a blockchain ecosystem launched with a core set of enthusiastic founders. Founders, however, need to commit to a plan for moving to more transparent and inclusive governance to attract a critical mass of additional adopters. Even Bitcoin started out with a benevolent dictator model before decision-making rights were distributed.[15] Each governance model is described below.

A **benevolent dictator** is a single person or single organization that solely holds decision making rights. The community trusts the person or organization to make decisions based on the best interests of the community. Initially, Satoshi Nakamoto over the Bitcoin whitepaper and Bitcoin Core and Vitalik Buterin over the idea for Ethereum, are examples of benevolent dictators over public blockchains.[16] These projects succeeded because the earliest of adopters—typically other like-minded coders—trusted the founders' intentions, even in the interesting case of Bitcoin where we do not know the identity of Nakamoto. Nathanial Popper, reporter for the *New York Times*, wrote:

> *"Satoshi's anonymity, if anything, seemed to increase the level of faith in the system. The anonymity suggested that Bitcoin was not created by a person seeking personal fame or success."*[17]

Traditional enterprises may prefer to call this governance model a **neutral facilitator** or **founder-led** model. For example, Chronicled is the neutral facilitator over MediLedger and iDatafy is the neutral facilitator over SmartResume.

If launched by a few partners, blockchain governance likely begins as an **oligarchy,** where power rests with a few. Most permissioned blockchains are being developed by a core group of partners, sometimes referred to as the **minimal viable ecosystem** (MVE). These partners—often comprising competitors as well as trading partners—form some sort of a council or consortium charged with developing and enforcing the rules for the initiative. WeTrade is one example. It began as an agreement among seven banks to build a **minimal viable product** (MVP). By their very nature, the rules represent a negotiated treaty among the founding partners, maximizing shared benefits. Founders will likely need to alter rules as they seek to attract additional partners after deployment.

'Staked' oligarchies, which we call **'stakeocracies'**, is a governance model where people pay to become part of the oligarchy. The Libra Association is an example. Council members (initially 28 firms) will need to buy *at least* $10 million in Libra Investment Tokens. The Libra Association refers to its decision-making process as 'proportional power', where voting powers of the council will be proportional to their stake, but with a cap to prevent an overtaking of the association.[18] As of 2020, the Libra Association lost some of its founding members—including PayPal, Mastercard, eBay, and Vodafone—after regulators expressed deep concerns, particularly over Facebook's influence as initiator of the project. Many people are concerned that Calibra (Facebook's digital wallet for libra coins) will have an unfair competitive advantage.[19] It is still early days, and the Libra Association's proposed governance model likely will evolve.[20]

Federations allow decentralized groups to specialize on parts of the project while coordinating with a central group to integrate solutions. The Hyperledger Project's overarching structure is a set of specialized projects. However, the Hyperledger Project's Technical Steering Committee is governed by what can be called a **representative meritocracy**, where people have to prove their merit to be eligible for election to a committee based on votes from other meritorious members. Working group leaders for Hyperledger's projects submit active contributors (there were 424 as of the last election) and all active participants vote to elect the 11 leaders. The 11-person Technical Steering Committee has decision rights over the admission of new projects, rules over projects, and status of projects (incubation/active).[21]

With a **meritocracy,** power is held by people based on their ability and goodwill. The aim is to elicit multiple views from informed stakeholders, debate views in open forums, and then stress-test ideas to find the best solution. Anyone, for example, can propose ideas to the Bitcoin Improvement Proposal (BIP). The whole Bitcoin community (miners, developers, and investors) can vote on the proposal based on its merit. By 2019, 322 BIPs had been submitted, of which 35 had been finalized.[22]

A **democracy** is the most decentralized form of governance, where one participant gets one vote. That's why many people like the fact that Bitcoin and Ethereum miners 'vote' by either installing or failing to install changes to the source code.

In addition to the governance structures covered above, enterprise blockchains often use a **steering committee** or an **advisory committee.** These committees may or may not have decision-making rights, but are nonetheless influential in guiding, recommending, and providing expertise on the development of the blockchain. Often used in conjunction with centralized governance structures, steering/advisory committees help ensure that decisions are transparent (at least to the members). The IBM Food Trust and MediLedger rely on such committees for direction.

The IBM Food Trust has an advisory council, comprising nine members as of July 2019: Walmart; Dole; Nestlé; Kroger; Carrefour; Danone; Driscoll's; Golden State Foods (GFS); and GS1. According to its website:

> *"An Advisory Council comprised of a range of industry representatives helps set the rules of engagement for the blockchain community, ensuring that the solution benefits all."*[23] Council members *"share, learn, discuss, prioritize and address the opportunities and challenges relevant to the food industry globally. They actively learn from each other and the market to provide meaningful direction to IBM Food Trust."*[24]

The chair of the Advisory Committee is elected for a two-year term by the other council members.

Founded by Chronicled, MediLedger is building in partnership with life science companies an open and decentralized network for the pharmaceutical supply chain. MediLedger has a steering committee that serves as the final word on any issue that could not be resolved with working teams, project managers, or the network owner. So, in this example, the steering committee *does* have decision-making rights.[25]

Within a blockchain-based solution, some decisions might be governed with one model and other decisions governed by another, forming a **governance portfolio**. For example, a steering committee might oversee data policies while a neutral facilitator oversees validation nodes. Moreover, the governance portfolio will likely evolve over time. Most blockchain-enabled applications/platforms/projects are launched by one entity or by a few partners. Initially, the founder or founding partners have full control over the suite of governance decisions, mainly because there is no one else to delegate power to yet. When the network launches and grows, blockchain governance should become—if not more decentralized—more transparent.

In summary, blockchain applications are ecosystem solutions that require enterprises to collaborate in new ways and to think differently about software governance. Traditional enterprises may struggle with these mind shifts. How does an enterprise establish a business case, estimate a return on investment, or otherwise justify building an application that has to be shared with trading partners and, very likely, with competitors? The blockchain evangelists within an enterprise may believe in the power of ecosystem solutions, but they will need the support of top management to be successful.

9.3. Selling the C-suite

Figure 9.5: Dilbert's boss is confused by blockchains

As the Dilbert Cartoon in Figure 9.5 so humorously depicts, the C-suite does not care about technology. Instead, the c-suite wants to know: How will coopetition and shared governance ultimately deliver any value to us? Where are the greatest opportunities for business value?

So far, this book has repeatedly talked about business value in terms of lower transaction costs and faster settlement times because parties trade directly with each other; no need for reconciliations because there is a reliable audit trail on the shared ledger, parties all agree *"this is what transpired"*; better traceability of assets from commissioning to decommissioning; reduced threat of vendor opportunism because smart contracts execute as pre-agreed by trading partners; heightened cyber security that de-risks critical infrastructure systems through distributed redundancy; and new revenue streams from expanding offerings to existing customers or from accessing new customers. While these value opportunities are powerful, they may be too generic to sway senior executives. To convince the C-suite, the following action principles are suggested:

✓ *Action Principle 3: The C-suite needs the blockchain evangelists to transform generic value propositions into a vivid, specific and compelling vision for the enterprise.*

Colonel James Allen Regenor, USAF (ret) and founder and CEO of VeriTX, is an advocate for selling the C-suite with scenario-based visions. To sell his idea for a business-to-business platform for the printing of parts and for the buying, selling, and tracking of digital and physical assets, recall his vision from Chapter 5:

> *"Imagine a scenario where lives depend upon a mission being flown off the deck of an aircraft carrier far out at sea. The only available aircraft has just been grounded with a failed critical part. There is no part inventory on the carrier. But we do have a 3-D printer and a stock of powder aboard. A technical data package is available for the part, and a replacement is quickly printed. You are the responsible person who needs to get this part quickly fitted to the aircraft and to sign the plane off as safe and ready to fly. How would you know if the newly printed additive manufacturing part you are holding in your hand is good for use?"*[26]

As another example, John Whelan, Managing Director, Digital Investment Bank for Santander, offered this simple yet compelling message to the C-suite:

"At its heart, a bank is a ledger, a way to track who owns what. Before blockchains, each bank has its own ledger and no banks trust the other banks' ledgers. After blockchains, banks do not need to trust each other—they trust the shared private ledger, transforming the banking industry architecture from 'many banks, many ledgers' to an industry with 'many banks, fewer ledgers'."

Often times, senior executives relate well to a very sharp, simple message. Compelling examples from our supply chain cases included the visions of 'farm to fork' for food; 'bait to plate' for seafood; 'grape to glass' for fine wines; and 'mine to finger' for diamond traceability.

✓ *Action Principle 4: Use success stories from early adopters as powerful examples of value delivered.*

Observability, defined as the 'degree to which the results of an innovation are visible to others', is a powerful way to convince C-suite executives.[27] Carrefour, for example, has boosted sales for some of its products that are traced on a blockchain and are accessible to consumers via QR codes.[28] While this book has highlighted many such solutions, we take this opportunity to introduce another solution, called KoreConX. KoreConX is a blockchain-enabled solution that provides private companies access to global capital markets. The KoreConX platform has been in live production since December 2016, and KoreConX's blockchain (KoreChain) was launched in October 2019.

KoreConX

More than 80,000 public companies have easy access to global investors who can use their cell phones to issue trades in seconds. In contrast, the 450 million private companies have very limited access to investors. Small, privately-owned companies rely on local dealers and brokers when trying to raise capital. Each deal is unique, and typically takes weeks for a private company to find a counterparty, negotiate an agreement, and gain approvals from their boards. Moreover, there is little automation; most private companies rely on local spreadsheets. The idea behind KoreConX is a platform:

"to give small-to-medium-sized enterprises (SMEs) a single location to manage all of their corporate records, funding, investors and investment brokers so they could efficiently take advantage of innovative new capital-raising opportunities."[29]

Kiran Garimella, Chief Scientist and CTO for KoreConX, describes the platform as …

"an infrastructure of trust that welcomes all regulated entities."[30]

Besides running the platform, KoreConX is a transfer agent that also operates on the platform, but more than 600 KorePartners that include broker-dealers, securities lawyers, secondary market operators, and other service providers provide the bulk of the business operations on the platform. For example, providers ensure KYC, such as certifications for accredited investors that prove their net worth and income levels, and identity verification for non-accredited investors.

The platform provides an easy way to digitize digital securities, including equity; options; warrants; debentures; SAFE, bonds; convertible bonds; promissory notes; loans; and liens. KoreConX also digitizes intellectual property because IP is part of a company's valuation. However, issuing digital assets is a one-time event and represents a small portion of the transaction activity. The platform provides services for ongoing trades and corporate actions like shareholders meetings; pre-emptive rights; exercise of first rights of refusal; tag-along rights; drag-along rights; dividend distributions; exits; and mergers and acquisitions. The platform's features include portfolio management; CapTable management; minute books; deal rooms; investor relations; transfer agency; capital markets; secondary markets; and compliance. Basic services are free for everyone to use. Kore Plus+ features cost $150 per month, and include services like telephone support, investor relations dashboards, and shareholder reports. For KoreConX, it mainly earns revenues from its professional transfer agent services (prices vary). Numerous private issuers have chosen the KoreConX platform. Examples include BrewDog, LegionM, GoldenSeed, TastyEquity, Quadrant, Atomic Video, and S2A Modular.

As far as business valued delivered, Oscar A. Jofre, CEO of KoreConX said:

> *"In our daily conversations with companies (issuers), investors, broker-dealers, board members, and other stakeholders, we come across many examples of how efficient processes are valuable. Unlike in disconnected systems, when transactions on this platform are made efficient for one party, the benefits quickly spread to, and are shared by all the other parties involved in the transaction. Process efficiencies and reduced costs are the most obvious benefits, but the value goes beyond to improved user experience and stronger, sustained long-term relationships, and trust."*

Table 9.1 highlights the improvements to transaction speeds.

Process	Old way	KoreConX Way
Issuer due diligence	60-120 days	30 days or less
Verification	days to weeks	seconds
KYC	days to weeks	minutes
Capital raising round closing	weeks, months	minutes
Shareholder onboarding	months	seconds to minutes

Table 9.1: KoreConX transaction speed improvements

Source: KoreConX

As of Q1 2020, KoreConX's blockchain (KoreChain) is deployed in 23 countries, on five different cloud platforms (IBM, AWS, Azure, Google, Digital Ocean), and has the capacity to process 10 billion transactions per year (about 318 transactions per second). KoreConX has 75,000 private companies on the platform, 1.2 billion shares, 32 million options, and 1.2 million warrants. As CTO, Garimella is enthusiastic about the technology, but he says that neither the investors nor the C-suite care about blockchains, leading us to the next lesson:

✓ *Action Principle 5: Put blockchains in the background, just focus on the value of the solution.*

C-suite executives do not care about the underlying technology, they care about what technology enables. Kiran Garimella, said:

> *"It's not blockchain alone that solves the problem. It's the application sitting on the blockchain that solves the problem."*

For the KoreConX solution, the company varies the messages to the C-suites by ecosystem players. For the C-suite of private companies, the messages focuses on guaranteed compliance, better issuance (multi-jurisdiction) and liquidity. For the C-suite of private equity investors, the message focuses on access to global market opportunities, safety, protection, and due diligence. For broker-dealers, the messaging is on improved deal flow, compliance, and syndication. For securities attorneys, it is about efficient compliance, more clients and business, managing regulatory and contract risks. For providers (transfer agents, KYC/AML, custodians), the main advantage is scalability.

The action principle was evident in other cases. At Walmart, for example, the C-suite cares deeply about food safety, food quality, and food waste reduction. These were the reasons that compelled Walmart to adopt the IBM Food Trust and VeChain. The fact that the food traceability solutions happen to be based on blockchain technologies was just a back story.

✓ *Action Principle 6: The C-suite can also be convinced of blockchain's value by highlighting the consequences of inaction.*

Blockchain applications have the potential to disrupt many current business models. No CEO wants to be blind-sided by her company's 'Uber' or 'Blockbuster' moment. Many times, the price of inaction is extinction. Mike Walker, Sr. Director, Applied Innovation Team for Microsoft made this provocative warning to accounting firms:

> *"Reconciliations are on the endangered species list."*

It's no wonder that the Big Four Accounting firms—Deloitte, EY, KPMG and PwC— have all built blockchain competencies. Banks are another example; many may find that their future competitors are tech firms that offer better financial services at a fraction of the costs. Recall also the words of John Whelan, Managing Director, Digital Investment Bank for Santander, from Chapter 4:

> *"If we do not build it, somebody else will. So, I think the banks realize that our competitors are not just other banks, but our competitors are also big tech, whether it's Facebook, Google, Alibaba or TenCent. In many respects, money and value are just ones and zeros in a machine and that's an engineering problem, not a financial problem."* [31]

9.4. Blockchain strategy: an ecosystem perspective

> *"Large banks are obviously enamored by blockchain. They all have innovation labs that are digging into it, but I don't see the change coming from there. Going from proof-of-concept to actual production is a huge, long road. It's hard to basically cannibalize your own business. It's hard to give up centralized control. Large institutions are calcified, they benefit form the status quo. So that's why we don't focus that much on large banks. We spend most of our time on these smaller, innovative financial institutions because they're able to move much quicker."*

Jed McCaleb, Cofounder and CTO of Stellar Development Foundation [32]

> *"I think that there are selective examples where a blockchain can be disruptive, but for the vast majority of our clients, blockchains are at the forefront of transformations that will reduce costs."*

Eamonn Maguire, Global Lead, Digital Ledger Services, KPMG [33]

In these early days of blockchain development, we see multiple platforms being developed for essentially the same use cases, such as food traceability; maritime tracking; trade finance; and credentials. We are seeing a proliferation of ecosystems of ecosystems.

Some ecosystems will fail, some ecosystems will consolidate (like Batavia did when it disbanded and joined WeTrade), and hopefully many will be interoperable. One of the powerful implications of a coopetition mindset is that the partners are going to need a business strategy at the ecosystem level.

The lessons from the great business theoretician Professor Clayton Christensen apply. Beginning with his first book on the subject, the *Innovator's Dilemma,* published in 1997, Christensen defined **disruptive innovation** as a *process* by which an innovation creates a new market that eventually disrupts an existing market, thereby displacing traditional enterprises.[34,35] Christensen observed that traditional enterprises find it very difficult to break their successful business models by cannibalizing revenues from existing products with a disruptive innovation. But don't rule out traditional enterprises, for the theory asserts that traditional enterprises can create disruption through a separate spinoff, and furthermore, can use technologies for what Christensen terms as **sustaining innovations**—those innovations that improve products and services within existing markets. Sustaining innovations can deliver substantial business value to the entire ecosystem; disruption does not have to be the strategic choice. To apply the Theory of Disruptive Innovation to blockchain ecosystems, one just needs to elevate the unit of analysis from the firm-level to the ecosystem-level. Here are the lessons:

✓ *Action Principle 7: Pursue sustaining innovations for ecosystems comprising mostly traditional enterprises.*

So many traditional enterprises we have spoken to have appropriated the language of 'disruption' when in fact they were building 'sustaining' innovations. Sustaining innovations add value by improving the performance of today's products and services for its most demanding customers. Not every innovation needs to rip an industry apart.

When ecosystem partners join forces successfully, they do not wipe out trusted third parties or by-pass intermediaries (although their roles may change). Rather, successful endeavors happen when partners work together on the shared objectives of reducing friction amongst themselves, and ultimately benefiting their customers. In short, many of the enterprise blockchain solutions embody the motto 'Rising tides raise all ships'. KoreConX, Santander's Bond Issuance, IBM Food Trust, MediLedger, and WeTrade are examples of traditional enterprises coming together to uplifts all parties rather than to eliminate any one of them. No parties were threatened with disintermediation.

Rather than help to build sustaining innovations, traditional enterprises can also decide to buy them:

✓ *Action Principle 8: Buy sustaining innovations as a service.*

Incumbent enterprises do not necessarily have to build sustaining innovations with ecosystem partners. They can allow others to build them and then buy them as a service. While followers bear little investment risk with this model, they may end up with suboptimal choices.

From Chapter 4, we learned that Ripple's customers are primarily institutional enterprises like banks, corporates, payment providers and exchanges. They gain benefits from engaging Ripple, but did not necessarily participate or invest in its development. For banking customers, Ripple promises that banks will capture new revenue by booking new corporate and consumer clients, reduce their transaction costs, and provide one integration point and a consistent experience for rules, standards and governance.[36]

State Street, a US-based global financial services firm, reached the buy/partner-versus-build conclusion after years of internal development. In September of 2016, State Street hired a new Chief Technology Architect (CTA), in part because of his long history with open-source projects. Over the next few years, the blockchain team grew to over 100 people. It was using Hyperledger Fabric to build an open source permissioned blockchain solution to create a single book of record. The idea was to eliminate the need for reconciliations across hundreds of databases.[37] In May 2019, the CTA left State Street to co-found a startup. In December of 2019, State Street cut at least 100 blockchain developers. Doug Brown, head of alternative financing solutions at State

Street, told Coindesk:

> *"There is a real question about whether it's worth their time to build that infrastructure, the cost to do it, the staffing to do it."* [38]

Rather than build an in-house DLT solution, State Street thought it was time to rely more on outside providers. According to Ralph Achkar, managing director of digital products at State Street in London:

> *"I think the choice in approaching that space was, do we need to have all of these resources internally, or can we actually build partnerships and work with other providers in the market?"* [39]

✓ *Action Principle 9: For traditional enterprises, be wary of attempting disruptive innovations.*

We have several examples of traditional enterprises working in consortia that failed to deliver any solution when they claimed the ambition to disrupt the industry. We highlight one example of a failed attempt.

Healthcare provider consortium

The head of innovation for one large health care provider was working with ecosystem partners to redesign healthcare. They knew the solution had to be disruptive rather than sustaining. He said:

> *"You see some things, particularly in radiology, where a patient pays $800 for an MRI in a physician's office, and ours cost $2,400. Which one do you think somebody's going to go to for an MRI? There's a point where you have to disrupt yourself."* [40]

He tried for a few years to evangelize the message to senior management. He continued:

> *"We need to design a consumer-centric, transparent healthcare system. I want to use blockchains to disrupt the current system, because it will be insolvent in ten years if we don't."*

Two years later, he left the company and the consortium after concluding that healthcare payers don't want to be disrupted—they make money by sitting on huge stores of cash. He said:

> *"Payers don't want claims to be streamlined with a blockchain. One of them told me he took it to their executives for review and was told, 'don't bring this back up…it is career limiting for you.' That's what we are fighting against. They can see losing money if claims are immediately adjudicated."*

Many of the blockchain innovation leaders we met in 2018 from large traditional enterprises left their organizations to start blockchain ventures or advisory firms. In addition to the head of innovation of the healthcare provider and the CTA of State Street mentioned above, blockchain leaders from CME Group, JP Morgan, Moog, and the State of Illinois also left to start their own companies. Blockchain leaders could not drive disruptive innovations from within because business sponsors within traditional enterprises blocked or failed to support disruption. One departed leader said, in 2020:

> *"It is very difficult to disrupt an organization from the inside. We were excited to build a digital ledger on top of systems of record, but the business sponsors just wanted to recreate the old models on the new world, so we lost support."*

When disruption does occur successfully, Professor Clayton Christensen observed that startups and spinoffs are the most likely producers of them.

✓ *Action Principle 10: Pursue disruptive innovations for ecosystems with nimble startups or spinoffs.*

Much of our empirical evidence aligned with theory. Most notably, Moog and Innogy—covered in Chapters 5 and 6 respectfully—were creating low-end market disruptions and new markets, and were doing so as predicted by Christensen. While working at Moog Aircraft, Colonel James Allen Regenor began working on a business-to-business blockchain-enabled solution for printed parts. This was a completely disruptive innovation, as it would pivot Moog from traditional manufactured parts to additive manufacturing. Ultimately, Regenor decided to depart Moog in 2018 to accelerate moving from POCs to live production. Regenor stayed on as a consultant with Moog as he launched VeriTX and Moog is one of its partners. As covered in Chapter 6, RWE's Innogy—the German-based electric utility—spun-off a separate company called Share&Charge from its corporate innovation center to launch a blockchain-based application that creates a market for individuals to buy and sell capacity from electric car charging stations.[41]

Moving beyond strategy to enactment, the next section covers action principles for the adoption journey from idea generation to deployment.

9.5. From idea to development

"From a blockchain point of view, we don't believe consortia efforts will scale broadly in the global commerce space and that it will take a big, open global village to accomplish this, which is what led me to 'coopetition'."

Dale Chrystie, Blockchain Strategist at FedEx,
Chair of BiTA Standards Council

Blockchain-based solutions may be led by a founder, by a few trading partners, or by a consortium. A founder-led solution is the fastest time-to-market governance model, but may result in a solution no one else wants to join.[42] A consortium-led solution is often the slowest time-to-market governance model because many parties need to agree, but can result in a solution that has deeply considered the needs of all ecosystem partners. A consortium-led solution also needs to create a legal entity to move a solution from sandbox to production. Solutions led by a few trading partners is the middle model. Here we explore the rationale behind the extreme models: A founder-led model for development and production versus a consortium-led model for development and a new legal entity for production.

✓ *Action Principle 11: Select a founder-led approach only if the organization will be accepted as a benevolent dictator/neutral facilitator.*

Many of the blockchain applications covered in this book used a founder-led model, including KoreConX; LO3 Energy; MediLedger; Ripple; SmartResume; TradeLens; and VeriTX. As previously stated, the benefits of founder-led governance include swift decisions, quick execution, high efficiency, and clear control and accountability. Arun et al. (2019) also highlighted this benefit: the founder establishes itself as a leader in the ecosystem and may derive the most benefits, including new revenue streams and adjacent business models.[43] However, the founder bears the risks and burdens of financing the initiative, attracting top talent, and delivering a solution that will also benefit targeted ecosystem partners.

Founder-led models work best when the founders serve as neutral facilitators that are not in direct competition with targeted ecosystem partners. For example, Chronicled is the founder of MediLedger. Chronicled is not part of the pharmaceutical supply chain, so it is not in competition with its targeted ecosystem partners comprising pharmaceutical manufacturers, wholesalers, distributers and retail pharmacies. Susanne Somerville, CEO of Chronicled, said:

> *"A neutral facilitator, who can establish trust among parties, can serve as a benevolent dictator—at least initially—because they are incentivized to solve the problem for everyone."*[44]

iDatafy also chose a founder-led model for its SmartResume platform, with iDatafy serving as the benevolent dictator entrusted with driving results. iDatafy is a neutral party that does not compete against any partners of SmartResume because it's not a credentialing or hiring organization. Wengel said:

> *"iDatafy is a kind of middle person, but we're also able to stay laser focused on this, and I think it has become very clear that a dedicated persistence is needed to drive new things forward."*

Wengel self-funded the project.

Although both Chronicled and iDatafy are the founders, each worked closely with ecosystem participants. It is fair to say these neutral facilitators coalesced a consortium of partners to design the solutions.

In contrast to MediLedger and SmartResume, some founder-led consortia are operated by a key industry partner (an insider), which make competitors reticent to join. For example, Maersk led the development (with IBM) of TradeLens, a platform to track shipping containers, but competitors were initially skittish about joining. Competitors have since joined due to positive actions taken by Maersk, such as announcing an advisory board that includes competitors.

General Electric (GE) offered one unique lesson about founder-led models: build it to get a return on investment even if no other competitors join.[45] GE built TRUEngine, a blockchain-enabled application for GE's aircraft parts supply chain. GE Aviation supplies parts to 60 percent of the airline industry and needed a better way to track the entire lifecycle of a GE part from manufacturing to decommissioning. Microsoft is GE's technology partner. Mike Walker, senior director of applied innovation and digital transformation at Microsoft, said that GE …

> *"stitched together its entire supply chain into one view—so you've got a full understanding of all the partners; you've got one ecosystem repository instead of hundreds, if not thousands."*[46]

Once launched into live production, founders will need to evolve the governance structure to convince additional competitors and smaller-sized participants in the ecosystem to join. Industry giants need to purposely dissipate control to convince others they are working for the greater good, and not attempting to build their own competitive advantage at the expense of others within the network.

✓ *Action Principle 12: Select a consortium-led approach for standards and early stage development.*

Many blockchain-enabled solutions will need competitors on the platform to achieve network effects. An industry-focused consortium is a common way to gather competitors to work on joint initiatives. Industry consortia are ideal places for learning mastery of the coopetition mindset. R3, the BiTA Standards Council, and WeTrade are examples covered in this book. With a consortium, participants maintain their own legal status and typically sign very light legal commitments, such as a memorandum of understanding. Consortia are very effective at defining standards and experimenting with POCs in sandboxes. However, the mounting evidence suggests that consortia are not the best model for moving solutions from sandboxes into production-ready systems. One leader told us:

> *"Consortia do not work; there are 60 plus consortia and they haven't delivered anything. If there is no legislation to drive it, nothing happens. Partners get together and agree on how to work together, then lawyers come in and it takes forever to get agreement; it doesn't scale; add one more person and you get another modified agreement."*

We interviewed leaders and members from consortia that required members to sign non-disclosure agreements, but they did not all have signed IP agreements. One interviewee from a large bank explained:

> *"Our industry is behind some other industries in our management of shared IP and our ability to collaborate and cooperate. We all jumped in to explore a use case and did some joint design thinking with two or three traditional competitors without thinking about who owns the intellectual capital that comes out the tail end of that workshop. Then, if you do highlight the need for some agreement there, getting to common ground on what that agreement needs to look like and who should own the IP, it's sometimes weeks or even months in lead time. We as an industry need to work faster on those kind of repeatable processes."*

For one healthcare consortium, the group did not want to delay the project to wait for large members to maneuver through the onerous process of signing an IP agreement. To protect the group's IP in the absence of formal IP agreements, the head of the consortium recorded all meetings so that none of its members could subsequently file a patent.

Roberto Mancone, a co-founder and first COO of WeTrade, said that the banks in the consortium agreed up front that all IP would be shared. He also suggested that consortia will progress faster if consortium partners commit to decision-making based on majority or super majority rule rather than on unanimity, as the WeTrade consortium partners did. Mancone also asserted that consortia are best used for technical design, but that a separate legal entity is needed to launch a product. WeTrade used a consortium with a simple Memorandum of Understanding (MoU) to build the application, and then created the joint venture as the legal entity to launch and license the solution. The lesson is:

✓ *Action Principle 13: For consortium-led development, launch a new entity to move solutions from sandboxes to production.*

9.6. Design principles

Whether founder-led, partner-led, or consortium-led, the target solution should be designed to attract participants beyond the initial minimal viable ecosystem to maximize network effects. Everett Roger's Diffusion of Innovation Theory suggests that attributes of an innovation account for between 49 to 87 percent of the variance in adoption rates. For Rogers, the five attributes that make people want to adopt innovations are relative advantage; trialability; compatibility; observability (discussed above); and complexity (see Figure 9.6). [47]

For a blockchain-based solution, our case study research suggests that solutions with the following attributes may increase adoption rates: open source software; guaranteed regulatory compliance; adaptability; and low obstacles to onboarding. We discuss each in turn.

✓ *Action principle 14: Go open or go home.*

Innovation Attribute	Description	Effect on Adoption Rate
Relative Advantage	'The degree to which an innovation is perceived as better than an idea it supersedes.' The innovation may be better economically, functionally, or socially.	⬆
Trialability	'The degree to which an innovation may be experimented with on a limited basis.' Trialability reduces uncertainty.	⬆
Compatibility	'The degree to which an innovation is perceived as being consistent with the existing values, past experiences, and needs of potential adopters.'	⬆
Observability	'The degree to which the results of an innovation are visible to others.'	⬆
Complexity	'The degree to which an innovation is perceived as difficult to understand and use.' The more complex the solution, the slower it will be adopted.	⬇

Figure 9.6. Five attributes of innovations

Source: Rogers(2006)

"Open source means we inherit the contributions of thousands of highly-qualified developers."

Amber Baldet, previous Program Lead for J.P. Morgan's Blockchain Center of Excellence[48]

"How do you get companies over the hurdle of going from a no to a yes to open innovation?"

General Manager for a large multinational conglomerate[49]

Our message to founders who hope to gain a critical mass of adopters is that open source solutions will provide a **relative advantage** over competing platforms with proprietary code bases. Potential adopters fear vendor lock-in if solutions are based on proprietary code. This is not always a welcomed message, for many founders quite rightly expect a return on their investment. It's perhaps the greatest tussle we've seen within organizations—the old ideas for competitive advantage based on protecting intellectual property with the news ideas of coopetition based on open intellectual property.

There are pros and cons to open source software. On the positive side, when source code developed by an open community has had time to mature, it can be more secure, less expensive, and provide greater interoperability and auditability compared to proprietary software—provided there is a vibrant community of core developers, co-developers, bug reporters, and users.[50] Open source software also means that there are low barriers to entry—anyone can download the software and start experimenting, providing easy **trialability**. On the other hand, immature open source code means that vulnerabilities are public. Furthermore, an open source community does not always agree on the path a code base should follow.

Of course, many enterprises will convert open source code bases to proprietary applications. This was indeed the route several enterprises in our study were considering. At one healthcare provider, the innovation director said:

> *"For healthcare, we are working with a private company developing proprietary source code because it's harder to hack than open source software. It can sit on top of open source, but will be shielded with proprietary code."*

At another organization, the Vice President for a global bank said:

> *"Open source through the Linux foundation allows a company to do plug-ins. So, if you had differentiation in, for example, a consent model, you could develop your own plug-in to support a differentiated business model."[51]*

✓ *Action Principle 15: Design for regulatory compliance.*

What's unique about blockchains is that records are immutable; once transactions are added to the digital ledger, they remain there forever unless some emergency requires a roll-back and forking of the ledger. Potential adopters beyond the founders want guarantees that solutions are **compatible** and compliant with all laws and regulations that grant individuals the right to be forgotten. Designing for immutability also requires using quantum-resistant cryptography so that the cryptography we use today will remain secure in the future. This means using larger-sized cryptographic keys compared to the key sizes we use today, which will have implications for storage and scalability. There are redactable blockchains under development that will enable reliable edits without creating a hard fork (see glossary).[52]

How can one possibly anticipate all the privacy regulations, company policies, and cybersecurity practices, now and in the future? The CTO of iDatafy offered this advice:

> *"Think of a blockchain as nothing more than a receipt that is validated by everybody who has touched it."*

The safest blockchain-based solutions store the hash of the receipt of a transaction on the ledger, but they never store sensitive or personal data (not even encrypted versions). The private keys to interpret the receipts are held offline and can be deleted to comply with regulations or a company's data retirement policy. This simple measure, however, will be insufficient to comply fully with privacy regulations like the EU's General Data Protection Regulation (GDPR).

In addition to rights of erasure and rectification of errors, GDPR requires an ***identifiable authority*** to be responsible for compliance and in charge of lawful bases for processing personal data. How can distributed blockchain solutions comply with a regulation that seems to assume centralized control over data processing and compliance? Researchers from the universities of Augsburg, Bayreuth, and Luxembourg identified three approaches for ensuring data privacy compliance for blockchain solutions. With a central authority approach, the blockchain network nominates a single central authority to act as the network's controller and all parties sign a contract with it. With a shared authority approach, the blockchain network selects some or even all participants to act as controllers and all parties sign an agreement. With a pseudonymization approach, data stored on the chain is only qualified to be personal data when it is combined with additional off-chain data.[i] Only the participants who possess the additional information required for attribution serve as controllers, and this off-chain data can be erased.[53]

---

[i] **Pseudonymization** is a data management and de-identification procedure by which personally identifiable information fields within a data record are replaced by one or more artificial identifiers, or pseudonyms.

Regulatory concerns also influence the platform selection. Many enterprise blockchain-enabled solutions are built on permissioned blockchains, usually Corda, Fabric or Quorum. For example, the IBM Food Trust, KoreConX, SmartResume, TradeLens, and WeTrade built their solutions on Hyperledger Fabric. Garimella explained why it chose a permissioned blockchain protocol:

> *"Today, public blockchains with probabilistic finality and settlement will not fly in private capital markets. Private blockchains provide definitive settlement."*

Other enterprises, most notably EY, strongly believe that enterprises will eventually migrate to public solutions like Ethereum. Until traditional enterprises are ready to go to a public blockchain, EY often builds client solutions on Quorum, the permissioned version of Ethereum. This way, the necessary recoding to transition private applications to public platforms is minimized.

✓ *Action Principle 16: Design with agility.*

Agile software development methods are suitable when requirements are uncertain at the start. Participants test and provide feedback on multiple iterations to rapidly produce a minimal viable product. iDatafy serves as an example.

iDatafy actively sought feedback on each iteration of the SmartResume platform. Early on, it was evident that most people have credentials from multiple universities, but what if a SmartResume user has a degree from an institution that has not yet joined the consortium? iDatafy allows users to add uncredentialed degrees, but guides them to use the federal government's standard naming convention. This way, as-yet-to-be verified credentials accumulate, iDatafy can approach those institutions with evidence for joining. The SmartResume platform can grab all the uniformly-named institutions for review.

User feedback also prompted another change, namely, to stop displaying older credentials when newer ones are activated, such as transitioning from a student to a graduate. Most importantly, feedback very early-on convinced iDatafy to adopt the opt-in model. This was the right thing to do to protect users' privacy and to get a more engaged user, even though it slowed the rollout. Wengel said other competitors who create public data without user knowledge will scale quickly, but may ultimately fail when users start getting unsolicited contacts. He concluded:

> *"Listening to feedback from the most important users of the system is a central tenant of why we have gotten where we are so quickly. Their feedback helped us to make the platform usable, and to make it easy for them to get engaged."*

Equally important is knowing how to balance stakeholder feedback with scope creep and dealing effectively with suggestions that are counter to the philosophy of the platform. One stakeholder, for example, wanted iDatafy to mask the credentialing organization in addition to the other data fields. While this suggestion would help job candidates from lesser-known institutions, it would be counter to the value proposition of promoting and protecting a credentialing organization's brand.

✓ Action Principle 17: Simplify the membership onboarding process.

Rogers (2006) recognizes that **complex** innovations deter adoption. Therefore, blockchain solutions that make it easy for new members to onboard and to try out the innovation without financial or time commitments are good design principles. KoreConX serves as a model; users may sign-up for free in an onboarding process that takes 30 seconds (see Figure 9.7).

Standard license agreements are another design principle. At WeTrade, one of the reasons for launching a JV after the consortium designed the solution was to move to one license agreement. Roberto Mancone explained:

> *"In the consortium, we had 12 banks as partners. We did not want 12 different agreements, and then a new agreement every time another bank joined."*

At iDatafy, CEO Dave Wengel designed an easy onboarding process for individuals. Once a credentialing organization launches a SmartResume on behalf of the individual, the individual is sent an email notifying them of the creation of their SmartResume. Individuals just click on the link in the email to opt-in to the platform. If an individual does not activate their SmartResume, it is not accessible by any third party.

Figure 9.7: KoreConX's onboarding process

https://www.koreconx.com/

9.7. From deployment to critical mass

Whether founder-led, partner-led, or consortium-led, most blockchain solutions will aim to attract a critical mass of adopters beyond the minimal viable ecosystem after launch. As of 2020, few blockchain-based solutions have reached the final phase of a critical mass of adopters. Among all the challenges discussed in this book, gaining a critical mass is the greatest one. For those blockchain platforms ready to gain critical mass but do not know how, theory again informs the process. Specifically, theories from behavioral economics and institutionalism offer guidance.

✓ *Action Principle 18: Behavioral incentives: Offer unique value propositions for each type of participant.*

Mike Walker, Sr. Director, Applied Innovation Team at Microsoft stated that financial incentives are the most powerful drivers of behaviors. Founders of ecosystem solutions need to provide a compelling value proposition for each new participant they aim to attract to the platform. The participants who get the most business value from the solution will be willing to pay the most fees. In some blockchain solutions, target participants who perceive little value, but who are key to the success of the solution, may need to be incentivized to join by offering the service for free.[54]

For the SmartResume solution, iDatafy considered unique value propositions for the three types of participants: credentialing organizations, individual smart resume holders, and hiring companies. Credentialing organizations gain value by protecting their brand—the SmartResume platform prevents users from claiming credentials they did not earn. They also gain efficiencies by credentialing a person once, rather than re-affirming credentials every time a person changes employment. Despite this value, iDatafy decided not to charge credentialing organizations; it needs them to create the credentials. Job seekers gain value by having access to hiring companies, but again Idatafy decided not to charge resume holders any fees. Individual resume holders are often financially-strapped students. Wengel said:

> *"There's a good business reason... in addition to just being the right thing to do, it's the key to scaling something like this quickly."*

Once scaled, hiring organizations will gain the most value from the solution by having access to a pool of certified talent, and they will be charged fees for the platform. But iDatafy delayed charging hiring organizations until the credentialing organizations had launched enough SmartResumes. Wengel continued:

"We're not charging you a dime unless we help you hire someone. We're motivated to make sure that we get this done right."

> ✓ *Action Principle 19: Evolve the governance portfolio to become more transparent and more decentralized when moving from development to deployment to critical mass.*

How do governance portfolios typically evolve? The benevolent dictators of Bitcoin and Ethereum moved quickly to distribute power to fellow believers. Specifically, Satoshi Nakamoto gave Martti Malmi and Gavin Andresen access rights to update Bitcoin's website and source code;[55] Buterin recruited Mihai Alisie; Amir Chetrit; Charles Hoskinson; and Anthony Di Iorio, and soon brought on Joseph Lubin; Gavin Wood; and Jeffrey Wilke, as Ethereum co-founders.

The same evolutionary patterns are needed to govern permissioned blockchains. A minimal viable ecosystem (MVE) comprising a few key trading partners competitors that build the minimal viable product (MVP), will likely be governed as an oligarchy or stakeocracy. To achieve network effects in the longer term, however, the initial MVE will need to attract many more participants to adopt its software. In order to do so, the founders likely will need to evolve aspects of the governance model, particularly the funding model, to convince potential adopters.

o, for example, gave their rights away to control the source code for HyperLedger Fabric by giving it to the Linux Foundation to manage as open source. Moreover, IBM has no data visibility into the blockchain platforms it hosts in its cloud environment. Only the trading partners within channels have the access keys needed to interpret the data stored on permissioned ledgers. IBM is also opening up its blockchain solutions to run on other cloud provider platforms.[56]

TradeLens provides another example of an evolving governance structure. Initially, Maersk was internally working on improving containerized shipping by itself in the wake of the Global Financial Crisis. In another part of Maersk, IBM was helping Maersk on paperless trade (the digitization of shipping documents).[57] In 2016, the projects were joined, and thanks to IBM's early foray into blockchain technologies, IBM showed Maersk the value of moving the project to a blockchain-enabled platform.[58] In January of 2018, TradeLens was announced as a 51/49 percent joint venture between Maersk and IBM.[59] Initially, each company intended to use their own sales channels, but IBM did not have the same global level of trade permissions as Maersk, so the TradeLens governance was changed again, this time to a subsidiary of Maersk in late 2018 with IBM as the solution provider. The next phase of governance involves more transparency and the creation of a Customer Advisory Board to move to a more transparent governance model.[60]

✓ *Action Principle 20: Exploit three influence sources to gain a critical mass of adopters.*

The Theory of Institutional Isomorphism models the process of homogenization among organizations facing similar environmental conditions.[61] Essentially, the theory seeks to answer the question: Why do organizations within an industry eventually change (from the Latin root 'morph') to become more alike (from the Latin root 'iso')? Paul DiMaggio and Walter Powell (1991) posited that organizations eventually adopt similar structures, processes, philosophies, practices, and technologies through three mechanisms of influence, namely, coercive, normative, and mimetic (see Figure 9.8):[62]

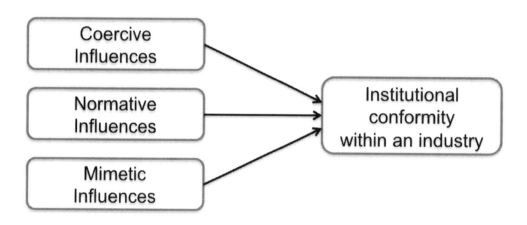

Figure 9.8: Three influences that pressure institutions to conform

Source: Adapted from DiMaggio and Powell (1991)[63]

Coercive influences

Coercive influences come from political pressures exerted on an organization by other organizations upon which they are dependent. Government regulations and powerful trading partners' mandates are examples of coercive influences. Although 'coercive' has a negative connotation, coercive influences can be effective for promoting a greater good. Government regulations, for example, aim to protect consumers, investors, citizens, children and the environment.

Within the context of blockchains, several interviewees thought government regulations would be the fastest route to mass adoption. For example, one interviewee thought new US government regulations would be the way to force the adoption of better healthcare processes that could be enabled with blockchains. He said:

> *"The government may need to step in at some point. All we have to do is have a couple of use cases, and then we go public about it and say, 'This is the kind of thing we could do. Why can't we do this with healthcare?' We let the government ask, 'Why aren't you doing this?' Then, there's going to be a bunch of payers who say, 'Oh, this is going to be bad for the consumer.' What are they talking about? Consumers are getting screwed to the nth degree right now. There have never been higher insurance rates."*

Powerful trading partners can also influence adoption: In September of 2018, Walmart and Sam's Club required its major suppliers of fresh, leafy greens to join the IBM Food Trust. Direct suppliers were required to conform to one-step back traceability by January 31, 2019 and end-to-end traceability through vertical partners by September 30, 2019. Its letter to suppliers explained that food safety (a greater good) is a shared responsibility that is only achieved through collaboration with supply chain partners. Recognizing that adoption would place burdens on its suppliers, the letter reads in part:

> *"To assist you in meeting this new Walmart business requirement, we have worked closely with IBM and other food companies to create a user-friendly, low-cost, blockchain-enabled traceability solution that meets our requirements and creates shared value for the entire leafy green farm to table continuum."*[64]

Normative influences

Normative influences arise from duties, obligations, and norms of professionalism, including formal education and professional and trade associations that seek to legitimize their existence.[65] In the context of blockchains, standards-making bodies like GS1, IEEE, and BiTA provide normative influences. Powerful blockchain advisors like CapGemini; Cognizant; Deloitte; EY; KPMG; HfS; IBM; PwC; and Wipro influence their client's blockchain directions. Tapscotts' Blockchain Research Institute is also a major influencer in the space, featuring early enterprise adopters in its programs and offering thought leadership on creating an 'Internet of Value'.

Mimetic influences

Mimetic influences arise from the perception that peer organizations are more successful; by mimicking peer behavior, the organization aims to achieve similar results. Mimetic influences are particularly strong when environmental uncertainty is high, goals are ambiguous, and when technologies are poorly understood.[66] iDatafy has built three successful consortia since 2011, with the SmartResume being the most recent. CEO Dave Wengel said that whenever he approaches a new consortium member, the first question asked is usually, *"Who else is using this?"* It's important to pick early adopters who are influential and well-regarded in the ecosystem. For the SmartResume project, Wengel knew he had to start the consortium with a large, influential academic credentialing organization. (Wengel would not recruit any hiring organizations until the career network was large enough to warrant their attention.) Wengel invited Matt Waller, the dean of the Sam M. Walton College of Business at the University of Arkansas, to become the first member in summer of 2018. As the flagship business school in the state, Walton College had the prominence to influence other adopters.

IBM's strategy to attract 'anchor tenants' like Maersk and Walmart for its major blockchain applications can be considered mimetic influences.[67] One interviewee thought this was an effective strategy:

> *"There's also a little bit of a herd mentality. People are afraid to be left out."*

DiMaggio and Powell stress that the three influences are analytically distinctive but may not be empirically indistinguishable.

9.7. Conclusion

In this chapter, we presented 20 **action principles** for making blockchain-enabled solutions a reality based on early adopters. We can learn from and improve on the practices used by early adopters. It's up to all of us to make them happen. As more blockchain-enabled solutions come online, the action principles may be further corroborated, fine-tuned, or even refuted. There will long-term outcomes. Blockchain is a slow train ... but it's definitely coming! Let's thank the pioneers for sharing their adoption journeys and lessons. Progress without them would be even more challenging.

Citations

[1] Wieck, M. (December 11, 2019), '2019 Saw the End of Blockchain Tourism', *Coindesk*, https://www.coindesk.com/2019-saw-the-end-of-blockchain-tourism

[2] Lacity, M. and Willcocks, L. (2018), *Robotic Process and Cognitive Automation: The Next Phase*, SB Publishing, Stratford-upon-Avon, UK

[3] Gupta, S., Snowden, J., and Mondal, T. (2020), *Ignore Blockchain at your own peril, but don't drive blindly*, HfS Research.

[4] Lacity, M. and Willcocks, L. (2018), *Robotic Process and Cognitive Automation: The Next Phase*, SB Publishing, Stratford-upon-Avon, UK

[5] Quoted in Lacity, M., Zach, S., Paul, C. (2019), *Blockchain Governance Models: Insights for Enterprises,* Blockchain Center of Excellence white paper, University of Arkansas.

[6] *Bridget van Kralingen & Mike White at Blockchain Revolution Global 2019.* https://youtu.be/7crOWQnz9tw

[7] LeRoy, F. and Benjamin, M. (2018), *Looking for the historical origins of coopetition:back to Antique Romans traders*, XXVIIe Conférence Internationale de Management Stratégique, https://www.strategie-aims.com/events/conferences/29-xxviieme-conference-de-l-aims/communications/5021-looking-for-the-historical-origins-of-coopetition-back-to-antique-romans-traders/download

[8] Dagnino, G., ; Padula, G. (2002), *Coopetition Strategy: Towards a New Kind of Interfirm Dynamics for Value Creation*, EURAM 2nd Annual Conference, Stockholm School of Entrepreneurship, Sweden.

[9] Volschenk, J., Ungerer, M., and Smit, E. (2016), 'Creation and appropriation of socio-environmental value in coopetition', *Industrial Marketing Management*, 57, pp. 109-118

[10] Dagnino, G., ; Padula, G. (2002), *Coopetition Strategy: Towards a New Kind of Interfirm Dynamics for Value Creation*, EURAM 2nd Annual Conference, Stockholm School of Entrepreneurship, Sweden.

[11] The behaviors needed for effective blockchain consortia were also found in our years of study on outsourcing relationships. Lacity, M., and Willcocks, L. (2015), *Nine Keys to World Class BPO*, Bloomsbury, London.

[12] Ibid.

[13] Wieck, M. (December 11, 2019), '2019 Saw the End of Blockchain Tourism', *Coindesk*, https://www.coindesk.com/2019-saw-the-end-of-blockchain-tourism

[14] Lacity, M., Zach, S., Paul, C. (2019), *Blockchain Governance Models: Insights for Enterprises*, Blockchain Center of Excellence white paper, BCoE-2019-02, University of Arkansas.

[15] Lacity, M., Zach, S., Paul, C. (2019), *Blockchain Governance Models: Insights for Enterprises*, Blockchain Center of Excellence white paper, BCoE-2019-02, University of Arkansas.

[16] Popper, N. (2015), *Digital Gold*, HarperCollins, New York, p. 82.

[17] Popper, N. (2015), *Digital Gold*, HarperCollins, New York, p. 82.

[18] The Libra Association, https://libra.org/en-US/association-council-principles/#overview

[19] Fisher, C. (July 15, 2019), *US Treasury has serious concerns Libra could be used for terrorism*, https://www.engadget.com/2019/07/15/facebook-libra-cryptocurrency-us-treasury-department-concerns/

Alexandre, A. (August 5, 2019), *UK Data Protection Watchdog Raises Concerns Over Facebook's Libra*,

CoinTelegragh, https://cointelegraph.com/news/uk-data-protection-watchdog-raises-concerns-over-facebooks-libra

[20] Lacity, M., Zach, S., Paul, C. (2019), *Blockchain Governance Models: Insights for Enterprises,* Blockchain Center of Excellence white paper, BCoE-2019-02, University of Arkansas.

[21] Hyperledger (September 6, 2017), *ABCs of Open Governance,* https://www.hyperledger.org/blog/2017/09/06/abcs-of-open-governance

[22] https://github.com/bitcoin/bips/blob/master/README.mediawiki

[23] https://www.ibm.com/blockchain/solutions/food-trust/food-industry-technology

[24] *What is the Advisory Council?* https://www.ibm.com/blockchain/solutions/food-trust/food-industry-technology#1797811

[25] Lacity, M., Zach, S., Paul, C. (2019), *Blockchain Governance Models: Insights for Enterprises,* Blockchain Center of Excellence white paper, BCoE-2019-02, University of Arkansas.

[26] Small, G., *Additive Manufacturing Reshaping Logistics,* http://www.moog.com/news/blog-new/IntroducingVeripart_Issue3.html

[27] Rogers, E.M., *Diffusion of Innovations,* New York, Free Press, 2006, fifth edition.

[28] Wieck, M. (December 11, 2019), '2019 Saw the End of Blockchain Tourism', *Coindesk,* https://www.coindesk.com/2019-saw-the-end-of-blockchain-tourism

[29] https://www.koreconx.com/about/

[30] Presentation by Kiran Garimella, Chief Scientist and CTO, presentation to the Blockchain Center of Excellence, University of Arkansas, December 3rd, 2019.

[31] Presentation by John Whelan, Managing Director, Digital Investment Bank, Santander, to the Blockchain Center of Excellence, University of Arkansas, December 3rd, 2019.

[32] Quoted in Lacity, M. (2018), *A Manager's Guide to Blockchains for Business,* SB Publishing, Stratford-upon-Avon, UK

[33] Quoted in Lacity, M. (2018), *A Manager's Guide to Blockchains for Business,* SB Publishing, Stratford-upon-Avon, UK

[34] The theory of disruptive innovation was developed by Clayton Christensen over two decades, beginning with his first book published in 1997, *The innovator's dilemma: when new technologies cause great firms to fail,* Harvard Business School Press. For a thoughtful and current synopsis of the theory, see Christensen, C., Raynor, M. and McDonald, R. "What Is Disruptive Innovation?," *Harvard Business Review* (93:12), December 2015, pp. 45-53.

[35] https://www.christenseninstitute.org/disruptive-innovations/

[36] https://ripple.com/use-cases/

[37] Lacity, M. (2018), *A Manager's Guide to Blockchains for Business*, SB Publishing, Stratford-upon-Avon, UK

[38] Quoted in Allison, I. (August 8, 2018), 'Inside State Street Bank's Blockchain Deliberations', *Coindesk*, https://www.coindesk.com/state-street-opens-up-about-its-internal-blockchain-debate

[39] Allison, I. (December 3, 2019), 'State Street Slashes DLT Developer Team as Bank Rethinks Blockchain Strategy', *Coindesk* https://www.coindesk.com/state-street-slashes-dlt-developer-team-as-bank-rethinks-blockchain-strategy

[40] Personal interview with Mary Lacity

[41] See http://shareandcharge.com/en/; Lielacher, A. (May 5th 2017), *Innogy Charges Electric Car Fleet Using Ethereum Blockchain*, https://www.nasdaq.com/article/innogy-charges-new-electric-car-fleet-using-ethereum-blockchain-cm785270

[42] Lacity, M., Zach, S., Paul, C. (2019), *Blockchain Governance Models: Insights for Enterprises* (02nd ed., vol. 2019), Blockchain Center of Excellence, University of Arkansas.

[43] Arun, J., Cuomo, J., and Gaur, N. (2019), *Blockchain for Business*, Addison-Wesley, Boston.

[44] Susanne Somerville, presentation to the Blockchain Center of Excellence, University of Arkansas, 2019.

[45] Presentation by Sean Moser, Chief Product Officer at GE Aviation's Digital Group, at San Francisco blockchain week, October 2019.

[46] Quote from Allison, I. (May 12, 2019). Codename 'TRUEngine': GE Aviation, Microsoft Reveal Aircraft Parts Blockchain, Coindesk, https://www.coindesk.com/codename-truengine-ge-aviation-and-microsoft-reveal-aircraft-parts-certification-blockchain

[47] Rogers, E.M., *Diffusion of Innovations*, New York, Free Press, 2006, fifth edition.

[48] Personal interview with Mary Lacity

[49] Personal Interview with Jeanne Ross and Kate Moloney in 2017

[50] Bahamdain, S. (2015), 'Open Source Software Quality Assurance: A Survey Paper', *Procedia Computer Science*, Vol. 56, 459-464

Spinellis, D, Gousios, G. Karakoidas, V.and Louridas, P. (2009), 'Evaluating the Quality of Open Source Software', *Electronic Notes in Theoretical Computer Science,* Issue 233, 5–28

Spinellis, D., *Code Quality: The Open Source Perspective*, Addison-Wesley, Boston, MA, 2006

[51] Personal interview with Mary Lacity and Kate Moloney in 2017

[52] Ateniese, G., B. Magri, D. Venturi and E. Andrade (2017), *Redactable Blockchain – or – Rewriting History in Bitcoin and Friends*, 2017 IEEE European Symposium on Security and Privacy (EuroS&P), Paris, pp. 111-126.

[53] Reiger, A., Guggenmos, F., Lockl, J., Fridgen, G. and Urbach, N. (2019), 'Building a Blockchain Application that Complies with the EU General Data Protection Regulation', *MIS Quarterly Executive*, 18(4), pp. 263-279.

[54] Ibid.

[55] Popper, N. (2015), *Digital Gold*, HarperCollins, New York, p. 82.

[56] IBM Press Release (October 23, 2018), *IBM and Microsoft Announce Partnership Between Cloud Offerings*, https://www.pbsnow.com/ibm-news/ibm-and-microsoft-announce-partnership-between-cloud-offerings/

[57] Jensen, T., Hedman, J., and Henningson, S. (2019), 'How TradeLens Delivers Business Value With Blockchain Technology', *MIS Quarterly Executive*, 18(4), pp. 221-243.

[58] Jensen, T. (December 12, 2018), *Blockchain Strategize Digital Infrastructuring: Blockchain technology bridging the Document Platforms towards real business value in Maritime Supply Chains*, Pre-ICIS Workshop, San Francisco.

[59] IBM Press Release (January 16, 2018), *Maersk and IBM to Form Joint Venture Applying Blockchain to Improve Global Trade and Digitize Supply Chains*, https://www-03.ibm.com/press/us/en/pressrelease/53602.wss

[60] TradeLens Advisory Board, https://www.tradelens.com/about/

[61] Mizruchi, M., and Fein, L. (1999), 'The Social Construction of Organizational Knowledge: A Study of the Uses of Coercive, Mimetic, and Normative Isomorphism', *Administrative Science Quarterly*, Vol. 44, 4, 653-683

[62] DiMaggio, P. and Powell, W. (1991), 'The Iron Cage Revisited: Industrial Isomorphism and Collective Rationality in Organizational Fields', *The New Institutionalism in Organizational Analysis*, (Powell, W. and DiMaggio, editors), University of Chicago Press, Chicago, 63-82.

[63] DiMaggio, P. and Powell, W. (1991), 'The Iron Cage Revisited: Industrial Isomorphism and Collective Rationality in Organizational Fields', *The New Institutionalism in Organizational Analysis*, (Powell, W. and DiMaggio, editors), University of Chicago Press, Chicago, 63-82.

[64] *Walmart Food Traceability Initiative Fresh Leafy Greens* (September 24, 2018). https://corporate.walmart.com/media-library/document/blockchain-supplier-letter-september-2018/_proxyDocument?id=00000166-088d-dc77-a7ff-4dff689f0001

[65] DiMaggio, P. and Powell, W. (1991), 'The Iron Cage Revisited: Industrial Isomorphism and Collective Rationality in Organizational Fields', *The New Institutionalism in Organizational Analysis*, (Powell, W. and DiMaggio, editors), University of Chicago Press, Chicago, 63-82.

[66] Ibid, p. 71.

Mizruchi, M., and Fein, L. (1999), 'The Social Construction of Organizational Knowledge: A Study of the Uses of Coercive, Mimetic, and Normative Isomorphism', *Administrative Science Quarterly*, Vol. 44, 4, 653-683.

[67] Marie Wieck, GM of IBM Blockchain, speaking at Consensus 2017: https://ibmgo.com/interconnect2017/search/?q=blockchain&tags=all&categoryType=video

Chapter 10

The Future of Blockchains

"Blockchain technology is transforming the way industries exchange information. Soon, we'll start seeing large-scale adoption of enterprise blockchains underpinned by interoperable networks and digital identities."

Archana Sristy, Senior Director, Walmart Global Tech

"We are hurtling toward a hyperconnected economy. Ecosystems across organizations that service the specific needs of a customer are emerging. No single organization owns the entire customer experience, and competitors and peers need to figure out how to collaborate. Blockchain, in combination with other emerging technologies like IoT and artificial intelligence (AI), will provide a way to make it happen."

Saurabh Gupta, Chief Research Officer, HFS

10.1. Introduction

Bitcoin celebrated its eleventh birthday on January 3, 2020. It serves as our most visible example of the power of the 'Internet of Value'. Built on blockchain technologies, Bitcoin's tamper-resistant distributed ledger has remained intact despite its honeypot of value.[i] While Bitcoin comes from a community of cypherpunks and libertarians,

---

[i] Recall from Chapter 3 that nearly all of the Bitcoin heists ones hears about happened by stealing off-chain private key, NOT by tampering with the distributed ledger.

traditional enterprises soon saw the threats and opportunities it posed. For the past five years, traditional enterprises across the globe have vetted blockchain technologies with thousands of proofs of concept, but mostly for private blockchain solutions. Live enterprise production deployments have been slow to come because ecosystem partners have to agree on standards, IP rights, shared governance, and business models. Early enterprise adopters show us the possibilities of the business and social value that can be created by sharing applications.

In this book, we have examined numerous blockchain platforms and applications that are marching us towards an 'Internet of Value'. Bitcoin; Ripple; Stellar; WeTrade; Sandander; and KoreConX show us that the future of financial services is upon us. The IBM Food Trust; EY's WineChain; Everledger; GE's TRUEngine; MediLedger; TradeLens; VeChain; and VeriTX illustrate asset authenticity and traceability through global supply chains. LO3 Energy and Share&Charge show us new markets for energy where individuals have platforms to share their excess energy capacity with other individuals. SmartResume shows us how to combine verified credentials with digital resumes to improve job markets. Each of these blockchain applications is a result of dedicated focus by founders and deep cooperation among ecosystem partners. Each was aiming to solve specific business and social problems that happened to be well-suited for blockchain technologies. The commonality across these contexts is this: ***Blockchain-based solutions are uniquely suited to verify, share and secure data for contexts that involve multiple trading parties who do not trust each other.*** Lack of trust does not mean one doubts the goodwill of trading partners; lack of trust means that one party is not willing to let another party execute agreements or to create or modify records pertaining to that agreement without verification. A well-designed blockchain application allows multiple parties to execute agreements as promised and to record, share and update transactions pertaining to those agreements safely.

However, as of 2020, blockchain-enabled solutions operate as islands. The current state is that these solutions are happening at the application level, not at the infrastructure level. We are still missing universal components to realize the full vision for an 'Internet of Value'. We have not yet realized the full power of individual self-sovereignty, asset/ token transfers across chains, and a truly seamless and friendly user experience. But today we can more easily see the possibilities.

So, what does the future of blockchains hold? As argued in Chapter 2, I believe that the future of blockchains is not deterministic; individuals and organizations do not just sit around and wait for the future to happen, they actively create it. Since the future of blockchains is a set of design choices, I discuss two final prescriptions (rather than predictions) in this chapter:

1. Use blockchain-enabled solutions to address 'butterfly defects' caused by globalization.
2. Beyond regulatory compliance, design ethical blockchain-enabled solutions.

For this final chapter on the future of blockchains, I've also sought the advice of people on the front lines of enterprise solutions. Their insights are inserted throughout this chapter in their own words. Several experts chose to ruminate upon the current, global COVID-19 pandemic, as the timing of my request for their thoughts happened in late March of 2020, when all of us were sequestered because of COVID-19. When speaking more broadly—beyond the pandemic—the experts agreed that blockchain-enabled solutions are uniquely suited for inter-organizational contexts but require many people working together to drive standards and to develop workable governance frameworks. All concur that we need the power of blockchains now more than ever.

10.2. Butterfly defects

"The tidal wave of globalization that has engulfed the planet over the past two decades has brought unprecedented opportunity. But it has also brought new risks that threaten to overwhelm us. Systemic risk cannot be removed because it is endemic to globalization. It is a process to be managed, not a problem to be solved."

Ian Goldin and Mike Mariathasan[1]

Since starting this book in January of 2020 and completing this final chapter five months later in May, the world has experienced unprecedented levels of devastation caused by COVID-19. The pandemic has revealed the weaknesses in our supply chains, our inability to deploy resources where they are most needed, and difficulties in capturing and sharing the data needed to make rapid decisions. But the underlying problem is much larger than this single pandemic. COVID-19 is just a single, specific manifestation of the systemic risks caused by globalization. Global warming; income disparity; the rise of xenophobia; nuclear weapon armament; and the depletion of natural resources, are other manifestations. The world is so hyper-connected that what happens locally swiftly magnifies and spreads globally. It makes us feel uncertain and somewhat helpless. How can we surmount the seemingly insurmountable?

Professor Ian Goldin from the University of Oxford and Dr. Mike Mariathasan from KU Leuven University, described the systemic risks of globalization in their provocative 2014 book, *The Butterfly Defect*. The authors wrote it after the 2008 Global Financial Crisis, another pandemic—this time a financial one—that began in the US subprime mortgage market, and quickly spread worldwide. Their book title relates to Chaos Theory, which describes how small changes in initial conditions can have exponential consequences. The ***butterfly effect*** is based on the popular explanation of Chaos Theory: a butterfly flaps its wings (a small perpetration to initial conditions) and prompts a hurricane weeks later. The metaphor comes from Ray Bradbury's short story *A Sound of Thunder*, written in 1952. In Bradbury's story, time travelers from the year 2055 go back 66 million years to hunt dinosaurs, but one hunter falls off the levitation path that prevents time warps. He crushes a butterfly that gets stuck on his shoe, and subsequently causes a devastating ripple through time that completely alters the evolution of the atmosphere, human language, and political outcomes.[2]

Goldin and Mariathasan transformed the popular metaphor from ***butterfly effect*** to ***butterfly defect***. The authors describe our hyperconnected supply chains, financial systems, and infrastructures (transportation, energy, and the Internet) and how interconnectivity amplifies environmental risks like global warming, economic and social inequality, and health risks such as pandemics. Within this broader framework, COVID-19 is just one of many 'butterfly defects' coming our way.

Alas, all is not lost. The authors argue that systemic risks can be managed. The authors call for shared governance across multiple borders. They write:

> *"Because systemic risks transcends national borders, it is vital that the governance of these risks also becomes coordinated internationally."*

Moreover, they argue that global governance must be *transparent*. For businesses, the authors argue that a focus on quarterly earnings causes enterprises to become too lean, and results in a significant loss of resiliency. Firm value, they argue, also should be assessed on investments in resiliency, including enough cash on hand, spare parts inventory, and redundancy in infrastructure. Their tome has many other prescriptions for addressing systemic global risks, but here we focus on how blockchain-enabled solution have already helped with COVID-19.

My colleague, Professor Remko Van Hoek from the Supply Chain Department at the Sam M. Walton College of Business, and I have been investigating blockchain solutions to address the pandemic. Blockchain solutions that have been under development for years have been repurposed and unleashed to address the pandemic. Sometimes a crisis can help accelerate the obstacles to technology adoption.

Consider the case of VeriTX. As we covered in Chapter 5, Colonel James Allen Regenor, USAF (ret) has been building a blockchain-powered platform since 2017 for the buying, selling, and tracing of 3-D printed parts (as well as traditional parts). Regenor and his team built the platform to enable a completely decentralized manufacturing process in which customers can order and print parts where they need them, when they need them. The blockchain ensures tamper-proof design and printing instructions. When Regenor realized that his platform could help with the medical devices needed to battle COVID-19, he leapt into action. He founded a new company, Rapid Medical Parts, in March 2020. He rallied his global network of partners, and in just 12 days, the

Pentagon awarded his company a contract for converting the abundant supply of sleep apnea machines into ventilators. The conversion requires additional parts that Rapid Medical Parts will print, and at a tenth of the cost of a new ventilator. The units should be in hospitals by mid-May.[3] In sharing his story with us, Regenor said:

> *"We all answer the call. Some run towards the cannons and others dig in. I have always run towards the cannons."*

It's not just the nimble startups that are leveraging blockchain solutions to fight the virus. Organizations including the World Health Organization; IBM; Oracle; Microsoft; other tech companies; government agencies; and international health organizations are partnering in building the blockchain-based open data hub called MiPasa. The platform, created by the enterprise blockchain firm HACERA, aims to quickly and precisely detect Covid-19 carriers and infection hotspots around the world. MiPasa will securely share information among individuals, hospitals, and authorities that will aid in public health analysis without revealing personal data.[4]

Don and Alex Tapscott highlight more blockchain solutions for the pandemic in their 74 page call for innovation and transformation in public health. They write:

> *"traditional systems have failed and it's time for a new paradigm."*

The authors detail a framework for applying blockchain technologies to improve public health which includes self-sovereignty over health records; just-in-time supply chain solutions, rapid response registries, and incentive models to reward responsible behaviors.[5]

Our experts also offered additional insights on COVID-19:

Insights from Ramesh Gopinath, Vice President of Blockchain Solutions for IBM:

> *"Supply chains are usually going to experience strain in a crisis, and in the current pandemic, we're seeing shortages for crucial personal protective equipment for medical workers on the front lines. In rectifying*

these shortages, collaboration across different industries has been critical. Many California companies, for example, had large stores of N-95 surgical masks acquired in response to the 2019 wildfire season and have moved to donate surplus to nearby hospitals. Rather than relying on a patchwork of donations, however, blockchain could connect a 'network of networks' for all of the different companies and organizations with the capacity to donate or manufacture needed equipment. If they could all communicate and share trusted data, they could better and more quickly allocate resources to where they're needed most."

Insights from Dale Chrystie, Blockchain Strategist at FedEx, Chair of BiTA Standards Council:

"This notion we have been discussing for some time of a big, open global village working together really resonates at this moment, not only in blockchain, but also beyond. Immediately after 9/11, we experienced in the US what was likely a very brief moment where we weren't competitors, or of different political parties, we were just American citizens. Today, I believe we are in another of those moments where many of the things we think of as differences at the surface level must be pushed aside for the greater good. This moment is the definition of 'coopetition,' and we need to move this technology and these efforts forward based on greatest need and applicability of the technology. From a FedEx point of view, because we have customers in 220 countries and territories, essentially our default position is from the International Space Station on blockchain and everything else. This is a moment of clarity, and today, as global citizens, we must quickly mobilize those who can to help those who, for whatever reason, can't, for the sake of us all. Today, we face a common enemy. We must not focus on where we traditionally compete, but, rather, where we can agree. And I would challenge the great thinkers in this group to ponder how we can scale this technology quickly, starting with key areas to help our fellow global citizens fight this common enemy."

To use blockchains—and other technologies—to help build a better future, leaders must protect data privacy and be transparent about data usage. Too often, crises can prompt widespread erosion of individual freedoms. ***The power of blockchain is the ability to share data without revealing personal information, if they are designed to do that***. We urge leaders to design blockchain solutions that capture and secure the data our decision makers need without eroding our democratic values. That is done by ethical design.

10.3. Ethical blockchains by design

In Chapter 9, action principles covered design features to attract a critical mass of adopters. In this final chapter, we elevate the notion of design from the practical to the ethical. Blockchain-enabled solutions should be designed on ethical principles rather than just on legal compliance. It helps to have an overarching ethical framework, so here we rely on a study by the Berkman Klein Center for Internet and Society at Harvard University to identify ethical design principles. Researchers at the center, Fjeld et al. (2020), published a research paper on the principles of ethical Artificial Intelligence (AI). Their ethical AI principles are broad-reaching and apply to any technology solution and seem particularly relevant to blockchain-enabled solutions.

Based on a review of 36 ethics documents published by civil societies, governments, inter-government organizations and the private sector, the authors extracted eight themes of ethical and rights-based approaches to design. These are:

1. Privacy
2. Accountability
3. Safety and security
4. Transparency and explainability

5. Fairness and non-discrimination
6. Human control of technology
7. Professional responsibility
8. Promotion of human values.[6]

Within these eight themes, there are nearly 50 specific ethical principles, some of which are highlighted in Table 10.1 and discussed below.

Ethical themes	Examples of specific principles	
1. Privacy	• Privacy by design • Rights of rectification • Rights to erasure	• Consent • Control over the use of data • Ability to restrict processes
2. Accountability	• Verifiability and replicability • Auditing • Impact assessments • Environmental responsibility	• Creation of a monitoring body • Ability to appeal • Liability and legal responsibility
3. Safety and security	• Safe by design • Secure by design • Predictable	
4. Transparency and explainability	• Transparent by design • Explainable by design • Open source • Regular reporting	• Notification when technology makes a decision about an individual
5. Fairness and non-discrimination	• Inclusive by design • Non-discrimination and prevention of bias • Representative data	• High quality data • Fairness • Equality
6. Human control of technology	• Human review of automated decisions • Human control of the technology • Ability to opt-out	
7. Professional responsibility	• Responsible by design • Accuracy of algorithms • Consideration of long-term effects	• Multi-stakeholder collaboration • Scientific integrity
8. Promotion of human values	• Leveraged to benefit society • Human values and human flourishing	

Table 10.1 Ethical design principles

Source: Extracted from Fjeld et al. (2020)

391

1. Privacy

As an ethical design principle, the right to privacy is viewed as an inalienable human right. Individuals have the right to control the access to and processing of data collected about them. They have the right to have that data rectified in cases of errors, and the right to erasure.

Public blockchains like Bitcoin, Monero and Zcash value anonymity as the ultimate right to privacy. Individuals control access to their own data through private keys stored in their own digital wallets. However, many individuals do not yet have the technical sophistication to protect their own private keys—the majority of people end up relying on trusted third parties like exchanges to protect private keys on their behalf. But individuals have the option, and through continued education, will develop the competencies needed for self-sovereignty.

Private blockchains value confidentiality, where identities need to be known, but data is only shared with authorized parties. If that data pertains to individual's personal information, ethical privacy design calls for consent from individuals and individuals should be given the rights of access to information collected about them. As an example from our cases, SmartResume holders are told when their resumes are created by a credentialing organization. Once individuals opt in to activate them, they control who gets to view their resumes. Otherwise, an individual's SmartResume is unviewable. As far as rights of erasure, Chapter 9 covered the options with *Action Principle 15: Design for regulatory compliance*.

2. Accountability

Who is accountable for decisions made by a technology? Fjeld et al. (2020) cover the mechanisms for accountability, including the verifiability and replicability of results; reliable audit trails; assessments of impacts including environmental impacts; creation of a neutral monitoring body; and legal liability for damages caused by the technology. Software liability laws are particularly complicated, but in general, it's very difficult to hold authors of software liable. Courts have generally ruled that hackers, not software providers, are responsible for data breaches.[7]

As applied to blockchain-based solutions, blockchains provide automatic verifiability because they 'confirm before posting' rather than 'confirm after the fact'. Blockchains are inherently auditable. In fact, the digital ledger *is* the audit trail.

However, governance is needed to address other accountability principles, particularly as it pertains to a neutral monitoring body. While public blockchains rely on a global network of volunteers to monitor network activity, private blockchains rely typically on more centralized governance structures.

3. Safety and security

Fjeld et al. (2020) express requirements for system safety, performance as intended, and resistance to being compromised by unauthorized parties. As applied to blockchains, the safety and security of many blockchain-based solutions are routinely assessed by deploying test nets before main nets. White-hat hackers are invited to discover security weaknesses so that holes can be plugged before live deployment. Once deployed, blockchain's distributed design inherently de-risks critical infrastructure systems through redundancy. KoreConX provides an example.

Insights by Kiran Garimella, Chief Scientist and CTO for KoreConX:

> *"Blockchains by nature are resilient because they are distributed. When a node is unavailable for whatever reason and then reconnected to the network, the node automatically re-syncs with the rest of the network. Node failures, therefore, don't affect the network as long as the minimum number of nodes for forming consensus is available. In our tests, when we brought down major areas of our global network and reconnected them, they 'heal' automatically. The process is totally hands-off. While this is an advantage of blockchains in general, we have further strengthened the KoreChain's resilience by distributing the nodes across multiple countries, cloud providers, and deployment technologies."*

4. Transparency and explainability

These ethical principles address the right to understand how technologies process information. In the case of AI, Fjeld et al. (2020) recognize that deep learning AI algorithms often mask how inputs are processed into outputs, the so called 'black box' problem. Here, blockchain-enabled solutions have an inherent advantage. Blockchains not only post the audit trail, but also post the coding for smart contracts. Public blockchains post these for everyone; private blockchains post these for authorized parties. In short, blockchain solutions are deterministic by nature, so they are inherently transparent and explainable. Moreover, blockchains are being used to open the 'black box' for AI, as the next story reveals.

At the University of Arkansas, Justin Zhan, professor of data science at the Department of Computer Science is working with the University of Arkansas for Medical Sciences to predict how the corona virus's genome will mutate so that we can maximize the efficacy of a vaccine. Using multiple shared data sources from around the world, the team is looking at changes in the genome over time and from location to location. The predictive model uses deep learning algorithms, but the big downside of that technology is it's black box—we see inputs and outputs, but we don't have good explanations of what is happening inside the box. Dr. Zhan created the notion of blockchain-based explainable artificial intelligence which creates an immutable log of each iteration of inputs and outputs, so people can understand the reasons why AI results change over time.

5. Fairness and non-discrimination

Fjeld et al. (2020)'s fairness and non-discrimination principles call for systems to be designed and used to maximize fairness, promote inclusivity, and avoid bias. As an ethical design principle, SmartResume was designed so that hiring organizations search for qualified candidates based only on their skills, as all demographic and personal information are masked. Dave Wengel, Founder and CEO of iDatafy explained:

"When XYZ freight company gets a SmartResume, they don't know the gender, race or ethnicity of the individual. And that's a benefit. So, we can help them prove that they're not showing any bias in candidate selection."

6. Human control of technology

Fjeld et al. (2020) argue that any important decisions made by technologies should be subject to human review. For the blockchain context, this principle calls for human governance over blockchain-enabled solutions. As we covered in Chapter 9, blockchain governance comprises a portfolio of decision rights, and while some rights might be automated on chain, so far, nearly all public and private chains rely on off-chain human governance. Vitalik Buterin, inventor of Ethereum, argued in favor of human governance:

"I argue that 'tightly coupled' on-chain voting is overrated, the status quo of 'informal governance', as practiced by Bitcoin, Bitcoin Cash, Ethereum, Zcash and similar systems, is much less bad than commonly thought, that people who think that the purpose of blockchains is to completely expunge soft mushy human intuitions and feelings in favor of completely algorithmic governance (emphasis on 'completely') are absolutely crazy."[8]

The 'human control of technology' principle requires deep consideration of on-chain governance before adoption. On-chain governance is unalterable without a significant software fork or intervention approved by the majority of the participants. It's meant to provide a guarantee—a programmed-in commitment, as it were—to how decisions will be made in the blockchain network now and in the future.[9] EOS is its most visible poster child. It launched its blockchain network with guaranteed democratic voting rights. Whereas Bitcoin and Ethereum miners vote on changes, EOS shifted the decision rights from developers and miners to users. As of May 5, 2020, 77,000 of 1.3 million EOS account holders participated in 1,696 votes taken since its launch, but the on-chain voting still remains at less than 5 percent of the total participants, indicating that not all participants in a blockchain may be an active participant in the governance process, but instead simply users of the developed platform.[10]

Other blockchain networks with on-chain governance include DFINITY (a blockchain-based cloud computing project aiming to reduce the costs of cloud computing); Tezos (a blockchain-based project aiming to improve smart contract safety); and Decred (a cryptocurrency like bitcoin but with on-chain governance). *The arguments for on-chain governance are guaranteed inclusion and decentralization. The arguments against are unanticipated consequences; the inability to adapt; ill-informed voters; and low voter turn-out.*[11]

7. Professional responsibility

Fjeld et al. (2020) recognize that humans design technologies and call on their professionalism and integrity to ensure that the appropriate stakeholders are consulted, and long-term effects are considered. As blockchain developers, we have a responsibility to make sure that solutions are accurate, multiple parties are invited to collaborate, and scientific methods are used to assess results. Concerning this last point, Dr Naseem Naqvi, the Co-founder of the British Blockchain Association and Editor-in-Chief of its flagship journal, advocates for evidence-based blockchain research. Here are his insights:

Insights from Dr. Naseem Naqvi, Chair, Centre for Evidence Based Blockchain; Editor in Chief, The JBBA:

> *"Evidence Based Blockchain, defined as 'conscientious, explicit and judicious decision making based on professional expertise and the best available organisational, stakeholder and scientific evidence' should be the cornerstone of applied blockchain. Evidence-based decision making cuts failure rates by 50 percent and increases the number of right business decisions by six-fold. The evidence required for better decision making in blockchain might not always be available, but that is not an excuse for relying solely on casual benchmarking, ideology and intuition to guide institutional practices. In a world of hyper-competition, evidence-based blockchain can be your biggest competitive advantage."*

8. Promotion of human values

Fjeld et al. (2020) discuss the principles of promoting human values by using technologies to help humans flourish; by providing access to many; and by leveraging technologies to better society. Depending on how a blockchain-enabled solution is designed, considerable human value can arise. Throughout this book, we've highlighted several of them. For example, Stellar values financial inclusion by making access to financial services convenient and inexpensive; food and goods traceability solutions, like the IBM Food Trust, provide confidence in product quality by knowing the source and journey of what we consume; KoreConX opened up capital markets to small private companies so they can thrive; LO3 Energy and Share&Charge's empower individuals to make energy choices. New examples come to light each day. For example, EY recently helped the Italian newspaper giant, ANSA, prevent fake news by proving the legitimacy of the news source with a token stored on public Ethereum.[12]

If we fulfill the promises of blockchain-based solutions, we will also see humans flourish by having self-sovereignty over one's own data; political inclusion by making it easier for people to participate and to vote; greater distributive justice by deploying resources to where they are most needed; and better health care and outcomes. Kathryn Carlisle, Senior Managing Director of BCoE at the University of Arkansas, is a strong advocate for designing blockchain solutions for social good. Here are her insights:

Insights from Kathryn Carlisle, Senior Managing Director of BCoE, University of Arkansas:

"Our financial economy will be introduced to new people, new business models and new standards. New people are referring to blockchain's ability to provide financial inclusion for the 1.7 billion unbanked around the world. These benefits are not only for developing nations, but developed ones as well. Imagine every citizen having a self-sovereign identity on the blockchain that would be interoperable with a government-issued digital wallet. Each individual over the age of 18 could be airdropped a Universal Basic Income

in cryptocurrency each month or a certain amount of 'democracy dollars' to spend towards political campaigning every four years. New business models will be created from automation driven by smart contracts, as will new financial asset classes. This will open the door to making innovations possible, like decentralized autonomous cars with smart wallets; micro-tipping and microtransactions for individual songs, news articles and donations. New standards will be formed in regards to price, speed, and privacy of transactions. Consumers will expect private transactions with instant settlement at a low cost."

10.3. Blockchain visionaries: In their own words

Blockchain leaders from EY, the University of Arkansas, WeTrade, Microsoft, and IBM close out this book with their insights on the future of blockchains. Paul Brody and Professor Dan Conway focus on the value of interorganizational blockchain solutions, and how they might enable small companies to compete effectively with large ones. Roberto Mancone points to the rise of Asia in leading blockchain investments and predicts that fewer blockchain applications will be developed by consortia. Mike Walker focuses on new business models and opportunities. Marie Wieck calls for more open innovations on three key areas of development. Their views are shared in their own words.

Paul Brody, Principal & Global Blockchain Leader, EY:

"Blockchains will do for business ecosystems what Enterprise Resource Planning (ERP) did for the single enterprise. Over the past few decades, companies have transformed themselves through digital integration, much of it driven through the way that ERP systems approach end-to-end processes like procure-to-pay or order-to-cash. Yet while companies have transformed themselves internally, the tools they use to transact externally have changed little. With blockchain technology, the same level of digital integration will be possible across enterprise boundaries.

The impact on the future size and shape of enterprises is likely to be profound. The most complex and challenging work going on at most companies today is the work required to manage external partners, and the truth is that most really large companies today are not so much individual enterprises as they are orchestrators of vast networks. The challenges of managing those networks are enormous and the efficiencies to be gained are equally large. Blockchains may also, in the long run, pose a challenge to the nature of large enterprises themselves. If a network of small companies linked through blockchain technology can act as rapidly as an integrated global firm, then some of the big advantages of size and scale may recede, leading to a whole new world of thriving small and medium size enterprises."

Dan Conway, Professor and Associate Director of BCoE, University of Arkansas:

"Databases have always been built with a single organizational focus, and thus applications using databases have inherited this limited focus. Opening and extending these systems has proven complex and rarely has accomplished value beyond transaction automation. Blockchain flips this script. The focus now is on the interorganizational entity itself. Blockchain has created the opportunity of a generation—the opportunity to leverage the enormous value released by a having an ecosystem of trust and transparency. The demand for interorganizational trust and transparency has never been greater."

Roberto Mancone, a co-founder and former COO of WeTrade:

"As far as investment trends, investments in blockchain moved from West to East. In 2017, US deals represented 51 percent of the total investment, while China accounted for only two percent. In 2019, the ratio was 31 percent US and 22 percent China. Entreprise blockchain projects do not attract necessary funding compared to investment in cryptocurrencies. $700 million was invested in enterprise blockchains cumulatively in 2018 and 2019 compared to $6.3 billion cumulative investment in non-enterprise blockchains. We are definitely moving away from consortium and exploring killer applications that

can increase competitive advantage versus others players in the same market. In 2020 I see increased interest by Central Banks for CBDC (Central Bank Digital Currencies), an increase of institutional investors placing deposits in crypto, and valuable blockchain solutions for custody such as Anchorage, Ledgeer and Knox proposing solutions to insurances without the needs to create consortium."

Mike Walker, Senior Director of Applied Innovation, Microsoft Corp:

"Organizations are continuously being pressured by their governments, shareholders, and customers to digitize their business in two major ways. The first way is to improve their operations by optimizing costs using digital technologies, implementing practices and technologies to avoid data security breaches, and use customer data ethically and responsibly. The second way is to use technology innovation to create new business models and compelling customer experiences that improve the way people live and work. Gradually over the next five years blockchain will enable this by creating new forms of collaboration between people, businesses, and things in the form of digital ecosystems. A blockchain-enabled digital ecosystem provides the basis of a value exchange network that harnesses the unique capabilities of blockchain such as: data self-sovereignty, tamper resistant data, peer-to-peer data collaboration, and distributed governance."

Marie Wieck, General Manager, IBM Blockchain

"In the last few years, blockchain has evolved from the hype and headlines around Bitcoin and crypto-currencies to the creation of enterprise platforms driving real-world benefits in finance, global trade and healthcare. While the technical viability of blockchain is now clear, ubiquitous cross-industry adoption remains elusive due to a lack of common standards and governance models. In the short-term, we will see efforts focused on interoperability between similar enterprise platforms, but in the longer term I think we need continued open-source innovation in three key areas:

Identity standards that will enable faster on-boarding and facilitate interoperability for permissioned enterprise use cases. Once a digital identity for blockchain has been established, granting access and validating context can be accelerated. These efforts could also open up the business model economics of decentralized public blockchains that are typically anonymous for more enterprise use cases,

Continued innovation in consensus methods to drive stepwise improvements in performance and the cost of data sharing as network adoption grows. Transaction speed has not been an issue in current use cases, but if for example, we want to provide provenance across the supply chain, transaction costs must be negligible, and

Blockchain governance models must be extended to easily specify data usage rights and lifecycle management that extend across networks. Blockchain provides trusted access, but proving that a supplier can't see a competitor's pricing on a shared platform still requires significant time and effort in new network formation. Providing standard methods for documenting access controls by role and automatically testing the validity of these data usage rights will accelerate industry adoption.

We've shown that the benefits of blockchain increase with adoption, so tackling these areas will drive exponential value creation, and mark the next frontier in bringing blockchain from the enterprise to the masses."

10.4. Conclusion

Hopefully, readers by now have been given enough evidence to agree that something big is indeed afoot. Blockchains have the potential to change the way we exchange value, just as the Internet changed the way we exchange information. Blockchains show us new ways to mitigate counter-party risks, to provide reliable bookkeeping records, and to secure networks by using cryptography, digital tokens, consensus algorithms, distributed ledgers and smart contracts. It's not just a pipe dream; public blockchains have over a decade of operations and a decent track record so far. When blunders like the DAO or a 51 percent attack occurs, we learn from them. Communities improve the technologies with each iteration of software development and upgrades. Private blockchains have a shorter history, but early enterprise adopters are proving the concept and realizing the value of sharing solutions across ecosystem partners.

The degree to which public and private blockchains will continue to develop in parallel, converge, intersect, or otherwise have one supplant the other, remains uncertain. Early indications suggest that confidential (rather than anonymous) transactions over public blockchains may become the dominant model. Personally, I do not consider the public versus private blockchains as either/or options. As informed by General Systems Theory, *equifinality* is an inherent property of open systems, whereby an end state can be reached by many paths.[13] In my opinion, the end state of an 'Internet of Value' will likely be public *and* private solutions; *and* hybrid solutions; *and* blockchain solutions that interface with existing systems of record. It's not really about the technology anyway; it's what the technology is ethically designed to do and the value it can deliver that keeps me—and hopefully readers—engaged.

Citations

[1] Goldin, I., and Mariathasan, M. (2014), *The Butterfly Defect*, University of Princeton Press, Princeton New Jersey.

[2] Bradbury, R. (June 28, 1952), 'The Sound of Thunder', *Collier's Magazine*.

[3] Van Hoek, R., and Lacity, M. (April 27, 2020), 'How the Pandemic Is Pushing Blockchain Forward', *Harvard Business Review*, https://hbr.org/2020/04/how-the-pandemic-is-pushing-blockchain-forward

[4] Van Hoek, R., and Lacity, M. (April 27, 2020), 'How the Pandemic Is Pushing Blockchain Forward', *Harvard Business Review*, https://hbr.org/2020/04/how-the-pandemic-is-pushing-blockchain-forward

[5] Tapscott, D., and Tapscott, A. (2020), *Blockchain Solutions in Pandemics*, A Blockchain Research Institute Special Report, https://www.blockchainresearchinstitute.org/blockchain-and-pandemics/

[6] Fjeld, J., Achten, N., Hilligoss, H., Nagy, A., and Srikumar, M. (2020), *Principled Artificial Intelligence: Mapping Consensus in Ethical and Rights-based Approaches to Principles for AI*, Research Publication No. 2020-1, The Berkman Klein Center for Internet & Society, https://cyber.harvard.edu/publication/2020/principled-ai

[7] Insureon (January 28, 2016), *The State of Software Liability*, https://www.insureon.com/technology-business-insurance

[8] Buterin, V. (2017), *Notes on Blockchain Governance*, https://vitalik.ca/general/2017/12/17/voting.html

[9] Frankenfield, J. (April 4, 2018), *On-chain governance*, Investopedia. https://www.investopedia.com/terms/o/onchain-governance.asp

[10] *EOS Block Producer Elections*, https://eosauthority.com/producers_schedules

Lacity, M., Zach, S., Paul, C. (2019), *Blockchain Governance Models: Insights for Enterprises* (02nd ed., vol. 2019), Blockchain Center of Excellence.

[11] Buterin, V. (2017), *Notes on Blockchain Governance*, https://vitalik.ca/general/2017/12/17/voting.html

[12] EY Global Blockchain Conference: *Going Public*. April 20, 2020.

[13] Bertalanffy, Ludwig von (1969), *General System Theory; Foundations, Development, Applications*, Braziller, New York.

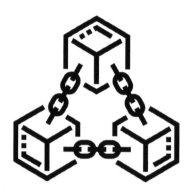

Glossary

This glossary covers terms, major events and supplemental information

Action principle: A management practice that facilitates the success of a business project. Action principles are similar to 'best practices' in that both seek to share knowledge from prior experiences. However, whereas 'best practices' imply that mimicry is always recommended and will always produce similar results, action principles recognize that context matters. The thoughtful practitioner decides the usefulness of an action principle depending on the objectives the organization is trying to achieve; whether the organization has the absorptive capacity to implement the action principle effectively; and timing—there are better times than others to act.

Altcoins: Alternative coins are cryptocurrencies that are alternatives to bitcoin. Typically, altcoins were created by downloading the Bitcoin Core, altering the programming code, and launching a new network. Namecoin and litecoin are examples. As time went on, the term has become outdated.

Anonymity: In the context of blockchains, the identity of the senders and receivers of transactions is unknown. Anonymity is different from confidentiality (see entry below).

Anti-Money Laundering (AML): Regulations that require financial institutions to report suspicious activity of money laundering, which is defined as an illegal practice that converts profits from crimes into what appears to be a legitimate source of cash. Sample AML regulations include the US Bank Secrecy Act of 1970; the UK Sanctions and Anti-Money Laundering Act 2018; and the European Union's AML directives in 2015 and 2020.[1]

Application Programming Interface (API): An API is a piece of software that connects two software applications so that one application can send a message to and receive a response from another application. Bitcoin, for example, has over 100 APIs. Sample Bitcoin APIs include programming code to indicate the number of blocks in the longest chain ('GetBlockCount'); to create a new bitcoin wallet ('CreateWallet'); and to list the IP addresses of all banned nodes ('ListBanned'). See https://bitcoin.org/en/developer-reference.

Asymmetric key algorithm: A type of cryptography that uses a pair of mathematically related numbers called 'keys'—one public key and one private key. Users can digitally sign messages by encrypting them with their private keys. *'This is effective since any message recipient can verify that the user's public key can decrypt the message, and thus prove that the user's secret key was used to encrypt it. If the user's secret key is, in fact, secret, then it follows that the user, and not some impostor, really sent the message.'*[2] **RSA, DSA,** and **ECC** are three specific examples of asymmetric key algorithms (see entries below for each).

Atomic swap: Ensures that *all* of the actions associated with a transaction execute, or *all* the actions fail; no partial executions should be allowed. For example, if Alice wants to send some value to Bob, an atomic swap ensures that either (a) Alice's account is debited AND Bob's account is credited, or (b) that NEITHER action occurs.

Benevolent dictator: A governance model in which a single person or single organization holds decision making rights, and bases decisions on the best interests of the community.

Bitcoin: This term bitcoin refers to both the Bitcoin application as a whole and to its native digital asset, the bitcoin cryptocurrency.

Bitcoin (application): The Bitcoin application is a peer-to-peer payment application. Conceived of by Satoshi Nakamoto in 2008 by combining many existing innovations, the Bitcoin network was launched live in 2009.[3] Nakamoto adopted public-private key encryption to authenticate asset ownership, a Proof-of-Work consensus protocol for validating transactions and adding them to the ledger, and the use of hashes and Merkle trees to secure transactions within a completely distributed, peer-to-peer, public network. Among its advances were a digital ledger structured as a chain of blocks and the creation of a native digital asset called bitcoins.

Bitcoin (cryptocurrency): Bitcoins are the native digital asset within the Bitcoin blockchain. Bitcoin was designed to be a scarce resource with a maximum money supply of 21 million bitcoins. The first 50 bitcoins were released in 2009, and the last will be released in the year 2140. Bitcoins are added to the money supply, on average, every ten minutes to reward miners for creating a new block of transactions. Every 210,000 blocks, the miner's reward cuts in half, so that more bitcoins are released in its earlier years than in later years. As of early 2020, about 85 percent of the money supply has been released.

Block header: Each block within a blockchain contains a header with important information such as the block's unique ID; the number of transactions in the block; when the block was created; the size of the block (in terms of computer storage); and the pointer to the previous block. Figure G.1 provides an example of Bitcoin's block header.

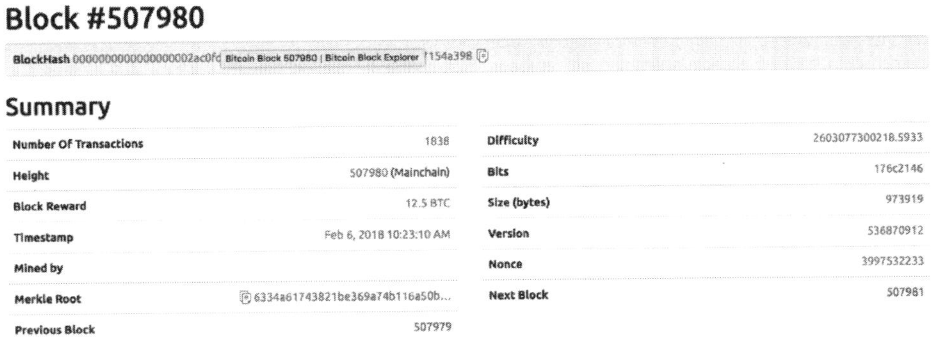

Block #507980

BlockHash 000000000000000000002ac0fd Bitcoin Block 507980 | Bitcoin Block Explorer 154a398

Summary

Number Of Transactions	1838	Difficulty	2603077300218.5933
Height	507980 (Mainchain)	Bits	176c2146
Block Reward	12.5 BTC	Size (bytes)	973919
Timestamp	Feb 6, 2018 10:23:10 AM	Version	536870912
Mined by		Nonce	3997532233
Merkle Root	6334a61743821be369a74b116a50b...	Next Block	507981
Previous Block	507979		

Figure G.1: Example of a block header for Bitcoin

407

In this example, we are looking at the 507,980th block in the Bitcoin blockchain. The summary data in the header indicates that there are 1,838 transactions in the block's payload; its *'height'* is equal to its sequence in the blockchain (block 507980); *'block reward'* indicates that the winning miner earned 12.5 bitcoins for using its computer's resources to validate the transactions and to create the block; the *'timestamp'* indicates the exact second the block was created on February 6th 2018; the *'Merkle root'* shows the result of the Merkle hashing sequences (see **Merkle root** entry below) used to secure the block; the *'previous block'* is the pointer to this block's predecessor. The *'bits'* and *'size'* indicate how much computer storage is required to store this block. The *'version'* indicates which set of Bitcoin's blockchains rules to follow. The *'difficulty'* and *'nonce'* are associated with Bitcoin's Proof-of-Work consensus algorithm. Functionally, the difficulty indicates the number of lead zeros the miner's computer(s) had to find (after trillions of random tries) in order to find a unique *'blockhash'*. In this block, notice the blockhash has 18 lead zeros. The difficulty is part of the proof that the miner's computer did some serious calculations to earn the block reward (see entry for **Proof-of-Work**).

Blockchain: This term is used several ways. Sometimes the term refers broadly to what we are calling a 'blockchain application'. For example, people call Bitcoin and Ethereum 'blockchains'. The term can also be used to describe the structure of the digital ledger. With a blockchain structure, newly submitted transactions are sequenced and collected into a block (see Figure G.2). The block comprises a header and payload of transactions. The block header includes a pointer to the previous block of transactions, forming a chain of sequenced blocks over time all the way back to the first block, called the 'genesis block'.

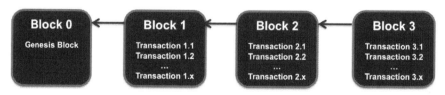

Figure G.2: Distributed ledger structured as a chain of blocks

Blockchain application: A blockchain application is a peer-to-peer system for validating, time-stamping, and permanently storing transactions on a shared *distributed ledger*. *Digital assets*, native to each blockchain application, exist only in digital form and come with rights of use. *Cryptography* and *consensus* algorithms are used to validate transactions, to update the ledger, and to keep the ledger and network secure. Most blockchains also use *smart contracts* that apply rules to automatically execute transactions based upon pre-agreed conditions.

Byzantine Fault Tolerance of a system: The ability of a distributed network to function properly given that a certain number of nodes are faulty or even malicious. A general rule is that peer-to-peer distributed systems like blockchains can function properly even when up to a third of the participating nodes are faulty.

Byzantine Generals' Problem: A conceptual situation described by Leslie Lamport, Robert Shostak, and Marshall Pease (1982) to investigate how decentralized communication networks can reach agreement if some unknown number of nodes is faulty. In their metaphor, a Byzantine General represents a computer node; some generals are loyal (i.e. not faulty) and some generals are disloyal (i.e. faulty). Lamport et al. (1982) proved that decentralized networks could reach a consensus provided that two thirds of the nodes function properly.[4]

Centralized network: See entry for **Network structures**

Code base: The set of programming instructions based on the agreed upon rules, i.e. protocols.

Coercive influences: See entry for **Institutional Isomorphism**

Confidentiality: In the context of blockchains, only authorized parties are allowed to know the identities of the parties involved or the details of the transaction.

Consensus protocol: Consensus protocols are rules for making sure copies of the distributed ledger agree. Consensus protocols are used to counteract the **tragedy of**

the commons and the **Byzantine Generals' Problem** (see separate entries). Although consensus protocols vary in their validation procedures, in general, all consensus protocols seek to authenticate ownership and ensure that transactions are funded (i.e. no double spending) before adding them to the official distributed ledger. The process of validation begins when a new transaction is broadcast to the network. Computer algorithms verify legitimate ownership of the asset (based on the owner's digital signature with his or her private key) and check that the asset has not been given away before by scanning the ledger, thus preventing double spending. Which node gets to collect verified transactions and add them to the official ledger depends on the network's consensus protocol. Many consensus protocols have been used and proposed, including Proof-of-Work; Proof-of-Stake; Proof-of-Activity (which combines Proof-of-Stake with Proof-of-Work); Proof-of-Authority; Proof-of-Burn; Proof-of-Capacity; Proof-of-Elapsed Time; Proof-of-Listening; and Proof-of-Luck.

Consortium-led innovation: In the context of a blockchain, a consortium provides a structure for competitors and ecosystem partners to cooperate on shared blockchain initiatives.

Coopetition: A portmanteau of two words—'cooperation' and 'competition'. Coopetition recognizes that firms have complex interdependencies. In some realms, firms that compete for market share also cooperate to achieve mutual benefits such as to define standards, to build component parts, or to reduce shared administrative and infrastructure costs.[5]

Corda: An open-source, distributed ledger platform developed by the R3 Consortium. Corda was designed to increase privacy, reduce data redundancy and increase scalability. Corda uses public-private key encryptions and hashes, and creates permanent, immutable records between trading partners. As a private protocol, participants are assigned a cryptographic identity, which is tied to a 'real world' identity, such as a legal entity identifier.[6] Once on-boarded, a party can transform a legal contract into smart contract code to transact with another Corda party or parties. Rather than distribute the entire ledger to everyone on the network, Corda creates node-to-node transactions directly between/among the parties involved in the transaction as defined in the smart contract.[7] Each Corda participant only sees the subset of data for which they are privy. This feature is implemented using Multiple Composite Keys (see entry below).[8]

Corda has configurable consensus, meaning parties to a contract can pick their preferred consensus protocol, which is likely to be Byzantine Fault Tolerance (BFT) or Raft.[9] The Corda ledger is built on relational database technology, and thus does not use a block structure. It chose this structure so that participants could easily query the ledger using SQL. Data is considered 'on-ledger' if at least two parties in the system agree about the transaction's validity, whereas data held by only one party is 'off-ledger'. Corda's design is scalable since there is less network traffic and data storage, more private than most DTL protocols, and settles transactions as soon as nodes agree.[10]

As time went on, Corda's architecture evolved to the point where some people no longer consider it a blockchain; Corda lacks some of the defining characteristics of public blockchains: It does not have a native digital asset, it does not broadcast transactions, and it does not distribute a shared ledger. Indeed, Corda's main architects call Corda 'blockchain-inspired'.[11] The initial version was released in November of 2016.[12]

Counterparty risk: The risk each trading party bears that the other party will not fulfill its contractual obligations.

Cross-chain oracle: One blockchain application reads data from another blockchain application. One-way reads are also called 'one-way pegs'.

Cross-chain transaction processing: Two or more blockchains coordinate operations so that a single asset can be used by more than one chain. These are also called 'two-way pegs'.

Cryptography: The science of securing data in the presence of third party adversaries using mathematical and computer algorithms.

CryptoNotes: A protocol that aims to increase the anonymity of blockchains.

Cryptocurrency exchange: A trusted third party that acts as a money transmitter or market maker for cryptocurrencies. Coinbase, Binance, and Huobi are examples.

Decentralized Autonomous Organization (DAO): A special kind of smart contract that runs an entire organization automatically based on codified rules in a smart contract. The idea of a DAO is to create a completely independent entity that is exclusively governed by the rules that you program into it and 'lives' on the chain. This is more than using the blockchain to manage a company: instead, the code is the entire company. And it cannot be stopped.[13]

Decentralized network: See entry for **Network structures**

Delegated Proof-of-Stake (DPoS): A consensus protocol created by Daniel Larimer, founder of BitShares, Steemit and EOS.[14] With this method, anyone who possesses the cryptocurrency can vote to elect validator nodes. The validator nodes with the most votes become a 'delegate' (see Figure G.3). The algorithm takes turns selecting a leader from among the panel of delegates for a current time period. After the time period elapses, another round of voting occurs to select the next panel of delegates. Delegates are rewarded with transaction fees. DPoS settles transactions faster and with fewer resources than proof-of-work, and is more democratic than permissioned protocols.[15] EOS uses DPoS.

Democracy: A governance model where any participant has an equal vote.

Denial of Service (DoS) attack: A type of malicious attack that floods a network with so many transactions that it disrupts service for legitimate users.

Digital signature: A way to sign a transaction using a computer rather than a hand signature, thus proving one is authorized to do so (see Chapter 3 for more details).

Digital wallet: Software that stores private keys associated with addresses that hold digital assets. A digital wallet is an entry point, or interface, to many blockchains. Stored off a blockchain, the private keys are the only way to prove that one owns an asset on the distributed ledger. If the digital wallet is destroyed or hacked, there is no way to retrieve it. Thus, digital wallets are the main source of vulnerability for blockchain applications.

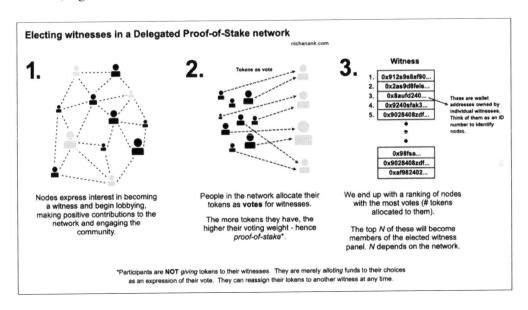

Figure G3: Delegated Proof-of-Stake (DPoS) voting process

Source: https://en.bitcoinwiki.org/upload/en/images/8/8b/Consensus-algorithms-pos-dpos.png

Directed Acyclic Graphs (DAG): A type of graph that flows in just one direction with no feedback loops. In the context of blockchains, one-way graphs can be used to represent the time sequence of transactions. Iota's 'tangle' structures its ledger based on a DAG (see Figure G.4).

Disruptive innovation: An innovation based on a new business model that targets underserved customers or creates new markets that may eventually threaten the traditional competitors' market shares. The term comes from Clayton Christensen's Theory of Disruptive Innovation.[16]

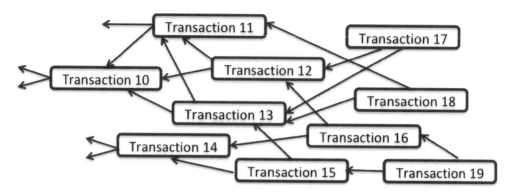

Figure G.4: Distributed ledger structured as a tangle of transactions

Distributed ledger: As a component of a blockchain application, a distributed ledger is a time-stamped, permanent record of all valid transactions that have occurred within a given blockchain application. Each node of the blockchain network has an identical copy; no node is in charge.

Distributed network: See entry for **Network structures**

DSA (Digital Signature Algorithm): An asymmetric key algorithm that generates private-public key pairs. Designed by David Kravitz, an NSA (National Security Agency) employee, the National Institute of Standards and Technology adopted it in the 1990s.[17]

Elliptic Curve Cryptography (ECC): ECC is a common method for generating private-public key pairs in blockchain applications. Basically, an ECC algorithm transforms a private key into a public key by bouncing around a large elliptic curve *n* number of times, where *n* is equal to the private key. It's theoretically impossible to figure out the private key if one only has the public key. The specific EC curve used in Bitcoin is y^2 = x3 + 7 (see Figure G.5). This is called SECP256K1. If we give someone the starting point G and the ending point public key (x, y), one cannot easily determine the n (the private key) even if one has this equation for the graph.

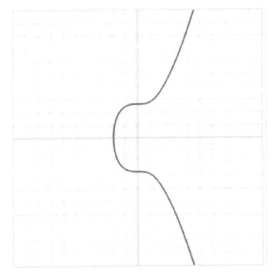

This is a graph of **secp256k1**'s elliptic curve $Y^2 = x^3 + 7$ over the real numbers. Note that because **secp256k1** is actually defined over the field Z_p, its graph will, in reality, appear as random scattered points, not anything like this.

The base point G in compressed form is:

• G = 02 9BE667E F9DCBBAC 55A06295 CE870B0F 029BFCDB 2DCE28D9 59F2815B 16F8179F

Indicates   Point on X axis   Point on Y axis
"compressed"

Figure G.5: Bitcoin's Elliptic Curve Cryptography

Source: https://en.bitcoin.it/wiki/Secp256k1

The algorithm begins at base point G and moves across the graph trillions upon trillion of times equal to the private key to land on a final (x,y) coordinate that becomes the public key.

EOS: EOS was developed by Daniel Larimer and Brendan Blumer, CTO and CEO, respectively, of Block.one. They wanted the advantages—open, secure, decentralized— of a public blockchain platform, like Ethereum, to build and operate decentralized applications, but without the latency, limited scalability, and resource intensity. The EOS mainnet was launched live in June of 2018. Anyone can view the blockchain (https://bloks.io/) and use EOS. Anyone can operate a validator node if they meet minimal criteria: an individual or organization must have a public website URL; at least one social media account; an ID on Steemit; sufficient hardware; plans to scale hardware; plans to benefit the community; telegram and testnet nodes; a roadmap; and a dividend position.[18] However, only 21 'block producers' can add blocks. The block producers are selected by a Delegated Proof-of-Stake mechanism (see glossary entry) in which owners of EOS cast votes in proportion to their stake.[19] Block producers are rewarded with the issuance of new EOS tokens. Blocks are produced about every 500 milliseconds, with each of the 21 producers getting a turn. On the day of this writing, EOS was trading at $2.35 and block producers were located in China (eight nodes), Singapore (three nodes), the Cayman Islands (two nodes), United States (two nodes) and BVI, Canada, Hong Kong, Japan, South Korea, and Ukraine (operating one node each).

ERC-20 tokens: Standard for creating a token for *fungible digital assets* that can be exchanged with other fungible tokens on Ethereum. Each token is interchangeable and has the same value. The token must meet mandatory requirements for defining the total money supply, specifying the number of tokens than can be transferred to a user account, providing a way to extract the balance of an account, allowing the transfer of tokens to other accounts, and checking a transaction against the money supply to prevent counterfeits. Optionally, ERC-20 tokens can be assigned a token name, symbol, and decimal value (up to 18 decimal places).[20] Aion (AION); Augur (REP); EOS (EOS); Golem (GNT); Maker (MKR); TRON (TRX); and VeChain(VET) are examples of ERC-20 tokens.

ERC-721 tokens: Standard for creating a token for *nonfungible digital assets* on Ethereum, whereby each token is unique and can have a different value than others of its kind. ERC-721 tokens can only be exchanged with other tokens of its same kind. ERC-721 tokens must meet required functions, including balance of an address; owner of a token; approval and transfer of a token. [21] CryptoKitties was the first ERC-721 token, which gained popularity in 2017; each CryptoKitty is one of a kind. Whereas CryptoKitties are native digital assets that only exist inside Ethereum, ERC-721 tokens can be used to represent unique assets outside of Ethereum with a unique digital twin inside Ethereum. EY's WineChain token is an example; EY tokenized 11 million unique wine bottles with an ERC-721 token.[22]

Ether: Ethereum's native digital asset. Ether is not intended so much as a cryptocurrency, as much as it is a 'crypto-fuel', meaning it's a token whose main function is to pay for the Ethereum platform.[23] Like bitcoin, ether is released through the process of mining blocks, and miners also receive the ether that senders append to their transactions to pay for them to be validated and added to the ledger. Ethereum's block reward was initially 5 ether, but it was reduced to 3 ether in 2017 and to 2 ether in 2019.[24] As of August 26, 2019, ether was trading at $188.49; the network had 8,977 active nodes, and 8,426,754 blocks had been added to the ledger.[25] The total ether money supply amount is unclear;a maximum of 18 million ether can be mined per year. [26,27]

Ethereum: Vitalik Buterin wrote the 2013 Ethereum white paper that would become the Ethereum platform when he was only 19 years old. Vitalik Buterin, Gavin Wood and Jeffrey Wilcke began work on Ethereum by launching The Ethereum Foundation, a non-profit organization based in Switzerland. According to the Ethereum Foundation: *"Ethereum is a community-driven project aiming to decentralize the Internet and return it to its democratic roots. It is a platform for building and deploying applications which do not need to rely on trust and cannot be controlled by any central authority."*[28] Ethereum's smart contracts are the primary innovation that extends a blockchain from a transaction verification and settlement protocol to a platform to launch decentralized applications (DApps). DApps can create and transact new native digitals assets besides ether, provided that they conform to **ERC-20** or **ERC-711** guidelines (see separate entries above).

Ethereum Foundation: Vitalik Buterin, Gavin Wood and Jeffrey Wilcke began work on Ethereum by launching The Ethereum Foundation, a non-profit organization based in Switzerland. The foundation was first funded in August 2014 using an Initial Coin Offering for its native digital asset called 'ether'. Ethereum went live in July of 2015, with a presale release of 60 million ether and 20 million ether retained by The Ethereum Foundation.[29] It raised over $16 million.[30]

Exchange: see **Cryptocurrency Exchange** entry.

Fabric: See **Hyperledger Fabric** entry.

Federation: A governance model in which decentralized groups specialize on parts of a project while coordinating with a central group.

Fork: A divergence of a blockchain into two or more separate paths. Soft forks are temporary, whereas hard forks are permanent (see Figure G.6).

Fork (Hard): Hard forks are permanent, divergent paths of a blockchain. Hard forks typically occur under two circumstances. First, someone may create their own blockchain or digital asset by copying and modifying source code. Second, hard forks can occur when the open source community disagrees on the rules of the next version of the protocol. For example, Bitcoin forked into 'Bitcoin' and 'Bitcoin Cash' when miners disagreed over a proposed upgrade in 2017. In another example, Ethereum split into 'Ethereum' and 'Ethereum Classic' when the community disagreed about remediating The DAO hack (see story in Chapter 8).

Fork (Soft): Sometimes two nodes create the next block at the same time, resulting in two versions called a soft fork. For a short while, different nodes in the network will be working off of different branches of the ledger until one is established as the longest and therefore the valid branch. Soft forks also occur during planned upgrades to the open source software. A temporary divergence in the blockchain happens when non-upgraded nodes do not follow the new consensus rules.[31] The non-upgraded nodes can still mine for a set time period, so it is up to the upgraded nodes to mine faster and become the longest, and thus, most valid chain.[32] In practice, the open source community tries to get most people to agree to the soft fork in advance.

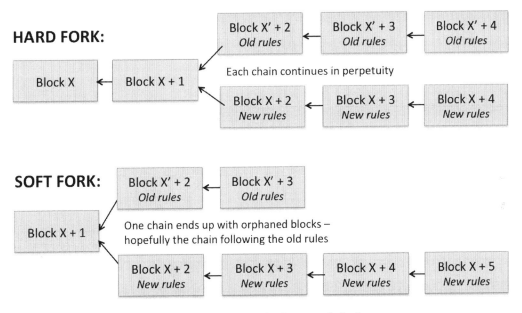

Figure G.6: Hard fork vs. soft forks

A hard fork is a permanent divergence in a blockchain. A soft fork is a temporary divergence in a blockchain while nodes upgrade to the new rules; mining under old rules will not win blocks, so nodes will eventually join the new chain if everything goes as planned.

Governance: Defines the decision-making rights over a blockchain initiative.

Hash: An algorithm for transforming one input into a different output. Given a specific input, the identical output will always be reproduced. A good hash algorithm makes it practically impossible to determine the input value based on the output value, which is why hashes are called 'one way' functions. SHA-256 is commonly used in blockchains. Blockchains use hashes in many places to add layers of security. Public keys are hashed into addresses; addresses and amounts within a transaction are hashed to create a unique and secure transaction ID; transaction IDs within a block are hashed together multiple

419

times to produce a **Merkle root** (see entry below) that resides in a block header; and all the data in the block header is hashed to create a unique and secure block ID.

Hash-Time Locked Contracts (HTLC): A type of smart contract that locks the sender's value into the contract until either the receiver retrieves the value in the address using the secret key and their digital signature (this is the 'hash lock'), or the contract expires and returns the value to the sender (this is the 'time lock').

Heisenbug: A computer programming logic error that changes its behavior unpredictably.[33] The bug is named after the Heisenberg Uncertainty Principle which asserts that the more precisely one thing is known about a particle—like its position— the less precisely another thing is known about the particle—like its momentum.

Hexadecimal: A numbering system with 16 base numbers, often used in blockchain cryptography. The 16 numbers are usually represented as 0,1,2,3,4,5,6,7,8,9,A,B,C,D,E, and F.

Hyperledger Fabric: Hyperledger Fabric is one of the projects sponsored by the Hyperledger Project, a non-profit organization launched by the Linux Foundation in December of 2015 to advance the application of enterprise-grade blockchains across industries.[34] Although the Hyperledger Project has other major blockchain frameworks, Fabric has received considerable media attention, thanks to its adoption by enterprises such as IBM, Wal-Mart, and Maersk.[35] Digital Asset Holdings and IBM initially contributed to Hyperledger Fabric's code base. Twenty-six other companies—including Fujitsu, GE, Hitachi, State Street, and SAP—contributed to the open source code that was released in 2017.[36] Fabric's ledger is structured as a chain of blocks and has two subsystems: 'the world state' and the 'transaction log' of all the transactions that led up to the current world state. Participants can create their own channels, which is a separate transaction ledger. Within a channel, every node gets copies of the same ledger.[37] Fabric also has a smart contracting feature, called Chaincode, which is used to connect outside applications to the world state ledger.

Hyperledger Project (HLP):   The Linux Foundation launched this non-profit organization in December of 2015 to advance the application of enterprise-grade blockchains across industries.[38]   Brian Behlendorf, the developer of the Apache Web server, serves as Executive Director. As of January 2020, 275 corporate members are listed on its website. As of 2020, HLP oversees six major distributed ledger projects: Fabric (see entry above); Sawtooth; Iroha; Burrow; Indy; and BESU. HLP is also developing four tools (Avalon, Caliper, Cello, and Explorer) and building libraries (Quilt for blockchain interoperability; Ursa for cryptograpy; Transact for smart contracts; and Aries for digital credentials).[39] Hyperledger GRID was donated by Cargill to serve as a reference implementation for supply chains and includes data types, data models, and smart contract business logic.[40]

Immutability: As it relates to blockchains, immutability means that a transaction or smart contract that has been added to the digital ledger can never be changed. For public blockchains like Bitcoin and Ethereum, immutability means that errors cannot be fixed unless 51 percent of the nodes agree to the fix by rolling back the ledger and creating a hard fork. For private blockchains, authorized parties may submit transactions that reverse a prior error, but the entire transaction history that led to the current account balance will be maintained. The benefit of immutability is that trading partners can rely on one historical record for data provenance and auditability. Immutability may conflict with regulations or corporate policies that require data destruction after an elapsed period of time, but there are a number of practices to address this, such as keeping private data off chain.[41]

Initial Coin Offering (ICO): With an ICO, startups announce that they want to raise cash using an ICO by launching a new coin, i.e. a new cryptocurrency. Investors buy the coins instead of shares in a company. While there are many legitimate ICOs, investors are warned to fully vet ICO projects to avoid being scammed.

Initial Exchange Offering (IEO): A funding round conducted on a cryptocurrency exchange. Investors fund their exchange wallets with coins and use those funds to buy the fundraising company's tokens. Binance, Huobi, OKEX, KuCoin, and BitMax are examples of exchanges with IEO services.[42]

Institutional Isomorphism: A theory that describes the process by which competitors within an industry become more alike in structure and adopt similar practices over time. Paul DiMaggio and Walter Powell first articulated the theory.[43] The theory identifies three pressures that lead institutions to conform: mimetic, coercive, and normative. *Mimetic influences* arise from the perception that peer organizations are more successful; by mimicking peer behavior, the organization aims to achieve similar results. *Coercive influences* come from both formal and informal political pressures exerted on an organization by other organizations upon which they are dependent. Government regulations, legal requirements, and ceremonial practices to boost legitimacy, are examples of coercive influences. *Normative influences* arise from duties, obligations, and norms of professionalism, including formal education and professional and trade associations that seek to legitimize their existence. DiMaggio and Powell wrote, *"Many professional career tracks are so closely guarded, both at the entry level and throughout career progression, that individuals who make it to the top are virtually indistinguishable".*[44]

Interface (blockchain): An access point to a blockchain application through an application programming interface (API). For end users, interfaces include digital wallets; gateways; anchors; exchanges; web portals; and IoT devices.

Interledger Protocol (ILP): Two Ripple engineers published the ILP's white paper back in 2015. For a given payment, the ILP protocol sends many micropayments with confirmations between micropayments to minimize the risk that a node could steal or fail to send a payment through a network.

Internet-of-Things (IoT): A term that refers to connecting devices with unique identifiers to the Internet so that data can be collected from and sent to those devices.

Internet Protocol (IP) address: This is a unique number assigned to every device connected to the Internet. It's like a street, city, state, and zip code for each device. A sample IP address (in version 4) is '172.16.254.1'.

Interoperability: The ability for one system to use another system.[45] In relation to blockchains, interoperability means one blockchain could be connected to different blockchains or to different systems of record.

Know Your Customer (KYC): Regulations that require financial institutions to verify the identity, suitability, and risks involved with maintaining a business relationship with a customer. Examples of KYC regulations include the USA Patriot Act of 2001 and the UK Money Laundering Regulation of 2017.[46]

Lightning Network: A protocol that tracks intermediate transfers of funds off a blockchain and only posts the value of the initial credit and the final account balance transfers to the blockchain. The solution helps unclutter the blockchain network by getting rid of intermediate transactions.

Mandelbug: A computer programming logic error that is obscure and complex and therefore hard to detect.[47] It is named after the mathematician Benoit Mandelbrot, who showed that complex phenomena could arise from simple rules.

Meritocracy: A governance model in which power is held by individuals or organizations based on their proven ability.

Merkle root: Named after the US computer scientist, Ralph Merkle, the Merkle root is the result of a sequence of hashes between pairs of numbers. In blockchain applications, the numbers are pairs of transactions (see Figure G.7). The process to calculate the Merkle root produces a very secure block because if a single digit is altered in any individual transaction, a subsequent calculation check of the Merkle root would reveal an alteration. For a given block, the Merkle root is added to the block's header.

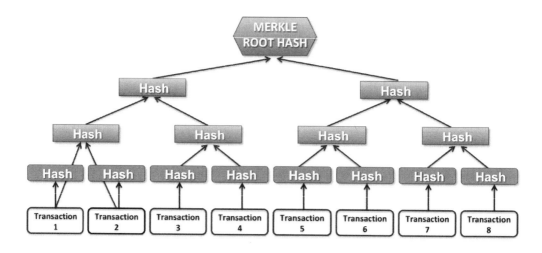

Figure G.7: Merkle tree

In this example, a block comprises 8 transactions. Each transaction is secured with a hash. Then, the transaction hashes are secured again by hashing four pairs of transactions. Next, two pairs of the hashes are hashed. Then the last hash pair is hashed again, resulting in the root hash called the Merkle root.

Mimetic influences: See entry for **Institutional Isomorphism**

Minimal viable ecosystem (MVE): The minimum number of ecosystem partners that are needed to successfully launch a minimal viable product. Too many participants will slow development; too few and the solution will not be useful or attractive. In the context of blockchains, IBM recommends that competitors should be included in an MVE to establish trust.[48]

Minimal viable product (MVP): An initial version of a product that has enough functionality to attract early adopters. The early adopters provide feedback to improve the product, such as proposing new features and functionality. The purposes of an MVP are to test a product with minimal resources; accelerate learning through feedback from early adopters; lay claim to the solution before competitors; and to start building a brand.[49]

Mining: See entry for **Proof-of-Work**

Mining pool: Groups of miners who pool their resources and agree to share block rewards in proportion to their contributed mining hash power. Mining pools are desirable to the average miner because they smooth out rewards and make them more predictable.[50]

Mission: A formal statement that expresses the aspirations and values of an organization or community.

Money laundering with cryptocurrencies: Criminals around the world have used cryptocurrencies for money laundering, which converts profits from crimes into what appears to be a legitimate source of cash. For example, ten men were arrested in the Netherlands in January 2016 for laundering large sums of money using bitcoins.[51] In another example, a Russian man was arrested in Greece for laundering $4 billion into virtual currency.[52] The US Drug Enforcement Agency (DEA) is concerned about the increased use of cryptocurrencies as a way to launder the revenue generated from crime, which is worth approximately $300 billion annually in the US.[53] In a 2017 report, the DEA stated, *"Emerging as a money laundering vulnerability, Bitcoin and other virtual currencies enable TCOs (Transnational Criminal Organizations) to easily transfer illicit proceeds internationally."*[54] Most exchanges now comply with Anti-Money Laundering (AML) requirements.

MultiChain: MultiChain is the code base developed by Coin Sciences Ltd. According to its whitepaper, *"MultiChain is an off-the-shelf platform for the creation and deployment of private blockchains, either within or between organizations. It aims to overcome a key obstacle to the deployment of blockchain technology in the institutional financial sector, by providing the privacy and control required in an easytouse package. Rather than supporting a single blockchain like Bitcoin Core, MultiChain is easy to configure and can work with different blockchains at the same time."*[55] Its consensus protocol relies on 'mining diversity'; a round robin schedule of pre-authorized nodes assigned the tasks of validating new transactions and adding them to the ledger.

Multiple Composite Keys: In contrast to a single private-key pair, multiple private keys are needed to authorize a transaction. It's a way for multiple parties to share an asset.

Network sructures:

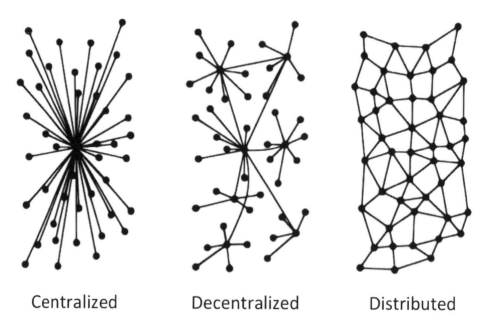

Centralized   Decentralized   Distributed

Figure G.8: Three network structures

Source: http://www.truthcoin.info/images/cent-dec-dist.jpg

A network structure describes the relationships among nodes in a network (see Figure G.8). With a centralized structure, one node is in control; the centralized node (server) receives all incoming data from other nodes and, in turn, routes data to other nodes. In a distributed network, all nodes are peers; no one node is in charge. Data travels to its closest neighbors until all targeted recipient nodes receive the data. In computer science, a decentralized network is a hybrid, resulting in a distributed network of centralized networks.[56] However, many people use the terms 'decentralized' and 'distributed' as synonyms in common vernacular.

Node: According to the Hyperledger Blockchain Performance Metrics white paper (2019), *"In the context of a blockchain network, a node is an independent computing entity that communicates with other nodes in a network to work together collectively to complete transactions. A node is a virtual entity, in the sense that it could be running on physical hardware, or as a Virtual Machine (VM) or containerized environment. In the latter case, a node could share physical hardware with other nodes in the same network. A set of nodes may be managed by the same organization. For example, think of a mining pool operated by one company where a group of machines run as individual nodes doing proof of work (PoW) on a network. In most blockchain networks (Bitcoin, Ethereum, Hyperledger Burrow, Hyperledger Indy, Hyperledger Iroha, Hyperledger Sawtooth) each node plays a uniform class of roles in the network, such as generating blocks, propagating blocks, and so on. In these networks, nodes are usually referred to as peers. Such networks might require one or more nodes to take on a temporary role as a leader. This leadership role may be passed to other nodes in certain well-determined conditions. However, in some blockchain networks (such as Hyperledger Fabric), nodes are assigned one or more possible roles, such as endorsing peers, ordering services, or validating peers."[57]*

Normative influences: See entry for **Institutional Isomorphism**.

Notary: Pertaining to blockchains, a notary is a trusted third party that coordinates cross-chain operations. Cryptocurrency exchanges are common examples. Exchanges allow users to easily buy and sell cryptocurrencies and to exchange cryptocurrencies for fiat currencies; but that convenience comes at the acceptance and trust of centralized control, and with the risks of a single point of failure.

Oligarchy: A governance model in which a few people or a few institutions hold decision making rights.

Oracle: In a blockchain application, an oracle is an agent that finds and verifies real-world occurrences and submits this information to a blockchain to be used by smart contracts.[58]

Performance: See entry for **Systems Performance**.

Permissioned Protocol: Within a blockchain application, a permissioned protocol restricts access and confines which nodes are allowed to observe, transact, validate and add transactions to the permanent record (i.e. the distributed ledger).

Permissionless Protocol: Within a blockchain application, a permissionless protocol does not restrict access. Anyone can operate a full node and compete (or be semi-randomly assigned or voted upon) to validate and add transactions to the permanent record (i.e. the distributed ledger).

Plasma: Designed for Ethereum by Vitalik Buterin and Joseph Poon, Plasma is a 'layer 2' blockchain option designed to increase Ethereum's throughput, allowing more transactions per second.[59] *As of 2020, it is still being debated by the Ethereum community.*[60]

Practical Byzantine Fault Tolerance (PBFT): A consensus protocol created by Miguel Castro and Barbara Liskov in 1999.[61] With PBFT, nodes need permission to serve as validator nodes, forming a member list. Each round, a node from the member list is selected as leader (see Figure G.9). A client node sends a request to the leader node to validate a transaction. The leader node multicasts the request to all the other authorized nodes. The authorized nodes execute the request independently and then send the confirmation to each other and to the client. The client waits for a certain percentage of replies to confirm validation, typically waiting for 2/3 of the nodes to agree. The leader node changes for the next round.

As a *class* of consensus algorithms, there are many versions of PBFT, including Redundant Byzantine Fault Tolerance (RBFT) used by Hyperledger Indy[62]; Delegated

Byzantine Fault Tolerance used by Antshares;[63] Quorum used by JP Morgan;[64] and Federated Byzantine Agreement used by Stellar[65]—to name but a few. PBFT versions differ by how authorized nodes are chosen and by how nodes are assigned roles. Ripple and Stellar, for example, allow participants to pick which nodes they want as validators;[66] Antshares separates bookkeeping nodes from user nodes, with the former being operated by professionals; Quorum delegates nodes to observer, voter, and maker roles;[67] R3 Corda authorizes notary and observer nodes; Hyperledger Fabric defines endorser, orderer, and committer nodes.

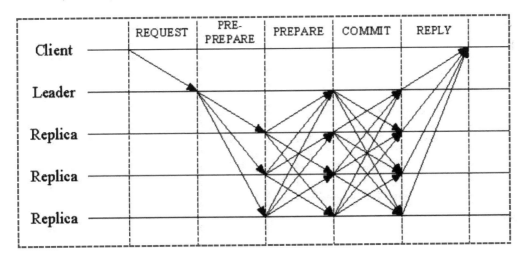

Figure G.9: Practical Byzantine Fault Tolerance (PBFT) Consensus Process

Source: Castro & Liskov (1999) https://theintelligenceofinformation.files.wordpress.com/2017/02/hotdep_ img_1.jpg

Privacy coin: A cryptocurrency that aims to maximize anonymity by using protocols and cryptography to mask the senders, receivers, and/or amounts while still preventing a double spend. Monero and zcash are examples.

Private-public key pair: Two numbers that are mathematically related such that it is nearly impossible to figure out the private key if one only has access to the public key.

Both keys are needed to prove ownership of a digital asset. Together, the pair serves as a digital signature. In practice, the owner of the digital asset holds the private key off the blockchain, either in a wallet the owner stores on his/her own device or in a wallet stored on an exchange or third-party provider. The public key is stored on the blockchain. (In Bitcoin, the public key is transformed into an address using a hash function.) Both keys need to 'turn' to send value. Figure G.10 is an example of a legitimate private-public key pair. (Don't bother searching for this address on a blockchain, a program created the private-public key pair for illustrative purposes.)[68]

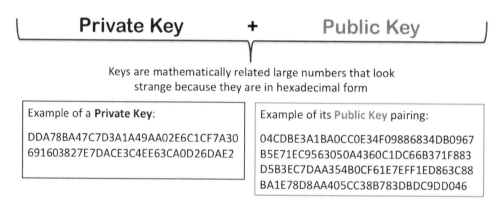

Figure G.10: Example of a private-public key pair

Source: http://minetopics.blogspot.com/2013/01/hiding-bitcoins-in-your-brain.html

Notice how long the hexadecimal public key is: 04CDBE3A1BA0CC0E34F09886834 DB0967B5E71EC9563050A4360C1DC66B371F883D5B3EC7DAA354B0CF61E7EF F1ED863C88BA1E78D8AA405CC38B783DBDC9DD046

To store on a blockchain, the public key gets shortened through a series of hashing processes, so it would look like this on a blockchain:

17A16QmavnUfCW11DAApiJxp7ARnxN5pGX

Proof-of-Authority (PoA): A consensus mechanism that preauthorizes nodes with the authority to validate and add transactions to a distributed ledger. The algorithm takes turns selecting a leader from among the list of authorized nodes (see Figure G.11). The leader node checks each transaction in the transaction queue; organizes valid transactions into a block; signs the block with the node's private key; and distributes the block to other nodes. The other nodes validate that the block was signed by the current leader and recheck each transaction within the block, resulting in an acceptance or a rejection of the entire block. As a permissioned consensus algorithm, it settles transactions faster and with fewer resources than permissionless algorithms, but it is more centralized.[69]

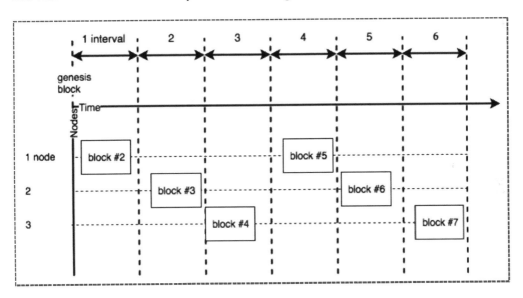

Figure G.11: Proof of Authority: Authorized nodes take turns creating blocks

Source: https://apla.readthedocs.io/en/latest/_images/block-generation.png

Proof-of-Stake: Sunny King and Scott Nadal created the 'proof-of-stake' consensus protocol for blockchains in a 2012 white paper.[70] Instead of 'mining' for coins, the protocol selects a member to 'forge' new currency as a reward for validating the transactions and creating the next block. Essentially, the selected member node is awarded a transaction fee. The member node is selected in a semi-random way; it's called a 'proof-of-stake' because the members with the highest 'stake' (i.e. have the largest account balances) are giving priority in the selection algorithm. Participants in the blockchain can estimate with some certainty which member will likely be the next 'forger'. A 'proof-of-stake' process uses much less energy than a 'Proof-of-Work' process. However, critics claim it is less secure than Proof-of-Work because people with small stakes have little to lose by voting for multiple blockchain histories, which leads to consensus never resolving.[71] Peercoin and Nxt use Proof-of-Stake. Ethereum may migrate to PoS.

Proof-of-Work: Cynthia Dwork and Moni Naor created the 'Proof-of-Work' protocol in 1993 to prevent junk email.[72] Satoshi Nakamoto adopted the 'Proof-of-Work' consensus protocol for Bitcoin in the 2008 white paper.[73] Ethereum also uses Proof-of-Work (for now). Nakamoto needed a way to find independent verifiers to validate transactions and add blocks to the blockchain without relying on trusted third parties. Nakamoto proposed to reward other nodes in the network with newly issued bitcoins when they validate all recently submitted transactions and create the next block. So that validator nodes take the task seriously, Nakamoto proposed a competition among computer nodes in the blockchain network to be the first to collect recently verified transactions into a block and then to find an acceptable block identification number (known as the blockhash) for the next block in the blockchain. It's not easy to find an acceptable number... it takes a lot of computing power to perform the brute force guesses to find a hash number that is less than the current mining 'difficulty'. The difficulty is part of the proof that the miner's computer did a significant amount of work to earn the block reward. Figure G.12 shows how it works.

For the Bitcoin blockchain, a block's winning miner—or more likely, the winning mining pool—receives a set amount of bitcoins, which was 12.5 bitcoins as of March 2020, plus all the small fees that people offered miners to include their transactions in the block. A new block is mined every ten minutes on average. The miner's block reward halves every 210,000 blocks, so miners earn fewer coins with time, but the value of those coins might be substantially higher over time.

For the Ethereum blockchain, winning miners are awarded two ether per block, which are created about every 15 seconds. Sometimes ether is sent to a miner who found a solution but whose block was not included, called an uncle (or aunt) reward.[74]

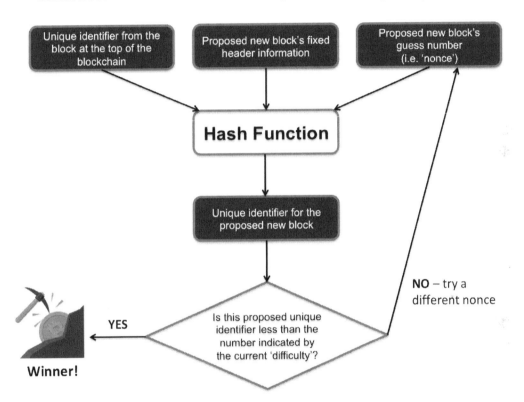

Figure G.12: The Proof-of-Work mining competition algorithm

A miner's computer takes the unique identifier (i.e. the blockhash) from the block at the top of the chain and hashes that number with the proposed next block's header of fixed information— the protocol version number, the root hash of the Merkle tree, the current time, and the difficulty—and a randomly selected number called a 'nonce'. The hash is then checked to see if it is less than the current mining difficulty. If the hash is greater than the target difficulty, the algorithm tries another guess. If it is less than the target difficulty, the miner wins the competition and is awarded newly created coins.

The Proof-of-Work protocol creates a highly secure ledger, as an attacker would need to gain control of more than 50 percent of the hashing power of the network, rewrite history and find all new hashes that adhere to the protocol before other nodes notice. The cons of the protocol include slower transaction settlement times, fewer transactions processed per second, and higher electricity consumption compared to other protocols.

Protocol: A common set of rules that allow different nodes in a computer network to communicate. For example, the Internet uses the Transmission Control Protocol/Internet Protocol (TCP/IP), which is a set of protocols that specify how data should be structured, addressed, transmitted, routed, and received by nodes on the Internet. Blockchain protocols specify rules for how transactions are structured; addressed; transmitted; routed; validated; sequenced; secured; and added to the permanent record (i.e. the distributed ledger) by nodes in a blockchain network.

Pseudo-anonymity: A blockchain application that aims to mask the identity of parties to a transaction, but whose identity may be revealed through meta data. For example, IP addresses may reveal the sender of a transaction. More commonly, when Party A sends value to an address owned by Party B on one date, Party A can later determine additional addresses owned by Party B when Party B spends the coins.

Quantum computing: A computing architecture based on quantum bits, called 'qubits', which can simultaneously represent multiple states and therefore do multiple calculations at the same time. Quantum computing will speed computers in such a way that brute force guesses of private cryptographic keys that are impractical today could be practical in the future.

Quick response (QR) code: A QR code is a two dimensional code that is machine readable. QR codes are often used to track goods, and may contain information such as the manufacturer, lot number, and item number. Any number or text can be converted to a QR code. For example, Figure G.13 is QR code for 'The University of Arkansas'. If you take your camera phone and scan the QR code, you will see that the QR code is interpreted correctly.

G.13. Machine-readable QR code for 'The University of Arkansas'

Quorum: Quorum is an enterprise-ready distributed ledger and smart contract platform based on Ethereum.[75] The Enterprise Ethereum Alliance officially supports Quorum.[76] Quorum was developed by J.P. Morgan, the world's third largest financial services firm, by assets of over $2.5 trillion, as an open-source, enterprise grade version of Ethereum.[77] Quorum is a private/permissioned blockchain that requires institutions to apply for permission to operate a node.[78] A key benefit is that it is designed to process and settle hundreds of transactions per second. J.P. Morgan licensed Quorum with a General Purpose License (GPL) so that the platform will be free to use. It plans to co-evolve in cooperation with Ethereum.[79] Quorum's architecture sits on top of the public Ethereum blockchain. QuorumChain is the original consensus protocol, with other Raft and Istanbul BFT protocols[80] added later.[81] As an open source project, any person or enterprise can download Quorum for experimentation. Notable adopters include Reuters;[82] Microsoft;[83] Synechron;[84] BlockApps;[85] AMIS Technologies;[86] and Chronicled. Microsoft added Quorum to the Azure cloud marketplace for a trusted execution environment that is an additional layer of security.[87]

QuorumChain: The main consensus protocol used in Quorum. QuorumChain is a time-based, majority-voting algorithm that uses a smart contract to identify which nodes participate in consensus. QuorumChain has three types of nodes: voter nodes, maker nodes, and observer nodes. Voter nodes vote on which block should be added to the blockchain. Maker nodes are authorized to add the blocks after enough votes have been cast. Observer nodes receive and validate blocks, but do not vote or make blocks.[88] The ledger is segmented into a private state database and a public state database. Participants can execute private and public smart contracts. While all nodes validate public transactions, nodes can only validate private transactions if they are party to the private smart contract.[89]

R3: A blockchain consortium founded in 2014 by David Rutter, with the aim to develop a blockchain platform that could be used by global financial institutions. See Chapter 2 for more information.

Raft: A consensus protocol used in several blockchains, including Quorum. According to the Quorum white paper, *"Raft separates the key elements of consensus, such as leader election, log replication, and safety, and it enforces a stronger degree of coherency to reduce the number of states that must be considered."*[90] The elected leader node accepts requests from client nodes, replicates them to the network, and responds to the client when a quorum (>50 percent) has been reached. Raft can ensure settlement finality and has throughput of over a thousand transactions per second.

Raiden Network: A protocol that builds another layer on top of a blockchain. It was initially launched to allow for micropayments on Ethereum.[91] Described as similar to the Lightning Network, the basic idea is to switch from a model where all transactions hit the shared ledger on the blockchain (which is the bottleneck) to a model where users can privately exchange messages, which sign the transfer of value. Raiden nodes connect to Ethereum nodes using an API and claims that a million transactions per second of confidential transactions are possible (because they are not added to the blockchain).[92]

Redactable blockchain: A technical innovation that allows blockchains to be edited reliably without creating a hard fork by using secret trap door keys. The keys can only be used by authorized parties. The keys are used to find a hash collision, where two different inputs can create the same hash output. According to the seminal paper by Ateniese et al. (2017), *"The best way to grasp the concept of a redactable blockchain is to think of adding a lock to each link of the hash chain: Without the lock key it is hard to find collisions and the chain remains immutable, but given the lock key it is possible to efficiently find collisions and thus replace the content of any block in the chain. With the knowledge of the key, any redaction is then possible: deletion, modification, and insertion of any number of blocks. Note that if the lock key is lost or destroyed, then a redactable blockchain reverts to an immutable one."*[93] The secret keys are meant to be invoked infrequently, such as in the case of remedying egregious errors or attacks (like the DAO).

Representative meritocracy: A governance model where people or institutions that have proven their merit are eligible to be elected to a council based on votes from other meritorious members.

RSA: RSA is an asymmetric key algorithm designed by three MIT professors—Rivest, Shamir, and Adleman—in 1977 based on multiplying two really large prime numbers.

Sandbox: A test environment that isolates software code from the live production environment, allowing people to test and experiment with the software.

Scalability: See entry for **System Scalability**.

Schrödinbug: An error in computer programming logic, which manifests only when somebody debugging it finds out that it shouldn't work at all.[94] The name comes from Schrödinger's cat thought experiment, which essentially described situations where we cannot know whether something is true or false until we observe it. (The actual thought experiment went something like this: *If a cat and something that could kill the cat was left in a sealed box, one cannot ascertain whether the cat is dead or alive until one opens the box. Until the box is opened, it's equally valid to surmise that the cat is both dead and alive.*)

Security Token Offerings (STOs): An STO is a legally compliant, licensed initial coin offering, which is only available to accredited investors.

Segregated Witness (SegWit): A protocol that increases the number of transactions that can be included in a Bitcoin block. Instead of appending a digital signature to each address within a transaction, the protocol calls for a single digital signature at block header level, thus reducing the size of transactions, enabling more transactions per block.[95]

Self-Sovereign Identity: Individuals and organizations own and control their personal data.

SHA-256: A secure, one-way hash function commonly used in blockchains. It was designed by the US National Security Agency. It takes any-sized input value and produces a 32-byte output value using hexadecimal notation. The same input will always produce the exact same output.

Sharding: A protocol that segments the validation process for new transactions in a blockchain so that not every node validates every transaction. Its purpose is to improve system performance.

Sidechains/relays: Sidechains and relays provide the functions of a notary, but rely on automatically executing algorithms instead of on custodians. Back et al. (2014) first conceived of 'pegged sidechains' as a way for bitcoins and other ledger assets to be transferred between multiple, independent blockchains.[96] For these authors, a sidechain is a two-way peg to a parent chain (or main chain) that allows assets to be interchanged at a predetermined rate. But the term is relative to the asset, not to the network. For this reason, Vitalik Buterin laments the term 'sidechain' in his white paper on interoperability. He argued that it is better to use the phrase, *"a relay of chain A exists on chain B"* or *"D is a cross-chain portable digital asset with home ledger A that can also be used on chain B."*[97]

Silk Road: Silk Road was an anonymous marketplace, and Bitcoin's most visible example of a nefarious use case. Ross William Ulbricht founded Silk Road in 2011, when he was just 27 years old.[98] The marketplace combined the anonymity of Bitcoin with the obscurity of Tor, the network protocol that masks the identity of servers. (One can spot a Tor website by the website address's suffix '.onion'). One can hardly believe the audacity of Silk Road's openness (see Figure G.14 for a screen shot showing illegal drugs available for sale). After an intense search that comprised cyber and behavioral investigative methods—such as posing as drug buyers—the US Federal Bureau of Investigation (FBI) arrested Ulbricht in 2013. He was sentenced to life in prison without the possibility of parole.[99] This story is nuanced in a way that will not be covered here, but the documentary film, *Deep Web*, by Director Alex Winter, provides thorough coverage of the rise and fall of Silk Road.

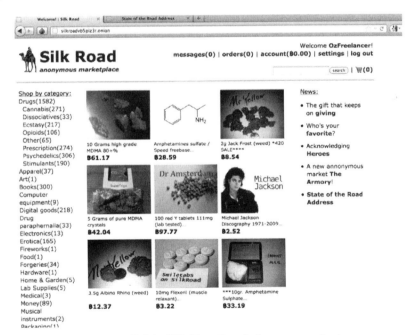

Figure G.14: Silk Road website screenshot

Source: Techrepublic[100]

Simple Payment Verification (SPV): Nakamoto (2008) described SPV as a way to verify itcoin transactions without running a full network node. Rather, one only needs to maintain a copy of the block headers and then find the security links (called a **Merkle tree** branch) to the transaction to prove it was verified and accepted by the network. SPV shows that *"tokens have been locked up on one chain so validators can safely unlock an equivalent value on the other chain."*[101]

Smart Contract–Deterministic: Once deployed on the blockchain, a deterministic smart contract can execute autonomously without the need for any outside information. See Chapter 3 for more information.

Smart Contract–Non-Deterministic: Once deployed on the blockchain, a non-deterministic smart contract requires outside information to execute the terms of the agreement. The outside information is called an 'oracle'. See Chapter 3 for more information.

Smart contract: A smart contract—a concept developed by Nick Szabo in 1994—is a piece of software that stores rules for negotiating the terms of a contract, automatically verifies the contract and then executes the terms.[102] See Chapter 3 for more information.

Stable coin: A cryptocurrency that aims to create a stable store of value by pegging the digital coin to a stable asset outside of the network, such as pegging a digital coin to a fiat currency or to a commodity like gold or a barrel of oil. Tether; USD Coin; gemini; JPM Coin; and libra are examples.

Stakeocracy: A 'Pay to Play' governance model where individuals' or institutions' votes are weighted by the size of their investment.

Sustaining innovation: An innovation that improves the performance of an enterprise's current product or services to meet the needs of its most demanding customers. The term comes from Clayton Christensen's Theory of Disruptive Innovation.[103]

Sybil attack: A single malicious node in a network that replicates itself so many times, it takes over the network. Blockchains like Bitcoin, Ethereum and Stellar use cryptocurrencies to prevent Sybil attacks, as a Sybil attacker would run out of money.

System performance: A term used to measure how long it takes a network to process a transaction. Blockchain applications generally vary in their performance from minutes to seconds.

System scalability: A system's ability to handle an increase in workload, such as when new users are added to a system.[104] Scalability refers to the throughput, i.e. how many transactions can be processed per second.

Tragedy of the commons: This concept is defined as a situation within a shared-resource system where individual users acting independently according to their own self-interest behave contrary to the common good of all users by depleting or spoiling that resource through their collective action.[105]

Transaction costs: The effort, time, and costs incurred in searching, creating, negotiating, monitoring, and administrating a transaction between trading partners.

Transmission Control Protocol/Internet Protocol (TCP/IP): As the Internet's primary protocol, it breaks messages into packets and routes them to their destination as defined by a unique address called an 'IP address'. Every device connected to the Internet has a unique IP address including computers; mobile phones; laptops; printers; IoT devices; servers; routers, etc.

Transaction malleability: When a user creates a transaction, the digital wallet signs and sends off the transaction to the network in order to get validated and added to the digital ledger. Transactions are automatically assigned a unique transaction-ID based on its content. While the transaction is still making its way through the network, there is a way to slightly change the transaction so that it is still a valid transaction that correctly moves money as the original author intended. The small change, however, will generate a different unique transaction-ID based on the slightly revised content. The result is that a sender sending a transaction cannot be certain that the transaction will have the same ID from the moment is was created to when it finally gets mined in a block.[106]

Trust: In general, trust is the confidence in another party's benevolence. In reference to blockchains, trust often refers to the confidence that records on the distributed ledger agree.

Trust protocol: In the context of a blockchain application, the term 'trust protocol' is defined to mean the reliance on computer algorithms rather than trusted third party institutions to verify transactions and to ensure all copies of the digital ledgers agree across nodes.

Trusted third parties: Trusted third parties—like banks, certificate authorities, and credit card companies—exist to mitigate counterparty risks, i.e. the risk each party bears that the other party will not fulfill its contractual obligations. Trusted third parties perform many vital functions, such as authenticating asset ownership and making sure accounts are funded to prevent double spending.

Turing complete: A term that refers to a computer programming language that has a full set of commands to execute every algorithm that another Turing complete programming language can execute. For example, a simple calculator with basic arithmetic functions is not Turing complete because it cannot execute if-then-else or loop logic. As it relates to blockchain codebases, a Turing complete, smart contracting feature provides the ability to code many types of agreements; but with more coding capabilities comes more risks of software vulnerabilities. Ethereum and Hyperledger Fabric, for example, do have Turing complete programming languages to code smart contracts; Ethereum's smart contracting language is called Solidity; Hyperledger Fabric's is called Chaincode. Bitcoin and Stellar do not have Turing complete smart contracts.

Zero-knowledge proof: Shafi Goldwasser, Charles Rackoff, and Silvio Micali developed the concept in 1985.[107] Zero knowledge proofs are a method for one party (or node) to verify possession of a piece of information to other parties (or nodes) without revealing the information. In general, there are two types of zero-knowledge proofs: *challenge-response* which coordinates an interaction for known parties and *non-interactive*, which do not require iterations. In blockchain applications, zero-knowledge proofs are used to guarantee that transactions are valid without revealing information about the sender, receiver, and/or transaction. Zcash, EY's Nightfall, MediLedger, and many other blockchains use zero knowledge proofs.

zk-SNARK (Zero-Knowledge Succinct Non-Interactive Argument of Knowledge): A zero-knowledge proof used in some blockchain protocols. Here is an explanation of zk-SNARKs:

'*Suppose Bob is given a hash **H** of some value, and he wishes to have a proof that Alice knows the value s that hashes to **H**. Normally Alice would prove this by giving s to Bob, after which Bob would compute the hash and check that it equals **H**. However, suppose Alice doesn't want to reveal the value s to Bob but instead she just wants to prove that she knows the value. She can use a zk-SNARK for this. We can describe Alice's scenario using the following program, here written as a Javascript function:*

```
function C(x, w) {
  return ( sha256(w) == x );
}
```

*In other words: the program takes in a public hash **x** and a secret value **w** and returns true if the **SHA–256 hash** of **w** equals **x**. Translating Alice's problem using the function C(x,w) we see that Alice needs to create a proof that she possesses s such that **C(H, s)** == **true**, without having to reveal s. This is the general problem that zk-SNARKs solve.*[108]

Citations

[1] https://en.wikipedia.org/wiki/Money_laundering#Anti-money_laundering

[2] *Definition of Asymmetric Encryption*, http://hitachi-id.com/resource/itsec-concepts/asymmetric_encryption.html

Mapt course, *Asymmetric Cryptography*, https://www.packtpub.com/mapt/book/big_data_and_business_intelligence/9781787125445/3/ch03lvl1sec28/asymmetric-cryptography

[3] Nakamoto, S. (2008), *Bitcoin: A Peer-to-Peer Electronic Cash System*, https://bitcoin.org/bitcoin.pdf

[4] Lamport, L.; Shostak, R.; Pease, M. (1982), T'he Byzantine Generals Problem', *ACM Transactions on Programming Languages and Systems*. 4 (3): 387–389.

[5] Dagnino, G., ; Padula, G. (2002), *Coopetition Strategy: Towards a New Kind of Interfirm Dynamics for Value Creation*, EURAM 2nd Annual Conference, Stockholm School of Entreprencurship, Sweden.

[6] *How is Consensus achieved in Corda?* https://discourse.corda.net/t/how-is-consensus-achieved-on-corda/1148

[7] *Welcome to Corda*, https://docs.corda.net/

[8] Corda survey responses as reported in Seibold, S., and Samman, G. (2016), *Consensus: Immutable Agreement for the Internet of Value*, KPMG White Paper

[9] Brown, R., Carlyle, J., Grigg, I., and Hearn, M. (2016), *Corda: An Introduction*, Corda White Paper, https://docs.corda.net/_static/corda-introductory-whitepaper.pdf

[10] Corda survey responses as reported in Seibold, S., and Samman, G. (2016), *Consensus: Immutable Agreement for the Internet of Value*, KPMG White Paper

[11] *Welcome to Corda*, https://docs.corda.net/

[12] Lee, P. (November 30th 2017), *R3 releases Corda as Blockchain strains start to show*, https://www.euromoney.com/article/b12kqb9hqwgp2d/r3-releases-corda-as-blockchain-strains-start-to-show

[13] Diedrich, H. (2016), *Ethereum: blockchains, digital assets, smart contracts, decentralized autonomous organizations*, Wildfire Publishing.

[14] https://en.bitcoinwiki.org/wiki/DPoS

[15] Delegated Proof of Stake, https://lisk.io/academy/blockchain-basics/how-does-blockchain-work/delegated-proof-of-stake

[16] Clayton Christensen has developed the theory of disruptive innovation over two decades, beginning with this first book, published in 1997, *The innovator's dilemma: when new technologies cause great firms to fail,* (Boston, Massachusetts, Harvard Business School Press). For a thoughtful and current synopsis of the theory, see Christensen, C., Raynor, M., and McDonald, R. (2015), *Disruptive Innovations, Harvard Business Review*, 93(12): 45-53

[17] https://en.wikipedia.org/wiki/Digital_Signature_Algorithm

[18] Ben Sigman (May 8, 2018), *EOS Block Producer FAQ* https://medium.com/@bensig/eos-block-producer-faq-8ba0299c2896

[19] To view the 21 EOS validator nodes and block producers, see https://bloks.io/vote

[20] William, M. (May 12, 2018), *ERC-20 Tokens, Explained*, Cointelegraph, https://cointelegraph.com/explained/erc-20-tokens-explained

[21] http://erc721.org/

[22] Sharma, T. (July 16th, 2019), *Know the Authenticity of Your Wines*, https://www.blockchain-council.org/blockchain/know-the-authenticity-of-your-wines-eys-blockchain-platform-for-wine-traceability/.

[23] Beigel, O. (March 3rd 2017), *What is Ethereum?* https://99bitcoins.com/guide-buy-ether-ethereum/

[24] ConsenSys (January 10, 2019), *The Thirdening: What You Need To Know*, https://media.consensys.net/the-thirdening-what-you-need-to-know-df96599ad857

[25] https://www.ethernodes.org/network/1

[26] According to discussions within the open source community, the total money supply for ether has not been established, https://ethereum.stackexchange.com/questions/443/what-is-the-total-supply-of-ether

[27] *Is the ether supply infinite?* https://www.ethereum.org/ether

[28] http://wiki.p2pfoundation.net/Ethereum, *A Next-Generation Smart Contract and Decentralized Application Platform*, posted on https://github.com/ethereum/wiki/wiki/White-Paper

[29] *Is the ether supply infinite?* https://www.ethereum.org/ether

[30] Levi, A. (May 21, 2017), *Corporate Trends in Blockchain*, CB Insights webinar presentation.

[31] *The Differences Between Hard and Soft Forks*, We Use Coins, August 23rd 2016, https://www.weusecoins.com/hard-fork-soft-fork-differences/

Glossary

[32] *Hard & Soft Forking Explained*, by Loshil and @MLPFrank, https://www.youtube.com/watch?v=pdaXY1OOiWQ

[33] Martin, L. (2016) *Blockchain for developers: Is it right for your application?* Techbeacon, https://techbeacon.com/blockchain-it-right-your-app

[34] The Linux Foundation (January 22nd 2016), *The Hyperledger Project Charter,* https://www.hyperledger.org/about/charter

[35] Connell, J. (June 2017), *On Byzantine Fault Tolerance in Blockchain Systems*, https://cryptoinsider.com/byzantine-fault-tolerance-blockchain-systems/

[36] Groenfeldt, T. (July 13th 2017), 'Linux Foundation's Hyperledger Fabric 1.0 Ready For Production', *Forbes Magazine,* https://www.forbes.com/sites/tomgroenfeldt/2017/07/13/linux-foundats-hyperledger-fabric-1-0-ready-for-production/ - 624d7632902e

[37] Hyperledger Foundation, *Hyperledger Architecture, Volume 1*, https://www.hyperledger.org/wp-content/uploads/2017/08/HyperLedger_Arch_WG_Paper_1_Consensus.pdf

[38] The Linux Foundation (January 22nd 2016), *The Hyperledger Project Charter,* https://www.hyperledger.org/about/charter

[39] https://www.hyperledger.org/projects

[40] https://www.hyperledger.org/projects

[41] Reiger, A.; Guggenmos, F., Locki, J., Fridgen, G., and Urbach, N. (2019), 'Building a Blockchain Application that Complies with the EU General Data Protection Regulation', *MIS Quarterly Executive*, 18(4), pp. 263-279.

[42] Winslet, T (2019), 'Top 3 Initial Exchange Offerings (IEOs) to Watch in the Crypto Market' *The Daily Hodl*, https://dailyhodl.com/2019/04/11/top-3-initial-exchange-offerings-ieos-to-watch-in-the-crypto-market/

[43] DiMaggio, P., and Powell, W. (1991), 'The Iron Cage Revisited: Institutional Isomorphism and Collective Rationality in Organizational Fields', *The New Institutionalism in Organizational Analysis,* (Powell & DiMaggio eds), The University of Chicago Press, 63-82

[44] DiMaggio, P., and Powell, W. (1991), 'The Iron Cage Revisited: Institutional Isomorphism and Collective Rationality in Organizational Fields', *The New Institutionalism in Organizational Analysis,* (Powell & DiMaggio eds), The University of Chicago Press, 63-82

[45] Ross, C. (December 5th 2016), *Blockchain Brings Us Into The Future, But Only After It Drags Up The Past: Interoperability Becomes An Actual Issue Again,* http://www.horsesforsources.com/blog/christine-ferrusi-ross/the-interoperability-problems-blockchain-brings_120616

Ross, C. (April 18th 2017), *Simplify Blockchain by Refusing to Let Interoperability Issues Bog You Down*, http://www.horsesforsources.com/Simplify-Blockchain-Refusing-Interoperability-Issues_041817

[46] https://en.wikipedia.org/wiki/Know_your_customer

[47] Martin, L. (2016) *Blockchain for developers: Is it right for your application?* Techbeacon, https://techbeacon.com/blockchain-it-right-your-app

[48] Arun, J., Cuomo, J., and Gaur, N. (2019). *Blockchain for Business*, Addison-Wesley, Boston.

[49] Lenarduzzi, V., Taibi, D. (August 2016), *MVP Explained: A Systematic Mapping Study on the Definitions of Minimal Viable Product*, 2016 42th Euromicro Conference on Software Engineering and Advanced Applications (SEAA). Cyprus. pp. 112–119.

[50] Tuwiner, J. (July 13th 2017), *Bitcoin Mining Pools*, https://www.buybitcoinworldwide.com/mining/pools/

[51] The Guardian (January 20th 2016), *Ten arrested in Netherlands over bitcoin money-laundering allegations*, https://www.theguardian.com/technology/2016/jan/20/bitcoin-netherlands-arrests-cars-cash-ecstasy

[52] Lee, T. (July 26th 2017), *Officials arrest suspect in $4 billion Bitcoin money laundering scheme*, https://arstechnica.com/tech-policy/2017/07/officials-arrest-suspect-in-4-billion-bitcoin-money-laundering-scheme/

[53] De, N. (Oct 25th 2017), *DEA Report: Bitcoin Used for Trade-Based Money Laundering*, https://www.coindesk.com/dea-report-bitcoin-used-trade-based-money-laundering/

[54] The US Department of Justice Drug Enforcement Administration (October 2017), *2017 National Drug Threat Assessment*, https://www.dea.gov/docs/DIR-040-17_2017-NDTA.pdf

[55] MultiChain White Paper (2015), https://www.MultiChain.com/download/MultiChain-White-Paper.pdf

[56] Institute of Network Cultures, *Beyond distributed and decentralized: what is a federated network?*, http://networkcultures.org/unlikeus/resources/articles/what-is-a-federated-network/

[57] Hyperledger Blockchain Performance Metrics White Paper (2019). https://www.hyperledger.org/resources/publications/blockchain-performance-metrics

[58] https://blockchainhub.net/blockchain-oracles/

[59] Robinson, Dan (2019). https://events.technologyreview.com/video/watch/dan-robinson-scaling-interoperability/

[60] Cuen, L. (February 11, 2020), *Plasma Became Optimism and It Might Just Save Ethereum*, Coindesk,

https://www.coindesk.com/plasma-became-optimism-and-it-might-just-save-ethereum

[61] *Practical Byzantine Fault Tolerance*, Proceedings of the Third Symposium on Operating Systems Design and Implementation, New Orleans, USA, February 1999, http://pmg.csail.mit.edu/papers/osdi99.pdf

[62] Hyperledger Foundation, *Hyperledger Architecture, Volume 1*, https://www.hyperledger.org/wp-content/uploads/2017/08/HyperLedger_Arch_WG_Paper_1_Consensus.pdf

[63] Connell, J. (June 2017), *On Byzantine Fault Tolerance in Blockchain Systems*, https://cryptoinsider.com/byzantine-fault-tolerance-blockchain-systems/

[64] Quorum White Paper, https://github.com/jpmorganchase/quorum-docs/blob/master/Quorum Whitepaper v0.1.pdf

[65] Maziières, D. (2016), *The Stellar Consensus Protocol: A Federated Model for Internet-level Consensus*, White Paper, https://www.stellar.org/papers/stellar-consensus-protocol.pdf

[66] Maziières, D. (2016), *The Stellar Consensus Protocol: A Federated Model for Internet-level Consensus*, White Paper, https://www.stellar.org/papers/stellar-consensus-protocol.pdf

[67] Maziières, D. (2016), *The Stellar Consensus Protocol: A Federated Model for Internet-level Consensus*, White Paper, https://www.stellar.org/papers/stellar-consensus-protocol.pdf

[68] http://minetopics.blogspot.com/2013/01/hiding-bitcoins-in-your-brain.html

[69] Proof-of-Authority Consensus https://apla.readthedocs.io/en/latest/concepts/consensus.html#advantages-of-poa-consensus

[70] King, S., and Nadal, S. (2012), *PPCoin: Peer-to-Peer Crypto-Currency with Proof-of-Stake*, https://peercoin.net/assets/paper/peercoin-paper.pdf

[71] *Distributed Consensus from Proof of Stake is Impossible, Andrew Poelstra,* https://www.smithandcrown.com/open-research/distributed-consensus-from-proof-of-stake-is-impossible/

[72] Dwork, C., and Naor, M. (1993), *Pricing via processing: Combatting Junk Mail*, http://www.hashcash.org/papers/pvp.pdf

[73] Nakamoto, S. (2008), *Bitcoin: A Peer-to-Peer Electronic Cash System*, https://bitcoin.org/bitcoin.pdf

[74] Beigel, O. (March 3rd 2017), *What is Ethereum?*, https://99bitcoins.com/guide-buy-ether-ethereum/

[75] J.P. Morgan, Quorum, https://www.jpmorgan.com/country/US/EN/Quorum

[76] Enterprise Ethereum Alliance (July 7th 2017), *Enterprise Ethereum Alliance Announces Support for*

Blockchain Consensus Algorithm Integration, https://entethalliance.org/enterprise-ethereum-alliance-announces-support-blockchain-consensus-algorithm-integration/

[77] The Quorum White Paper, https://github.com/jpmorganchase/quorum-docs/blob/master/Quorum Whitepaper v0.1.pdf

[78] Hackett, R. (October 4th 2016), 'Why J.P. Morgan Chase Is Building a Blockchain on Ethereum', *Fortune Magazine*, http://fortune.com/2016/10/04/jp-morgan-chase-blockchain-ethereum-quorum/

[79] J.P. Morgan, Quorum, https://www.jpmorgan.com/country/US/EN/Quorum

[80] https://www.ethnews.com/amis-technologies-new-algorithm-handles-more-transactions-per-second

https://github.com/ethereum/EIPs/issues/650

https://ethereumfoundation.org/devcon3/sessions/bft-for-geth/

[81] Quorum White Paper, https://github.com/jpmorganchase/quorum-docs/blob/master/Quorum Whitepaper v0.1.pdf

[82] http://www.ibtimes.co.uk/how-ihs-markits-syndicated-loans-blockchain-arrived-cash-1622304

[83] Castillo, M (February 28th 2017), *Microsoft Adds JPMorgan's 'Quorum' Blockchain to Azure Platform*, https://www.coindesk.com/microsoft-azure-jpmorgans-quorum-blockchain/

[84] http://www.financemagnates.com/cryptocurrency/innovation/synechron-releases-quorum-maker-enterprise-ethereum-alliance/

[85] http://blockapps.net/

[86] Nation, J. (July 5th 2017), *AMIS Technologies' New Algorithm Handles More Transactions-Per-Second*, https://www.ethnews.com/amis-technologies-new-algorithm-handles-more-transactions-per-second

[87] Castillo, M (February 28th 2017), *Microsoft Adds JPMorgan's 'Quorum' Blockchain to Azure Platform*, https://www.coindesk.com/microsoft-azure-jpmorgans-quorum-blockchain/

[88] *QuorumChain Consensus*, https://github.com/jpmorganchase/quorum/wiki/QuorumChain-Consensus

[89] Quorum White Paper, https://github.com/jpmorganchase/quorum-docs/blob/master/Quorum Whitepaper v0.1.pdf

[90] Raft White Paper, Ongaro, D., and Ousterhout, J. (2014), *In Search of an Understandable Consensus Algorithm*, https://raft.github.io/raft.pdf

[91] Hertig, A. (May 31st 2016), *Will Ethereum Beat Bitcoin to Mainstream Microtransactions?* https://

Glossary

www.coindesk.com/ethereum-bitcoin-mainstream-microtransactions/

[92] *The Raiden Network: High Speed Asset Transfers for Ethereum*, http://raiden.network/

[93] Ateniese, G., B. Magri, D. Venturi and E. Andrade (2017), *Redactable Blockchain – or – Rewriting History in Bitcoin and Friends*, 2017 IEEE European Symposium on Security and Privacy (EuroS&P), Paris, pp. 111-126.

[94] https://en.wiktionary.org/wiki/schroedinbug

[95] For a technical explanation of segregated witness, see http://learnmeabitcoin.com/faq/segregated-witness

[96] Back, A., Corallo, M., Dashjr, L., Friedenbach, M., Maxwell, G., Miller, A., Poelstra, A., Timón, J., and Wuille, P. (Oct 22 2014), *Enabling Blockchain Innovations with Pegged Sidechains*, https://blockstream.com/sidechains.pdf

[97] Buterin, V. (September 9, 2016), *Chain Interoperability*, https://static1.squarespace.com/static/55f73743e4b051cfcc0b02cf/t/5886800ecd0f68de303349b1/1485209617040/C hain+Interoperability.pdf

[98] Popper, N. (2015), *Digital Gold: Bitcoin and the Inside History of the Misfits and Millionaires Trying to Reinvent Money*, Harper, New York.

[99] Weiser, B. (May 29th 2015), 'Ross Ulbricht, Creator of Silk Road Website, Is Sentenced to Life in Prison', *The New York Times*, posted https://www.nytimes.com/2015/05/30/nyregion/ross-ulbricht-creator-of-silk-road-website-is-sentenced-to-life-in-prison.html

[100] Reese, H. (May 10th 2017), *How the founder of the Silk Road made millions on his illegal startup on the Dark Web*, https://www.techrepublic.com/article/how-online-marketplace-silk-road-became-the-craigslist-for-illegal-drugs/

https://tr2.cbsistatic.com/hub/i/r/2017/05/10/709e488c-6c51-407f-ae13-5115b14d86c4/resize/770x/ac1af6 17d15f84b986b574770d9a67de/screen-shot-2012-04-24-at-2-02-25-am.png

[101] *SPV, Simplified Payment Verification*, Bitcoin.Org glossary.

[102] *The Future of Blockchains: Smart Contracts*, Technode, http://technode.com/2016/11/14/the-future-of-blockchain-technology-smart-contracts/

[103] Clayton Christensen has developed the theory of disruptive innovation over two decades, beginning with this first book, published in 1997, *The innovator's dilemma: when new technologies cause great firms to fail*, (Boston, Massachusetts, Harvard Business School Press). For a thoughtful and current synopsis of the theory, see Christensen, C., Raynor, M., and McDonald, R. (2015), *Disruptive Innovations, Harvard Business Review*, 93(12): 45-53

[104] Castor, A. (June 14th 2017), *Hyperledger Takes on Blockchain Scaling with New Working Group*, https://www.coindesk.com/hyperledger-takes-on-blockchain-scaling-with-new-working-group/

[105] 'The tof the commons' is defined as 'an economic theory of a situation within a shared-resource system where individual users acting independently according to their own self-interest behave contrary to the common good of all users by depleting or spoiling that resource through their collective action.' https://en.wikipedia.org/wiki/Tragedy_of_the_commons

[106] *Transaction Malleability*, https://en.bitcoinwiki.org/wiki/Transaction_Malleability

[107] https://blockonomi.com/zero-knowledge-proofs/

[108] Lundkvist, C. (2017), *Introduction to zk-SNARKs with examples*, https://media.consensys.net/introduction-to-zksnarks-with-examples-3283b554fc3b

Index

Index

C

Index

Index

E

ECC. *See* Elliptic Curve Cryptography
EEA. *See* Enterprise Ethereum Alliance
Elliptic Curve Cryptography 134, **414**, 415
Enterprise Ethereum Alliance 73, **76-77**, 130, 187, 435
EOS 51, 65, 117, 121, 122, **123-124**, 283, 395, 412, 415, 416
ERC-20 9, 130, 192, 303, **416**, 417
ERC-721 130, **416–417**
Ernst & Young 25, 52, 127
ether 59, **130**, 174, 286, 287, **417**, 418, 432
Ethereum 9, 10, 16, 23, 27, 51, 59, 60, 65, 66, 71, 73, 76, 89, 117, 118, 121, 122, 126, 128,
    130, 135, 136, 139, 141, 142, 143, 146, 148, 187, 188, 189, 191, 192, 214, 238, 245,
    247, 271, 280, 281, **285–298**, 300, 303, 306, 311, 315, 317, 341, 347, 348, 369, 373, 395,
    397, 408, **415–418**, 421, 427, 428, 432, 435, 436, 441, 442
Ethereum Foundation 286, **417–418**
ethical blockchains **390–398**
eTradeConnect 184
Everledger 6, 9, **215–216**, 226, 384
exchange 13, 29, 42, 48, 50, **56–63**, **65–69**, 84, 86, 87, 91, 96, 113, 115, 128, 144, 145, 160,
    162, 164, 165, 167, 171, 174, 175, 178, 255, 284, 291, 298, 303, 318, 320, 321, 323,
    358, 383, 392, 400, 401, 412, 418, 421, 422, 425, 427, 429, 436
EY. *See* Ernst & Young

F

Fabric 10, 23, 71, 75, 117, 118, 126, 135, 142, 175, 182, 210, 215, 265, 299, 310, 311, 319,
    358, 369, 373, 418, **420–421**, 427, 429, 442
federation 271, **320–323**, 345, 348, 418
FedEx 55, 77, 92, 337, 342, 361, 389
fork 57, 66, 98, 141, 210, 286, 287, 291, 295, 297, 345, 352, 368, 395, **418–419**, 421, 436

G

Garimella, Kiran 353, 354, 355, 369, 393
Gartner 8, 57, 70, 72, 94, 95, 96

Index

I

IBM 9, 16, 25, 36, 51, 53, 70, 72, 75, 82, 83, 89, 92, 95, **126–127**, 175, 179, 180, 182, 208, **210–212**, 213, 215, 226, 231, 299, 311, 337, 341, 344, 349, 354, 355, 358, 363, 369, 373, 374, 375, 376, 384, 388, 398, 400, 420, 424

IBM Food Trust 9, 36, 51, 83, 126, 127, 208, **210–212**, 226, 341, 349, 355, 358, 369, 375, 384

IBM World Wire 175, 198

ICO. *See* Initial Coin Offering

iDatafy 256, 258, 259, **264–271**, 347, 362, 363, 368, 369, 370, 371, 372, 376, 394

IEEE 79, 80, 376

IEO. *See* Initial Exchange offering

ILP. *See* Interledger Protocol

immutability 51, 149, 367, **421–422**

influences 375–377

Initial Coin Offering (ICO) 11, 62, **65–68**, 84, 100, 418, 421

Initial Exchange Offering (IEO) **67**, 421

institutional isomorphism 374, 409, **422**, 424, 427

interface 9, 23, 122, 123, **144–151**, 171, 179, 236, 240, 263, 264, 267, 402, 406, 412, **422**

Interledger Protocol 10, **325–326**, 422

Internet-of-Things (IoT) 29, **144**, 422

Internet Protocol (IP) 42, 225, **423**, 434, 441

Internet Protocol (IP) address 423

interoperability 7, 10, 22, 25, 52, 75, 79, 83, 184, 186, 253, 280, 298, **311–326**, 367, 400, 401, 421, 423, 438

    Aion **219**, 311, 416

    atomic swap 191, 406

    cross-chain oracle 313, **315-317**, 411

    cross-chain transaction processing **313–317**, 411

    Hash-Time Locked Contracts (HTLC) 10, 317, **323–324**, 420

    Interledger Protocol 10, **325–326**, 422

    Internet Protocol (IP) 42, 225, **423**, 434, 441

    notary 10, **317–321**, 323, 427, 429, 438

    sidechains/relays 317, **321–323**, 438

    Simple Payment Verification (SPV) 10, 315, **322–323**, 440

O

P

Robotic and Cognitive Automation

Despite the massive hype surrounding RPA, cognitive automation, artificial intelligence (AI), and blockchain, these emerging technologies are becoming more real, relevant and impactful every day.

Our objective, on this website, is to dispel myths and misinformation about risks and effective practices, through insightful, research-based commentary that is independent, objective, rigorous, ahead of the curve, and highly practical.

We are focusing on the bigger picture consequences of automation. This will lead us into interactive discussions on major issues as they arise, such as:

- ✿ **The Future of Work**
- ✿ **Technology and ethics**
- ✿ **Physical and psychological health**
- ✿ **Quality of work**
- ✿ **Risk mitigation**
- ✿ **Automation and the economy**
- ✿ **Automation and the environment**
- ✿ **Political and social challenges**
- ✿ **Emerging technologies**
- ✿ **Blockchain technology**

We will also be connecting up service automation and blockchain technologies with the broader digital transformation ongoing over the next ten years or more—especially in light of the 2020 Covid-19 pandemic. We will be running discerning and sceptical eyes and brains over emerging technologies in business and work contexts, to find out their capabilities, limitations, and likely diffusion—using our customary searching, evidence-based assessments.

There is a plethora of information available on the website, including free, downloadable reasearch papers; regular blogs; links to RPA & CA advisors and providers; and video interviews—where we anwser questions on robotic process and cognitive automation.

*"Whether you are an existing adopter of RPA & CA; thinking of moving in that direction; or just have a keen interest in where the trechnology is at right now, you can join us on the journey that is **Automation and The Future of Work**"*

Professor Leslie Willcocks and **Professor Mary Lacity**